ELSIE VENNER

ELSIE VENNER

A ROMANCE OF DESTINY

BY

OLIVER WENDELL HOLMES

Dolphin Books
Doubleday & Company, Inc.
Garden City, New York

Printed in the United States of America

To
THE SCHOOLMISTRESS
WHO HAS FURNISHED SOME OUTLINES MADE USE OF
IN THESE PAGES AND ELSEWHERE,
THIS STORY IS DEDICATED
BY HER OLDEST SCHOLAR

PREFACE

This tale was published in successive parts in the "Atlantic Monthly," under the name of "The Professor's Story," the first number having appeared in the third week of December 1859. The critic who is curious in coincidences must refer to the Magazine for the date of publication of the Chapter he is examining.

In calling this narrative a "romance," the Author wishes to make sure of being indulged in the common privileges of the poetic license. Through all the disguise of fiction a grave scientific doctrine may be detected lying beneath some of the delineations of character. He has used this doctrine as a part of the machinery of his story without pledging his absolute belief in it to the extent to which it is asserted or implied. It was adopted as a convenient medium of truth rather than as an accepted scientific conclusion. The reader must judge for himself what is the value of various stories cited from old authors. He must decide how much of what has been told he can accept either as having actually happened, or as possible and more or less probable. The Author must be permitted, however, to say here, in his personal character, and as responsible to the students of the human mind and body, that since this story has been in progress he has received the most startling confirmation of the possibility of the existence of a character like that which he had drawn as a purely imaginary conception in Elsie Venner.

BOSTON, January, 1861

A SECOND PREFACE

This is the story which a dear old lady, my very good friend, spoke of as "a medicated novel," and quite properly refused to read. I was always pleased with her discriminating criticism. It *is* a medicated novel, and if she wished to read for mere amusement and helpful recreation there was no need of troubling herself with a story written with a different end in view.

This story has called forth so many curious inquiries that it seems worth while to answer the more important questions which have occurred to its readers.

In the first place, it is not based on any well-ascertained physiological fact. There are old fables about patients who have barked like dogs or crowed like cocks, after being bitten or wounded by those animals. There is nothing impossible in the idea that Romulus and Remus may have imbibed wolfish traits of character from the wet nurse the legend assigned them, but the legend is not sound history, and the supposition is nothing more than a speculative fancy. Still, there is a limbo of curious evidence bearing on the subject of pre-natal influences sufficient to form the starting point of an imaginative composition.

The real aim of the story was to test the doctrine of "original sin" and human responsibility for the disordered volition coming under that technical denomination. Was Elsie Venner, poisoned by the venom of a crotalus before she was born, morally responsible for the "volitional" aberrations, which translated into acts become what is known as sin, and, it may be, what is punished as crime? If, on presentation of the evidence, she becomes by the verdict of the human conscience a proper object of divine pity, and not of divine wrath, as a subject of moral poisoning, wherein lies the difference between her position at the bar of judgment, human or divine, and that of the unfortunate victim who received a moral poison from a remote ancestor before he drew his first breath?

It might be supposed that the character of Elsie Venner was suggested by some of the fabulous personages of classical or mediæval story. I remember that a French critic spoke of her as *cette pauvre Melusine*. I ought to have been ashamed, perhaps, but I had not the slightest idea who Melusina was until I hunted up the story, and found that she was a fairy, who for some offence was changed every Saturday to a serpent from her waist downward. I was of course familiar with Keats's Lamia, another imaginary being, the subject of magical transformation into a serpent. My story was well advanced before Hawthorne's wonderful "Marble Faun," which might be thought to have furnished me with the hint of a mixed nature,—human, with an alien element,—was published or known to me. So that my poor heroine found her origin, not in fable or romance, but in a physiological conception, fertilized by a theological dogma.

I had the dissatisfaction of enjoying from a quiet corner a well-meant effort to dramatize "Elsie Venner." Unfortunately, a physiological romance, as I knew beforehand, is hardly adapted for the melodramatic efforts of stage representation. I can therefore say, with perfect truth, that I was not disappointed. It is to the mind, and not to the senses, that such a story must appeal, and all attempts to render the character and events objective on the stage, or to make them real by artistic illustrations, are almost of necessity failures. The story has won the attention and enjoyed the favor of a limited class of readers, and if it still continues to interest others of the same tastes and habits of thought I can ask nothing more of it.

January 23, 1883

CONTENTS

I.	THE BRAHMIN CASTE OF NEW ENGLAND	15
II.	THE STUDENT AND HIS CERTIFICATE	20
III.	MR. BERNARD TRIES HIS HAND	32
IV.	THE MOTH FLIES INTO THE CANDLE	47
V.	AN OLD-FASHIONED DESCRIPTIVE CHAPTER	56
VI.	THE SUNBEAM AND THE SHADOW	68
VII.	THE EVENT OF THE SEASON	77
VIII.	THE MORNING AFTER	106
IX.	THE DOCTOR ORDERS THE BEST SULKY (WITH A DIGRESSION ON "HIRED HELP")	119
X.	THE DOCTOR CALLS ON ELSIE VENNER	123
XI.	COUSIN RICHARD'S VISIT	131
XII.	THE APOLLINEAN INSTITUTE (WITH EXTRACTS FROM THE "REPORT OF THE COMMITTEE")	143
XIII.	CURIOSITY	154
XIV.	FAMILY SECRETS	166
XV.	PHYSIOLOGICAL	175
XVI.	EPISTOLARY	187
XVII.	OLD SOPHY CALLS ON THE REVEREND DOCTOR	198
XVIII.	THE REVEREND DOCTOR CALLS ON BROTHER FAIRWEATHER	212

XIX.	THE SPIDER ON HIS THREAD	219
XX.	FROM WITHOUT AND FROM WITHIN	229
XXI.	THE WIDOW ROWENS GIVES A TEA-PARTY	239
XXII.	WHY DOCTORS DIFFER	261
XXIII.	THE WILD HUNTSMAN	274
XXIV.	ON HIS TRACKS	285
XXV.	THE PERILOUS HOUR	295
XXVI.	THE NEWS REACHES THE DUDLEY MANSION	315
XXVII.	A SOUL IN DISTRESS	330
XXVIII.	THE SECRET IS WHISPERED	338
XXIX.	THE WHITE ASH	359
XXX.	THE GOLDEN CORD IS LOOSED	368
XXXI.	MR. SILAS PECKHAM RENDERS HIS ACCOUNT	381
XXXII.	CONCLUSION	395

ELSIE VENNER

CHAPTER I

THE BRAHMIN CASTE OF NEW ENGLAND

There is nothing in New England corresponding at all to the feudal aristocracies of the Old World. Whether it be owing to the stock from which we were derived, or to the practical working of our institutions, or to the abrogation of the technical "law of honor," which draws a sharp line between the personally responsible class of "gentlemen" and the unnamed multitude of those who are not expected to risk their lives for an abstraction,—whatever be the cause, we have no such aristocracy here as that which grew up out of the military systems of the Middle Ages.

What we mean by "aristocracy" is merely the richer part of the community, that live in the tallest houses, drive real carriages, (not "kerridges,") kid-glove their hands, and French-bonnet their ladies' heads, give parties where the persons who call them by the above title are not invited, and have a provokingly easy way of dressing, walking, talking, and nodding to people, as if they felt entirely at home, and would not be embarrassed in the least, if they met the Governor, or even the President of the United States, face to face. Some of these great folks are really well-bred, some of them are only purse-proud and assuming,—but they form a class, and are named as above in the common speech.

It is in the nature of large fortunes to diminish rapidly, when subdivided and distributed. A million is the unit of wealth, now and here in America. It splits into four handsome properties; each of these into four good inheritances; these, again, into scanty competences for four ancient maidens,—with whom it is best the family should die out, unless it can begin again as its great-grandfather did. Now a million is a kind of golden cheese, which represents in a compendious form the summer's growth of a fat meadow of craft or commerce; and as this kind of meadow rarely bears more than one crop, it is pretty certain that sons and grandsons will not get another golden cheese out of it, whether they milk the same cows or turn in new ones. In other words, the millionocracy, considered in a large way, is not at all an affair of persons and families, but a perpetual fact of money with a variable human element, which a philosopher might leave out of consideration without falling into serious error. Of course, this trivial and fugitive fact of personal wealth does not create a permanent class, unless some special means are taken to arrest the process of disintegration in the third generation. This is so rarely done, at least successfully, that one need not live a very long life to see most of the rich families he knew in childhood more or less reduced, and the millions shifted into the hands of the country-boys who were sweeping stores and carrying parcels when the now decayed gentry were driving their chariots, eating their venison over silver chafing-dishes, drinking Madeira chilled in embossed coolers, wearing their hair in powder, and casing their legs in long boots with silken tassels.

There is, however, in New England, an aristocracy, if you choose to call it so, which has a far greater character of permanence. It has grown to be a *caste*,—not in any odious sense,—but, by the repetition of the same influences, generation after generation, it has acquired a distinct organization and physiognomy, which not to recognize is mere stupidity, and not to be willing to describe would show a distrust of the good-nature and intelligence of our readers, who like to have us see all we can and tell all we see.

If you will look carefully at any class of students in one of our colleges, you will have no difficulty in selecting specimens of two different aspects of youthful manhood. Of course I shall choose extreme cases to illustrate the contrast between them. In the first, the figure is perhaps robust, but often otherwise,—inelegant, partly from careless attitudes, partly from ill-dressing,—the face is uncouth in feature, or at least common,—the mouth coarse and unformed,—the eye unsympathetic, even if bright,—the movements of the face are clumsy, like those of the limbs,—the voice is unmusical,—and the enunciation as if the words were coarse castings, instead of fine carvings. The youth of the other aspect is commonly slender,—his face is smooth, and apt to be pallid,—his features are regular and of a certain delicacy,—his eye is bright and quick,—his lips play over the thought he utters as a pianist's fingers dance over their music,—and his whole air, though it may be timid, and even awkward, has nothing clownish. If you are a teacher, you know what to expect from each of these young men. With equal willingness, the first will be slow at learning; the second will take to his books as a pointer or a setter to his field-work.

The first youth is the common country-boy, whose race has been bred to bodily labor. Nature has adapted the family organization to the kind of life it has lived. The hands and feet by constant use have got more than their share of development,—the organs of thought and expression less than their share. The finer instincts are latent and must be developed. A youth of this kind is raw material in its first stage of elaboration. You must not expect too much of any such. Many of them have force of will and character, and become distinguished in practical life; but very few of them ever become great scholars. A scholar is, in a large proportion of cases, the son of scholars or scholarly persons.

That is exactly what the other young man is. He comes of the *Brahmin caste of New England*. This is the harmless, inoffensive, untitled aristocracy referred to, and which many readers will at once acknowledge. There are races of scholars among us, in which aptitude for learning, and all these marks of it I have spoken of, are congenital and hereditary. Their names are always on some college catalogue or other. They break out every generation or two in some learned labor which calls them up after they seem to have died out. At last some newer name takes their place, it may be,—but you inquire a little and you find it is the blood of the Edwardses or the Chauncys or the Ellerys or some of the old historic scholars, disguised under the altered name of a female descendant.

There probably is not an experienced instructor anywhere in our Northern States who will not recognize at once the truth of this general distinction. But the reader who has never been a teacher will very probably object, that some of our most illustrious public men have come direct from the homespun-clad class of the people,—and he may, perhaps, even find a noted scholar or two whose parents were masters of the English alphabet, but of no other.

It is not fair to pit a few chosen families against the great multitude of those who are continually working their way up into the intellectual classes. The results which are habitually reached by hereditary training are occasionally brought about without it. There are natural filters as well as artificial ones; and though the great rivers are commonly more or less turbid, if you will look long enough, you may find a spring that sparkles as no water does which drips through your apparatus of sands and sponges. So there are families which refine themselves into intellectual aptitude without having had much opportunity for intellectual acquirements. A series of felicitous crosses develops an improved strain of blood, and reaches its maximum perfection at last in the large uncombed youth who goes to college and startles the hereditary class-leaders by striding past them all. That is Nature's republicanism; thank God for it, but do not let it make you illogical. The race of the hereditary scholar has exchanged a certain portion of its animal vigor for its new instincts, and it is hard to lead men without a good deal of animal vigor. The scholar who comes by Nature's special grace from an unworn stock of broad-chested sires and deep-bosomed mothers must always overmatch an equal intelligence with a compromised and lowered vitality. A man's breathing and digestive apparatus (one is tempted to add *muscular*) are just as important to him on the floor of the Senate as his thinking organs. You broke down in your great speech, did you? Yes, your grandfather had an attack of dyspepsia in '82, after working too hard on his famous Election Sermon. All this does not touch the main fact: our scholars come chiefly from a privileged order, just as our best fruits come from well-known grafts,—though now and then a seedling apple, like the

Northern Spy, or a seedling pear, like the Seckel, springs from a nameless ancestry and grows to be the pride of all the gardens in the land.

Let me introduce you to a young man who belongs to the Brahmin caste of New England.

CHAPTER II

THE STUDENT AND HIS CERTIFICATE

Bernard C. Langdon, a young man attending Medical Lectures at the school connected with one of our principal colleges, remained after the Lecture one day and wished to speak with the Professor. He was a student of mark,—first favorite of his year, as they say of the Derby colts. There are in every class half a dozen bright faces to which the teacher naturally directs his discourse, and by the intermediation of whose attention he seems to hold that of the mass of listeners. Among these some one is pretty sure to take the lead, by virtue of a personal magnetism, or some peculiarity of expression, which places the face in quick sympathetic relations with the lecturer. This was a young man with such a face; and I found,—for you have guessed that I was the "Professor" above-mentioned,—that, when there was anything difficult to be explained, or when I was bringing out some favorite illustration of a nice point, (as, for instance, when I compared the cell-growth, by which Nature builds up a plant or an animal, to the glassblower's similar mode of beginning,—always with a hollow sphere, or vesicle, whatever he is going to make,) I naturally looked in his face and gauged my success by its expression.

It was a handsome face,—a little too pale, perhaps, and would have borne something more of fulness without becoming heavy. I put the organization to which it belongs in Section B of Class 1 of my Anglo-American Anthropology (unpublished). The jaw in this section is but *slightly* narrowed,—just enough to make the width of the forehead tell more decidedly. The moustache often grows vigorously, but the whiskers are thin. The skin is like that of Jacob, rather than like Esau's. One string of the animal nature has been taken away, but this gives only a greater predominance to the intellectual chords. To see just how the vital energy has been toned down, you must contrast one of this section with a specimen of Section A of the same class,—say, for instance, one of the old-fashioned, full-whiskered, red-faced, roaring, big Commodores of the last generation, whom you remember, at least by their portraits, in ruffled shirts, looking as hearty as butchers and as plucky as bull-terriers, with their hair combed straight up from their foreheads, which were not commonly very high or broad. The special form of physical life I have been describing gives you a right to expect more delicate perceptions and a more reflective nature than you commonly find in shaggy-throated men, clad in heavy suits of muscles.

The student lingered in the lecture-room, looking all the time as if he wanted to say something in private, and waiting for two or three others, who were still hanging about, to be gone.

Something is wrong!—I said to myself, when I noticed his expression.—Well, Mr. Langdon,—I said to him, when we were alone,—can I do anything for you to-day?

You can, Sir,—he said.—I am going to leave the class, for the present, and keep school.

Why, that's a pity, and you so near graduating! You'd better stay and finish this course and take your degree in the spring, rather than break up your whole plan of study.

I can't help myself, Sir,—the young man answered.—There's trouble at home, and they cannot keep me here as they have done. So I must look out for myself for a while. It's what I've done before, and am ready to do again. I came to ask you for a certificate of my fitness to teach a common school, or a high school, if you think I am up to that. Are you willing to give it to me?

Willing? Yes, to be sure,—but I don't want you to go. Stay; we'll make it easy for you. There's a fund will do something for you, perhaps. Then you can take both the annual prizes if you like,—and claim them in money, if you want that more than medals.

I have thought it all over,—he answered,—and have pretty much made up my mind to go.

A perfectly gentlemanly young man, of courteous address and mild utterance, but means at least as much as he says. There are some people whose rhetoric consists of a slight habitual understatement. I often tell Mrs. Professor that one of her "I think it's sos" is worth the Bible-oath of all the rest of the household that they "know it's so." When you find a person a little better than his word, a little more liberal than his promise, a little more than borne out in his statement by his facts, a little larger in deed than in speech, you recognize a kind of eloquence in that person's utterance not laid down in Blair or Campbell.

This was a proud fellow, self-trusting, sensitive, with family-recollections that made him unwilling to accept the kind of aid which many students would have thankfully welcomed. I knew him too well to urge him, after the few words which implied that he was determined to go. Besides, I have great confidence in young men who believe in themselves, and are accustomed to rely on their own resources from an early period. When a resolute young fellow steps up to the great bully, the World, and takes him boldly by the beard, he is often surprised to find it come off in his hand, and that it was only tied on to scare away timid adventurers. I have seen young men more than once, who came to a great city without a single friend, support themselves and pay for their education, lay up money in a few years, grow rich enough to travel, and establish themselves in life, without ever asking a dollar of any person which they had not earned. But these are exceptional cases. There are horse-tamers, born so, as we all know; there are woman-tamers who bewitch the sex as the pied piper bedeviled the children of Hamelin; and there are world-tamers, who can make any community, even a Yankee one, get down and let them jump on its back as easily as Mr. Rarey saddled Cruiser.

Whether Langdon was of this sort or not I could not say positively; but he had spirit, and, as I have said, a family-pride which would not let him be dependent. The New England Brahmin caste often gets blended with connections of political influence or commercial distinction. It is a charming thing for the scholar, when his fortune carries him in this way into some of the "old families" who have fine old houses, and city-lots that have risen in the market, and names written in all the stock-books of all the dividend-paying companies. His narrow study expands into a stately library, his books are counted by thousands instead of hundreds, and his favorites are dressed in gilded calf in place of plebeian sheepskin or its pauper substitutes of cloth and paper.

The Reverend Jedediah Langdon, grandfather of our young gentleman, had made an advantageous alliance of this kind. Miss Dorothea Wentworth had read one of his sermons which had been printed "by request," and became deeply interested in the young author, whom she had never seen. Out of this circumstance grew a correspondence, an interview, a declaration, a matrimonial alliance, and a family of half a dozen children. Wentworth Langdon, Esquire, was the oldest of these, and lived in the old family-mansion. Unfortunately, that principle of the diminution of estates by division, to which I have referred, rendered it somewhat difficult to maintain the establishment upon the fractional income which the proprietor received from his share of the property. Wentworth Langdon, Esq., represented a certain intermediate condition of life not at all infrequent in our old families. He was the connecting link between the generation which lived in ease, and even a kind of state, upon its own resources, and the new brood, which must live mainly by its wits or industry, and make itself rich, or shabbily subside into that lower stratum known to social geologists by a deposit of Kidderminster carpets and the peculiar aspect of the fossils constituting the family furniture and wardrobe. This *slack-water* period of a race, which comes before the rapid ebb of its prosperity, is familiar to all who live in cities. There are no more quiet, inoffensive people than these children of rich families, just above the necessity of active employment, yet not in a condition to place their own children advantageously, if they happen to have families. Many of them are content to live unmarried. Some mend their broken fortunes by prudent alliances, and some leave a numerous progeny to pass into the obscurity from which their ancestors emerged; so that you may see on hand-carts and cobblers' stalls names which, a few generations back, were upon parchments with broad seals, and tombstones with armorial bearings.

In a large city, this class of citizens is familiar to us in the streets. They are very courteous in their salutations; they have time enough to bow and take their hats off,—which, of course, no business-man can afford to do. Their beavers are smoothly brushed, and their boots well polished; all their appointments are tidy; they look the respectable walking gentleman to perfection. They are prone to habits,—they frequent reading-rooms, insurance-offices,—they walk the same streets at the same hours,—so that one becomes familiar with their faces and persons, as a part of the street-furniture.

There is one curious circumstance, that all city-people must have noticed, which is often illustrated in our experience of the slack-water gentry. We shall know a certain person by his looks, familiarly, for years, but never have learned his name. About this person we shall have accumulated no little circumstantial knowledge;—thus his face, figure, gait, his mode of dressing, of saluting, perhaps even of speaking, may be familiar to us; yet who he is we know not. In another department of our consciousness, there is a very familiar *name*, which we have never found the person to match. We have heard it so often, that it has idealized itself, and become one of that multitude of permanent shapes which walk the chambers of the brain in velvet slippers in the company of Falstaff and Hamlet and General Washington and Mr. Pickwick. Sometimes the person dies, but the name lives on indefinitely. But now and then it happens, perhaps after years of this independent existence of the name and its shadowy image in the brain, on the one part, and the person and all its real attributes, as we see them daily, on the other, that some accident reveals their relation, and we find the name we have carried so long in our memory belongs to the person we have known so long as a fellow-citizen. Now the slack-water gentry are among the persons most likely to be the subjects of this curious divorce of title and reality,—for the reason, that, playing no important part in the community, there is nothing to tie the floating name to the actual individual, as is the case with the men who belong in any way to the public, while yet their names have a certain historical currency, and we cannot help meeting them, either in their haunts, or going to and from them.

To this class belonged Wentworth Langdon, Esq. He had been "dead-headed" into the world some fifty years ago, and had sat with his hands in his pockets staring at the show ever since. I shall not tell you, for reasons before hinted, the whole name of the place in which he lived. I will only point you in the right direction, by saying that there are three towns lying in a line with each other, as you go "down East," each of them with a *Port* in its name, and each of them having a peculiar interest which gives it individuality, in addition to the Oriental character they have in common. I need not tell you that these towns are Newburyport, Portsmouth, and Portland. The Oriental character they have in common consists in their large, square, palatial mansions, with sunny gardens round them. The two first have seen better days. They are in perfect harmony with the condition of weakened, but not impoverished, gentility. Each of them is a "paradise of demi-fortunes." Each of them is of that intermediate size between a village and a city which any place has outgrown when the presence of a well-dressed stranger walking up and down the main street ceases to be a matter of public curiosity and private speculation, as frequently happens, during the busier months of the year, in considerable commercial centres like Salem. They both have grand old recollections to fall back upon,—times when they looked forward to commercial greatness, and when the portly gentlemen in cocked hats, who built their now decaying wharves and sent out their ships all over the world, dreamed that their fast-growing port was to be the Tyre or the Carthage of the rich British Colony. Great houses, like that once lived in by Lord Timothy Dexter, in Newburyport, remain as evidence of the fortunes amassed in these places of old. Other mansions—like the Rockingham House in Portsmouth (look at the white horse's tail before you mount the broad staircase) show that there was not only wealth, but style and state, in these quiet old towns during the last century. It is not with any thought of pity or depreciation that we speak of them as in a certain sense decayed towns; they did not fulfil their early promise of expansion, but they remain incomparably the most interesting places of their size in any of the three northernmost New England States. They have even now prosperity enough to keep them in good condition, and offer the most attractive residences for quiet families, which, if they had been English, would have lived in a *palazzo* at Genoa or Pisa, or some other Continental Newburyport or Portsmouth.

As for the last of the three Ports, or Portland, it is getting too prosperous to be as attractive as its less northerly neighbors. Meant for a fine old town, to ripen like a Cheshire cheese within its walls of ancient rind, burrowed by crooked alleys and mottled with venerable mould, it seems likely to sacrifice its mellow future to a vulgar material prosperity. Still it remains invested with many of its old charms, as yet, and will forfeit its place among this admirable trio only when it gets a hotel with unequivocal marks of having been built and organized in the present century.

——It was one of the old square palaces of the North, in which Bernard Langdon, the son of Wentworth, was born. If he had had the luck to be an only child, he might have lived as his father had done, letting his meagre competence smoulder on almost without consuming, like the fuel in an air-tight stove. But after Master Bernard came Miss Dorothea Elizabeth Wentworth Langdon, and then Master William Pepperell Langdon, and others, equally well named,— a string of them, looking, when they stood in a row in prayer-time, as if they would fit a set of Pandean pipes, of from three feet upward in dimensions. The door of the air-tight stove has to be opened, under such circumstances, you may well suppose! So it happened that our young man had been obliged, from an early period, to do something to support himself, and found himself stopped short in his studies by the inability of the good people at home to furnish him the present means of support as a student.

You will understand now why the young man wanted me to give him a certificate of his fitness to teach, and why I did not choose to urge him to accept the aid which a meek country-boy from a family without ante-Revolutionary recollections would have thankfully received. Go he must,—that was plain enough. He would not be content otherwise. He was not, however, to give up his studies; and as it is customary to allow *half-time* to students engaged in school-keeping,—that is, to count a year, so employed, if the student also keep on with his professional studies, as equal to six months of the three years he is expected to be under an instructor before applying for his degree,—he would not necessarily lose more than a few months of time. He had a small library of professional books, which he could take with him.

So he left my teaching and that of my estimable colleagues, carrying with him my certificate, that Mr. Bernard C. Langdon was a young gentleman of excellent moral character, of high intelligence and good education, and that his services would be of great value in any school, academy, or other institution, where young persons of either sex were to be instructed.

I confess, that expression, "either sex," ran a little thick, as I may say, from my pen. For, although the young man bore a very fair character, and there was no special cause for doubting his discretion, I considered him altogether too good-looking, in the first place, to be let loose in a roomfull of young girls. I didn't want him to fall in love just then,—and if half a dozen girls fell in love with him, as they most assuredly would, if brought into too near relations with him, why, there was no telling what gratitude and natural sensibility might bring about.

Certificates are, for the most part, like ostrich-eggs; the giver never knows what is hatched out of them. But once in a thousand times they act as curses are said to,—come home to roost. Give them often enough, until it gets to be a mechanical business, and, some day or other, you will get caught warranting somebody's ice not to melt in any climate, or somebody's razors to be safe in the hands of the youngest children.

I had an uneasy feeling, after giving this certificate. It might be all right enough; but if it happened to end badly, I should always reproach myself. There was a chance, certainly, that it would lead him or others into danger or wretchedness. Any one who looked at this young man could not fail to see that he was capable of fascinating and being fascinated. Those large, dark eyes of his would sink into the white soul of a young girl as the black cloth sunk into the snow in Franklin's famous experiment. Or, on the other hand, if the rays of a passionate nature should ever be concentrated on them, they would be absorbed into the very depths of his nature, and then his blood would turn to flame and burn his life out of him, until his cheeks grew as white as the ashes that cover a burning coal.

I wish I had not said *either sex* in my certificate. An academy for young gentlemen, now; that sounds cool and unimaginative. A boys' school, that would be a very good place for him;—some of them are pretty rough, but there is nerve enough in that old Wentworth strain of blood; he can give any country fellow, of the common stock, twenty pounds, and hit him out of time in ten minutes. But to send such a young fellow as that out a girl's-nesting! to give this falcon a free pass into all the dove-cotes! I was a fool, —that's all.

I brooded over the mischief which might come out of these two words until it seemed to me that they were charged with destiny. I could hardly sleep for thinking what a train I might have been laying, which might take a spark any day, and blow up nobody knows whose peace or prospects. What I dreaded most was one of those miserable matrimonial misalliances where a young fellow who does not know himself as yet flings his magnificent future into the checked apron-lap of some fresh-faced, half-bred country-girl, no more fit to be mated with him than her father's horse to go in double harness with Flora Temple. To think of the eagle's wings being clipped so that he shall never lift himself over the farm-yard fence! Such things happen, and always must,—because, as one of us said awhile ago, a man always loves a woman, and a woman a man, unless some good reason exists to the contrary. You think yourself a very fastidious young man, my friend; but there are probably at least five thousand young women in these United States, any one of whom you would certainly marry, if you were thrown much into her company, and nobody more attractive were near, and she had no objection. And you, my dear young lady, justly pride yourself on your discerning delicacy; but if I should say that there are twenty thousand young men, any one of whom, if he offered his hand and heart under favorable circumstances, you would

"First endure, then pity, then embrace,"

I should be much more imprudent than I mean to be, and you would, no doubt, throw down a story in which I hope to interest you.

I had settled it in my mind that this young fellow had a career marked out for him. He should begin in the natural way, by taking care of poor patients in one of the public charities, and work his way up to a better kind of practice, —better, that is, in the vulgar, worldly sense. The great and good Boerhaave used to say, as I remember very well, that the poor were his best patients; for God was their paymaster. But everybody is not as patient as Boerhaave, nor as deserving; so that the rich, though not, perhaps, the best patients, are good enough for common practitioners. I suppose Boerhaave put up with them when he could not get poor ones, as he left his daughter two millions of florins when he died.

Now if this young man once got into the *wide streets*, he would sweep them clear of his rivals of the same standing; and as I was getting indifferent to business, and old Dr. Kilham was growing careless, and had once or twice prescribed morphine when he meant quinine, there would soon be an opening into the Doctor's Paradise,—the *streets with only one side to them*. Then I would have him strike a bold stroke,—set up a nice little coach, and be driven round like a first-class London doctor, instead of coasting about in a shabby one-horse concern and casting anchor opposite his patients' doors like a Cape-Ann fishing-smack. By the time he was thirty, he would have knocked the social pawns out of his way, and be ready to challenge a wife from the row of great pieces in the background. I would not have a man marry above his level, so as to become the appendage of a powerful family-connection; but I would not have him marry until he knew his level,—that is, again, looking at the matter in a purely worldly point of view, and not taking the sentiments at all into consideration. But remember, that a young man, using large endowments wisely and fortunately, may put himself on a level with the highest in the land in ten brilliant years of spirited, unflagging labor. And to stand at the very top of your calling in a great city is something in itself,—that is, if you like money and influence, and a seat on the platform at public lectures, and gratuitous tickets to all sorts of places where you don't want to go, and, what is a good deal better than any of these things, a sense of power, limited, it may be, but absolute in its range, so that all the Cæsars and Napoleons would have to stand aside, if they came between you and the exercise of your special vocation.

That is what I thought this young fellow might have come to; and now I have let him go off into the country with my certificate, that he is fit to teach in a school for either sex! Ten to one he will run like a moth into a candle, right into one of those girls'-nests, and get tangled up in some sentimental folly or other, and there will be the end of him. Oh, yes! country doctor,—half a dollar a visit,—drive, drive, drive all day,—get up at night and harness your own horse,—drive again ten miles in a snow-storm,—shake powders out of two phials, (*pulv. glycyrrhiz., pulv. gum. acac. āā partes equales,*)—drive back again, if you don't happen to get stuck in a drift,—no home, no peace, no continuous meals, no unbroken sleep, no Sunday, no holiday, no social intercourse, but one eternal jog, jog, jog, in a sulky, until you feel like the mummy of an Indian who had been buried in the sitting posture, and was dug up a hundred years afterwards! Why didn't I warn him about love and all that nonsense? Why didn't I tell him he had nothing to do with it, yet awhile? Why didn't I hold up to him those awful examples I could have cited, where poor young fellows who could just keep themselves afloat have hung a matrimonial millstone round their necks, taking it for a life-preserver?

All this of two words in a certificate!

CHAPTER III

MR. BERNARD TRIES HIS HAND

Whether the Student advertised for a school, or whether he fell in with the advertisement of a school-committee, is not certain. At any rate, it was not long before he found himself the head of a large district, or, as it was called by the inhabitants, "deestric" school, in the flourishing inland village of Pequawkett, or, as it is commonly spelt, Pigwacket Centre. The natives of this place would be surprised, if they should hear that any of the readers of a work published in Boston were unacquainted with so remarkable a locality. As, however, some copies of it may be read at a distance from this distinguished metropolis, it may be well to give a few particulars respecting the place, taken from the Universal Gazetteer.

"PIGWACKET, sometimes spelt Pequawkett. A post-village and township in —— Co., State of ——, situated in a fine agricultural region, 2 thriving villages, Pigwacket Centre and Smithville, 3 churches, several school-houses, and many handsome private residences. Mink River runs through the town, navigable for small boats after heavy rains. Muddy Pond at N. E. section, well stocked with horn pouts, eels, and shiners. Products, beef, pork, butter, cheese. Manufactures, shoe-pegs, clothes-pins, and tin-ware. Pop. 1373."

The reader may think there is nothing very remarkable implied in this description. If, however, he had read the town-history, by the Rev. Jabez Grubb, he would have learned, that, like the celebrated Little Pedlington, it was distinguished by many *very* remarkable advantages. Thus:—

"The situation of Pigwacket is eminently beautiful, looking down the lovely valley of Mink River, a tributary of the Musquash. The air is salubrious, and many of the inhabitants have attained great age, several having passed the allotted period of 'three-score years and ten' before succumbing to any of the various 'ills that flesh is heir to.' Widow Comfort Leevins died in 1836, Æt. LXXXVII. years. Venus, an African, died in 1841, supposed to be C. years old. The people are distinguished for intelligence, as has been frequently remarked by eminent lyceum-lecturers, who have invariably spoken in the highest terms of a Pigwacket audience. There is a public library, containing nearly a hundred volumes, free to all subscribers. The preached word is well attended, there is a flourishing temperance society, and the schools are excellent. It is a residence admirably adapted to refined families who relish the beauties of Nature and the charms of society. The Honorable John Smith, formerly a member of the State Senate, was a native of this town."

That is the way they all talk. After all, it is probably pretty much like other inland New England towns in point of "salubrity,"—that is, gives people their choice of dysentery or fever every autumn, with a season-ticket for consumption, good all the year round. And so of the other pretences. "Pigwacket audience," forsooth! Was there ever an audience anywhere, though there wasn't a pair of eyes in it brighter than pickled oysters, that didn't think it was "distinguished for intelligence"?—"The preachèd word"! That means the Rev. Jabez Grubb's sermons. "Temperance society"! "Excellent schools"! Ah, that is just what we were talking about.

The truth was, that District No. 1, Pigwacket Centre, had had a good deal of trouble of late with its schoolmasters. The committee had done their best, but there were a number of well-grown and pretty rough young fellows who had got the upperhand of the masters, and meant to keep it. Two dynasties had fallen before the uprising of this fierce democracy. This was a thing that used to be not very uncommon; but in so "intelligent" a community as that of Pigwacket Centre, in an era of public libraries and lyceum-lectures, it was portentous and alarming.

The rebellion began under the ferule of Master Weeks, a slender youth from a country college, under-fed, thin-blooded, sloping-shouldered, knock-kneed, straight-haired, weak-bearded, pale-eyed, wide-pupilled, half-colored; a common type enough in in-door races, not rich enough to pick and choose in their alliances. Nature kills off a good many of this sort in the first teething-time, a few in later childhood, a good many again in early adolescence; but every now and then one runs the gauntlet of her various diseases, or rather forms of one disease, and grows up, as Master Weeks had done.

It was a very foolish thing for him to try to inflict personal punishment on such a lusty young fellow as Abner Briggs, Junior, one of the "hardest customers" in the way of a rough-and-tumble fight that there were anywhere round. No doubt he had been insolent, but it would have been better to overlook it. It pains me to report the events which took place when the master made his rash attempt to maintain his authority. Abner Briggs, Junior, was a great, hulking fellow, who had been bred to butchering, but urged by his parents to attend school, in order to learn the elegant accomplishments of reading and writing, in which he was sadly deficient. He was in the habit of talking and laughing pretty loud in school-hours, of throwing wads of paper reduced to a pulp by a natural and easy process, of occasional insolence and general negligence. One of the soft, but unpleasant missiles just alluded to, flew by the master's head one morning, and flattened itself against the wall, where it adhered in the form of a convex mass in *alto rilievo*. The master looked round and saw the young butcher's arm in an attitude which pointed to it unequivocally as the source from which the projectile had taken its flight.

Master Weeks turned pale. He must "lick" Abner Briggs, Junior, or abdicate. So he determined to lick Abner Briggs, Junior.

"Come here, Sir!" he said; "you have insulted me and outraged the decency of the schoolroom often enough! Hold out your hand!"

The young fellow grinned and held it out. The master struck at it with his black ruler, with a will in the blow and a snapping of the eyes, as much as to say that he meant to make him smart this time. The young fellow pulled his hand back as the ruler came down, and the master hit himself a vicious blow with it on the right knee. There are things no man can stand. The master caught the refractory youth by the collar and began shaking him, or rather shaking himself against him.

"Le' go o' that are cŏat, naow," said the fellow, "or I'll make ye! 'T'll take tew on ye t' handle me, I tell ye, 'n' then ye caänt dew it!"—and the young pupil returned the master's attention by catching hold of *his* collar.

When it comes to that, the *best man*, not exactly in the moral sense, but rather in the material, and more especially the muscular point of view, is very apt to have the best of it, irrespectively of the merits of the case. So it happened now. The unfortunate schoolmaster found himself taking the measure of the sanded floor, amidst the general uproar of the school. From that moment his ferule was broken, and the school-committee very soon had a vacancy to fill.

Master Pigeon, the successor of Master Weeks, was of better stature, but loosely put together, and slender-limbed. A dreadfully nervous kind of man he was, walked on tiptoe, started at sudden noises, was distressed when he heard a whisper, had a quick, suspicious look, and was always saying, "Hush!" and putting his hands to his ears. The boys were not long in finding out this nervous weakness, of course. In less than a week a regular system of torments was inaugurated, full of the most diabolical malice and ingenuity. The exercises of the conspirators varied from day to day, but consisted mainly of foot-scraping, solos on the slate-pencil, (making it *screech* on the slate,) falling of heavy books, attacks of coughing, banging of desk-lids, boot-creaking, with sounds as of drawing a cork from time to time, followed by suppressed chuckles.

Master Pigeon grew worse and worse under these inflictions. The rascally boys always had an excuse for any one trick they were caught at. "Couldn' help coughin', Sir." "Slipped out o' m' han', Sir." "Didn' go to, Sir." "Didn' dew 't o' purpose, Sir." And so on,—always the best of reasons for the most outrageous of behavior. The master weighed himself at the grocer's on a platform balance, some ten days after he began keeping the school. At the end of a week he weighed himself again. He had lost two pounds. At the end of another week he had lost five. He made a little calculation, based on these data, from which he learned that in a certain number of months, going on at this rate, he should come to weigh precisely nothing at all; and as this was a sum in subtraction he did not care to work out in practice, Master Pigeon took to himself wings and left the school-committee in possession of a letter of resignation and a vacant place to fill once more.

This was the school to which Mr. Bernard Langdon found himself appointed as master. He accepted the place conditionally, with the understanding that he should leave it at the end of a month, if he were tired of it.

The advent of Master Langdon to Pigwacket Centre created a much more lively sensation than had attended that of either of his predecessors. Looks go a good way all the world over, and though there were several good-looking people in the place, and Major Bush was what the natives of the town called a "hahnsome mahn," that is, big, fat, and red, yet the sight of a really elegant young fellow, with the natural air which grows up with carefully-bred young persons, was a novelty. The Brahmin blood which came from his grandfather as well as from his mother, a direct descendant of the old Flynt family, well known by the famous tutor, Henry Flynt, (see Cat. Harv. Anno 1693,) had been enlivened and enriched by that of the Wentworths, which had had a good deal of ripe old Madeira and other generous elements mingled with it, so that it ran to gout sometimes in the old folks and to high spirit, warm complexion, and curly hair in some of the younger ones. The soft curling hair Mr. Bernard had inherited,—something, perhaps, of the high spirit; but that we shall have a chance of finding out by-and-by. But the long sermons and the frugal board of his Brahmin ancestry, with his own habits of study, had told upon his color, which was subdued to something more of delicacy than one would care to see in a young fellow with rough work before him. This, however, made him look more interesting, or, as the young ladies at Major Bush's said, "interéstin'."

When Mr. Bernard showed himself at meeting, on the first Sunday after his arrival, it may be supposed that a good many eyes were turned upon the young schoolmaster. There was something heroic in his coming forward so readily to take a place which called for a strong hand, and a prompt, steady will to guide it. In fact, his position was that of a military chieftain on the eve of a battle. Everybody knew everything in Pigwacket Centre; and it was an understood thing that the young rebels meant to put down the new master, if they could. It was natural that the two prettiest girls in the village, called in the local dialect, as nearly as our limited alphabet will represent it, Alminy Cutterr, and Arvilly Braowne, should feel and express an interest in the good-looking stranger, and that, when their flattering comments were repeated in the hearing of their indigenous admirers, among whom were some of the older "boys" of the school, it should not add to the amiable dispositions of the turbulent youth.

Monday came, and the new schoolmaster was in his chair at the upper end of the schoolhouse, on the raised platform. The rustics looked at his handsome face, thoughtful, peaceful, pleasant, cheerful, but sharply cut round the lips and proudly lighted about the eyes. The ringleader of the mischief-makers, the young butcher who has before figured in this narrative, looked at him stealthily, whenever he got a chance to study him unobserved; for the truth was, he felt uncomfortable, whenever he found the large, dark eyes fixed on his own little, sharp, deep-set, gray ones. But he managed to study him pretty well,—first his face, then his neck and shoulders, the set of his arms, the narrowing at the loins, the make of his legs, and the way he moved. In short, he examined him as he would have examined a steer, to see what he could do and how he would cut up. If he could only have gone to him and felt of his muscles, he would have been entirely satisfied. He was not a very wise youth, but he did know well enough, that, though big arms and legs are very good things, there is something besides size that goes to make a man; and he had heard stories of a fighting-man, called "The Spider," from his attenuated proportions, who was yet a terrible hitter in the ring, and had whipped many a big-limbed fellow, in and out of the roped arena.

Nothing could be smoother than the way in which everything went on for the first day or two. The new master was so kind and courteous, he seemed to take everything in such a natural, easy way, that there was no chance to pick a quarrel with him. He in the mean time thought it best to watch the boys and young men for a day or two with as little show of authority as possible. It was easy enough to see that he would have occasion for it before long.

The schoolhouse was a grim, old, red, one-story building, perched on a bare rock at the top of a hill,—partly because this was a conspicuous site for the temple of learning, and partly because land is cheap where there is no chance even for rye or buckwheat, and the very sheep find nothing to nibble. About the little porch were carved initials and dates, at various heights, from the stature of nine to that of eighteen. Inside were old unpainted desks,—unpainted, but browned with the umber of human contact,—and hacked by innumerable jack-knives. It was long since the walls had been whitewashed, as might be conjectured by the various traces left upon them, wherever idle hands or sleepy heads could reach them. A curious appearance was noticeable on various higher parts of the wall, namely, a wart-like eruption, as one would be tempted to call it, being in reality a crop of the soft missiles before mentioned, which, adhering in considerable numbers, and hardening after the usual fashion of *papier-mâché*, formed at last permanent ornaments of the edifice.

The young master's quick eye soon noticed that a particular part of the wall was most favored with these ornamental appendages. Their position pointed sufficiently clearly to the part of the room they came from. In fact, there was a nest of young mutineers just there, which must be broken up by a *coup d'état*. This was easily effected by redistributing the seats and arranging the scholars according to classes, so that a mischievous fellow, charged full of the rebellious imponderable, should find himself between two non-conductors, in the shape of small boys of studious habits. It was managed quietly enough, in such a plausible sort of way that its motive was not thought of. But its effects were soon felt; and then began a system of correspondence by signs, and the throwing of little scrawls done up in pellets, and announced by preliminary *a'h'ms!* to call the attention of the distant youth addressed. Some of these were incendiary documents, devoting the schoolmaster to the lower divinities, as "a —— stuck-up dandy," as "a —— purse-proud aristocrat," as "a —— sight too big for his, etc.," and holding him up in a variety of equally forcible phrases to the indignation of the youthful community of School District No. 1, Pigwacket Centre.

Presently the draughtsman of the school set a caricature in circulation, labelled, to prevent mistakes, with the schoolmaster's name. An immense bell-crowned hat, and a long, pointed, swallow-tailed coat showed that the artist had in his mind the conventional dandy, as shown in prints of thirty or forty years ago, rather than any actual human aspect of the time. But it was passed round among the boys and made its laugh, helping of course to undermine the master's authority, as "Punch" or the "Charivari" takes the dignity out of an obnoxious minister. One morning, on going to the schoolroom, Master Langdon found an enlarged copy of this sketch, with its label, pinned on the door. He took it down, smiled a little, put it into his pocket, and entered the schoolroom. An insidious silence prevailed, which looked as if some plot were brewing. The boys were ripe for mischief, but afraid. They had really no fault to find with the master, except that he was dressed like a gentleman, which a certain class of fellows always consider a personal insult to themselves. But the older ones were evidently plotting, and more than once the warning *a'h'm!* was heard, and a dirty little scrap of paper rolled into a wad shot from one seat to another. One of these happened to strike the stove-funnel, and lodged on the master's desk. He was cool enough not to seem to notice it. He secured it, however, and found an opportunity to look at it, without being observed by the boys. It required no *immediate* notice.

He who should have enjoyed the privilege of looking upon Mr. Bernard Langdon the next morning, when his toilet was about half finished, would have had a very pleasant gratuitous exhibition. First he buckled the strap of his trousers pretty tightly. Then he took up a pair of heavy dumb-bells, and swung them for a few minutes; then two great "Indian clubs," with which he enacted all sorts of impossible-looking feats. His limbs were not very large, nor his shoulders remarkably broad; but if you knew as much of the muscles as all persons who look at statues and pictures with a critical eye ought to have learned,—if you knew the *trapezius*, lying diamond-shaped over the back and shoulders like a monk's cowl,—or the *deltoid*, which caps the shoulder like an epaulette,—or the *triceps*, which furnishes the *calf* of the upper arm,—or the hard-knotted *biceps*,—any of the great sculptural landmarks, in fact,—you would have said there was a pretty show of them, beneath the white satiny skin of Mr. Bernard Langdon. And if you had seen him, when he had laid down the Indian clubs, catch hold of a leather strap that hung from the beam of the old-fashioned ceiling, and lift and lower himself over and over again by his left hand alone, you might have thought it a very simple and easy thing to do, until you tried to do it yourself.—Mr. Bernard looked at himself with the eye of an expert. "Pretty well!" he said;—"not so much fallen off as I expected." Then he set up his bolster in a very knowing sort of way, and delivered two or three blows straight as rulers and swift as winks. "That will do," he said. Then, as if determined to make a certainty of his condition, he took a dynamometer from one of the drawers in his old veneered bureau. First he squeezed it with his two hands. Then he placed it on the floor and lifted, steadily, strongly. The springs creaked and cracked; the index swept with a great stride far up into the high figures of the scale; it was a good lift. He was satisfied. He sat down on the edge of his bed and looked at his cleanly-shaped arms. "If I strike one of those boobies, I am afraid I shall spoil him," he said. Yet this young man, when weighed with his class at the college, could barely turn one hundred and forty-two pounds in the scale,—not a heavy weight, surely; but some of the middle weights, as the present English champion, for instance, seem to be of a far finer quality of muscle than the bulkier fellows.

The master took his breakfast with a good appetite that morning, but was perhaps rather more quiet than usual. After breakfast he went up-stairs and put on a light loose frock, instead of that which he commonly wore, which was a close-fitting and rather stylish one. On his way to school he met Alminy Cutterr, who happened to be walking in the other direction. "Good morning, Miss Cutter," he said; for she and another young lady had been introduced to him, on a former occasion, in the usual phrase of polite society in presenting ladies to gentlemen,—"Mr. Langdon, let me make y' acquainted with Miss Cutterr;—let me make y' acquainted with Miss Braowne." So he said, "Good morning"; to which she replied, "Good mornin', Mr. Langdon. Haow's your haälth?" The answer to this question ought naturally to have been the end of the talk; but Alminy Cutterr lingered and looked as if she had something more on her mind.

A young fellow does not require a great experience to read a simple country-girl's face as if it were a signboard. Alminy was a good soul, with red cheeks and bright eyes, kind-hearted as she could be, and it was out of the question for her to hide her thoughts or feelings like a fine lady. Her bright eyes were moist and her red cheeks paler than their wont, as she said, with her lips quivering,—"Oh, Mr. Langdon, them boys 'll be the death of ye, if ye don't take caär!"

"Why, what's the matter, my dear?" said Mr. Bernard.— Don't think there was anything very odd in that "my dear," at the second interview with a village belle;—some of these woman-tamers call a girl "My dear," after five minutes' acquaintance, and it sounds all right *as they say it*. But you had better not try it at a venture.

It sounded all right to Alminy, as Mr. Bernard said it.—

"I'll tell ye what's the mahtterr," she said, in a frightened voice. "Ahbner's go'n' to car' his dog, 'n' he'll set him on ye 'z sure 'z y' 'r' alive. 'T 's the same cretur that haäf ēat up Eben Squires's little Jo, a year come nex' Faäst day."

Now this last statement was undoubtedly overcolored; as little Jo Squires was running about the village,—with an ugly scar on his arm, it is true, where the beast had caught him with his teeth, on the occasion of the child's taking liberties with him, as he had been accustomed to do with a good-tempered Newfoundland dog, who seemed to like being pulled and hauled round by children. After this the creature was commonly muzzled, and, as he was fed on raw meat chiefly, was always ready for a fight,—which he was occasionally indulged in, when anything stout enough to match him could be found in any of the neighboring villages.

Tiger, or, more briefly, Tige, the property of Abner Briggs, Junior, belonged to a species not distinctly named in scientific books, but well known to our country-folks under the name "Yallah dog." They do not use this expression as they would say *black* dog or *white* dog, but with almost as definite a meaning as when they speak of a terrier or a spaniel. A "yallah dog," is a large canine brute, of a dingy old-flannel color, of no particular breed except his own, who hangs round a tavern or a butcher's shop, or trots alongside of a team, looking as if he were disgusted with the world, and the world with him. Our inland population, while they tolerate him, speak of him with contempt. Old ——, of Meredith Bridge, used to twit the sun for not shining on cloudy days, swearing, that, if he hung up his "yallah dog," he would make a better show of daylight. A country fellow, abusing a horse of his neighbor's, vowed, that, "if he had such a hoss, he'd swap him for a 'yallah dog,'—and then shoot the dog."

Tige was an ill-conditioned brute by nature, and art had not improved him by cropping his ears and tail and investing him with a spiked collar. He bore on his person, also, various not ornamental scars, marks of old battles; for Tige had fight in him, as was said before, and as might be guessed by a certain bluntness about the muzzle, with a projection of the lower jaw, which looked as if there might be a bull-dog stripe among the numerous bar-sinisters of his lineage.

It was hardly fair, however, to leave Alminy Cutterr waiting while this piece of natural history was telling.— As she spoke of little Jo, who had been "haäf ēat up" by Tige, she could not contain her sympathies, and began to cry.

"Why, my dear little soul," said Mr. Bernard, "what are you worried about? I used to play with a *bear* when I was a boy; and the bear used to hug me, and I used to kiss him,— so!"

It was too bad of Mr. Bernard, only the second time he had seen Alminy; but her kind feelings had touched him, and that seemed the most natural way of expressing his gratitude. Alminy looked round to see if anybody was near; she saw nobody, so of course it would do no good to "holler." She saw nobody; but a stout young fellow, leading a yellow dog, muzzled, saw *her* through a crack in a picket fence, not a great way off the road. Many a year he had been "hangin' 'raoun'" Alminy, and never did he see any encouraging look, or hear any "Behave, naow!" or "Come, naow, a'n't ye 'shamed?" or other forbidding phrase of acquiescence, such as village belles understand as well as ever did the nymph who fled to the willows in the eclogue we all remember.

No wonder he was furious, when he saw the schoolmaster, who had never seen the girl until within a week, touching with his lips those rosy cheeks which he had never dared to approach. But that was all; it was a sudden impulse; and the master turned away from the young girl, laughing, and telling her not to fret herself about him,— he would take care of himself.

So Master Langdon walked on toward his schoolhouse, not displeased, perhaps, with his little adventure, nor immensely elated by it; for he was one of the natural class of the sex-subduers, and had had many a smile without asking, which had been denied to the feeble youth who try to win favor by pleading their passion in rhyme, and even to the more formidable approaches of young officers in volunteer companies, considered by many to be quite irresistible to the fair who have once beheld them from their windows in the epaulettes and plumes and sashes of the "Pigwacket Invincibles," or the "Hackmatack Rangers."

Master Langdon took his seat and began the exercises of his school. The smaller boys recited their lessons well enough, but some of the larger ones were negligent and surly. He noticed one or two of them looking toward the door, as if expecting somebody or something in that direction. At half past nine o'clock, Abner Briggs, Junior, who had not yet shown himself, made his appearance. He was followed by his "yallah dog," without his muzzle, who squatted down very grimly near the door, and gave a wolfish look round the room, as if he were considering which was the plumpest boy to begin with. The young butcher, meanwhile, went to his seat, looking somewhat flushed, except round the lips, which were hardly as red as common, and set pretty sharply.

"Put out that dog, Abner Briggs!"—The master spoke as the captain speaks to the helmsman, when there are rocks foaming at the lips, right under his lee.

Abner Briggs answered as the helmsman answers, when he knows he has a mutinous crew round him that mean to run the ship on the reef, and is one of the mutineers himself. "Put him aout y'rself, 'f ye a'n't afeard on him!"

The master stepped into the aisle. The great cur showed his teeth,—and the devilish instincts of his old wolf-ancestry looked out of his eyes, and flashed from his sharp tusks, and yawned in his wide mouth and deep red gullet.

The movements of animals are so much quicker than those of human beings commonly are, that they avoid blows as easily as one of us steps out of the way of an ox-cart. It must be a very stupid dog that lets himself be run over by a fast driver in his gig; he can jump out of the wheel's way after the tire has already touched him. So, while one is lifting a stick to strike or drawing back his foot to kick, the beast makes his spring, and the blow or the kick comes too late.

It was not so this time. The master was a fencer, and something of a boxer; he had played at single-stick, and was used to watching an adversary's eye and coming down on him without any of those premonitory symptoms by which unpractised persons show long beforehand what mischief they meditate.

"Out with you!" he said, fiercely,—and explained what he meant by a sudden flash of his foot that clashed the yellow dog's white teeth together like the springing of a bear-trap. The cur knew he had found his master at the first word and glance, as low animals on four legs, or a smaller number, always do; and the blow took him so by surprise, that it curled him up in an instant, and he went bundling out of the open schoolhouse-door with a most pitiable yelp, and his stump of a tail shut down as close as his owner ever shut the short, stubbed blade of his jack-knife.

It was time for the other cur to find who his master was.

"Follow your dog, Abner Briggs!" said Master Langdon.

The stout butcher-youth looked round, but the rebels were all cowed and sat still.

"I'll go when I'm ready," he said,—"'n' I guess I won't go afore I'm ready."

"You're ready now," said Master Langdon, turning up his cuffs so that the little boys noticed the yellow gleam of a pair of gold sleeve-buttons, once worn by Colonel Percy Wentworth, famous in the Old French War.

Abner Briggs, Junior, did not apparently think he was ready, at any rate; for he rose up in his place, and stood with clenched fists, defiant, as the master strode towards him. The master knew the fellow was really frightened, for all his looks, and that he must have no time to rally. So he caught him suddenly by the collar, and, with one great pull, had him out over his desk and on the open floor. He gave him a sharp fling backwards and stood looking at him.

The rough-and-tumble fighters all *clinch*, as everybody knows; and Abner Briggs, Junior, was one of that kind. He remembered how he had floored Master Weeks, and he had just "spunk" enough left in him to try to repeat his former successful experiment on the new master. He sprang at him, open-handed, to clutch him. So the master had to strike, —once, but very hard, and just in the place to tell. No doubt, the authority that doth hedge a schoolmaster added to the effect of the blow; but the blow was itself a neat one, and did not require to be repeated.

"Now go home," said the master, "and don't let me see you or your dog here again." And he turned his cuffs down over the gold sleeve-buttons.

This finished the great Pigwacket Centre School rebellion. What could be done with a master who was so pleasant as long as the boys behaved decently, and such a terrible fellow when he got "riled," as they called it? In a week's time everything was reduced to order, and the school-committee were delighted. The master, however, had received a proposition so much more agreeable and advantageous, that he informed the committee he should leave at the end of his month, having in his eye a sensible and energetic young college-graduate who would be willing and fully competent to take his place.

So, at the expiration of the appointed time, Bernard Langdon, late master of the School District No. 1, Pigwacket Centre, took his departure from that place for another locality, whither we shall follow him, carrying with him the regrets of the committee, of most of the scholars, and of several young ladies; also two locks of hair, sent unbeknown to payrents, one dark and one warmish auburn, inscribed with the respective initials of Alminy Cutterr and Arvilly Braowne.

CHAPTER IV

THE MOTH FLIES INTO THE CANDLE

The invitation which Mr. Bernard Langdon had accepted came from the Board of Trustees of the "Apollinean Female Institute," a school for the education of young ladies, situated in the flourishing town of Rockland. This was an establishment on a considerable scale, in which a hundred scholars or thereabouts were taught the ordinary English branches, several of the modern languages, something of Latin, if desired, with a little natural philosophy, metaphysics, and rhetoric, to finish off with in the last year, and music at any time when they would pay for it. At the close of their career in the Institute, they were submitted to a grand public examination, and received diplomas tied in blue ribbons, which proclaimed them with a great flourish of capitals to be graduates of the Apollinean Female Institute.

Rockland was a town of no inconsiderable pretensions. It was ennobled by lying at the foot of a mountain,—called by the working-folks of the place "*the* Maounting,"—which sufficiently showed that it was the principal high land of the district in which it was situated. It lay to the south of this, and basked in the sunshine as Italy stretches herself before the Alps. To pass from the town of Tamarack on the north of the mountain to Rockland on the south was like crossing from Coire to Chiavenna.

There is nothing gives glory and grandeur and romance and mystery to a place like the impending presence of a high mountain. Our beautiful Northampton with its fair meadows and noble stream is lovely enough, but owes its surpassing attraction to those twin summits which brood over it like living presences, looking down into its streets as if they were its tutelary divinities, dressing and undressing their green shrines, robing themselves in jubilant sunshine or in sorrowing clouds, and doing penance in the snowy shroud of winter, as if they had living hearts under their rocky ribs and changed their mood like the children of the soil at their feet, who grow up under their almost parental smiles and frowns. Happy is the child whose first dreams of heaven are blended with the evening glories of Mount Holyoke, when the sun is firing its treetops, and gilding the white walls that mark its one human dwelling! If the other and the wilder of the two summits has a scowl of terror in its overhanging brows, yet is it a pleasing fear to look upon its savage solitudes through the barred nursery-windows in the heart of the sweet, companionable village. —And how the mountains love their children! The sea is of a facile virtue, and will run to kiss the first comer in any port he visits; but the chaste mountains sit apart, and show their faces only in the midst of their own families.

The Mountain which kept watch to the north of Rockland lay waste and almost inviolate through much of its domain. The catamount still glared from the branches of its old hemlocks on the lesser beasts that strayed beneath him. It was not long since a wolf had wandered down, famished in the winter's dearth, and left a few bones and some tufts of wool of what had been a lamb in the morning. Nay, there were broad-footed tracks in the snow only two years previously, which could not be mistaken;—the black bear alone could have set that plantigrade seal, and little children must come home early from school and play, for he is an indiscriminate feeder when he is hungry, and a little child would not come amiss when other game was wanting.

But these occasional visitors may have been mere wanderers, which, straying along in the woods by day, and perhaps stalking through the streets of still villages by night, had worked their way along down from the ragged mountain-spurs of higher latitudes. The one feature of The Mountain that shed the brownest horror on its woods was the existence of the terrible region known as Rattlesnake Ledge, and still tenanted by those damnable reptiles, which distil a fiercer venom under our cold northern sky than the cobra himself in the land of tropical spices and poisons.

From the earliest settlement of the place, this fact had been, next to the Indians, the reigning nightmare of the inhabitants. It was easy enough, after a time, to drive away the savages; for "a screeching Indian Divell," as our fathers called him, could not crawl into the crack of a rock to escape from his pursuers. But the venomous population of Rattlesnake Ledge had a Gibraltar for their fortress that might have defied the siege-train dragged to the walls of Sebastopol. In its deep embrasures and its impregnable casemates they reared their families, they met in love or wrath, they twined together in family knots, they hissed defiance in hostile clans, they fed, slept, hybernated, and in due time died in peace. Many a foray had the town's-people made, and many a stuffed skin was shown as a trophy,—nay, there were families where the children's first toy was made from the warning appendage that once vibrated to the wrath of one of these "cruel serpents." Sometimes one of them, coaxed out by a warm sun, would writhe himself down the hillside into the roads, up the walks that led to houses,—worse than this, into the long grass, where the bare-footed mowers would soon pass with their swinging scythes,—more rarely into houses,—and on one memorable occasion, early in the last century, into the meeting-house, where he took a position on the pulpit-stairs,—as is narrated in the "Account of Some Remarkable Providences," etc., where it is suggested that a strong tendency of the Rev. Didymus Bean, the Minister at that time, towards the Arminian Heresy may have had something to do with it, and that the Serpent supposed to have been killed on the Pulpit-Stairs was a false show of the Dæmon's Contrivance, he having come in to listen to a Discourse which was a sweet Savour in his Nostrils, and, of course, not being capable of being killed Himself. Others said, however, that, though there was good Reason to think it was a Dæmon, yet he did come with Intent to bite the Heel of that faithful Servant, —etc.

One Gilson is said to have died of the bite of a rattlesnake in this town early in the present century. After this there was a great snake-hunt, in which very many of these venomous beasts were killed,—one in particular, said to have been as big round as a stout man's arm, and to have had no less than *forty* joints to his rattle,—indicating, according to some, that he had lived forty years, but, if we might put any faith in the Indian tradition, that he had killed forty human beings,—an idle fancy, clearly. This hunt, however, had no permanent effect in keeping down the serpent population. Viviparous creatures are a kind of specie-paying lot, but oviparous ones only give their notes, as it were for a future brood,—an egg being, so to speak, a promise to pay a young one by-and-by, if nothing happen. Now the domestic habits of the rattlesnake are not studied very closely, for obvious reasons; but it is, no doubt, to all intents and purposes oviparous. Consequently it has large families, and is not easy to kill out.

In the year 184–, a melancholy proof was afforded to the inhabitants of Rockland, that the brood which infested The Mountain was not extirpated. A very interesting young married woman, detained at home at the time by the state of her health, was bitten in the entry of her own house by a rattlesnake which had found its way down from The Mountain. Owing to the almost instant employment of powerful remedies, the bite did not prove immediately fatal; but she died within a few months of the time when she was bitten.

All this seemed to throw a lurid kind of shadow over The Mountain. Yet, as many years passed without any accident, people grew comparatively careless, and it might rather be said to add a fearful kind of interest to the romantic hillside, that the banded reptiles, which had been the terror of the red men for nobody knows how many thousand years, were there still, with the same poison-bags and spring-teeth at the white men's service, if they meddled with them.

The other natural features of Rockland were such as many of our pleasant country-towns can boast of. A brook came tumbling down the mountain-side and skirted the most thickly settled portion of the village. In the parts of its course where it ran through the woods, the water looked almost as brown as coffee flowing from its urn,—to say like *smoky quartz* would perhaps give a better idea,—but in the open plain it sparkled over the pebbles white as a queen's diamonds. There were huckleberry-pastures on the lower flanks of The Mountain, with plenty of the sweet-scented bayberry mingled with the other bushes. In other fields grew great store of high-bush blackberries. Along the roadside were barberry-bushes, hung all over with bright red coral pendants in autumn and far into the winter. Then there were swamps set thick with dingy alders, where the three-leaved arum and the skunk's-cabbage grew broad and succulent,—shelving down into black boggy pools here and there, at the edge of which the green frog, stupidest of his tribe, sat waiting to be victimized by boy or snapping-turtle long after the shy and agile leopard-frog had taken the six-foot spring that plumped him into the middle of the pool. And on the neighboring banks the maiden-hair spread its flat disk of embroidered fronds on the wire-like stem that glistened polished and brown as the darkest tortoise-shell, and pale violets cheated by the cold skies of their hues and perfume, sunned themselves like white-cheeked invalids. Over these rose the old forest-trees,—the maple, scarred with the wounds which had drained away its sweet life-blood,—the beech, its smooth gray bark mottled so as to look like the body of one of those great snakes of old that used to frighten armies,—always the mark of lovers' knives, as in the days of Musidora and her swain,— the yellow birch, rough as the breast of Silenus in old marbles,—the wild cherry, its little bitter fruit lying unheeded at its foot,—and, soaring over all, the huge, coarse-barked, splintery-limbed, dark-mantled hemlock, in the depth of whose aerial solitudes the crow brooded on her nest unscared, and the gray squirrel lived unharmed till his incisors grew to look like ram's-horns.

Rockland would have been but half a town without its pond; Quinnepeg Pond was the name of it, but the young ladies of the Apollinean Institute were very anxious that it should be called Crystalline Lake. It was here that the young folks used to sail in summer and skate in winter; here, too, those queer, old, rum-scented good-for-nothing, lazy, storytelling, half-vagabonds, who sawed a little wood or dug a few potatoes now and then under the pretence of working for their living used to go and fish through the ice for pickerel every winter. And here those three young people were drowned, a few summers ago, by the upsetting of a sailboat in a sudden flaw of wind. There is not one of these smiling ponds which has not devoured more youths and maidens than any of those monsters the ancients used to tell such lies about. But it was a pretty pond, and never looked more innocent—so the native "bard" of Rockland said in his elegy—than on the morning when they found Sarah Jane and Ellen Maria floating among the lily-pads.

The Apollinean Institute, or Institoot, as it was more commonly called, was, in the language of its Prospectus, a "first-class Educational Establishment." It employed a considerable corps of instructors to rough out and finish the hundred young lady scholars it sheltered beneath its roof. First, Mr. and Mrs. Peckham, the Principal and the Matron of the school. Silas Peckham was a thorough Yankee, born on a windy part of the coast, and reared chiefly on salt-fish. Everybody knows the type of Yankee produced by this climate and diet: thin, as if he had been split and dried; with an ashen kind of complexion, like the tint of the food he is made of; and about as sharp, tough, juiceless, and biting to deal with as the other is to the taste. Silas Peckham kept a young ladies' school exactly as he would have kept a hundred head of cattle,—for the simple, unadorned purpose of making just as much money in just as few years as could be safely done. Mr. Peckham gave very little personal attention to the department of instruction, but was always busy with contracts for flour and potatoes, beef and pork, and other nutritive staples, the amount of which required for such an establishment was enough to frighten a quartermaster. Mrs. Peckham was from the West, raised on Indian corn and pork, which give a fuller outline and a more humid temperament, but may perhaps be thought to render people a little coarse-fibred. Her specialty was to look after the feathering, cackling, roosting, rising, and general behavior of these hundred chicks. An honest, ignorant woman, she could not have passed an examination in the youngest class. So this distinguished institution was under the charge of a commissary and a housekeeper, and its real business was making money by taking young girls in as boarders.

Connected with this, however, was the incidental fact, which the public took for the principal one, namely, the business of instruction. Mr. Peckham knew well enough that it was just as well to have good instructors as bad ones, so far as cost was concerned, and a great deal better for the reputation of his feeding-establishment. He tried to get the best he could without paying too much, and, having got them, to screw all the work out of them that could possibly be extracted.

There was a master for the English branches, with a young lady assistant. There was another young lady who taught French, of the *ahvahng* and *pahndahng* style, which does not exactly smack of the asphalt of the Boulevards. There was also a German teacher of music, who sometimes helped in French of the *ahfaung* and *bauntaung* style,—so that, between the two, the young ladies could hardly have been mistaken for Parisians, by a Committee of the French Academy. The German teacher also taught a Latin class after his fashion,—*benna*, a ben, *gahboot*, a head, and so forth.

The master for the English branches had lately left the school for private reasons, which need not be here mentioned,—but he had gone, at any rate, and it was his place which had been offered to Mr. Bernard Langdon. The offer came just in season,—as, for various causes, he was willing to leave the place where he had begun his new experience.

It was on a fine morning, that Mr. Bernard, ushered in by Mr. Peckham, made his appearance in the great school-room of the Apollinean Institute. A general rustle ran all round the seats when the handsome young man was introduced. The principal carried him to the desk of the young lady English assistant, Miss Darley by name, and introduced him to her.

There was not a great deal of study done that day. The

young lady assistant had to point out to the new master the whole routine in which the classes were engaged when their late teacher left, and which had gone on as well as it could since. Then Master Langdon had a great many questions to ask, some relating to his new duties, and some, perhaps, implying a degree of curiosity not very unnatural under the circumstances. The truth is, the general effect of the schoolroom, with its scores of young girls, all their eyes naturally centring on him with fixed or furtive glances, was enough to bewilder and confuse a young man like Master Langdon, though he was not destitute of self-possession, as we have already seen.

You cannot get together a hundred girls, taking them as they come, from the comfortable and affluent classes, probably anywhere, certainly not in New England, without seeing a good deal of beauty. In fact, we very commonly mean by *beauty* the way young girls look when there is nothing to hinder their looking as Nature meant them to. And the great schoolroom of the Apollinean Institute did really make so pretty a show on the morning when Master Langdon entered it, that he might be pardoned for asking Miss Darley more questions about his scholars than about their lessons.

There were girls of all ages: little creatures, some pallid and delicate-looking, the offspring of invalid parents,—much given to books, not much to mischief, commonly spoken of as particularly good children, and contrasted with another sort, girls of more vigorous organization, who were disposed to laughing and play, and required a strong hand to manage them;—then young growing misses of every shade of Saxon complexion, and here and there one of more Southern hue: blondes, some of them so translucent-looking, that it seemed as if you could see the souls in their bodies, like bubbles in glass, if souls were objects of sight; brunettes, some with rose-red colors, and some with that swarthy hue which often carries with it a heavily-shaded lip, and which with pure outlines and outspoken reliefs, gives us some of our handsomest women,—the women whom ornaments of plain gold adorn more than any other *parures*; and again, but only here and there, one with dark hair and gray or blue eyes, a Celtic type, perhaps, but found in our native stock occasionally; rarest of all, a light-haired girl with dark eyes, hazel, brown, or of the color of that mountain-brook spoken of in this chapter, where it ran through shadowy woodlands. With these were to be seen at intervals some of maturer years, full-blown flowers among the opening buds, with that conscious look upon their faces which so many women wear during the period when they never meet a single man without having his monosyllable ready for him,—tied as they are, poor things! on the rock of expectation, each of them an Andromeda waiting for her Perseus.

"Who is that girl in ringlets,—the fourth in the third row on the right?" said Master Langdon.

"Charlotte Ann Wood," said Miss Darley;—"writes very pretty poems."

"Oh!—And the pink one, three seats from her? Looks bright; anything in her?"

"Emma Dean,—day-scholar,—Squire Dean's daughter,—nice girl,—second medal last year."

The master asked these two questions in a careless kind of way, and did not seem to pay any too much attention to the answers.

"And who and what is that," he said,—"sitting a little apart there,—that strange, wild-looking girl?"

This time he put the real question he wanted answered; —the other two were asked at random, as masks for the third.

The lady-teacher's face changed;—one would have said she was frightened or troubled. She looked at the girl doubtfully, as if she might hear the master's question and its answer. But the girl did not look up;—she was winding a gold chain about her wrist, and then uncoiling it, as if in a kind of reverie.

Miss Darley drew close to the master and placed her hand so as to hide her lips. "Don't look at her as if we were talking about her," she whispered softly;—"that is Elsie Venner."

CHAPTER V

AN OLD-FASHIONED DESCRIPTIVE CHAPTER

It was a comfort to get to a place with something like society, with residences which had pretensions to elegance, with people of some breeding, with a newspaper, and "stores" to advertise in it, and with two or three churches to keep each other alive by wholesome agitation. Rockland was such a place.

Some of the natural features of the town have been described already. The Mountain, of course, was what gave it its character, and redeemed it from wearing the commonplace expression which belongs to ordinary country-villages. Beautiful, wild, invested with the mystery which belongs to untrodden spaces, and with enough of terror to give it dignity, it had yet closer relations with the town over which it brooded than the passing stranger knew of. Thus, it made a local climate by cutting off the northern winds and holding the sun's heat like a garden-wall. Peach-trees, which, on the northern side of the mountain, hardly ever came to fruit, ripened abundant crops in Rockland.

But there was still another relation between the mountain and the town at its foot, which strangers were not likely to hear alluded to, and which was oftener thought of than spoken of by its inhabitants. Those high-impending forests,—"hangers," as White of Selborne would have called them,—sloping far upward and backward into the distance, had always an air of menace blended with their wild beauty. It seemed as if some heaven-scaling Titan had thrown his shaggy robe over the bare, precipitous flanks of the rocky summit, and it might at any moment slide like a garment flung carelessly on the nearest chance-support, and, so sliding, crush the village out of being, as the Rossberg when it tumbled over on the valley of Goldau.

Persons have been known to remove from the place, after a short residence in it, because they were haunted day and night by the thought of this awful green wall piled up into the air over their heads. They would lie awake of nights, thinking they heard the muffled snapping of roots, as if a thousand acres of the mountain-side were tugging to break away, like the snow from a house-roof, and a hundred thousand trees were clinging with all their fibres to hold back the soil just ready to peel away and crash down with all its rocks and forest-growths. And yet, by one of those strange contradictions we are constantly finding in human nature, there were natives of the town who would come back thirty or forty years after leaving it, just to nestle under this same threatening mountain-side, as old men sun themselves against southward-facing walls. The old dreams and legends of danger added to the attraction. If the mountain should ever slide, they had a kind of feeling as if they ought to be there. It was a fascination like that which the rattlesnake is said to exert.

This comparison naturally suggests the recollection of that other source of danger which was an element in the every-day life of the Rockland people. The folks in some of the neighboring towns had a joke against them, that a Rocklander couldn't hear a bean-pod rattle without saying, "The Lord have mercy on us!" It is very true, that many a nervous old lady has had a terrible start, caused by some mischievous young rogue's giving a sudden shake to one of these noisy vegetable products in her immediate vicinity. Yet, strangely enough, many persons missed the excitement of the possibility of a fatal bite in other regions, where there were nothing but black and green and striped snakes, mean ophidians, having the spite of the nobler serpent without his venom,—poor crawling creatures, whom Nature would not trust with a poison-bag. Many natives of Rockland did unquestionably experience a certain gratification in this infinitesimal sense of danger. It was noted that the old people retained their hearing longer than in other places. Some said it was the softened climate, but others believed it was owing to the habit of keeping their ears open whenever they were walking through the grass or in the woods. At any rate, a slight sense of danger is often an agreeable stimulus. People sip their *crème de noyau* with a peculiar tremulous pleasure, because there is a bare possibility that it may contain prussic acid enough to knock them over; in which case they will lie as dead as if a thunder-cloud had emptied itself into the earth through their brain and marrow.

But Rockland had other features which helped to give it a special character. First of all, there was one grand street which was its chief glory. Elm Street it was called, naturally enough, for its elms made a long, pointed-arched gallery of it through most of its extent. No natural Gothic arch compares, for a moment, with that formed by two American elms, where their lofty jets of foliage shoot across each other's ascending curves, to intermingle their showery flakes of green. When one looks through a long double row of these, as in that lovely avenue which the poets of Yale remember so well,—

"O, could the vista of my life but now as bright appear
As when I first through Temple Street looked down thine espalier!"

he beholds a temple not built with hands, fairer than any minister, with all its clustered stems and flowering capitals, that ever grew in stone.

Nobody knows New England who is not on terms of intimacy with one of its elms. The elm comes nearer to having a soul than any other vegetable creature among us. It loves man as man loves it. It is modest and patient. It has a small flake of a seed which blows in everywhere and makes arrangements for coming up by-and-by. So, in spring, one finds a crop of baby-elms among his carrots and parsnips, very weak and small compared to those succulent vegetables. The baby-elms die, most of them, slain, unrecognized or unheeded, by hand or hoe, as meekly as Herod's innocents. One of them gets overlooked, perhaps, until it has established a kind of right to stay. Three generations of carrot and parsnip-consumers have passed away, yourself among them, and now let your great-grandson look for the baby-elm. Twenty-two feet of clean girth, three hundred and sixty feet in the line that bounds its leafy circle, it covers the boy with such a canopy as neither glossy-leafed oak nor insect-haunted linden ever lifted into the summer skies.

Elm Street was the pride of Rockland, but not only on account of its Gothic-arched vista. In this street were most of the great houses, or "mansion-houses," as it was usual to call them. Along this street, also, the more nicely kept and neatly painted dwellings were chiefly congregated. It was the correct thing for a Rockland dignitary to have a house in Elm Street.

A New England "mansion-house" is naturally square, with dormer windows projecting from the roof, which has a balustrade with turned posts round it. It shows a good breadth of front-yard before its door, as its owner shows a respectable expanse of clean shirt-front. It has a lateral margin beyond its stables and offices, as its master wears his white wrist-bands showing beyond his coat-cuffs. It may not have what can properly be called grounds, but it must have elbow-room, at any rate. Without it, it is like a man who is always tight-buttoned for want of any linen to show. The mansion-house which has had to button itself up tight in fences, for want of green or gravel margin, will be advertising for boarders presently. The old English pattern of the New England mansion-house, only on a somewhat grander scale, is Sir Thomas Abney's place, where dear, good Dr. Watts said prayers for the family, and wrote those blessed hymns of his that sing us into consciousness in our cradles, and come back to us in sweet, single verses, between the moments of wandering and of stupor, when we lie dying, and sound over us when we can no longer hear them, bringing grateful tears to the hot, aching eyes beneath the thick, black veils, and carrying the holy calm with them which filled the good man's heart, as he prayed and sung under the shelter of the old English mansion-house.

Next to the mansion-houses, came the two-story trim, white-painted, "genteel" houses, which, being more gossipy and less nicely bred, crowded close up to the street, instead of standing back from it with arms akimbo, like the mansion-houses. Their little front-yards were very commonly full of lilac and syringa and other bushes, which were allowed to smother the lower story almost to the exclusion of light and air, so that, what with small windows and small window-panes, and the darkness made by these choking growths of shrubbery, the front parlors of some of these houses were the most tomb-like, melancholy places that could be found anywhere among the abodes of the living. Their garnishing was apt to assist this impression. Large-patterned carpets, which always look discontented in little rooms, hair-cloth furniture, black and shiny as beetles' wing cases, and centre-tables, with a sullen oil-lamp of the kind called astral by our imaginative ancestors, in the centre,—these things were inevitable. In set piles round the lamp was ranged the current literature of the day, in the form of Temperance Documents, unbound numbers of one of the Unknown Public's Magazines with worn-out steel engravings and high-colored fashion-plates, the Poems of a distinguished British author whom it is unnecessary to mention, a volume of sermons, or a novel or two, or both, according to the tastes of the family, and the Good Book, which is always Itself in the cheapest and commonest company. The father of the family with his hand in the breast of his coat, the mother of the same in a wide-bordered cap, sometimes a print of the Last Supper, by no means Morghen's, or the Father of his Country, or the old General, or the Defender of the Constitution, or an unknown clergyman with an open book before him,—these were the usual ornaments of the walls, the first two a matter of rigor, the others according to politics and other tendencies.

This intermediate class of houses, wherever one finds them in New England towns, are very apt to be cheerless and unsatisfactory. They have neither the luxury of the mansion-house nor the comfort of the farm-house. They are rarely kept at an agreeable temperature. The mansion-house has large fireplaces and generous chimneys, and is open to the sunshine. The farm-house makes no pretensions, but it has a good warm kitchen, at any rate, and one can be comfortable there with the rest of the family, without fear and without reproach. These lesser country-houses of genteel aspirations are much given to patent subterfuges of one kind and another to get heat without combustion. The chilly parlor and the slippery hair-cloth seat take the life out of the warmest welcome. If one would make these places wholesome, happy, and cheerful, the first precept would be,—The dearest fuel, plenty of it, and let half the heat go up the chimney. If you can't afford this, don't try to live in a "genteel" fashion, but stick to the ways of the honest farm-house.

There were a good many comfortable farm-houses scattered about Rockland. The best of them were something of the following pattern, which is too often superseded of late by a more pretentious, but infinitely less pleasing kind of rustic architecture. A little back from the road, seated directly on the green sod, rose a plain wooden building, two stories in front, with a long roof sloping backwards to within a few feet of the ground. This, like the "mansion-house," is copied from an old English pattern. Cottages of this model may be seen in Lancashire, for instance, always with the same honest, homely look, as if their roofs acknowledged their relationship to the soil out of which they sprung. The walls were unpainted, but turned by the slow action of sun and air and rain to a quiet dove- or slate-color. An old broken mill-stone at the door,—a well-sweep pointing like a finger to the heavens, which the shining round of water beneath looked up at like a dark unsleeping eye,—a single large elm a little at one side,—a barn twice as big as the house,—a cattle-yard, with

"The white horns tossing above the wall,"—

some fields, in pasture or in crops, with low stone walls round them,—a row of beehives,—a garden-patch, with roots, and currant-bushes, and many-hued hollyhocks, and swollen-stemmed, globe-headed, seedling onions, and marigolds and flower-de-luces, and lady's-delights, and peonies, crowding in together, with southernwood in the borders, and woodbine and hops and morning-glories climbing as they got a chance,—these were the features by which the Rockland-born children remembered the farm-house, when they had grown to be men. Such are the recollections that come over poor sailor-boys crawling out on reeling yards to reef topsails as their vessels stagger round the stormy Cape; and such are the flitting images that make the eyes of old country-born merchants look dim and dreamy, as they sit in their city palaces, warm with the after-dinner flush of the red wave out of which Memory arises, as Aphrodite arose from the green waves of the ocean.

Two meeting-houses stood on two eminences, facing each other, and looking like a couple of fighting-cocks with their necks straight up in the air,—as if they would flap their roofs, the next thing, and crow out of their upstretched steeples, and peck at each other's glass eyes with their sharp-pointed weathercocks.

The first was a good pattern of the real old-fashioned New England meeting-house. It was a large barn with windows, fronted by a square tower crowned with a kind of wooden bell inverted and raised on legs, out of which rose a slender spire with the sharp-billed weathercock at its summit. Inside, tall, square pews with flapping seats, and a gallery running round three sides of the building. On the fourth side the pulpit, with a huge, dusty sounding-board hanging over it. Here preached the Reverend Pierrepont Honeywood, D.D., successor, after a number of generations, to the office and the parsonage of the Reverend Didymus Bean, before mentioned, but not suspected of any of his alleged heresies. He held to the old faith of the Puritans, and occasionally delivered a discourse which was considered by the hard-headed theologians of his parish to have settled the whole matter fully and finally, so that now there was a good logical basis laid down for the Millennium, which might begin at once upon the platform of his demonstrations. Yet the Reverend Dr. Honeywood was fonder of preaching plain, practical sermons about the duties of life, and showing his Christianity in abundant good works among his people. It was noticed by some few of his flock, not without comment, that the great majority of his texts came from the Gospels, and this more and more as he became interested in various benevolent enterprises which brought him into relations with ministers and kind-hearted laymen of other denominations. He was in fact a man of a very warm, open, and exceedingly *human* disposition, and, although bred by a clerical father, whose motto was "*Sit anima mea cum Puritanis,*" he exercised his human faculties in the harness of his ancient faith with such freedom that the straps of it got so loose they did not interfere greatly with the circulation of the warm blood through his system. Once in a while he seemed to think it necessary to come out with a grand doctrinal sermon, and then he would lapse away for a while into preaching on men's duties to each other and to society, and hit hard, perhaps, at some of the actual vices of the time and place, and insist with such tenderness and eloquence on the great depth and breadth of true Christian love and charity, that his oldest deacon shook his head, and wished he had shown as much interest when he was preaching, three Sabbaths back, on Predestination, or in his discourse against the Sabellians. But he was sound in the faith; no doubt of that. Did he not preside at the council held in the town of Tamarack, on the other side of the mountain, which expelled its clergyman for maintaining heretical doctrines? As presiding officer, he did not vote, of course, but there was no doubt that he was all right; he had some of the Edwards blood in him, and that couldn't very well let him go wrong.

The meeting-house on the other and opposite summit was of a more modern style, considered by many a great improvement on the old New England model, so that it is not uncommon for a country parish to pull down its old meeting-house, which has been preached in for a hundred years or so, and put up one of these more elegant edifices. The new building was in what may be called the florid shingle-Gothic manner. Its pinnacles and crockets and other ornaments were, like the body of the building, all of pine wood,—an admirable material, as it is very soft and easily worked, and can be painted of any color desired. Inside, the walls were stuccoed in imitation of stone,—first a dark-brown square, then two light-brown squares, then another dark-brown square, and so on, to represent the accidental differences of shade always noticeable in the real stones of which walls are built. To be sure, the architect could not help getting his party-colored squares in almost as regular rhythmical order as those of a chess-board; but nobody can avoid doing things in a systematic and serial way; indeed, people who wish to plant trees in natural clumps know very well that they cannot keep from making regular lines and symmetrical figures, unless by some trick or other, as that one of throwing a peck of potatoes up into the air and sticking in a tree wherever a potato happens to fall. The pews of this meeting-house were the usual oblong ones, where people sit close together with a ledge before them to support their hymn-books, liable only to occasional contact with the back of the next pew's heads or bonnets, and a place running under the seat of that pew where hats could be deposited,—always at the risk of the owner, in case of injury by boots or crickets.

In this meeting-house preached the Reverend Chauncy Fairweather, a divine of the "Liberal" school, as it is commonly called, bred at that famous college which used to be thought, twenty or thirty years ago, to have the monopoly of training young men in the milder forms of heresy. His ministrations were attended with decency, but not followed with enthusiasm. "The beauty of virtue" got to be an old story at last. "The moral dignity of human nature" ceased to excite a thrill of satisfaction, after some hundred repetitions. It grew to be a dull business, this preaching against stealing and intemperance, while he knew very well that the thieves were prowling round orchards and empty houses, instead of being there to hear the sermon, and that the drunkards, being rarely church-goers, get little good by the statistics and eloquent appeals of the preacher. Every now and then, however, the Reverend Mr. Fairweather let off a polemic discourse against his neighbor opposite, which waked his people up a little; but it was a languid congregation, at best,—very apt to stay away from meeting in the afternoon, and not at all given to extra evening services. The minister, unlike his rival of the other side of the way, was a down-hearted and timid kind of man. He went on preaching as he had been taught to preach, but he had misgivings at times. There was a little Roman Catholic church at the foot of the hill where his own was placed, which he always had to pass on Sundays. He could never look on the thronging multitudes that crowded its pews and aisles or knelt bare-headed on its steps, without a longing to get in among them and go down on his knees and enjoy that luxury of devotional contact which makes a worshipping throng as different from the same numbers praying apart as a bed of coals is from a trail of scattered cinders.

"Oh, if I could but huddle in with those poor laborers and working-women!" he would say to himself. "If I could but breathe that atmosphere, stifling though it be, yet made holy by ancient litanies, and cloudy with the smoke of hallowed incense, for one hour, instead of droning over these moral precepts to my half-sleeping congregation!" The intellectual isolation of his sect preyed upon him; for, of all terrible things to natures like his, the most terrible is to belong to a minority. No person that looked at his thin and sallow cheek, his sunken and sad eye, his tremulous lip, his contracted forehead, or who heard his querulous, though not unmusical voice, could fail to see that his life was an uneasy one, that he was engaged in some inward conflict. His dark, melancholic aspect contrasted with his seemingly cheerful creed, and was all the more striking, as the worthy Dr. Honeywood, professing a belief which made him a passenger on board a shipwrecked planet, was yet a most good-humored and companionable gentleman, whose laugh on week-days did one as much good to listen to as the best sermon he ever delivered on a Sunday.

A mile or two from the centre of Rockland was a pretty little Episcopal church, with a roof like a wedge of cheese, a square tower, a stained window, and a trained rector, who read the service with such ventral depth of utterance and rrreduplication of the rrresonant letter, that his own mother would not have known him for her son, if the good woman had not ironed his surplice and put it on with her own hands.

There were two public-houses in the place: one dignified with the name of the Mountain House, somewhat frequented by city-people in the summer months, large-fronted, three-storied, balconied, boasting a distinct ladies'-

drawing-room, and spreading a *table d'hôte* of some pretensions; the other, "Pollard's Tahvern," in the common speech,—a two-story building, with a bar-room, once famous, where there was a great smell of hay and boots and pipes and all other bucolic-flavored elements,—where games of checkers were played on the back of the bellows with red and white kernels of corn, or with beans and coffee,—where a man slept in a box-settle at night, to wake up early passengers,—where teamsters came in, with wooden-handled whips and coarse frocks, reinforcing the bucolic flavor of the atmosphere, and middle-aged male gossips, sometimes including the squire of the neighboring law-office, gathered to exchange a question or two about the news, and then fall into that solemn state of suspended animation which the temperance bar-rooms of modern days produce in human beings, as the Grotta del Cane does in dogs in the well-known experiments related by travellers. This barroom used to be famous for drinking and story-telling, and sometimes fighting, in old times. That was when there were rows of decanters on the shelf behind the bar, and a hissing vessel of hot water ready, to make punch, and three or four *loggerheads* (long irons clubbed at the end) were always lying in the fire in the cold season, waiting to be plunged into sputtering and foaming mugs of flip,—a goodly compound, speaking according to the flesh, made with beer and sugar, and a certain suspicion of strong waters, over which a little nutmeg being grated, and in it the hot iron being then allowed to sizzle, there results a peculiar singed aroma, which the wise regard as a warning to remove themselves at once out of the reach of temptation.

But the bar of Pollard's Tahvern no longer presented its old attractions, and the loggerheads had long disappeared from the fire. In place of the decanters, were boxes containing "lozengers," as they were commonly called, sticks of candy in jars, cigars in tumblers, a few lemons, grown hard-skinned and marvellously shrunken by long exposure, but still feebly suggestive of possible lemonade,—the whole ornamented by festoons of yellow and blue cut fly-paper. On the front shelf of the bar stood a large German-silver pitcher of water, and scattered about were ill-conditioned lamps, with wicks that always wanted picking, which burned red and smoked a good deal, and were apt to go out without any obvious cause, leaving strong reminiscences of the whale-fishery in the circumambient air.

The common school-houses of Rockland were dwarfed by the grandeur of the Apollinean Institute. The master passed one of them, in a walk he was taking, soon after his arrival at Rockland. He looked in at the rows of desks, and recalled his late experiences. He could not help laughing, as he thought how neatly he had knocked the young butcher off his pins.

" 'A little *science* is a dangerous thing,'

as well as a little 'learning,' " he said to himself; "only it's dangerous to the fellow you try it on." And he cut him a good stick, and began climbing the side of The Mountain to get a look at that famous Rattlesnake Ledge.

CHAPTER VI

THE SUNBEAM AND THE SHADOW

The virtue of the world is not mainly in its leaders. In the midst of the multitude which follows there is often something better than in the one that goes before. Old generals wanted to take Toulon, but one of their young colonels showed them how. The junior counsel has been known not unfrequently to make a better argument than his senior fellow,—if, indeed, he did not make both their arguments. Good ministers will tell you they have parishioners who beat them in the practice of the virtues. A great establishment, got up on commercial principles, like the Apollinean Institute, might yet be well carried on, if it happened to get good teachers. And when Master Langdon came to see its management, he recognized that there must be fidelity and intelligence somewhere among the instructors. It was only necessary to look for a moment at the fair, open forehead, the still, tranquil eye of gentle, habitual authority, the sweet gravity that lay upon the lips, to hear the clear answers to the pupils' questions, to notice how every request had the force without the form of a command, and the young man could not doubt that the good genius of the school stood before him in the person of Helen Darley.

It was the old story. A poor country-clergyman dies, and leaves a widow and a daughter. In Old England the daughter would have eaten the bitter bread of a governess in some rich family. In New England she must keep a school. So, rising from one sphere to another, she at length finds herself the *prima donna* in the department of instruction in Mr. Silas Peckham's educational establishment.

What a miserable thing it is to be poor. She was dependent, frail, sensitive, conscientious. She was in the power of a hard, grasping, thin-blooded, tough-fibred, trading educator, who neither knew nor cared for a tender woman's sensibilities, but who paid her and meant to have his money's worth out of her brains, and as much more than his money's worth as he could get. She was consequently, in plain English, overworked, and an overworked woman is always a sad sight,—sadder a great deal than an overworked man, because she is so much more fertile in capacities of suffering than a man. She has so many varieties of headache,—sometimes as if Jael were driving the nail that killed Sisera into her temples,—sometimes letting her work with half her brain while the other half throbs as if it would go to pieces,—sometimes tightening round the brows as if her cap-band were a ring of iron,—and then her neuralgias, and her backaches, and her fits of depression, in which she thinks she is nothing and less than nothing, and those paroxysms which men speak slightingly of as hysterical,—convulsions, that is all, only not commonly fatal ones,—so many trials which belong to her fine and mobile structure, —that she is always entitled to pity, when she is placed in conditions which develop her nervous tendencies.

The poor young lady's work had, of course, been doubled since the departure of Master Langdon's predecessor. Nobody knows what the weariness of instruction is, as soon as the teacher's faculties begin to be overtasked, but those who have tried it. The *relays* of fresh pupils, each new set with its exhausting powers in full action, coming one after another, take out all the reserved forces and faculties of resistance from the subject of their draining process.

The day's work was over, and it was late in the evening, when she sat down, tired and faint, with a great bundle of girls' themes or compositions to read over before she could rest her weary head on the pillow of her narrow trundle-bed, and forget for a while the treadmill stair of labor she was daily climbing.

How she dreaded this most forlorn of all a teacher's tasks! She was conscientious in her duties, and would insist on reading every sentence,—there was no saying where she might find faults of grammar or bad spelling. There might have been twenty or thirty of these themes in the bundle before her. Of course she knew pretty well the leading sentiments they could contain: that beauty was subject to the accidents of time; that wealth was inconstant, and existence uncertain; that virtue was its own reward; that youth exhaled, like the dewdrop from the flower, ere the sun had reached its meridian; that life was o'ershadowed with trials; that the lessons of virtue instilled by our beloved teachers were to be our guides through all our future career. The imagery employed consisted principally of roses, lilies, birds, clouds, and brooks, with the celebrated comparison of wayward genius to a meteor. Who does not know the small, slanted, Italian hand of these girls'-compositions, —their stringing together of the good old traditional copybook phrases, their occasional gushes of sentiment, their profound estimates of the world, sounding to the old folks that read them as the experience of a bantam-pullet's last-hatched young one with the chips of its shell on its head would sound to a Mother Cary's chicken, who knew the great ocean with all its typhoons and tornadoes? Yet every now and then one is liable to be surprised with strange clairvoyant flashes, that can hardly be explained, except by the mysterious inspiration which every now and then seizes a young girl and exalts her intelligence, just as hysteria in other instances exalts the sensibility,—a little something of that which made Joan of Arc, and the Burney girl who prophesied "Evelina," and the Davidson sisters. In the midst of these commonplace exercises which Miss Darley read over so carefully were two or three that had something of individual flavor about them, and here and there there was an image or an epithet which showed the footprint of a passionate nature, as a fallen scarlet feather marks the path the wild flamingo has trodden.

The young lady teacher read them with a certain indifference of manner, as one reads proofs—noting defects of detail, but not commonly arrested by the matters treated of. Even Miss Charlotte Ann Wood's poem, beginning

"How sweet at evening's balmy hour,"

did not excite her. She marked the inevitable false rhyme of Cockney and Yankee beginners, *morn* and *dawn*, and tossed the verses on the pile of papers she had finished. She was looking over some of the last of them in a rather listless way,—for the poor thing was getting sleepy in spite of herself,—when she came to one which seemed to rouse her attention, and lifted her drooping lids. She looked at it a moment before she would touch it. Then she took hold of it by one corner and slid it off from the rest. One would have said she was afraid of it, or had some undefined antipathy which made it hateful to her. Such odd fancies are common enough in young persons in her nervous state. Many of these young people will jump up twenty times a day and run to dabble the tips of their fingers in water, after touching the most inoffensive objects.

This composition was written in a singular, sharp-pointed, long, slender hand, on a kind of wavy, ribbed paper. There was something strangely suggestive about the look of it,—but exactly of what, Miss Darley either could not or did not try to think. The subject of the paper was The Mountain,—the composition being a sort of descriptive rhapsody. It showed a startling familiarity with some of the savage scenery of the region. One would have said that the writer must have threaded its wildest solitudes by the light of the moon and stars as well as by day. As the teacher read on, her color changed, and a kind of tremulous agitation came over her. There were hints in this strange paper she did not know what to make of. There was something in its descriptions and imagery that recalled,—Miss Darley could not say what,—but it made her frightfully nervous. Still she could not help reading, till she came to one passage which so agitated her, that the tired and overwearied girl's self-control left her entirely. She sobbed once or twice, then laughed convulsively, and flung herself on the bed, where she worked out a set hysteric spasm as she best might, without anybody to rub her hands and see that she did not hurt herself. By-and-by she got quiet, rose and went to her book-case, took down a volume of Coleridge, and read a short time, and so to bed, to sleep and wake from time to time with a sudden start out of uneasy dreams.

Perhaps it is of no great consequence what it was in the composition which set her off into this nervous paroxysm. She was in such a state that almost any slight agitation would have brought on the attack, and it was the accident of her transient excitability, very probably, which made a trifling cause the seeming occasion of so much disturbance. The theme was signed, in the same peculiar, sharp, slender hand, E. Venner, and was, of course, written by that wild-looking girl who had excited the master's curiosity and prompted his question, as before mentioned.

The next morning the lady-teacher looked pale and wearied, naturally enough, but she was in her place at the usual hour, and Master Langdon in his own. The girls had not yet entered the school-room.

"You have been ill, I am afraid," said Mr. Bernard.

"I was not well yesterday," she answered. "I had a worry and a kind of fright. It is so dreadful to have the charge of all these young souls and bodies. Every young girl ought to walk locked close, arm in arm, between two guardian angels. Sometimes I faint almost with the thought of all that I ought to do, and of my own weakness and wants.— Tell me, are there not natures born so out of parallel with the lines of natural law that nothing short of a miracle can bring them right?"

Mr. Bernard had speculated somewhat, as all thoughtful persons of his profession are forced to do, on the innate organic tendencies with which individuals, families, and races are born. He replied, therefore, with a smile, as one to whom the question suggested a very familiar class of facts.

"Why, of course. Each of us is only the footing-up of a double column of figures that goes back to the first pair. Every unit tells,—and some of them are *plus*, and some *minus*. If the columns don't add up right, it is commonly because we can't make out all the figures. I don't mean to say that something may not be added by Nature to make up for losses and keep the race to its average, but we are mainly nothing but the answer to a long sum in addition and subtraction. No doubt there are people born with impulses at every possible angle to the parallels of Nature, as you call them. If they happen to cut these at right angles, of course they are beyond the reach of common influences. Slight obliquities are what we have most to do with in education. Penitentiaries and insane asylums take care of most of the right-angle cases.—I am afraid I have put it too much like a professor, and I am only a student, you know. Pray, what set you to asking me this? Any strange cases among the scholars?"

The meek teacher's blue eyes met the luminous glance that came with the question. She, too, was of gentle blood, —not meaning by that that she was of any noted lineage, but that she came of a cultivated stock, never rich, but long trained to intellectual callings. A thousand decencies, amenities, reticences, graces, which no one thinks of until he misses them, are the traditional right of those who spring from such families. And when two persons of this exceptional breeding meet in the midst of the common multitude, they seek each other's company at once by the natural law of elective affinity. It is wonderful how men and women know their peers. If two stranger queens, sole survivors of two shipwrecked vessels, were cast, half-naked, on a rock together, each would at once address the other as "Our Royal Sister."

Helen Darley looked into the dark eyes of Bernard Langdon glittering with the light which flashed from them with his question. Not as those foolish, innocent country-girls of the small village did she look into them, to be fascinated and bewildered, but to sound them with a calm steadfast purpose. "A gentleman," she said to herself, as she read his expression and his features with a woman's rapid, but exhausting glance. "A lady," he said to himself, as he met her questioning look,—so brief, so quiet, yet so assured, as of one whom necessity had taught to read faces quickly without offence, as children read the faces of parents, as wives read the faces of hard-souled husbands. All this was but a few seconds' work, and yet the main point was settled. If there had been any vulgar curiosity or coarseness of any kind lurking in his expression, she would have detected it. If she had not lifted her eyes to his face so softly and kept them there so calmly and withdrawn them so quietly, he would not have said to himself, "She is a *lady*," for that word meant a good deal to the descendant of the courtly Wentworths and the scholarly Langdons.

"There are strange people everywhere, Mr. Langdon," she said, "and I don't think our school-room is an exception. I am glad you believe in the force of transmitted tendencies. It would break my heart, if I did not think that there are faults beyond the reach of everything but God's special grace. I should die, if I thought that my negligence or incapacity was alone responsible for the errors and sins of those I have charge of. Yet there are mysteries I do not know how to account for." She looked all round the school-room, and then said, in a whisper, "Mr. Langdon, we had a girl that *stole*, in the school, not long ago. Worse than that, we had a girl who tried to set us on fire. Children of good people, both of them. And we have a girl now that frightens me so"——

The door opened, and three misses came in to take their seats: three types, as it happened, of certain classes, into which it would not have been difficult to distribute the greater number of the girls in the school.—*Hannah Martin.* Fourteen years and three months old. Short-necked, thick-waisted, round-cheeked, smooth, vacant forehead, large, dull eyes. Looks good-natured, with little other expression. Three buns in her bag, and a large apple. Has a habit of attacking her provisions in school-hours.—*Rosa Milburn.* Sixteen. Brunette, with a rareripe flush in her cheeks. Color comes and goes easily. Eyes wandering, apt to be downcast. Moody at times. Said to be passionate, if irritated. Finished in high relief. Carries shoulders well back and walks well, as if proud of her woman's life, with a slight rocking movement, being one of the wide-flanged pattern, but seems restless,—a hard girl to look after. Has a romance in her pocket, which she means to read in school-time.—*Charlotte Ann Wood.* Fifteen. The poetess before mentioned. Long, light ringlets, pallid complexion, blue eyes. Delicate child, half unfolded. Gentle, but languid and despondent. Does not go much with the other girls, but reads a good deal, especially poetry, underscoring favorite passages. Writes a great many verses, very fast, not very correctly; full of the usual human sentiments, expressed in the accustomed phrases. Undervitalized. Sensibilities not covered with their normal integuments. A negative condition, often confounded with genius, and sometimes running into it. Young people who *fall* out of line through weakness of the active faculties are often confounded with those who *step* out of it through strength of the intellectual ones.

The girls kept coming in, one after another, or in pairs or groups, until the school-room was nearly full. Then there was a little pause, and a light step was heard in the passage. The lady-teacher's eyes turned to the door, and the master's followed them in the same direction.

A girl of about seventeen entered. She was tall and slender, but rounded, with a peculiar undulation of movement, such as one sometimes sees in perfectly untutored country-girls, whom Nature, the queen of graces, has taken in hand, but more commonly in connection with the very highest breeding of the most thoroughly trained society. She was a splendid scowling beauty, black-browed, with a flash of white teeth which was always like a surprise when her lips parted. She wore a checkered dress, of a curious pattern, and a camel's-hair scarf twisted a little fantastically about her. She went to her seat, which she had moved a short distance apart from the rest, and, sitting down, began playing listlessly with her gold chain, as was a common habit with her, coiling it and uncoiling it about her slender wrist, and braiding it in with her long, delicate fingers. Presently she looked up. Black, piercing eyes, not large,—a low forehead, as low as that of Clytie in the Townley bust,—black hair, twisted in heavy braids,—a face that one could not help looking at for its beauty, yet that one wanted to look away from for something in its expression, and could not for those diamond eyes. They were fixed on the lady-teacher now. The latter turned her own away, and let them wander over the other scholars. But they could not help coming back again for a single glance at the wild beauty. The diamond eyes were on her still. She turned the leaves of several of her books, as if in search of some passage, and, when she thought she had waited long enough to be safe, once more stole a quick look at the dark girl. The diamond eyes were still upon her. She put her kerchief to her forehead, which had grown slightly moist; she sighed once, almost shivered, for she felt cold; then, following some ill-defined impulse, which she could not resist, she left her place and went to the young girl's desk.

"*What do you want of me, Elsie Venner?*" It was a strange question to put, for the girl had not signified that she wished the teacher to come to her.

"Nothing," she said. "I thought I could make you come." The girl spoke in a low tone, a kind of half-whisper. She did not lisp, yet her articulation of one or two consonants was not absolutely perfect.

"Where did you get that flower, Elsie?" said Miss Darley. It was a rare alpine flower, which was found only in one spot among the rocks of The Mountain.

"Where it grew," said Elsie Venner. "Take it." The teacher could not refuse her. The girl's finger-tips touched hers as she took it. How cold they were for a girl of such an organization!

The teacher went back to her seat. She made an excuse for quitting the school-room soon afterwards. The first thing she did was to fling the flower into her fireplace and rake the ashes over it. The second was to wash the tips of her fingers, as if she had been another Lady Macbeth. A poor, overtasked, nervous creature,—we must not think too much of her fancies.

After school was done, she finished the talk with the master which had been so suddenly interrupted. There were things spoken of which may prove interesting by-and-by, but there are other matters we must first attend to.

CHAPTER VII

THE EVENT OF THE SEASON

"Mr. and Mrs. Colonel Sprowle's compliments to Mr. Langdon and requests the pleasure of his company at a social entertainment on Wednesday evening next.

"*Elm St. Monday.*"

On paper of a pinkish color and musky smell, with a large ₷ at the top, and an embossed border. Envelop adherent, not sealed. Addressed

— *Langdon Esq.*

Present.

Brought by H. Frederic Sprowle, youngest son of the Colonel,—the H. of course standing for the paternal Hezekiah, put in to please the father, and reduced to its initial to please the mother, she having a marked preference for Frederic. Boy directed to wait for an answer.

"Mr. Langdon has the pleasure of accepting Mr. and Mrs. Colonel Sprowle's polite invitation for Wednesday evening."

On plain paper, sealed with an initial.

In walking along the main street, Mr. Bernard had noticed a large house of some pretensions to architectural display, namely, unnecessarily projecting eaves, giving it a mushroomy aspect, wooden mouldings at various available points, and a grandiose arched portico. It looked a little swaggering by the side of one or two of the mansion-houses that were not far from it, was painted too bright for Mr. Bernard's taste, had rather too fanciful a fence before it, and had some fruit-trees planted in the front-yard, which to this fastidious young gentleman implied a defective sense of the fitness of things, not promising in people who lived in so large a house, with a mushroom roof and a triumphal arch for its entrance.

This place was known as "Colonel Sprowle's villa," (genteel friends,)—as "the elegant residence of our distinguished fellow-citizen, Colonel Sprowle," (Rockland Weekly Universe,)—as "the neew haouse," (old settlers,) —as "Spraowle's Folly," (disaffected and possibly envious neighbors,)—and in common discourse, as "the Colonel's."

Hezekiah Sprowle, Esquire, Colonel Sprowle of the Commonwealth's Militia, was a retired "merchant." An India merchant he might, perhaps, have been properly called; for he used to deal in West India goods, such as coffee, sugar, and molasses, not to speak of rum,—also in tea, salt fish, butter and cheese, oil and candles, dried fruit, agricultural "p'dóose" generally, industrial products, such as boots and shoes, and various kinds of iron and wooden ware, and at one end of the establishment in calicoes and other stuffs,—to say nothing of miscellaneous objects of the most varied nature, from sticks of candy, which tempted in the smaller youth with coppers in their fists, up to ornamental articles of apparel, pocket-books, breast-pins, gilt-edged Bibles, stationery,—in short, everything which was like to prove seductive to the rural population. The Colonel had made money in trade, and also by matrimony. He had married Sarah, daughter and heiress of the late Tekel Jordan, Esq., an old miser, who gave the town-clock, which carries his name to posterity in large gilt letters as a generous benefactor of his native place. In due time the Colonel reaped the reward of well-placed affections. When his wife's inheritance fell in, he thought he had money enough to give up trade, and therefore sold out his "store," called in some dialects of the English language *shop*, and his business.

Life became pretty hard work to him, of course, as soon as he had nothing particular to do. Country people with money enough not to have to work are in much more danger than city people in the same condition. They get a specific look and character, which are the same in all the villages where one studies them. They very commonly fall into a routine, the basis of which is going to some lounging-place or other, a bar-room, a reading-room, or something of the kind. They grow slovenly in dress, and wear the same hat forever. They have a feeble curiosity for news perhaps, which they take daily as a man takes his bitters, and then fall silent and think they are thinking. But the mind goes out under this regimen, like a fire without a draught; and it is not very strange, if the instinct of mental self-preservation drives them to brandy-and-water, which makes the hoarse whisper of memory musical for a few brief moments, and puts a weak leer of promise on the features of the hollow-eyed future. The Colonel was kept pretty well in hand as yet by his wife, and though it had happened to him once or twice to come home rather late at night with a curious tendency to say the same thing twice and even three times over, it had always been in very cold weather,—and everybody knows that no one is safe to drink a couple of glasses of wine in a warm room and go suddenly out into the cold air.

Miss Matilda Sprowle, sole daughter of the house, had reached the age at which young ladies are supposed in technical language to have *come out*, and thereafter are considered to be *in company*.

"There's one piece o' goods," said the Colonel to his wife, "that we ha'n't disposed of, nor got a customer for yet. That's Matildy. I don't mean to set *her* up at vaandoo. I guess she can have her pick of a dozen."

"She's never seen anybody yet," said Mrs. Sprowle, who had had a certain project for some time, but had kept quiet about it. "Let's have a party, and give her a chance to show herself and see some of the young folks."

The Colonel was not very clear-headed, and he thought, naturally enough, that the party was his own suggestion, because his remark led to the first starting of the idea. He entered into the plan, therefore, with a feeling of pride as well as pleasure, and the great project was resolved upon in a family council without a dissentient voice. This was the party, then, to which Mr. Bernard was going. The town had been full of it for a week. "Everybody was asked." So everybody said that was invited. But how in respect of those who were not asked? If it had been one of the old mansion-houses that was giving a party, the boundary between the favored and the slighted families would have been known pretty well beforehand, and there would have been no great amount of grumbling. But the Colonel, for all his title, had a forest of poor relations and a brushwood swamp of shabby friends, for he had scrambled up to fortune, and now the time was come when he must define his new social position.

This is always an awkward business in town or country. An exclusive alliance between two powers is often the same thing as a declaration of war against a third. Rockland was soon split into a triumphant minority, invited to Mrs. Sprowle's party, and a great majority, uninvited, of which the fraction just on the border line between recognized "gentility" and the level of the ungloved masses was in an active state of excitement and indignation.

"Who is she, I should like to know?" said Mrs. Saymore, the tailor's wife. "There was plenty of folks in Rockland as good as ever Sally Jordan was, if she *had* managed to pick up a merchant. Other folks could have married merchants, if their families wasn't as wealthy as them old skinflints that willed her their money," etc. etc. Mrs. Saymore expressed the feeling of many beside herself. She had, however, a special right to be proud of the name she bore. Her husband was own cousin to the Saymores of Freestone Avenue (who write the name *Seymour*, and claim to be of the Duke of Somerset's family, showing a clear descent from the Protector to Edward Seymour, (1630,)—then a jump that would break a herald's neck to one Seth Saymore, (1783,)—from whom to the head of the present family the line is clear again). Mrs. Saymore, the tailor's wife, was not invited, because her husband *mended* clothes. If he had confined himself strictly to *making* them, it would have put a different face upon the matter.

The landlord of the Mountain House and his lady were invited to Mrs. Sprowle's party. Not so the landlord of Pollard's Tahvern and his lady. Whereupon the latter vowed that they would have a party at their house too, and made arrangements for a dance of twenty or thirty couples, to be followed by an entertainment. Tickets to this "Social

Ball" were soon circulated, and, being accessible to all at a moderate price, admission to the "Elegant Supper" included, this second festival promised to be as merry, if not as select, as the great party.

Wednesday came. Such doings had never been heard of in Rockland as went on that day at the "villa." The carpet had been taken up in the long room, so that the young folks might have a dance. Miss Matilda's piano had been moved in, and two fiddlers and a clarionet-player engaged to make music. All kinds of lamps had been put in requisition, and even colored wax-candles figured on the mantel-pieces. The costumes of the family had been tried on the day before: the Colonel's black suit fitted exceedingly well; his lady's velvet dress displayed her contours to advantage; Miss Matilda's flowered silk was considered superb; the eldest son of the family, Mr. T. Jordan Sprowle, called affectionately and elegantly "Geordie," voted himself "stunnin'"; and even the small youth who had borne Mr. Bernard's invitation was effective in a new jacket and trousers, buttony in front, and baggy in the reverse aspect, as is wont to be the case with the home-made garments of inland youngsters.

Great preparations had been made for the refection which was to be part of the entertainment. There was much clinking of borrowed spoons, which were to be carefully counted, and much clicking of borrowed china, which was to be tenderly handled,—for nobody in the country keeps those vast closets full of such things which one may see in rich city-houses. Not a great deal could be done in the way of flowers, for there were no green-houses, and few plants were out as yet; but there were paper ornaments for the candlesticks, and colored mats for the lamps, and all the tassels of the curtains and bells were taken out of those brown linen bags, in which, for reasons hitherto undiscovered, they are habitually concealed in some households. In the remoter apartments every imaginable operation was going on at once,—roasting, boiling, baking, beating, rolling, pounding in mortars, frying, freezing; for there was to be ice-cream to-night of domestic manufacture;—and in the midst of all these labors, Mrs. Sprowle and Miss Matilda were moving about, directing and helping as they best might, all day long. When the evening came, it might be feared they would not be in just the state of mind and body to entertain company.

——One would like to give a party now and then, if one could be a billionnaire.—"Antoine, I am going to have twenty people to dine to-day." "*Bien, Madame.*" Not a word or thought more about it, but get home in season to dress, and come down to your own table, one of your own guests.—"Giuseppe, we are to have a party a week from to-night,—five hundred invitations—there is the list." The day comes. "Madam, do you remember you have your party to-night?" "Why, so I have! Everything right? supper and all?" "All as it should be, Madam." "Send up Victorine." "Victorine, full toilet for this evening,—pink, diamonds, and emeralds. Coiffeur at seven. *Allez.*"—Billionism, or even millionism, must be a blessed kind of state, with health and clear conscience and youth and good looks,—but most blessed in this, that it takes off all the mean cares which give people the three wrinkles between the eyebrows, and leaves them free to have a good time and make others have a good time, all the way along from the charity that tips up unexpected loads of wood before widows' houses, and leaves foundling turkeys upon poor men's door-steps, and sets lean clergymen crying at the sight of anonymous fifty-dollar bills, to the taste which orders a perfect banquet in such sweet accord with every sense that everybody's nature flowers out full-blown in its golden-glowing, fragrant atmosphere.

——A great party given by the smaller gentry of the interior is a kind of solemnity, so to speak. It involves so much labor and anxiety,—its spasmodic splendors are so violently contrasted with the homeliness of every-day family-life,—it is such a formidable matter to break in the raw subordinates to the *manège* of the cloak-room and the table,—there is such a terrible uncertainty in the results of unfamiliar culinary operations,—so many feuds are involved in drawing that fatal line which divides the invited from the uninvited fraction of the local universe,—that, if the notes requested the pleasure of the guests' company on "this solemn occasion," they would pretty nearly express the true state of things.

The Colonel himself had been pressed into the service. He had pounded something in the great mortar. He had agitated a quantity of sweetened and thickened milk in what was called a cream-freezer. At eleven o'clock, A.M., he retired for a space. On returning, his color was noted to be somewhat heightened, and he showed a disposition to be jocular with the female help,—which tendency, displaying itself in livelier demonstrations than were approved at head-quarters, led to his being detailed to out-of-door duties, such as raking gravel, arranging places for horses to be hitched to, and assisting in the construction of an arch of winter-green at the porch of the mansion.

A whiff from Mr. Geordie's cigar refreshed the toiling females from time to time; for the windows had to be opened occasionally, while all these operations were going on, and the youth amused himself with inspecting the interior, encouraging the operatives now and then in the phrases commonly employed by genteel young men,—for he had perused an odd volume of "Verdant Green," and was acquainted with a Sophomore from one of the fresh-water colleges.—"Go it on the feed!" exclaimed this spirited young man. "Nothin' like a good spread. Grub enough and good liquor, that's the ticket. Guv'nor'll do the heavy polite, and let me alone for polishin' off the young charmers." And Mr. Geordie looked expressively at a handmaid who was rolling gingerbread, as if he were rehearsing for "Don Giovanni."

Evening came at last, and the ladies were forced to leave the scene of their labors to array themselves for the coming festivities. The tables had been set in a back room, the meats were ready, the pickles were displayed, the cake was baked, the blanc-mange had stiffened, and the ice-cream had frozen.

At half past seven o'clock, the Colonel, in costume, came into the front parlor, and proceeded to light the lamps. Some were good-humored enough and took the hint of a lighted match at once. Others were as vicious as they could be,—would not light on any terms, any more than if they were filled with water, or lighted and smoked one side of the chimney, or sputtered a few sparks and sulked themselves out, or kept up a faint show of burning, so that their ground glasses looked as feebly phosphorescent as so many invalid fireflies. With much coaxing and screwing and pricking, a tolerable illumination was at last achieved. At eight there was a grand rustling of silks, and Mrs. and Miss Sprowle descended from their respective bowers or boudoirs. Of course they were pretty well tired by this time, and very glad to sit down,—having the prospect before them of being obliged to stand for hours. The Colonel walked about the parlor, inspecting his regiment of lamps. By-and-by Mr. Geordie entered.

"Mph! mph!" he sniffed, as he came in. "You smell of lamp-smoke here."

That always galls people,—to have a newcomer accuse them of smoke or close air, which they have got used to and do not perceive. The Colonel raged at the thought of his lamps' smoking, and tongued a few anathemas inside of his shut teeth, but turned down two or three wicks that burned higher than the rest.

Master H. Frederic next made his appearance, with questionable marks upon his fingers and countenance. Had been tampering with something brown and sticky. His elder brother grew playful, and caught him by the baggy reverse of his more essential garment.

"Hush!" said Mrs. Sprowle,—"there's the bell!"

Everybody took position at once, and began to look very smiling and altogether at ease.—False alarm. Only a parcel of spoons,—"loaned," as the inland folks say when they mean lent, by a neighbor.

"Better late than never!" said the Colonel, "let me heft them spoons."

Mrs. Sprowle came down into her chair again as if all her bones had been bewitched out of her.

"I'm pretty nigh beat out a'ready," said she, "before any of the folks has come."

They sat silent awhile, waiting for the first arrival. How nervous they got! and how their senses were sharpened!

"Hark!" said Miss Matilda,—"what's that rumblin'?"

It was a cart going over a bridge more than a mile off, which at any other time they would not have heard. After this there was a lull, and poor Mrs. Sprowle's head nodded once or twice. Presently a crackling and grinding of gravel; —how much that means, when we are waiting for those whom we long or dread to see! Then a change in the tone of the gravel-crackling.

"Yes, they have turned in at our gate. They're comin'! Mother! mother!"

Everybody in position, smiling and at ease. Bell rings. Enter the first set of visitors. The Event of the Season has begun.

"Law! it's nothin' but the Cranes' folks! I do believe Mahala's come in that old green de-laine she wore at the Surprise Party!"

Miss Matilda had peeped through a crack of the door and made this observation and the remark founded thereon. Continuing her attitude of attention, she overheard Mrs. Crane and her two daughters conversing in the attiring-room, up one flight.

"How fine everything is in the great house!" said Mrs. Crane,—"jest look at the picters!"

"Matildy Sprowle's drawins," said Ada Azuba, the eldest daughter.

"I shoud think so," said Mahala Crane, her younger sister,—a wide-awake girl, who hadn't been to school for nothing, and performed a little on the lead pencil herself. "I should like to know whether that's a hay-cock or a mountain!"

Miss Matilda winced; for this must refer to her favorite monochrome, executed by laying on heavy shadows and stumping them down into mellow harmony,—the style of drawing which is taught in six lessons, and the kind of specimen which is executed in something less than one hour. Parents and other very near relatives are sometimes gratified with these productions, and cause them to be framed and hung up, as in the present instance.

"I guess we won't go down jest yet," said Mrs. Crane, "as folks don't seem to have come."

So she began a systematic inspection of the dressing-room and its conveniences.

"Mahogany four-poster,—come from the Jordans', I cal'late. Marseilles quilt. Ruffles all round the piller. Chintz curtings,—jest put up,—o' purpose for the party I'll lay ye a dollar.—What a nice washbowl!" (Taps it with a white knuckle belonging to a red finger.) "Stone chaney.—Here's a bran'-new brush and comb,—and here's a scent-bottle. Come here, girls, and fix yourselves in the glass, and scent your pocket-handkerchers."

And Mrs. Crane bedewed her own kerchief with some of the *eau de Cologne* of native manufacture,—said on its label to be much superior to the German article.

It was a relief to Mrs. and the Miss Cranes when the bell rang and the next guests were admitted. Deacon and Mrs. Soper,—Deacon Soper of the Rev. Mr. Fairweather's church, and his lady. Mrs. Deacon Soper was directed, of course, to the ladies' dressing-room, and her husband to the other apartment, where gentlemen were to leave their outside coats and hats. Then came Mr. and Mrs. Briggs, and then the three Miss Spinneys, then Silas Peckham, Head of the Apollinean Institute, and Mrs. Peckham, and more after them, until at last the ladies' dressing-room got so full that one might have thought it was a trap none of them could get out of. In truth, they all felt a little awkwardly. Nobody wanted to be first to venture down-stairs. At last Mr. Silas Peckham thought it was time to make a move for the parlor, and for this purpose presented himself at the door of the ladies' dressing-room.

"Lorindy, my dear!" he exclaimed to Mrs. Peckham,—"I think there can be no impropriety in our joining the family down-stairs."

Mrs. Peckham laid her large, flaccid arm in the sharp angle made by the black sleeve which held the bony limb her husband offered, and the two took the stair and struck out for the parlor. The ice was broken, and the dressing-room began to empty itself into the spacious, lighted apartments below.

Mr. Silas Peckham slid into the room with Mrs. Peckham alongside, like a shad convoying a jelly-fish.

"Good evenin', Mrs. Sprowle! I hope I see you well this evenin'. How's your haälth, Colonel Sprowle?"

"Very well, much obleeged to you. Hope you and your good lady are well. Much pleased to see you. Hope you'll enjoy yourselves. We've laid out to have everything in good shape,—spared no trouble nor ex"——

——"pense,"—said Silas Peckham.

Mrs. Colonel Sprowle, who, you remember, was a Jordan, had nipped the Colonel's statement in the middle of the word Mr. Peckham finished, with a look that jerked him like one of those sharp twitches women keep giving a horse when they get a chance to drive one.

Mr. and Mrs. Crane, Miss Ada Azuba, and Miss Mahala Crane made their entrance. There had been a discussion about the necessity and propriety of inviting this family, the head of which kept a small shop for hats and boots and shoes. The Colonel's casting vote had carried it in the affirmative.—How terribly the poor old green de-laine did cut up in the blaze of so many lamps and candles.

——Deluded little wretch, male or female, in town or country, going to your first great party, how little you know the nature of the ceremony in which you are to bear the part of victim! What! are not these garlands and gauzy mists and many-colored streamers which adorn you, is not this music which welcomes you, this radiance that glows about you, meant solely for your enjoyment, young miss of seventeen or eighteen summers, now for the first time swimming into the frothy, chatoyant, sparkling, undulating sea of laces and silks and satins, and white-armed, flower-crowned maidens struggling in their waves beneath the lustres that make the false summer of the drawing-room?

Stop at the threshold! This is a hall of judgment you are entering; the court is in session; and if you move five steps forward, you will be at its bar.

There was a tribunal once in France, as you may remember, called the *Chambre Ardente*, the Burning Chamber. It was hung all round with lamps, and hence its name. The burning chamber for the trial of young maidens is the blazing ball-room. What have they full-dressed you, or rather half-dressed you for, do you think? To make you look pretty, of course!—Why have they hung a chandelier above you, flickering all over with flames, so that it searches you like the noonday sun, and your deepest dimple cannot hold a shadow? To give brilliancy to the gay scene, no doubt!—No, my dear! Society is *inspecting* you, and it finds undisguised surfaces and strong lights a convenience in the process. The dance answers the purpose of the revolving pedestal upon which the "White Captive" turns, to show us the soft, kneaded marble, which looks as if it had never been hard, in all its manifold aspects of living loveliness. No mercy for you, my love! Justice, strict justice, you shall certainly have,—neither more nor less. For, look you, there are dozens, scores, hundreds, with whom you must be weighed in the balance; and you have got to learn that the "struggle for life" Mr. Charles Darwin talks about reaches to vertebrates clad in crinoline, as well as to mollusks in shells, or articulates in jointed scales, or anything that fights for breathing-room and food and love in any coat of fur or feather! Happy they who can flash defiance from bright eyes and snowy shoulders back into the pendants of the insolent lustres!

——Miss Mahala Crane did not have these reflections; and no young girl ever did, or ever will, thank Heaven! Her keen eyes sparkled under her plainly parted hair and the green de-laine moulded itself in those unmistakable lines of natural symmetry in which Nature indulges a small shopkeeper's daughter occasionally as well as a wholesale dealer's young ladies. She would have liked a new dress as much as any other girl, but she meant to go and have a good time at any rate.

The guests were now arriving in the drawing-room pretty fast, and the Colonel's hand began to burn a good deal with the sharp squeezes which many of the visitors gave it. Conversation, which had begun like a summer-shower, in scattering drops, was fast becoming continuous, and occasionally rising into gusty swells, with now and then a broad-chested laugh from some Captain or Major or other military personage,—for it may be noted that all large and loud men in the unpaved districts bear military titles.

Deacon Soper came up presently, and entered into conversation with Colonel Sprowle.

"I hope to see our pastor present this evenin'," said the Deacon.

"I don't feel quite sure," the Colonel answered. "His dyspepsy has been bad on him lately. He wrote to say, that, Providence permittin', it would be agreeable to him to take a part in the exercises of the evenin'; but I mistrusted he didn't mean to come. To tell the truth, Deacon Soper, I rather guess he don't like the idee of dancin', and some of the other little arrangements."

"Well," said the Deacon, "I know there's some condemns dancin'. I've heerd a good deal of talk about it among the folks round. Some have it that it never brings a blessin' on a house to have dancin' in it. Judge Tileston died, you remember, within a month after he had his great ball, twelve year ago, and some thought it was in the natur' of a judgment. I don't believe in any of them notions. If a man happened to be struck dead the night after he'd been givin' a ball," (the Colonel loosened his black stock a little, and winked and swallowed two or three times,) "I shouldn't call it a judgment,—I should call it a coincidence. But I'm a little afraid our pastor won't come. Somethin' or other's the matter with Mr. Fairweather. I should sooner expect to see the old Doctor come over out of the Orthodox parsonage-house."

"I've asked him," said the Colonel.

"Well?" said Deacon Soper.

"He said he should like to come, but he didn't know what his people would say. For his part, he loved to see young folks havin' their sports together, and very often felt as if he should like to be one of 'em himself. 'But,' says I, 'Doctor, I don't say there won't be a little dancin'.' 'Don't!' says he, 'for I want Letty to go,' (she's his granddaughter that's been stayin' with him,) 'and Letty's mighty fond of dancin'. You know,' says the Doctor, 'it isn't my business to settle whether other people's children should dance or not.' And the Doctor looked as if he should like to rigadoon and sashy across as well as the young one he was talkin' about. He's got blood in him, the old Doctor has. I wish our little man and him would swop pulpits."

Deacon Soper started and looked up into the Colonel's face, as if to see whether he was in earnest.

Mr. Silas Peckham and his lady joined the group.

"Is this to be a Temperance Celebration, Mrs. Sprowle?" asked Mr. Silas Peckham.

Mrs. Sprowle replied, "that there would be lemonade and srub for those that preferred such drinks, but that the Colonel had given folks to understand that he didn't mean to set in judgment on the marriage in Canaan, and that those that didn't like srub and such things would find somethin' that would suit them better."

Deacon Soper's countenance assumed a certain air of restrained cheerfulness. The conversation rose into one of its gusty paroxysms just then. Master H. Frederic got behind a door and began performing the experiment of stopping and unstopping his ears in rapid alternation, greatly rejoicing in the singular effect of mixed conversation chopped very small, like the contents of a mince-pie,—or meat pie, as it is more forcibly called in the deep-rutted villages lying along the unsalted streams. All at once it grew silent just round the door, where it had been loudest,—and the silence spread itself like a stain, till it hushed everything but a few corner-duets. A dark, sad-looking, middle-aged gentleman entered the parlor, with a young lady on his arm,—his daughter, as it seemed, for she was not wholly unlike him in feature, and of the same dark complexion.

"Dudley Venner," exclaimed a dozen people, in startled, but half-suppressed tones.

"What can have brought Dudley out to-night?" said Jefferson Buck, a young fellow, who had been interrupted in one of the corner-duets which he was executing in concert with Miss Susy Pettingill.

"How do I know, Jeff?" was Miss Susy's answer. Then, after a pause,—"Elsie made him come, I guess. Go ask Dr. Kittredge; he knows all about 'em both, they say."

Dr. Kittredge, the leading physician of Rockland, was a shrewd old man, who looked pretty keenly into his patients through his spectacles, and pretty widely at men, women, and things in general over them. Sixty-three years old,—just the year of the grand climacteric. A bald crown, as every doctor should have. A consulting practitioner's mouth; that is, movable round the corners while the case is under examination, but both corners well drawn down and kept so when the final opinion is made up. In fact, the Doctor was often sent for to act as "caounsel," all over the county, and beyond it. He kept three or four horses, sometimes riding in the saddle, commonly driving in a sulky, pretty fast, and looking straight before him, so that people got out of the way of bowing to him as he passed on the road. There was some talk about his not being so long-sighted as other folks, but his old patients laughed and looked knowing when this was spoken of.

The Doctor knew a good many things besides how to drop tinctures and shake out powders. Thus, he knew a horse, and, what is harder to understand, a horse-dealer, and was a match for him. He knew what a nervous woman is, and how to manage her. He could tell at a glance when she is in that condition of unstable equilibrium in which a rough word is like a blow to her, and the touch of unmagnetized fingers reverses all her nervous currents. It is not everybody that enters into the soul of Mozart's or Beethoven's harmonies; and there are vital symphonies in B flat, and other low, sad keys, which a doctor may know as little of as a hurdy-gurdy player of the essence of those divine musical mysteries. The Doctor knew the difference between what men say and what they mean as well as most people. When he was listening to common talk, he was in the habit of looking over his spectacles; if he lifted his head so as to look through them at the person talking, he was busier with that person's thoughts than with his words.

Jefferson Buck was not bold enough to confront the Doctor with Miss Susy's question, for he did not look as if he were in the mood to answer queries put by curious young people. His eyes were fixed steadily on the dark girl, every movement of whom he seemed to follow.

She was, indeed, an apparition of wild beauty, so unlike the girls about her that it seemed nothing more than natural, that, when she moved, the groups should part to let her pass through them, and that she should carry the centre of all looks and thoughts with her. She was dressed to please her own fancy, evidently, with small regard to the modes declared correct by the Rockland milliners and mantua-makers. Her heavy black hair lay in a braided coil, with a long gold pin shot through it like a javelin. Round her neck was a golden *torque*, a round, cord-like chain, such as the Gauls used to wear: the "Dying Gladiator" has it. Her dress was a grayish watered silk; her collar was pinned with a flashing diamond brooch, the stones looking as fresh as morning dew-drops, but the silver setting of the past generation; her arms were bare, round, but slender rather than large, in keeping with her lithe round figure. On her wrists she wore bracelets: one was a circlet of enamelled scales; the other looked as if it might have been Cleopatra's asp, with its body turned to gold and its eyes to emeralds.

Her father—for Dudley Venner was her father—looked like a man of culture and breeding, but melancholy and with a distracted air, as one whose life had met some fatal cross or blight. He saluted hardly anybody except his entertainers and the Doctor. One would have said, to look at him, that he was not at the party by choice; and it was natural enough to think, with Susy Pettingill, that it must have been a freak of the dark girl's which brought him there, for he had the air of a shy and sad-hearted recluse.

It was hard to say what could have brought Elsie Venner to the party. Hardly anybody seemed to know her, and she seemed not at all disposed to make acquaintances. Here and there was one of the older girls from the Institute, but she appeared to have nothing in common with them. Even in the school-room, it may be remembered, she sat apart by her own choice, and now in the midst of the crowd she made a circle of isolation round herself. Drawing her arm out of her father's, she stood against the wall, and looked, with a strange, cold glitter in her eyes, at the crowd which moved and babbled before her.

The old Doctor came up to her by-and-by.

"Well, Elsie, I am quite surprised to find you here. Do tell me how you happened to do such a good-natured thing as to let us see you at such a great party."

"It's been dull at the mansion-house," she said, "and I wanted to get out of it. It's too lonely there,—there's nobody to hate since Dick's gone."

The Doctor laughed good-naturedly, as if this were an amusing bit of pleasantry,—but he lifted his head and dropped his eyes a little, so as to see her through his spectacles. She narrowed her lids slightly, as one often sees a sleepy cat narrow hers,—somewhat as you may remember our famous Margaret used to, if you remember her at all, —so that her eyes looked very small, but bright as the diamonds on her breast. The old Doctor felt very oddly as she looked at him; he did not like the feeling, so he dropped his head and lifted his eyes and looked at her *over* his spectacles again.

"And how have you all been at the mansion-house?" said the Doctor.

"Oh, well enough. But Dick's gone, and there's nobody left but Dudley and I and the people. I'm tired of it. What kills anybody quickest, Doctor?" Then, in a whisper, "I ran away again the other day, you know."

"Where did you go?" The Doctor spoke in a low, serious tone.

"Oh, to the old place. Here, I brought this for you."

The Doctor started as she handed him a flower of the *Atragene Americana*, for he knew that there was only one spot where it grew, and that not one where any rash foot, least of all a thin-shod woman's foot, should venture.

"How long were you gone?" said the Doctor.

"Only one night. You should have heard the horns blowing and the guns firing. Dudley was frightened out of his wits. Old Sophy told him she'd had a dream, and that I should be found in Dead-Man's Hollow, with a great rock lying on me. They hunted all over it, but they didn't find me,—I was farther up."

Doctor Kittredge looked cloudy and worried while she was speaking, but forced a pleasant professional smile, as he said cheerily, and as if wishing to change the subject,—

"Have a good dance this evening, Elsie. The fiddlers are tuning up. Where's the young master? Has he come yet? or is he going to be late, with the other great folks?"

The girl turned away without answering, and looked toward the door.

The "great folks," meaning the mansion-house gentry, were just beginning to come; Dudley Venner and his daughter had been the first of them. Judge Thornton, white-headed, fresh-faced, as good at sixty as he was at forty, with a youngish second wife, and one noble daughter, Arabella, who, they said, knew as much law as her father, a stately, Portia-like girl, fit for a premier's wife, not like to find her match even in the great cities she sometimes visited; the Trecothicks, the family of a merchant, (in the larger sense,) who, having made himself rich enough by the time he had reached middle life, threw down his ledger as Sylla did his dagger, and retired to make a little paradise around him in one of the stateliest residences of the town, a family inheritance; the Vaughans, an old Rockland race, descended from its first settlers, Toryish in tendency in Revolutionary times, and barely escaping confiscation or worse; the Dunhams, a new family, dating its gentility only as far back as the Honorable Washington Dunham, M.C., but turning out a clever boy or two that went to college, and some showy girls with white necks and fat arms who had picked up professional husbands: these were the principal mansion-house people. All of them had made it a point to come; and as each of them entered, it seemed to Colonel and Mrs. Sprowle that the lamps burned up with a more cheerful light, and that the fiddles which sounded from the uncarpeted room were all half a tone higher and half a beat quicker.

Mr. Bernard came in later than any of them; he had been busy with his new duties. He looked well; and that is saying a good deal; for nothing but a gentleman is endurable in full dress. Hair that masses well, a head set on with an air, a neckerchief tied cleverly by an easy, practised hand, close-fitting gloves, feet well shaped and well covered,—these advantages can make us forgive the odious sable broadcloth suit, which appears to have been adopted by society on the same principle that condemned all the Venetian gondolas to perpetual and uniform blackness. Mr. Bernard, introduced by Mr. Geordie, made his bow to the Colonel and his lady and to Miss Matilda, from whom he got a particularly gracious curtsy, and then began looking about him for acquaintances. He found two or three faces he knew,—many more strangers. There was Silas Peckham,—there was no mistaking him; there was the inelastic amplitude of Mrs. Peckham; few of the Apollinean girls, of course, they not being recognized members of society,—but there is one with the flame in her cheeks and the fire in her eyes, the girl of vigorous tints and emphatic outlines, whom we saw entering the school-room the other day. Old Judge Thornton has his eyes on her, and the Colonel steals a look every now and then at the red brooch which lifts itself so superbly into the light, as if he thought it a wonderfully becoming ornament. Mr. Bernard himself was not displeased with the general effect of the rich-blooded school-girl, as she stood under the bright lamps, fanning herself in the warm, languid air, fixed in a kind of passionate surprise at the new life which seemed to be flowering out in her consciousness. Perhaps he looked at her somewhat steadily, as some others had done; at any rate, she seemed to feel that she was looked at, as people often do, and, turning her eyes suddenly on him, caught his own on her face, gave him a half-bashful smile, and threw in a blush involuntarily which made it more charming.

"What can I do better," he said to himself, "than have a dance with Rosa Milburn?" So he carried his handsome pupil into the next room and took his place with her in a cotillon. Whether the breath of the Goddess of Love could intoxicate like the cup of Circe,—whether a woman is ever phosphorescent with the luminous vapor of life that she exhales,—these and other questions which relate to occult influences exercised by certain women, we will not now discuss. It is enough that Mr. Bernard was sensible of a strange fascination, not wholly new to him, nor unprecedented in the history of human experience, but always a revelation when it comes over us for the first or the hundredth time, so pale is the most recent memory by the side of the passing moment with the flush of any newborn passion on its cheek. Remember that Nature makes every man love all women, and trusts the trivial matter of special choice to the commonest accident.

If Mr. Bernard had had nothing to distract his attention, he might have thought too much about his handsome partner, and then gone home and dreamed about her, which is always dangerous, and waked up thinking of her still, and then begun to be deeply interested in her studies, and so on, through the whole syllogism which ends in Nature's supreme *quod erat demonstrandum*. What was there to distract him or disturb him? He did not know,—but there was something. This sumptuous creature, this Eve just within the gate of an untried Paradise, untutored in the ways of the world, but on tiptoe to reach the fruit of the tree of knowledge,—alive to the moist vitality of that warm atmosphere palpitating with voices and music, as the flower of some diœcious plant which has grown in a lone corner and suddenly unfolding its corolla on some hot-breathing June evening, feels that the air is perfumed with strange odors and loaded with golden dust wafted from those other blossoms with which its double life is shared,—this almost overwomanized woman might well have bewitched him, but that he had a vague sense of a counter-charm. It was, perhaps, only the same consciousness that some one was looking at him which he himself had just given occasion to in his partner. Presently, in one of the turns of the dance, he felt his eyes drawn to a figure he had not distinctly recognized, though he had dimly felt its presence, and saw that Elsie Venner was looking at him as if she saw nothing else but him. He was not a nervous person, like the poor lady teacher, yet the glitter of the diamond eyes affected him strangely. It seemed to disenchant the air, so full a moment before of strange attractions. He became silent, and dreamy, as it were. The round-limbed beauty at his side crushed her gauzy draperies against him, as they trod the figure of the dance together, but it was no more to him than if an old nurse had laid her hand on his sleeve. The young girl chafed at his seeming neglect, and her imperious blood mounted into her cheeks; but he appeared unconscious of it.

"There is one of our young ladies I must speak to," he said,—and was just leaving his partner's side.

"Four hands all round!" shouted the first violin,—and Mr. Bernard found himself seized and whirled in a circle out of which he could not escape, and then forced to "cross over," and then to "dozy do," as the *maestro* had it,—and when, on getting back to his place, he looked for Elsie Venner, she was gone.

The dancing went on briskly. Some of the old folks looked on, others conversed in groups and pairs, and so the evening wore along, until a little after ten o'clock. About this time there was noticed an increased bustle in the passages, with a considerable opening and shutting of doors. Presently it began to be whispered about that they were going to have supper. Many, who had never been to any large party before, held their breath for a moment at this announcement. It was rather with a tremulous interest than with open hilarity that the rumor was generally received.

One point the Colonel had entirely forgotten to settle. It was a point involving not merely propriety, but perhaps principle also, or at least the good report of the house,— and he had never thought to arrange it. He took Judge Thornton aside and whispered the important question to him,—in his distress of mind, mistaking pockets and taking out his bandanna instead of his white handkerchief to wipe his forehead.

"Judge," he said, "do you think, that, before we commence refreshing ourselves at the tables, it would be the proper thing to—crave a—to request Deacon Soper or some other elderly person—to ask a blessing?"

The Judge looked as grave as if he were about giving the opinion of the Court in the great India-rubber case.

"On the whole," he answered, after a pause, "I should think it might, perhaps, be dispensed with on this occasion. Young folks are noisy, and it is awkward to have talking and laughing going on while a blessing is being asked. Unless a clergyman is present and makes a point of it, I think it will hardly be expected."

The Colonel was infinitely relieved. "Judge, will you take Mrs. Sprowle in to supper?" And the Colonel returned the compliment by offering his arm to Mrs. Judge Thornton.

The door of the supper-room was now open, and the company, following the lead of the host and hostess, began to stream into it, until it was pretty well filled.

There was an awful kind of pause. Many were beginning to drop their heads and shut their eyes, in anticipation of the usual petition before a meal; some expected the music to strike up,—others, that an oration would now be delivered by the Colonel.

"Make yourselves at home, ladies and gentlemen," said the Colonel; "good things were made to eat, and you're welcome to all you see before you."

So saying, he attacked a huge turkey which stood at the head of the table; and his example being followed first by the bold, then by the doubtful, and lastly by the timid, the clatter soon made the circuit of the tables. Some were shocked, however, as the Colonel had feared they would be, at the want of the customary invocation. Widow Leech, a kind of relation, who had to be invited, and who came with her old, back-country-looking string of gold beads round her neck, seemed to feel very serious about it.

"If she'd ha' known that folks would begrutch cravin' a blessin' over sech a heap o' provisions, she'd rather ha' staid t' home. It was a bad sign, when folks wasn't grateful for the baounties of Providence."

The elder Miss Spinney, to whom she made this remark, assented to it, at the same time ogling a piece of frosted cake, which she presently appropriated with great refinement of manner,—taking it between her thumb and forefinger, keeping the others well spread and the little finger in extreme divergence, with a graceful undulation of the neck, and a queer little sound in her throat, as of an *m* that wanted to get out and perished in the attempt.

The tables now presented an animated spectacle. Young fellows of the more dashing sort, with high stand-up collars and voluminous bows to their neckerchiefs, distinguished themselves by cutting up fowls and offering portions thereof to the buxom girls these knowing ones had commonly selected.

"A bit of the wing, Roxy, or of the—under limb?"

The first laugh broke out at this, but it was premature, a *sporadic* laugh, as Dr. Kittredge would have said, which did not become epidemic. People were very solemn as yet, many of them being new to such splendid scenes, and crushed, as it were, in the presence of so much crockery and so many silver spoons, and such a variety of unusual viands and beverages. When the laugh rose around Roxy and her saucy beau, several looked in that direction with an anxious expression, as if something had happened,—a lady fainted, for instance, or a couple of lively fellows come to high words.

"Young folks will be young folks," said Deacon Soper. "No harm done. Least said soonest mended."

"Have some of these shell-oysters?" said the Colonel to Mrs. Trecothick.

A delicate emphasis on the word *shell* implied that the Colonel knew what was what. To the New England inland native, beyond the reach of the east winds, the oyster unconditioned, the oyster absolute, without a qualifying adjective, is the *pickled* oyster. Mrs. Trecothick, who knew very well that an oyster long out of his shell (as is apt to be the case with the rural bivalve) gets homesick and loses his sprightliness, replied, with the pleasantest smile in the world, that the chicken she had been helped to was too delicate to be given up even for the greater rarity. But the word "shell-oysters" had been overheard; and there was a perceptible crowding movement towards their newly discovered habitat, a large soup-tureen.

Silas Peckham had meantime fallen upon another locality of these recent mollusks. He said nothing, but helped himself freely, and made a sign to Mrs. Peckham.

"Lorindy," he whispered, "shell-oysters!"

And ladled them out to her largely, without betraying any emotion, just as if they had been the natural inland or pickled article.

After the more solid portion of the banquet had been duly honored, the cakes and sweet preparations of various kinds began to get their share of attention. There were great cakes and little cakes, cakes with raisins in them, cakes with currants, and cakes without either; there were brown cakes and yellow cakes, frosted cakes, glazed cakes, hearts and rounds, and *jumbles,* which playful youth slip over the forefinger before spoiling their annular outline. There were moulds of *blo'monje,* of the arrowroot variety,—that being undistinguishable from such as is made with Russia isinglass. There were jellies, which had been shaking, all the time the young folks were dancing in the next room, as if they were balancing to partners. There were built-up fabrics, called *Charlottes,* caky externally, pulpy within; there were also *marangs,* and likewise custards,—some of the indolent-fluid sort, others firm, in which every stroke of the teaspoon left a smooth, conchoidal surface like the fracture of chalcedony, with here and there a little eye like what one sees in cheeses. Nor was that most wonderful object of domestic art called *trifle* wanting, with its charming confusion of cream and cake and almonds and jam and jelly and wine and cinnamon and froth; nor yet the marvellous *floating-island,*—name suggestive of all that is romantic in the imaginations of youthful palates.

"It must have cost you a sight of work, to say nothin' of money, to get all this beautiful confectionery made for the party," said Mrs. Crane to Mrs. Sprowle.

"Well, it cost some consid'able labor, no doubt," said Mrs. Sprowle. "Matilda and our girls and I made 'most all the cake with our own hands, and we all feel some tired; but if folks get what suits 'em, we don't begrudge the time nor the work. But I do feel thirsty," said the poor lady, "and I think a glass of srub would do my throat good; it's dreadful dry. Mr. Peckham, would you be so polite as to pass me a glass of srub?"

Silas Peckham bowed with great alacrity, and took from the table a small glass cup, containing a fluid reddish in hue and subacid in taste. This was *srub,* a beverage in local repute, of questionable nature, but suspected of owing its tint and sharpness to some kind of syrup derived from the maroon-colored fruit of the sumac. There were similar small cups on the table filled with lemonade, and here and there a decanter of Madeira wine, of the Marsala kind, which some prefer to, and many more cannot distinguish from, that which comes from the Atlantic island.

"Take a glass of wine, Judge," said the Colonel; "here is an article that I rather think 'll suit you."

The Judge knew something of wines, and could tell all the famous old Madeiras from each other,—"Eclipse," "Juno," the almost fabulously scarce and precious "Whitetop," and the rest. He struck the nativity of the Mediterranean Madeira before it had fairly moistened his lip.

"A sound wine, Colonel, and I should think of a genuine vintage. Your very good health."

"Deacon Soper," said the Colonel, "here is some Madary Judge Thornton recommends. Let me fill you a glass of it."

The Deacon's eyes glistened. He was one of those consistent Christians who stick firmly by the first miracle and Paul's advice to Timothy.

"A little good wine won't hurt anybody," said the Deacon. "Plenty,—plenty,—plenty. There!" He had not withdrawn his glass, while the Colonel was pouring, for fear it should spill, and now it was running over.

——It is very odd how all a man's philosophy and theology are at the mercy of a few drops of a fluid which the chemists say consists of nothing but C_4, O_2, H_6. The Deacon's theology fell off several points towards latitudinarianism in the course of the next ten minutes. He had a deep inward sense that everything was as it should be, human nature included. The little accidents of humanity, known collectively to moralists as sin, looked very venial to his growing sense of universal brotherhood and benevolence.

"It will all come right," the Deacon said to himself,— "I feel a joyful conviction that everything is for the best. I am favored with a blessed peace of mind, and a very precious season of good feelin' toward my fellow-creturs."

A lusty young fellow happened to make a quick step backward just at that instant, and put his heel, with his weight on top of it, upon the Deacon's toes.

"Aigh! What the d' d' didos are y' abou' with them great huffs o' yourn?" said the Deacon, with an expression upon his features not exactly that of peace and good-will to men. The lusty young fellow apologized; but the Deacon's face did not come right, and his theology backed round several points in the direction of total depravity.

Some of the dashing young men in stand-up collars and extensive neck-ties, encouraged by Mr. Geordie, made quite free with the "Madary," and even induced some of the more stylish girls—not of the mansion-house set, but of the tip-top two-story families—to taste a little. Most of these young ladies made faces at it, and declared it was "perfectly horrid," with that aspect of veracity peculiar to their age and sex.

About this time a movement was made on the part of some of the mansion-house people to leave the supper-table. Miss Jane Trecothick had quietly hinted to her mother that she had had enough of it. Miss Arabella Thornton had whispered to her father that he had better adjourn this court to the next room. There were signs of migration,—a loosening of people in their places,—a looking about for arms to hitch on to.

"Stop!" said the Colonel. "There's something coming yet. ——Ice-cream!"

The great folks saw that the play was not over yet, and that it was only polite to stay and see it out. The word "Ice-Cream" was no sooner whispered than it passed from one to another all down the tables. The effect was what might have been anticipated. Many of the guests had never seen this celebrated product of human skill, and to all the two-story population of Rockland it was the last expression of the art of pleasing and astonishing the human palate. Its appearance had been deferred for several reasons: first, because everybody would have attacked it, if it had come in with the other luxuries, secondly, because undue apprehensions were entertained (owing to want of experience) of its tendency to deliquesce and resolve itself with alarming rapidity into puddles of creamy fluid; and, thirdly, because the surprise would make a grand climax to finish off the banquet.

There is something so audacious in the conception of ice-cream, that it is not strange that a population undebauched by the luxury of great cities looks upon it with a kind of awe and speaks of it with a certain emotion. This defiance of the seasons, forcing Nature to do her work of congelation in the face of her sultriest noon, might well inspire a timid mind with fear lest human art were revolting against the Higher Powers, and raise the same scruples which resisted the use of ether and chloroform in certain contingencies. Whatever may be the cause, it is well known that the announcement at any private rural entertainment that there is to be ice-cream produces an immediate and profound impression. It may be remarked, as aiding this impression, that exaggerated ideas are entertained as to the dangerous effects this congealed food may produce on persons not in the most robust health.

There was silence as the pyramids of ice were placed on the table, everybody looking on in admiration. The Colonel took a knife and assailed the one at the head of the table. When he tried to cut off a slice, it didn't seem to understand it, however, and only tipped, as if it wanted to upset. The Colonel attacked it on the other side and it tipped just as badly the other way. It was awkward for the Colonel. "Permit me," said the Judge,—and he took the knife and struck a sharp slanting stroke which sliced off a piece just of the right size, and offered it to Mrs. Sprowle. This act of dexterity was much admired by the company.

The tables were all alive again.

"Lorindy, here's a plate of ice-cream," said Silas Peckham.

"Come, Mahaly," said a fresh-looking young fellow with a saucerful in each hand, "here's your ice-cream;—let's go in the corner and have a celebration, us two." And the old green de-laine, with the young curves under it to make it sit well, moved off as pleased apparently as if it had been silk velvet with thousand-dollar laces over it.

"Oh, now, Miss Green! do you think it's safe to put that cold stuff into your stomick?" said the Widow Leech to a young married lady, who, finding the air rather warm, thought a little ice would cool her down very nicely. "It's jest like eatin' snowballs. You don't look very rugged; and I should be dreadful afeard, if I was you"——

"Carrie," said old Dr. Kittredge, who had overheard this, —"how well you're looking this evening! But you must be tired and heated;—sit down here, and let me give you a good slice of ice-cream. How you young folks do grow up, to be sure! I don't feel quite certain whether it's you or your older sister, but I know it's somebody I call Carrie, and that I've known ever since"——

A sound something between a howl and an oath startled the company and broke off the Doctor's sentence. Everybody's eyes turned in the direction from which it came. A group instantly gathered round the person who had uttered it, who was no other than Deacon Soper.

"He's chokin'! he's chokin'!" was the first exclamation,—"slap him on the back!"

Several heavy fists beat such a tattoo on his spine that the Deacon felt as if at least one of his vertebræ would come up.

"He's black in the face," said Widow Leech,—"he's swallered somethin' the wrong way. Where's the Doctor? —let the Doctor get to him, can't ye?"

"If you will move, my good lady, perhaps I can," said Doctor Kittredge, in a calm tone of voice.—"He's not choking, my friends," the Doctor added immediately, when he got sight of him.

"It's apoplexy,—I told you so,—don't you see how red he is in the face?" said old Mrs. Peake, a famous woman for "nussin" sick folks,—determined to be a little ahead of the Doctor.

"It's not apoplexy," said Dr. Kittredge.

"What is it, Doctor? what is it? Will he die? Is he dead? —Here's his poor wife, the Widow Soper that is to be, if she a'n't a'ready"——

"Do be quiet, my good woman," said Dr. Kittredge.— "Nothing serious, I think, Mrs. Soper.—Deacon!"

The sudden attack of Deacon Soper had begun with the extraordinary sound mentioned above. His features had immediately assumed an expression of intense pain, his eyes staring wildly, and, clapping his hands to his face, he had rocked his head backward and forward in speechless agony.

At the Doctor's sharp appeal the Deacon lifted his head.

"It's all right," said the Doctor, as soon as he saw his face. "The Deacon had a smart attack of neuralgic pain. That's all. Very severe, but not at all dangerous."

The Doctor kept his countenance, but his diaphragm was shaking the change in his waistcoat-pockets with subterranean laughter. He had looked through his spectacles and seen at once what had happened. The Deacon, not being in the habit of taking his nourishment in the congealed state, had treated the ice-cream as a pudding of a rare species, and, to make sure of doing himself justice in its distribution, had taken a large mouthful of it without the least precaution. The consequence was a sensation as if a dentist were killing the nerves of twenty-five teeth at once with hot irons, or cold ones, which would hurt rather worse.

The Deacon swallowed something with a spasmodic effort, and recovered pretty soon and received the congratulations of his friends. There were different versions of the expressions he had used at the onset of his complaint,—some of the reported exclamations involving a breach of propriety, to say the least,—but it was agreed that a man in an attack of neuralgy wasn't to be judged of by the rules that applied to other folks.

The company soon after this retired from the supper-room. The mansion-house gentry took their leave, and the two-story people soon followed. Mr. Bernard had staid an hour or two, and left soon after he found that Elsie Venner and her father had disappeared. As he passed by the dormitory of the Institute, he saw a light glimmering from one of its upper rooms, where the lady teacher was still waking. His heart ached, when he remembered, that, through all these hours of gayety, or what was meant for it, the patient girl had been at work in her little chamber; and he looked up at the silent stars, as if to see that they were watching over her. The planet Mars was burning like a red coal; the northern constellation was slanting downward about its central point of flame; and while he looked, a falling star slid from the zenith and was lost.

He reached his chamber and was soon dreaming over the Event of the Season.

CHAPTER VIII

THE MORNING AFTER

Colonel Sprowle's family arose late the next morning. The fatigues and excitements of the evening and the preparation for it were followed by a natural collapse, of which somnolence was a leading symptom. The sun shone into the window at a pretty well opened angle when the Colonel first found himself sufficiently awake to address his yet slumbering spouse.

"Sally!" said the Colonel, in a voice that was a little husky,—for he had finished off the evening with an extra glass or two of "Madary," and had a somewhat rusty and headachy sense of renewed existence, on greeting the rather advanced dawn,—"Sally!"

"Take care o' them custard-cups! There they go!"

Poor Mrs. Spowle was fighting the party over in her dream; and as the visionary custard-cups crashed down through one lobe of her brain into another, she gave a start as if an inch of lightning from a quart Leyden jar had jumped into one of her knuckles with its sudden and lively *poonk!*

"Sally!" said the Colonel,—"wake up, wake up! What 'r' y' dreamin' abaout?"

Mrs. Sprowle raised herself, by a sort of spasm, *sur son séant*, as they say in France,—up on end, as we have it in New England. She looked first to the left, then to the right, then straight before her, apparently without seeing anything, and at last slowly settled down, with her two eyes, blank of any particular meaning, directed upon the Colonel.

"What time is't?" she said.

"Ten o'clock. What 'y' been dreamin' abaout? Y' giv a

jump like a hoppergrass. Wake up, wake up! Th' party's over, and y' been asleep all the mornin'. The party's over, I tell ye! Wake up!"

"Over!" said Mrs. Sprowle, who began to define her position at last,—"over! I should think 'twas time 'twas over! It's lasted a hundud year. I've been workin' for that party longer 'n Methuselah's lifetime, sence I been asleep. The pies wouldn' bake, and the blo'monge wouldn' set, and the ice-cream wouldn' freeze, and all the folks kep' comin' 'n' comin' 'n' comin',—everybody I ever knew in all my life,— some of 'em 's been dead this twenty year 'n' more,—'n' nothin' for 'em to eat nor drink. The fire wouldn' burn to cook anything, all we could do. We blowed with the belluses, 'n' we stuffed in paper 'n' pitch-pine kindlin's, but nothin' could make that fire burn; 'n' all the time the folks kep' comin', as if they'd never stop,—'n' nothin' for 'em but empty dishes, 'n' all the borrowed chaney slippin' round on the waiters 'n' chippin' 'n' crackin',—I wouldn' go through what I been through t'-night for all th' money in th' Bank, —I do believe it's harder t' have a party than t'"—

Mrs. Sprowle stated the case strongly.

The Colonel said he didn't know how that might be. She was a better judge than he was. It was bother enough, anyhow, and he was glad that it was over. After this, the worthy pair commenced preparations for rejoining the waking world, and in due time proceeded down-stairs.

Everybody was late that morning, and nothing had got put to rights. The house looked as if a small army had been quartered in it over night. The tables were of course in huge disorder, after the protracted assault they had undergone. There had been a great battle evidently, and it had gone against the provisions. Some points had been stormed, and all their defences annihilated, but here and there were centres of resistance which had held out against all attacks, —large rounds of beef, and solid loaves of cake, against which the inexperienced had wasted their energies in the enthusiasm of youth or uninformed maturity, while the longer-headed guests were making discoveries of "shell-oysters" and "pătridges" and similar delicacies.

The breakfast was naturally of a somewhat fragmentary

character. A chicken that had lost his legs in the service of the preceding campaign was once more put on duty. A great ham stuck with cloves, as Saint Sebastian was with arrows, was again offered for martyrdom. It would have been a pleasant sight for a medical man of a speculative turn to have seen the prospect before the Colonel's family of the next week's breakfasts, dinners, and suppers. The trail that one of these great rural parties leaves after it is one of its most formidable considerations. Every door-handle in the house is suggestive of sweetmeats for the next week, at least. The most unnatural articles of diet displace the frugal but nutritious food of unconvulsed periods of existence. If there is a walking infant about the house, it will certainly have a more or less fatal fit from overmuch of some indigestible delicacy. Before the week is out, everybody will be tired to death of sugary forms of nourishment and long to see the last of the remnants of the festival.

The family had not yet arrived at this condition. On the contrary, the first inspection of the tables suggested the prospect of days of unstinted luxury; and the younger portion of the household, especially, were in a state of great excitement as the account of stock was taken with reference to future internal investments. Some curious facts came to light during these researches.

"Where's all the oranges gone to?" said Mrs. Sprowle. "I expected there'd be ever so many of 'em left. I didn't see many of the folks eatin' oranges. Where's the skins of 'em? There ought to be six dozen orange-skins round on the plates, and there a'n't one dozen. And all the small cakes, too, and all the sugar things that was stuck on the big cakes. Has anybody counted the spoons? Some of 'em got swallered, perhaps. I hope they was plated ones, if they did!"

The failure of the morning's orange-crop and the deficit in other expected residual delicacies were not very difficult to account for. In many of the two-story Rockland families, and in those favored households of the neighboring villages whose members had been invited to the great party, there was a very general excitement among the younger people on the morning after the great event. "Did y' bring home somethin' from the party? What is it? What is it? Is it frût-cake? Is it nuts and oranges and apples? Give me some! Give *me* some!" Such a concert of treble voices uttering accents like these had not been heard since the great Temperance Festival with the celebrated "cōlation" in the open air under the trees of the Parnassian Grove,—as the place was christened by the young ladies of the Institute. The cry of the children was not in vain. From the pockets of demure fathers, from the bags of sharp-eyed spinsters, from the folded handkerchiefs of light-fingered sisters, from the tall hats of sly-winking brothers, there was a resurrection of the missing oranges and cakes and sugar-things in many a rejoicing family-circle, enough to astonish the most hardened "caterer" that ever contracted to feed a thousand people under canvas.

The tender recollection of those dear little ones whom extreme youth or other pressing considerations detain from scenes of festivity—a trait of affection by no means uncommon among our thoughtful people—dignifies those social meetings where it is manifested, and sheds a ray of sunshine on our common nature. It is "an oasis in the desert," —to use the striking expression of the last year's "Valedictorian" of the Apollinean Institute. In the midst of so much that is purely selfish, it is delightful to meet such disinterested care for others. When a large family of children are expecting a parent's return from an entertainment, it will often require great exertions on his part to freight himself so as to meet their reasonable expectations. A few rules are worth remembering by all who attend anniversary dinners in Faneuil Hall or elsewhere. Thus: Lobsters claws are always acceptable to children of all ages. Oranges and apples are to be taken *one at a time*, until the coat-pockets begin to become inconveniently heavy. Cakes are injured by sitting upon them; it is, therefore, well to carry a stout tin box of a size to hold as many pieces as there are children in the domestic circle. A very pleasant amusement, at the close of one of these banquets, is grabbing for the flowers with which the table is embellished. These will please the ladies at home very greatly, and, if the children are at the same time abundantly supplied with fruits, nuts, cakes, and any little ornamental articles of confectionery which are of a nature to be unostentatiously removed, the kind-hearted parent will make a whole household happy, without any additional expense beyond the outlay for his ticket.

There were fragmentary delicacies enough left, of one kind and another, at any rate, to make all the Colonel's family uncomfortable for the next week. It bid fair to take as long to get rid of the remains of the great party as it had taken to make ready for it.

In the mean time Mr. Bernard had been dreaming, as young men dream, of gliding shapes with bright eyes and burning cheeks, strangely blended with red planets and hissing meteors, and, shining over all, the white, unwandering star of the North, girt with its tethered constellations.

After breakfast he walked into the parlor, where he found Miss Darley. She was alone, and, holding a school-book in her hand, was at work with one of the morning's lessons. She hardly noticed him as he entered, being very busy with her book,—and he paused a moment before speaking, and looked at her with a kind of reverence. It would not have been strictly true to call her beautiful. For years,—since her earliest womanhood,—those slender hands had taken the bread which repaid the toil of heart and brain from the coarse palms which offered it in the world's rude market. It was not for herself alone that she had bartered away the life of her youth, that she had breathed the hot air of school-rooms, that she had forced her intelligence to posture before her will, as the exigencies of her place required,—waking to mental labor,—sleeping to dream of problems,—rolling up the stone of education for an endless twelve-month's term, to find it at the bottom of the hill again when another year called her to its renewed duties,—schooling her temper in unending inward and outward conflicts, until neither dulness nor obstinacy nor ingratitude nor insolence could reach her serene self-possession. Not for herself alone. Poorly as her prodigal labors were repaid in proportion to the waste of life they cost, her value was too well established to leave her without what, under other circumstances, would have been a more than sufficient compensation. But there were others who looked to her in their need, and so the modest fountain which might have been filled to its brim was continually drained through silent-flowing, hidden sluices.

Out of such a life, inherited from a race which had lived in conditions not unlike her own, *beauty*, in the common sense of the term, could hardly find leisure to develop and shape itself. For it must be remembered, that symmetry and elegance of features and figure, like perfectly formed crystals in the mineral world, are reached only by insuring a certain necessary repose to individuals and to generations. Human beauty is an agricultural product in the country, growing up in men and women as in corn and cattle, where the soil is good. It is a luxury almost monopolized by the rich in cities, bred under glass like their forced pine-apples and peaches. Both in city and country, the evolution of the physical harmonies which make music to our eyes requires a combination of favorable circumstances, of which alternations of unburdened tranquillity with intervals of varied excitement of mind and body are among the most important. Where sufficient excitement is wanting, as often happens in the country, the features, however rich in red and white, get heavy, and the movements sluggish; where excitement is furnished in excess, as is frequently the case in cities, the contours and colors are impoverished, and the nerves begin to make their existence known to the consciousness, as the face very soon informs us.

Helen Darley could not, in the nature of things, have possessed the kind of beauty which pleases the common taste. Her eye was calm, sad-looking, her features very still, except when her pleasant smile changed them for a moment, all her outlines were delicate, her voice was very gentle, but somewhat subdued by years of thoughtful labor, and on her smooth forehead one little hinted line whispered already that Care was beginning to mark the trace which Time sooner or later would make a furrow. She could not be a beauty; if she had been, it would have been much harder for many persons to be interested in her. For, although in the abstract we all love beauty, and although, if we were sent naked souls into some ultramundane warehouse of soulless bodies and told to select one to our liking, we should each choose a handsome one, and never think of the consequences,—it is quite certain that beauty carries an atmosphere of repulsion as well as of attraction with it, alike in both sexes. We may be well assured that there are many persons who no more think of specializing their love of the other sex upon one endowed with signal beauty, than they think of wanting great diamonds or thousand-dollar horses. No man or woman can appropriate beauty without paying for it,—in endowments, in fortune, in position, in self-surrender, or other valuable stock; and there are a great many who are too poor, too ordinary, too humble, too busy, too proud, to pay any of these prices for it. So the unbeautiful get many more lovers than the beauties; only, as there are more of them, their lovers are spread thinner and do not make so much show.

The young master stood looking at Helen Darley with a kind of tender admiration. She was such a picture of the martyr by the slow social combustive process, that it almost seemed to him he could see a pale lambent *nimbus* round her head.

"I did not see you at the great party last evening," he said, presently.

She looked up and answered, "No. I have not much taste for such large companies. Besides, I do not feel as if my time belonged to me after it has been paid for. There is always something to do, some lesson or exercise,—and it so happened, I was very busy last night with the new problems in geometry. I hope you had a good time."

"Very. Two or three of our girls were there. Rosa Milburn. What a beauty she is! I wonder what she feeds on! Wine and musk and chloroform and coals of fire, I believe; I didn't think there was such color and flavor in a woman outside the tropics."

Miss Darley smiled rather faintly; the imagery was not just to her taste: *femineity* often finds it very hard to accept the fact of *muliebrity*.

"Was"——?

She stopped short; but her question had asked itself.

"Elsie there? She was, for an hour or so. She looked

frightfully handsome. I meant to have spoken to her, but she slipped away before I knew it."

"I thought she meant to go to the party," said Miss Darley. "Did she look at you?"

"She did. Why?"

"And you did not speak to her?"

"No. I should have spoken to her, but she was gone when I looked for her. A strange creature! Isn't there an odd sort of fascination about her? You have not explained all the mystery about the girl. What does she come to this school for? She seems to do pretty much as she likes about studying."

Miss Darley answered in very low tones. "It was a fancy of hers to come, and they let her have her way. I don't know what there is about her, except that she seems to take my life out of me when she looks at me. I don't like to ask other people about our girls. She says very little to anybody, and studies, or makes believe to study, almost what she likes. I don't know what she is," (Miss Darley laid her hand, trembling, on the young master's sleeve,) "but I can tell when she is in the room without seeing or hearing her. Oh, Mr. Langdon, I am weak and nervous, and no doubt foolish, —but—if there were women now, as in the days of our Saviour, possessed of devils, I should think there was something not human looking out of Elsie Venner's eyes!"

The poor girl's breast rose and fell tumultuously as she spoke, and her voice labored, as if some obstruction were rising in her throat.

A scene might possibly have come of it, but the door opened. Mr. Silas Peckham. Miss Darley got away as soon as she well could.

"Why did not Miss Darley go to the party last evening?" said Mr. Bernard.

"Well, the fact is," answered Mr. Silas Peckham, "Miss Darley, she's pooty much took up with the school. She's an industris young woman,—yis, she *is* industris,—but perhaps she a'n't quite so spry a worker as some. Maybe, considerin' she's paid for her time, she isn't fur out o' the way in occoopyin' herself evenin's,—that is, if so be she a'n't smart enough to finish up all her work in the daytime. Edoocation is the great business of the Institoot. Amoosements are objec's of a secondary natur', accordin' to my v'oo." [The unspellable pronunciation of this word is the touchstone of New England Brahminism.]

Mr. Bernard drew a deep breath, his thin nostrils dilating, as if the air did not rush in fast enough to cool his blood, while Silas Peckham was speaking. The Head of the Apollinean Institute delivered himself of these judicious sentiments in that peculiar acid, penetrating tone, thickened with a nasal twang, which not rarely becomes hereditary after three or four generations raised upon east winds, salt fish, and large, white-bellied, pickled cucumbers. He spoke deliberately, as if weighing his words well, so that, during his few remarks, Mr. Bernard had time for a mental accompaniment with variations, accented by certain bodily changes, which escaped Mr. Peckham's observation. First there was a feeling of disgust and shame at hearing Helen Darley spoken of like a dumb working animal. That sent the blood up into his cheeks. Then the slur upon her probable want of force—*her* incapacity, who made the character of the school and left this man to pocket its profits—sent a thrill of the old Wentworth fire through him, so that his muscles hardened, his hands closed, and he took the measure of Mr. Silas Peckham, to see if his head would strike the wall in case he went over backwards all of a sudden. This would not do, of course, and so the thrill passed off and the muscles softened again. Then came that state of tenderness in the heart, overlying wrath in the stomach, in which the eyes grow moist like a woman's, and there is also a great boiling-up of objectionable terms out of the deep-water vocabulary, so that Prudence and Propriety and all the other pious Ps have to jump upon the lid of speech to keep them from boiling *over* into fierce articulation. All this was internal, chiefly, and of course not recognized by Mr. Silas Peckham. The idea, that any full-grown, sensible man should have any other notion than that of getting the most work for the least money out of his assistants, had never suggested itself to him.

Mr. Bernard had gone through this paroxysm, and cooled down, in the period while Mr. Peckham was uttering these words in his thin, shallow whine, twanging up into the frontal sinuses. What was the use of losing his temper and throwing away his place, and so, among the consequences which would necessarily follow, leaving the poor lady-teacher without a friend to stand by her ready to lay his hand on the grand-inquisitor before the windlass of his rack had taken one turn too many?

"No doubt, Mr. Peckham," he said, in a grave, calm voice, "there is a great deal of work to be done in the school; but perhaps we can distribute the duties a little more evenly after a time. I shall look over the girls' themes myself, after this week. Perhaps there will be some other parts of her labor that I can take on myself. We can arrange a new programme of studies and recitations."

"We can do that," said Mr. Silas Peckham. "But I don't propose mater'lly alterin' Miss Darley's dooties. I don't think she works to hurt herself. Some of the Trustees have proposed interdoosin' new branches of study, and I expect you will be pooty much occoopied with the dooties that belong to your place. On the Sahbath you will be able to attend divine service three times, which is expected of our teachers. I shall continoo myself to give Sahbath Scriptur'-readin's to the young ladies. That is a solemn dooty I can't make up my mind to commit to other people. My teachers enjoy the Lord's day as a day of rest. In it they do no manner of work,—except in cases of necessity or mercy, such as fillin' out diplomas, or when we git crowded jest at the end of a term, or when there is an extry number of p'oopils, or other Providential call to dispense with the ordinance."

Mr. Bernard had a fine glow in his cheeks by this time, —doubtless kindled by the thought of the kind consideration Mr. Peckham showed for his subordinates in allowing them the between meeting-time on Sundays except for some special reason. But the morning was wearing away; so he went to the school-room, taking leave very properly of his respected principal, who soon took his hat and departed.

Mr. Peckham visited certain "stores" or shops, where he made inquiries after various articles in the provision-line, and effected a purchase or two. Two or three barrels of potatoes, which had sprouted in a promising way, he secured at a bargain. A side of feminine beef was also obtained at a low figure. He was entirely satisfied with a couple of barrels of flour, which, being invoiced "slightly damaged," were to be had at a reasonable price.

After this, Silas Peckham felt in good spirits. He had done a pretty stroke of business. It came into his head whether he might not follow it up with a still more brilliant speculation. So he turned his steps in the direction of Colonel Sprowle's.

It was now eleven o'clock, and the battle-field of last evening was as we left it. Mr. Peckham's visit was unexpected, perhaps not very well timed, but the Colonel received him civilly.

"Beautifully lighted,—these rooms last night!" said Mr. Peckham. "Winter-strained?"

The Colonel nodded.

"How much do you pay for your winter-strained?"

The Colonel told him the price.

"Very hahnsome supper,—very hahnsome. Nothin' ever seen like it in Rockland. Must have been a great heap of things left over."

The compliment was not ungrateful, and the Colonel acknowledged it by smiling and saying, "I should think the' was a trifle! Come and look."

When Silas Peckham saw how many delicacies had survived the evening's conflict, his commercial spirit rose at once to the point of a proposal.

"Colonel Sprowle," said he, "there's meat and cakes and pies and pickles enough on that table to spread a hahnsome cōlation. If you'd like to trade reasonable, I think perhaps I should be willin' to take 'em off your hands. There's been a talk about our havin' a celebration in the Parnassian Grove, and I think I could work in what your folks don't want and make myself whole by chargin' a small sum for tickets. Broken meats, of course, a'n't of the same valoo as fresh provisions; so I think you might be willin' to trade reasonable."

Mr. Peckham paused and rested on his proposal. It would not, perhaps, have been very extraordinary, if Colonel

Sprowle had entertained the proposition. There is no telling beforehand how such things will strike people. It didn't happen to strike the Colonel favorably. He had a little red-blooded manhood in him.

"Sell you them things to make a cōlation out of?" the Colonel replied. "Walk up to that table, Mr. Peckham, and help yourself! Fill your pockets, Mr. Peckham! Fetch a basket, and our hired folks shall fill it full for ye! Send a cart, if y' like, 'n' carry off them leavin's to make a celebration for your pupils with! Only let me tell ye this:—as sure's my name's Hezekiah Spraowle, you'll be known through the taown 'n' through the caounty, from that day forrard, as the Principal of the Broken-Victuals Instıtoot!"

Even provincial human-nature sometimes has a touch of sublimity about it. Mr. Silas Peckham had gone a little deeper than he meant, and come upon the "hard pan," as the well-diggers call it, of the Colonel's character, before he thought of it. A militia-colonel standing on his sentiments is not to be despised. That was shown pretty well in New England two or three generations ago. There were a good many plain officers that talked about their "rigiment" and their "caounty" who knew very well how to say "Make ready!" "Take aim!" "Fire!"—in the face of a line of grenadiers with bullets in their guns and bayonets on them. And though a rustic uniform is not always unexceptionable in its cut and trimmings, yet there was many an ill-made coat in those old times that was good enough to be shown to the enemy's front rank too often to be left on the field with a round hole in its left lapel that matched another going right through the brave heart of the plain country captain or major or colonel who was buried in it under the crimson turf.

Mr. Silas Peckham said little or nothing. His sensibilities were not acute, but he perceived that he had made a miscalculation. He hoped that there was no offence,—thought it might have been mutooally agreeable, conclooded he would give up the idee of a cōlation, and backed himself out as if unwilling to expose the less guarded aspect of his person to the risk of accelerating impulses.

The Colonel shut the door,—cast his eye on the toe of his right boot, as if it had had a strong temptation,—looked at his watch, then round the room, and, going to a cupboard, swallowed a glass of deep-red brandy and water to compose his feelings.

CHAPTER IX

THE DOCTOR ORDERS THE BEST SULKY

(*With a Digression on "Hired Help"*)

"Abel! Slip Cassia into the new sulky, and fetch her round."

Abel was Dr. Kittredge's hired man. He was born in New Hampshire, a queer sort of State, with fat streaks of soil and population where they breed giants in mind and body, and lean streaks which export imperfectly nourished young men with promising but neglected appetites, who may be found in great numbers in all the large towns, or could be until of late years, when they have been half driven out of their favorite basement-stories by foreigners, and half coaxed away from them by California. New Hampshire is in more than one sense the Switzerland of New England. The "Granite State" being naturally enough deficient in pudding-stone, its children are apt to wander southward in search of that deposit,—in the unpetrified condition.

Abel Stebbins was a good specimen of that extraordinary hybrid or mule between democracy and chrysocracy, a native-born New-England serving-man. The Old World has nothing at all like him. He is at once an emperor and a subordinate. In one hand he holds one five-millionth part (be the same more or less) of the power that sways the destinies of the Great Republic. His other hand is in your boot, which he is about to polish. It is impossible to turn a fellow-citizen whose vote may make his master—say, rather, employer—Governor or President, or who may be one or both himself, into a flunky. That article must be imported ready-made from other centres of civilization. When a New Englander has lost his self-respect as a citizen and as a man, he is demoralized, and cannot be trusted with the money to pay for a dinner.

It may be supposed, therefore, that this fractional emperor, this continent-shaper, finds his position awkward when he goes into service, and that his employer is apt to find it still more embarrassing. It is always under protest that the hired man does his duty. Every act of service is subject to the drawback, "I am as good as you are." This is so common, at least, as almost to be the rule, and partly accounts for the rapid disappearance of the indigenous "domestic" from the basements above mentioned. Paleontologists will by-and-by be examining the floors of our kitchens for tracks of the extinct native species of serving-man. The female of the same race is fast dying out; indeed, the time is not far distant when all the varieties of young *woman* will have vanished from New England, as the dodo has perished in the Mauritius. The young *lady* is all that we shall have left, and the mop and duster of the last Almira or Loïzy will be stared at by generations of Bridgets and Noras as that famous head and foot of the lost bird are stared at in the Ashmolean Museum.

Abel Stebbins, the Doctor's man, took the true American view of his difficult position. He sold his time to the Doctor, and, having sold it, he took care to fulfil his half of the bargain. The Doctor, on his part, treated him, not like a gentleman, because one does not order a gentleman to bring up his horse or run his errands, but he treated him like a man. Every order was given in courteous terms. His reasonable privileges were respected as much as if they had been guaranteed under hand and seal. The Doctor lent him books from his own library, and gave him all friendly counsel, as if he were a son or a younger brother.

Abel had Revolutionary blood in his veins, and though he saw fit to "hire out," he could never stand the word "servant," or consider himself the inferior one of the two high contracting parties. When he came to live with the Doctor, he made up his mind he would dismiss the old gentleman, if he did not behave according to his notions of propriety. But he soon found that the Doctor was one of the right sort, and so determined to keep him. The Doctor soon found, on his side, that he had a trustworthy, intelligent fellow, who would be invaluable to him, if he only let him have his own way of doing what was to be done.

The Doctor's hired man had not the manners of a French valet. He was grave and taciturn for the most part, he never bowed and rarely smiled, but was always at work in the daytime, and always reading in the evening. He was hostler, and did all the housework that a man could properly do, would go to the door or "tend table," bought the provisions for the family,—in short, did almost everything for them but get their clothing. There was no office in a perfectly appointed household, from that of steward down to that of stable-boy, which he did not cheerfully assume. His round of work not consuming all his energies, he must needs cultivate the Doctor's garden, which he kept in one perpetual bloom, from the blowing of the first crocus to the fading of the last dahlia.

This garden was Abel's poem. Its half-dozen beds were so many cantos. Nature crowded them for him with imagery such as no Laureate could copy in the cold mosaic of language. The rhythm of alternating dawn and sunset, the strophe and antistrophe still perceptible through all the sudden shifts of our dithyrambic seasons and echoed in corresponding floral harmonies, made melody in the soul of Abel, the plain serving-man. It softened his whole otherwise rigid aspect. He worshipped God according to the strict way of his fathers; but a florist's Puritanism is always colored by the petals of his flowers,—and Nature never shows him a black corolla.

He may or may not figure again in this narrative; but as there must be some who confound the New-England *hired man*, native-born, with the *servant* of foreign birth, and as there is the difference of two continents and two civilizations between them, it did not seem fair to let Abel bring round the Doctor's mare and sulky without touching his features in half-shadow into our background.

The Doctor's mare, Cassia, was so called by her master from her cinnamon color, cassia being one of the professional names for that spice or drug. She was of the shade we call sorrel, or, as an Englishman would perhaps say, chestnut,—a genuine "Morgan" mare, with a low forehand, as is common in this breed, but with strong quarters and flat hocks, well ribbed up, with a good eye and a pair of lively ears,—a first-rate doctor's beast,—would stand until her harness dropped off her back at the door of a tedious case, and trot over hill and dale thirty miles in three hours, if there was a child in the next county with a bean in its windpipe and the Doctor gave her a hint of the fact. Cassia was not large, but she had a good deal of action, and was the Doctor's show-horse. There were two other animals in his stable: Quassia or Quashy, the black horse, and Caustic, the old bay, with whom he jogged round the village.

"A long ride to-day?" said Abel, as he brought up the equipage.

"Just out of the village,—that's all.—There's a kink in her mane,—pull it out, will you?"

"Goin' to visit some of the great folks," Abel said to himself. "Wonder who it is."—Then to the Doctor,—"Anybody get sick at Sprowles's? They say Deacon Soper had a fit, after eatin' some o' their frozen victuals."

The Doctor smiled. He guessed the Deacon would do well enough. He was only going to ride over to the Dudley mansion-house.

CHAPTER X

THE DOCTOR CALLS ON ELSIE VENNER

If that primitive physician, CHIRON, M.D., appears as a Centaur, as we look at him through the lapse of thirty centuries, the modern country-doctor, if he could be seen about thirty miles off, could not be distinguished from a wheel-animalcule. He *inhabits* a wheel-carriage. He thinks of stationary dwellings as Long Tom Coffin did of land in general; a house may be well enough for incidental purposes, but for a "stiddy" residence give him a "kerridge." If he is classified in the Linnæan scale, he must be set down thus: Genus *Homo;* Species *Rotifer infusorius,*—the wheel-animal of infusions.

The Dudley mansion was not a mile from the Doctor's; but it never occurred to him to think of walking to see any of his patients' families, if he had any professional object in his visit. Whenever the narrow sulky turned in at a gate, the rustic who was digging potatoes, or hoeing corn, or *swishing* through the grass with his scythe, in wave-like crescents, or stepping short behind a loaded wheelbarrow, or trudging lazily by the side of the swinging, loose-throated, short-legged oxen, rocking along the road as if they had just been landed after a three-months' voyage,—the toiling native, whatever he was doing, stopped and looked up at the house the Doctor was visiting.

"Somebody sick over there t' Haynes's. Guess th' old man's ailin' ag'in. Winder's haäf-way open in the chamber, —shouldn' wonder 'f he was dead and laid aout. Docterin' a'n't no use, when y' see th' winders open like that. Wahl, money a'n't much to speak of to th' old man naow! He don' want but *tew cents,*—'n' old Widah Peake, she knows what he wants them for!"

Or again,—

"Measles raound pooty thick. Briggs's folks buried two children with 'em laäs' week. Th' ol' Doctor, he'd h' ker'd 'em threugh. Struck in 'n' p'dooced mo't'f'cation,—so they say."

This is only meant as a sample of the kind of way they used to think or talk, when the narrow sulky turned in at the gate of some house where there was a visit to be made.

Oh, that narrow sulky! What hopes, what fears, what comfort, what anguish, what despair, in the roll of its coming or its parting wheels! In the spring, when the old people get the coughs which give them a few shakes and their lives drop in pieces like the ashes of a burned thread which have kept the threadlike shape until they were stirred,— in the hot summer noons, when the strong man comes in from the fields, like the son of the Shunamite, crying, "My head, my head,"—in the dying autumn days, when youth and maiden lie fever-stricken in many a household, still-faced, dull-eyed, dark-flushed, dry-lipped, low-muttering in their daylight dreams, their fingers moving singly like those of slumbering harpers,—in the dead winter, when the white plague of the North has caged its wasted victims, shuddering as they think of the frozen soil which must be quarried like rock to receive them, if their perpetual convalescence should happen to be interfered with by any untoward accident,—at every season, the narrow sulky rolled round freighted with unmeasured burdens of joy and woe.

The Doctor drove along the southern foot of The Mountain. The "Dudley Mansion" was near the eastern edge of this declivity, where it rose steepest, with baldest cliffs and densest patches of overhanging wood. It seemed almost too steep to climb, but a practised eye could see from a distance the zigzag lines of the sheep paths which scaled it like miniature Alpine roads. A few hundred feet up The Mountain's side was a dark deep dell, unwooded, save for a few spindling, crazy-looking hackmatacks or native larches, with pallid green tufts sticking out fantastically all over them. It shelved so deeply, that, while the hemlock-tassels were swinging on the trees around its border, all would be still at its springy bottom, save that perhaps a single fern would wave slowly backward and forward like a sabre with a twist as of a feathered oar,—and this when not a breath could be felt, and every other stem and blade were motionless. There was an old story of one having perished here in the winter of '86, and his body having been found in the spring,—whence its common name of "Dead-Man's Hollow." Higher up there were huge cliffs with chasms, and, it was thought, concealed caves, where in old times they said that Tories lay hid,—some hinted not without occasional aid and comfort from the Dudleys then living in the mansion-house. Still higher and farther west lay the accursed ledge,—shunned by all, unless it were now and then a daring youth, or a wandering naturalist who ventured to its edge in the hope of securing some infantile *Crotalus durissus*, who had not yet cut his poison-teeth.

Long, long ago, in old Colonial times, the Honorable Thomas Dudley, Esquire, a man of note and name and great resources, allied by descent to the family of "Tom Dudley," as the early Governor is sometimes irreverently called by our most venerable, but still youthful antiquary, —and to the other public Dudleys, of course,—of all of whom he made small account, as being himself an English gentleman, with little taste for the splendors of provincial office,—early in the last century, Thomas Dudley had built this mansion. For several generations it had been dwelt in by descendants of the same name, but soon after the Revolution it passed by marriage into the hands of the Venners, by whom it had ever since been held and tenanted.

As the Doctor turned an angle in the road, all at once the stately old house rose before him. It was a skilfully managed effect, as it well might be, for it was no vulgar English architect who had planned the mansion and arranged its position and approach. The old house rose before the Doctor, crowning a terraced garden, flanked at the left by an avenue of tall elms. The flower-beds were edged with box, which diffused around it that dreamy balsamic odor, full of ante-natal reminiscences of a lost Paradise, dimly fragrant as might be the bdellium of ancient Havilah, the land compassed by the river Pison that went out of Eden. The garden was somewhat neglected, but not in disgrace,

—and in the time of tulips and hyacinths, of roses, of "snowballs," of honeysuckles, of lilacs, of syringas, it was rich with blossoms.

From the front-windows of the mansion the eye reached a far blue mountain-summit,—no rounded heap, such as often shuts in a village-landscape, but a sharp peak, clean-angled as Ascutney from the Dartmouth green. A wide gap through miles of woods had opened this distant view, and showed more, perhaps, than all the labors of the architect and the landscape-gardener the large style of the early Dudleys.

The great stone-chimney of the mansion-house was the centre from which all the artificial features of the scene appeared to flow. The roofs, the gables, the dormer-windows, the porches, the clustered offices in the rear, all seemed to crowd about the great chimney. To this central pillar the paths all converged. The single poplar behind the house,—Nature is jealous of proud chimneys, and always loves to put a poplar near one, so that it may fling a leaf or two down its black throat every autumn,—the one tall poplar behind the house seemed to nod and whisper to the grave square column, the elms to sway their branches towards it. And when the blue smoke rose from its summit, it seemed to be wafted away to join the azure haze which hung around the peak in the far distance, so that both should bathe in a common atmosphere.

Behind the house were clumps of lilacs with a century's growth upon them, and looking more like trees than like shrubs. Shaded by a group of these was the ancient well, of huge circuit, and with a low arch opening out of its wall about ten feet below the surface,—whether the door of a crypt for the concealment of treasure, or of a subterranean passage, or merely of a vault for keeping provisions cool in hot weather, opinions differed.

On looking at the house, it was plain that it was built with Old-World notions of strength and durability, and, so far as might be, with Old-World materials. The hinges of the door stretched out like arms, instead of like hands, as we make them. The bolts were massive enough for a donjon-keep. The small window-panes were actually inclosed in the wood of the sashes instead of being stuck to them with putty, as in our modern windows. The broad staircase was of easy ascent, and was guarded by quaintly turned and twisted balusters. The ceilings of the two rooms of state were moulded with medallion-portraits and rustic figures, such as may have been seen by many readers in the famous old Philipse house,—Washington's head-quarters,—in the town of Yonkers. The fire-places, worthy of the wide-throated central chimney, were bordered by pictured tiles, some of them with Scripture stories, some with Watteau-like figures,—tall damsels in slim waists and with spread enough of skirt for a modern ballroom, with bowing, reclining, or musical swains of what everybody calls the "conventional" sort,—that is, the swain adapted to genteel society rather than to a literal sheep-compelling existence.

The house was furnished, soon after it was completed, with many heavy articles made in London from a rare wood just then come into fashion, not so rare now, and commonly known as mahogany. Time had turned it very dark, and the stately bedsteads and tall cabinets and claw-footed chairs and tables were in keeping with the sober dignity of the ancient mansion. The old "hangings" were yet preserved in the chambers, faded, but still showing their rich patterns,—properly entitled to their name, for they were literally hung upon flat wooden frames like trellis-work, which again were secured to the naked partitions.

There were portraits of different date on the walls of the various apartments, old painted coats-of-arms, bevel-edged mirrors, and in one sleeping-room a glass case of wax-work flowers and spangly symbols, with a legend signifying that E. M. (supposed to be Elizabeth Mascarene) wished not to be "forgot"

"When I am dead and lay'd in dust
And all my bones are"—

Poor E. M.! Poor everybody that sighs for earthly remembrance in a planet with a core of fire and a crust of fossils!

Such was the Dudley mansion-house,—for it kept its ancient name in spite of the change in the line of descent. Its spacious apartments looked dreary and desolate; for here

Dudley Venner and his daughter dwelt by themselves, with such servants only as their quiet mode of life required. He almost lived in his library, the western room on the ground-floor. Its window looked upon a small plat of green, in the midst of which was a single grave marked by a plain marble slab. Except this room, and the chamber where he slept, and the servants' wing, the rest of the house was all Elsie's. She was always a restless, wandering child from her early years, and would have her little bed moved from one chamber to another,—flitting round as the fancy took her. Sometimes she would drag a mat and a pillow into one of the great empty rooms, and, wrapping herself in a shawl, coil up and go to sleep in a corner. Nothing frightened her; the "haunted" chamber, with the torn hangings that flapped like wings when there was air stirring, was one of her favorite retreats.

She had been a very hard creature to manage. Her father could influence, but not govern her. Old Sophy, born of a slave mother in the house, could do more with her than anybody, knowing her by long instinctive study. The other servants were afraid of her. Her father had sent for governesses, but none of them ever stayed long. She made them nervous; one of them had a strange fit of sickness; not one of them ever came back to the house to see her. A young Spanish woman who taught her dancing succeeded best with her, for she had a passion for that exercise, and had mastered some of the most difficult dances.

Long before this period, she had manifested some most extraordinary singularities of taste or instinct. The extreme sensitiveness of her father on this point prevented any allusion to them; but there were stories floating round, some of them even getting into the papers,—without her name, of course,—which were of a kind to excite intense curiosity, if not more anxious feelings. This thing was certain, that at the age of twelve she was missed one night, and was found sleeping in the open air under a tree, like a wild creature. Very often she would wander off by day, always without a companion, bringing home with her a nest, a flower, or even a more questionable trophy of her ramble, such as showed that there was no place where she was afraid to venture. Once in a while she had stayed out over night, in which case the alarm was spread, and men went in search of her, but never successfully,—so that some said she hid herself in trees, and others that she had found one of the old Tory caves.

Some, of course, said she was a crazy girl, and ought to be sent to an Asylum. But old Dr. Kittredge had shaken his head, and told them to bear with her, and let her have her way as much as they could, but watch her, as far as possible, without making her suspicious of them. He visited her now and then, under the pretext of seeing her father on business, or of only making a friendly call.

The Doctor fastened his horse outside the gate, and walked up the garden-alley. He stopped suddenly with a start. A strange sound had jarred upon his ear. It was a sharp prolonged rattle, continuous, but rising and falling as if in rhythmical cadence. He moved softly towards the open window from which the sound seemed to proceed.

Elsie was alone in the room, dancing one of those wild Moorish fandangos, such as a *matador* hot from the *Plaza de Toros* of Seville or Madrid might love to lie and gaze at. She was a figure to look upon in silence. The dancing frenzy must have seized upon her while she was dressing; for she was in her bodice, bare-armed, her hair floating unbound far below the waist of her barred or banded skirt. She had caught up her castanets, and rattled them as she danced with a kind of passionate fierceness, her lithe body undulating with flexuous grace, her diamond eyes glittering, her round arms wreathing and unwinding, alive and vibrant to the tips of the slender fingers. Some passion seemed to exhaust itself in this dancing paroxysm; for all at once she reeled from the middle of the floor, and flung herself, as it were in a careless coil, upon a great tiger's-skin which was spread out in one corner of the apartment.

The old Doctor stood motionless, looking at her as she lay panting on the tawny, black-lined robe of the dead monster, which stretched out beneath her, its rude flattened outline recalling the Terror of the Jungle as he crouched for his fatal spring. In a few moments her head drooped upon her arm, and her glittering eyes closed,—she was sleeping. He stood looking at her still, steadily, thoughtfully, tenderly. Presently he lifted his hand to his forehead, as if recalling some fading remembrance of other years.

"Poor Catalina!"

This was all he said. He shook his head,—implying that his visit would be in vain to-day,—returned to his sulky, and rode away, as if in a dream.

CHAPTER XI

COUSIN RICHARD'S VISIT

The Doctor was roused from his reverie by the clatter of approaching hoofs. He looked forward and saw a young fellow galloping rapidly towards him.

A common New-England rider with his toes turned out, his elbows jerking and the daylight showing under him at every step, bestriding a cantering beast of the plebeian breed, thick at every point where he should be thin, and thin at every point where he should be thick, is not one of those noble objects that bewitch the world. The best horsemen outside of the cities are the unshod country-boys, who ride "bare-back," with only a halter round the horse's neck, digging their brown heels into his ribs, and slanting over backwards, but sticking on like leeches, and taking the hardest trot as if they loved it. This was a different sight on which the Doctor was looking. The streaming mane and tail of the unshorn, savage-looking, black horse, the dashing grace with which the young fellow in the shadowy *sombrero*, and armed with the huge spurs, sat in his high-peaked saddle, could belong only to the mustang of the Pampas and his master. This bold rider was a young man whose sudden apparition in the quiet inland town had reminded some of the good people of a bright, curly-haired boy they had known some eight or ten years before as little Dick Venner.

This boy had passed several of his early years at the Dudley mansion, the playmate of Elsie, being her cousin, two or three years older than herself, the son of Captain Richard Venner, a South American trader, who, as he changed his residence often, was glad to leave the boy in his brother's charge. The Captain's wife, this boy's mother, was a lady of Buenos Ayres, of Spanish descent, and had died while the child was in his cradle. These two motherless children were as strange a pair as one roof could well cover. Both handsome, wild, impetuous, unmanageable, they played and fought together like two young leopards, beautiful, but dangerous, their lawless instincts showing through all their graceful movements.

The boy was little else than a young *Gaucho* when he first came to Rockland; for he had learned to ride almost as soon as to walk, and could jump on his pony and trip up a runaway pig with the *bolas* or noose him with his miniature *lasso* at an age when some city-children would hardly be trusted out of sight of a nursery-maid. It makes men imperious to sit a horse; no man governs his fellows so well as from this living throne. And so, from Marcus Aurelius in Roman bronze, down to the "man on horseback" in General Cushing's prophetic speech, the saddle has always been the true seat of empire. The absolute tyranny of the human will over a noble and powerful beast develops the instinct of personal prevalence and dominion; so that horse-subduer and hero were almost synonymous in simpler times, and are closely related still. An ancestry of wild riders naturally enough bequeaths also those other tendencies which we see in the Tartars, the Cossacks, and our own Indian Centaurs,—and as well, perhaps, in the old-fashioned fox-hunting squire as in any of these. Sharp alternations of violent action and self-indulgent repose; a hard run, and a long revel after it: this is what over-much horse tends to animalize a man into. Such antecedents may have helped to make little Dick Venner a self-willed, capricious boy, and a rough playmate for Elsie.

Elsie was the wilder of the two. Old Sophy, who used to watch them with those quick, animal-looking eyes of hers, —she was said to be the granddaughter of a cannibal chief, and inherited the keen senses belonging to all creatures which are hunted as game,—Old Sophy, who watched them in their play and their quarrels, always seemed to be more afraid for the boy than the girl. "Massa Dick! Massa Dick!

don' you be too rough wi' dat gal! She scratch you las' week, 'n' some day she bite you; 'n' if she bite you, Massa Dick!" Old Sophy nodded her head ominously, as if she could say a great deal more; while, in grateful acknowledgment of her caution, Master Dick put his two little fingers in the angles of his mouth, and his forefingers on his lower eyelids, drawing upon these features until his expression reminded her of something she vaguely recollected in her infancy,—the face of a favorite deity executed in wood by an African artist for her grandfather, brought over by her mother, and burned when she became a Christian.

These two wild children had much in common. They loved to ramble together, to build huts, to climb trees for nests, to ride the colts, to dance, to race, and to play at boys' rude games as if both were boys. But wherever two natures have a great deal in common, the conditions of a first-rate quarrel are furnished ready-made. Relations are very apt to hate each other just because they are too much alike. It is so frightful to be in an atmosphere of family idiosyncrasies; to see all the hereditary uncomeliness or infirmity of body, all the defects of speech, all the failings of temper, intensified by concentration, so that every fault of our own finds itself multiplied by reflections, like our images in a saloon lined with mirrors! Nature knows what she is about. The centrifugal principle which grows out of the antipathy of like to like is only the repetition in character of the arrangement we see expressed materially in certain seed-capsules, which burst and throw the seed to all points of the compass. A house is a large pod with a human germ or two in each of its cells or chambers; it opens by dehiscence of the front-door by-and-by, and projects one of its germs to Kansas, another to San Francisco, another to Chicago, and so on; and this that Smith may not be Smithed to death and Brown may not be Browned into a mad-house, but mix in with the world again and struggle back to average humanity.

Elsie's father, whose fault was to indulge her in everything, found that it would never do to let these children grow up together. They would either love each other as they got older, and pair like wild creatures, or take some fierce antipathy, which might end nobody could tell where. It was not safe to try. The boy must be sent away. A sharper quarrel than common decided this point. Master Dick forgot Old Sophy's caution, and vexed the girl into a paroxysm of wrath, in which she sprang at him and bit his arm. Perhaps they made too much of it; for they sent for the old Doctor, who came at once when he heard what had happened. He had a good deal to say about the danger there was from the teeth of animals or human beings when enraged; and as he emphasized his remarks by the application of a pencil of lunar caustic to each of the marks left by the sharp white teeth, they were like to be remembered by at least one of his hearers.

So Master Dick went off on his travels, which led him into strange places and stranger company. Elsie was half pleased and half sorry to have him go; the children had a kind of mingled liking and hate for each other, just such as is very common among relations. Whether the girl had most satisfaction in the plays they shared, or in teasing him, or taking her small revenge upon him for teasing her, it would have been hard to say. At any rate, she was lonely without him. She had more fondness for the old black woman than anybody; but Sophy could not follow her far beyond her own old rocking-chair. As for her father, she had made him afraid of her, not for his sake, but for her own. Sometimes she would seem to be fond of him, and the parent's heart would yearn within him as she twined her supple arms about him; and then some look she gave him, some half-articulated expression, would turn his cheek pale and almost make him shiver, and he would say kindly, "Now go, Elsie, dear," and smile upon her as she went, and close and lock the door softly after her. Then his forehead would knot and furrow itself, and the drops of anguish stand thick upon it. He would go to the western window of his study and look at the solitary mound with the marble slab for its head-stone. After his grief had had its way, he would kneel down and pray for his child as one who has no hope save in that special grace which can bring the most rebellious spirit into sweet subjection. All this might seem like weakness in a parent having the charge of one sole daughter of his house and heart; but he had tried authority and tenderness by turns so long without any good effect, that he had become sore perplexed, and, surrounding her with cautious watchfulness as he best might, left her in the main to her own guidance and the merciful influences which Heaven might send down to direct her footsteps.

Meantime the boy grew up to youth and early manhood through a strange succession of adventures. He had been at school at Buenos Ayres,—had quarrelled with his mother's relatives,—had run off to the Pampas, and lived with the *Gauchos*,—had made friends with the Indians, and ridden with them, it was rumored, in some of their savage forays, —had returned and made up his quarrel,—had got money by inheritance or otherwise,—had troubled the peace of certain magistrates,—had found it convenient to leave the City of Wholesome Breezes for a time, and had galloped off on a fast horse of his, (so it was said), with some officers riding after him, who took good care (but this was only the popular story) not to catch him. A few days after this he was taking his ice on the Alameda of Mendoza, and a week or two later sailed from Valparaiso for New York, carrying with him the horse with which he had scampered over the Plains, a trunk or two with his newly purchased outfit of clothing and other conveniences, and a belt heavy with gold and with a few Brazilian diamonds sewed in it, enough in value to serve him for a long journey.

Dick Venner had seen life enough to wear out the earlier sensibilities of adolescence. He was tired of worshipping or tyrannizing over the bistred or umbered beauties of mingled blood among whom he had been living. Even that piquant exhibition which the Rio de Mendoza presents to the amateur of breathing sculpture failed to interest him. He was thinking of a far-off village on the other side of the equator, and of the wild girl with whom he used to play and quarrel, a creature of a different race from these degenerate mongrels.

"A game little devil she was, sure enough!"—and as Dick spoke, he bared his wrist to look for the marks she had left on it: two small white scars, where the two small sharp upper teeth had struck when she flashed at him with her eyes sparkling as bright as those glittering stones sewed up in the belt he wore.—"That's a filly worth noosing!" said Dick to himself, as he looked in admiration at the sign of her spirit and passion. "I wonder if she will bite at eighteen as she did at eight! She shall have a chance to try, at any rate!"

Such was the self-sacrificing disposition with which Richard Venner, Esq., a passenger by the Condor from Valparaiso, set foot upon his native shore, and turned his face in the direction of Rockland, The Mountain, and the mansion-house. He had heard something, from time to time, of his New-England relatives, and knew that they were living together as he left them. And so he heralded himself to "My dear Uncle" by a letter signed "Your loving nephew, Richard Venner," in which letter he told a very frank story of travel and mercantile adventure, expressed much gratitude for the excellent counsel and example which had helped to form his character and preserve him in the midst of temptation, inquired affectionately after his uncle's health, was much interested to know whether his lively cousin who used to be his playmate had grown up as handsome as she promised to be, and announced his intention of paying his respects to them both at Rockland. Not long after this came the trunks marked R. V. which he had sent before him, forerunners of his advent: he was not going to wait for a reply or an invitation.

What a sound that is,—the banging down of the preliminary trunk, without its claimant to give it the life which is borrowed by all personal appendages, so long as the owner's hand or eye is on them! If it announce the coming of one loved and longed for, how we delight to look at it, to sit down on it, to caress it in our fancies, as a lone exile walking out on a windy pier yearns towards the merchantman lying alongside, with the colors of his own native land at her peak, and the name of the port he sailed from long ago upon her stern! But if it tell the near approach of the undesired, inevitable guest, what sound short of the muffled noises made by the undertakers as they turn the corners in the dim-lighted house, with low shuffle of feet and whispered cautions, carries such a sense of knocking-kneed collapse with it as the thumping down in the front entry of the heavy portmanteau, rammed with the changes of uncounted coming weeks?

Whether the R. V. portmanteaus brought one or the other of these emotions to the tenants of the Dudley mansion, it might not be easy to settle. Elsie professed to be pleased with the thought of having an adventurous young stranger, with stories to tell, an inmate of their quiet, not to say dull, family. Under almost any other circumstances, her father would have been unwilling to take a young fellow of whom he knew so little under his roof; but this was his nephew, and anything that seemed like to amuse or please Elsie was agreeable to him. He had grown almost desperate, and felt as if any change in the current of her life and feelings might save her from some strange paroxysm of dangerous mental exaltation or sullen perversion of disposition, from which some fearful calamity might come to herself or others.

Dick had been several weeks at the Dudley mansion. A few days before, he had made a sudden dash for the nearest large city,—and when the Doctor met him, he was just returning from his visit.

It had been a curious meeting between the two young persons, who had parted so young and after such strange relations with each other. When Dick first presented himself at the mansion, not one in the house would have known him for the boy who had left them all so suddenly years ago. He was so dark, partly from his descent, partly from long habits of exposure, that Elsie looked almost fair beside him. He had something of the family beauty which belonged to his cousin, but his eye had a fierce passion in it, very unlike the cold glitter of Elsie's. Like many people of strong and imperious temper, he was soft-voiced and very gentle in his address, when he had no special reason for being otherwise. He soon found reasons enough to be as amiable as he could force himself to be with his uncle and his cousin. Elsie was to his fancy. She had a strange attraction for him, quite unlike anything he had ever known in other women. There was something, too, in early associations: when those who parted as children meet as man and woman, there is always a renewal of that early experience which followed the taste of the forbidden fruit,—a natural blush of consciousness, not without its charm.

Nothing could be more becoming than the behavior of "Richard Venner, Esquire, the guest of Dudley Venner, Esquire, at his noble mansion," as he was announced in the Court column of the "Rockland Weekly Universe." He was pleased to find himself treated with kindness and attention as a relative. He made himself very agreeable by abundant details concerning the religious, political, social, commercial, and educational progress of the South American cities and states. He was himself much interested in everything that was going on about the Dudley mansion, walked all over it, noticed its valuable wood-lots with special approbation, was delighted with the grand old house and its furniture, and would not be easy until he had seen all the family silver and heard its history. In return, he had much to tell of his father, now dead,—the only one of the Venners, beside themselves, in whose fate his uncle was interested. With Elsie, he was subdued and almost tender in his manner; with the few visitors whom they saw, shy and silent, —perhaps a little watchful, if any young man happened to be among them.

Young fellows placed on their good behavior are apt to get restless and nervous, all ready to fly off into some mischief or other. Dick Venner had his half-tamed horse with him to work off his suppressed life with. When the savage passion of his young blood came over him, he would fetch out the mustang, screaming and kicking as these amiable beasts are wont to do, strap the Spanish saddle tight to his back, vault into it, and, after getting away from the village, strike the long spurs into his sides and whirl away in a wild gallop, until the black horse was flecked with white foam, and the cruel steel points were red with his blood. When horse and rider were alike tired, he would fling the bridle on his neck and saunter homeward, always contriving to get to the stable in a quiet way, and coming into the house as calm as a bishop after a sober trot on his steady-going cob.

After a few weeks of this kind of life, he began to want

some more fierce excitement. He had tried making downright love to Elsie, with no great success as yet, in his own opinion. The girl was capricious in her treatment of him, sometimes scowling and repellent, sometimes familiar, very often, as she used to be of old, teasing and malicious. All this, perhaps, made her more interesting to a young man who was tired of easy conquests. There was a strange fascination in her eyes, too, which at times was quite irresistible, so that he would feel himself drawn to her by a power which seemed to take away his will for the moment. It may have been nothing but the common charm of bright eyes; but he had never before experienced the same kind of attraction.

Perhaps she was not so very different from what she had been as a child, after all. At any rate, so it seemed to Dick Venner, who, as was said before, had tried making love to her. They were sitting alone in the study one day; Elsie had round her neck that somewhat peculiar ornament, the golden *torque*, which she had worn to the great party. Youth is adventurous and very curious about necklaces, brooches, chains, and other such adornments, so long as they are worn by young persons of the female sex. Dick was seized with a great passion for examining this curious chain, and, after some preliminary questions, was rash enough to lean towards her and put out his hand toward the neck that lay in the golden coil. She threw her head back, her eyes narrowing and her forehead drawing down so that Dick thought her head actually flattened itself. He started involuntarily; for she looked so like the little girl who had struck him with those sharp flashing teeth, that the whole scene came back, and he felt the stroke again as if it had just been given, and the two white scars began to sting as they did after the old Doctor had burned them with that stick of gray caustic, which looked so like a slate pencil, and felt so much like the end of a red-hot poker.

It took something more than a gallop to set him right after this. The next day he mentioned having received a letter from a mercantile agent with whom he had dealings. What his business was is, perhaps, none of our business.

At any rate, it required him to go at once to the city where his correspondent resided.

Independently of this "business" which called him, there may have been other motives, such as have been hinted at. People who have been living for a long time in dreary country-places, without any emotion beyond such as are occasioned by a trivial pleasure or annoyance, often get crazy at last for a vital paroxysm of some kind or other. In this state they rush to the great cities for a plunge into their turbid life-baths, with a frantic thirst for every exciting pleasure, which makes them the willing and easy victims of all those who sell the Devil's wares on commission. The less intelligent and instructed class of unfortunates, who venture with their ignorance and their instincts into what is sometimes called the "life" of great cities, are put through a rapid course of instruction which entitles them very commonly to a diploma from the police court. But they only illustrate the working of the same tendency in mankind at large which has been occasionally noticed in the sons of ministers and other eminently worthy people, by many ascribed to that intense congenital hatred for goodness which distinguishes human nature from that of the brute, but perhaps as readily accounted for by considering it as the yawning and stretching of a young soul cramped too long in one moral posture.

Richard Venner was a young man of remarkable experience for his years. He ran less risk, therefore, in exposing himself to the temptations and dangers of a great city than many older men, who, seeking the livelier scenes of excitement to be found in large towns as a relaxation after the monotonous routine of family-life, are too often taken advantage of and made the victims of their sentiments or their generous confidence in their fellow-creatures. Such was not his destiny. There was something about him which looked as if he would not take bullying kindly. He had also the advantage of being acquainted with most of those ingenious devices by which the proverbial inconstancy of fortune is steadied to something more nearly approaching fixed laws, and the dangerous risks which have so often led young men to ruin and suicide are practically reduced to somewhat less than nothing. So that Mr. Richard Venner worked off his nervous energies without any troublesome adventure, and was ready to return to Rockland in less than a week, without having lightened the money-belt he wore round his body, or tarnished the long glittering knife he carried in his boot.

Dick had sent his trunk to the nearest town through which the railroad leading to the city passed. He rode off on his black horse and left him at the place where he took the cars. On arriving at the city station, he took a coach and drove to one of the great hotels. Thither drove also a sagacious-looking, middle-aged man, who entered his name as "W. Thompson" in the book at the office immediately after that of "R. Venner." Mr. "Thompson" kept a carelessly observant eye upon Mr. Venner during his stay at the hotel, and followed him to the cars when he left, looking over his shoulder when he bought his ticket at the station, and seeing him fairly off without obtruding himself in any offensive way upon his attention. Mr. Thompson, known in other quarters as Detective Policeman Terry, got very little by his trouble. Richard Venner did not turn out to be the wife-poisoner, the defaulting cashier, the river-pirate, or the great counterfeiter. He paid his hotel-bill as a gentleman should always do, if he has the money and can spare it. The detective had probably overrated his own sagacity when he ventured to suspect Mr. Venner. He reported to his chief that there was a knowing-looking fellow he had been round after, but he rather guessed he was nothing more than "one o' them Southern sportsmen."

The poor fellows at the stable where Dick had left his horse had had trouble enough with him. One of the ostlers was limping about with a lame leg, and another had lost a mouthful of his coat, which came very near carrying a piece of his shoulder with it. When Mr. Venner came back for his beast, he was as wild as if he had just been lassoed, screaming, kicking, rolling over to get rid of his saddle,— and when his rider was at last mounted, jumping about in a way to dislodge any common horseman. To all this Dick replied by sticking his long spurs deeper and deeper into his flanks, until the creature found he was mastered, and dashed off as if all the thistles of the Pampas were pricking him.

"One more gallop, Juan!" This was in the last mile of the road before he came to the town which brought him in sight of the mansion-house. It was in this last gallop that the fiery mustang and his rider flashed by the old Doctor. Cassia pointed her sharp ears and shied to let them pass. The Doctor turned and looked through the little round glass in the back of his sulky.

"Dick Turpin, there, will find more than his match!" said the Doctor.

CHAPTER XII

THE APOLLINEAN INSTITUTE

(With Extracts from the "Report of the Committee")

The readers of this narrative will hardly expect any elaborate details of the educational management of the Apollinean Institute. They cannot be supposed to take the same interest in its affairs as was shown by the Annual Committees who reported upon its condition and prospects. As these Committees were, however, an important part of the mechanism of the establishment, some general account of their organization and a few extracts from the Report of the one last appointed may not be out of place.

Whether Mr. Silas Peckham had some contrivance for packing his Committees, whether they happened always to be made up of optimists by nature, whether they were cajoled into good-humor by polite attentions, or whether they were always really delighted with the wonderful acquirements of the pupils and the admirable order of the school, it is certain that their Annual Reports were couched in language which might warm the heart of the most coldblooded and calculating father that ever had a family of daughters to educate. In fact, these Annual Reports were considered by Mr. Peckham as his most effective advertisements.

The first thing, therefore, was to see that the Committee was made up of persons known to the public. Some wornout politician, in that leisurely and amiable transition-state which comes between official extinction and the paralysis which will finish him as soon as his brain gets a little softer, made an admirable Chairman for Mr. Peckham, when he had the luck to pick up such an article. Old reputations, like old fashions, are more prized in the grassy than in the stony districts. An effete celebrity, who would never be heard of again in the great places until the funeral sermon waked up his memory for one parting spasm, finds himself in full flavor of renown a little farther back from the changing winds of the sea-coast. If such a public character was not to be had, so that there was no chance of heading the Report with the name of the Honorable Mr. Somebody, the next best thing was to get the Reverend Dr. Somebody to take that conspicuous position. Then would follow two or three local worthies with Esquire after their names. If any stray literary personage from one of the great cities happened to be within reach, he was pounced upon by Mr. Silas Peckham. It was a hard case for the poor man, who had travelled a hundred miles or two to the outside suburbs after peace and unwatered milk, to be pumped for a speech in this unexpected way. It was harder still, if he had been induced to venture a few tremulous remarks, to be obliged to write them out for the "Rockland Weekly Universe," with the chance of seeing them used as an advertising certificate as long as he lived, if he lived as long as the late Dr. Waterhouse did after giving his certificate in favor of Whitwell's celebrated Cephalic Snuff.

The Report of the last Committee had been signed by the Honorable ——, late —— of ——, as Chairman. (It is with reluctance that the name and titles are left in blank; but our public characters are so familiarly known to the whole community that this reserve becomes necessary.) The other members of the Committee were the Reverend Mr. Butters, of a neighboring town, who was to make the prayer before the Exercises of the Exhibition, and two or three notabilities of Rockland, with geoponic eyes, and glabrous, bumpless foreheads. A few extracts from the Report are subjoined:—

"The Committee have great pleasure in recording their unanimous opinion, that the Institution was never in so flourishing a condition. . . .

"The health of the pupils is excellent; the admirable quality of food supplied shows itself in their appearance; their blooming aspect excited the admiration of the Committee, and bears testimony to the assiduity of the excellent Matron.

". . . . . moral and religious condition most encouraging, which they cannot but attribute to the personal efforts and instruction of the faithful Principal, who considers religious instruction a solemn duty which he cannot commit to other people.

". . . . . . . great progress in their studies, under the intelligent superintendence of the accomplished Principal, assisted by Mr. Badger, [Mr. Langdon's predecessor,] Miss Darley, the lady who superintends the English branches, Miss Crabs, her assistant and teacher of Modern Languages, and Mr. Schneider, teacher of French, German, Latin, and Music. . . . .

"Education is the great business of the Institute. Amusements are objects of a secondary nature; but these are by no means neglected. . . .

". . . . . English compositions of great originality and beauty, creditable alike to the head and heart of their accomplished authors. . . . . . several poems of a very high order of merit, which would do honor to the literature of any age or country. . . . . life-like drawings, showing great proficiency. . . . Many converse fluently in various modern languages. . . . . . perform the most difficult airs with the skill of professional musicians. . . .

". . . . . advantages unsurpassed, if equalled by those of any Institution in the country, and reflecting the highest honor on the distinguished Head of the Establishment, SILAS PECKHAM, Esquire, and his admirable Lady, the MATRON, with their worthy assistants. . . . ."

The perusal of this Report did Mr. Bernard more good than a week's vacation would have done. It gave him such a laugh as he had not had for a month. The way in which Silas Peckham had made his Committee say what he wanted them to—for he recognized a number of expressions in the Report as coming directly from the lips of his principal, and could not help thinking how cleverly he had *forced* his phrases, as jugglers do the particular card they wish their dupe to take—struck him as particularly neat and pleasing.

He had passed through the sympathetic and emotional stages in his new experience, and had arrived at the philosophical and practical state, which takes things coolly, and goes to work to set them right. He had breadth enough of view to see that there was nothing so very exceptional in this educational trader's dealings with his subordinates, but he had also manly feeling enough to attack the particular individual instance of wrong before him. There are plenty of dealers in morals, as in ordinary traffic, who confine themselves to wholesale business. They leave the small necessity of their next-door neighbor to the retailers, who are poorer in statistics and general facts, but richer in the every-day charities. Mr. Bernard felt, at first, as one does who sees a gray rat steal out of a drain and begin gnawing at the bark of some tree loaded with fruit or blossoms, which he will soon girdle, if he is let alone. The first impulse is to murder him with the nearest ragged stone. Then one remembers that he is a rodent, acting after the law of his kind, and cools down and is contented to drive him off and guard the tree against his teeth for the future. As soon as this is done, one can watch his attempts at mischief with a certain amusement.

This was the kind of process Mr. Bernard had gone through. First, the indignant surprise of a generous nature, when it comes unexpectedly into relations with a mean one. Then the impulse of extermination,—a divine instinct, intended to keep down vermin of all classes to their working averages in the economy of Nature. Then a return of cheerful tolerance,—a feeling, that, if the Deity could bear with rats and sharpers, he could; with a confident trust, that, in the long run, terriers and honest men would have the upperhand, and a grateful consciousness that he had been sent just at the right time to come between a patient victim and the master who held her in peonage.

Having once made up his mind what to do, Mr. Bernard was as good-natured and hopeful as ever. He had the great advantage, from his professional training, of knowing how to recognize and deal with the nervous disturbances to which overtasked women are so liable. He saw well enough that Helen Darley would certainly kill herself or lose her wits, if he could not lighten her labors and lift off a large part of her weight of cares. The worst of it was, that she was one of those women who naturally overwork themselves, like those horses who will go at the top of their pace until they drop. Such women are dreadfully unmanageable. It is as hard reasoning with them as it would have been reasoning with Io, when she was flying over land and sea, driven by the sting of the never-sleeping gadfly.

This was a delicate, interesting game that he played. Under one innocent pretext or another, he invaded this or that special province she had made her own. He would collect the themes and have them all read and marked, answer all the puzzling questions in mathematics, make the other teachers come to him for directions, and in this way gradually took upon himself not only all the general superintendence that belonged to his office, but stole away so many of the special duties which might fairly have belonged to his assistant, that, before she knew it, she was looking better and feeling more cheerful than for many and many a month before.

When the nervous energy is depressed by any bodily cause, or exhausted by overworking, there follow effects which have often been misinterpreted by moralists, and especially by theologians. The conscience itself becomes neuralgic, sometimes actually inflamed, so that the least touch is agony. Of all liars and false accusers, a sick conscience is the most inventive and indefatigable. The devoted daughter, wife, mother, whose life has been given to unselfish labors, who has filled a place which it seems to others only an angel would make good, reproaches herself with incompetence and neglect of duty. The humble Christian, who has been a model to others, calls himself a worm of the dust on one page of his diary, and arraigns himself on the next for coming short of the perfection of an archangel.

Conscience itself requires a conscience, or nothing can be more unscrupulous. It told Saul that he did well in persecuting the Christians. It has goaded countless multitudes of various creeds to endless forms of self-torture. The cities of India are full of cripples it has made. The hill-sides of Syria are riddled with holes, where miserable hermits, whose lives it had palsied, lived and died like the vermin they harbored. Our libraries are crammed with books written by spiritual hypochondriacs, who inspected all their moral secretions a dozen times a day. They are full of interest, but they should be transferred from the shelf of the theologian to that of the medical man who makes a study of insanity.

This was the state into which too much work and too much responsibility were bringing Helen Darley, when the new master came and lifted so much of the burden that was crushing her as must be removed before she could have a chance to recover her natural elasticity and buoyancy. Many of the noblest women, suffering like her, but less fortunate in being relieved at the right moment, die worried out of life by the perpetual teasing of this inflamed, neuralgic conscience. So subtile is the line which separates the true and almost angelic sensibility of a healthy, but exalted nature, from the soreness of a soul which is sympathizing with a morbid state of the body that it is no wonder they are often confounded. And thus many good women are suffered to perish by that form of spontaneous combustion in which the victim goes on toiling day and night with the hidden fire consuming her, until all at once her cheek whitens, and, as we look upon her, she drops away, a heap of ashes. The more they overwork themselves, the more exacting becomes the sense of duty,—as the draught of the locomotive's furnace blows stronger and makes the fire burn more fiercely, the faster it spins along the track.

It is not very likely, as was said at the beginning of this chapter, that we shall trouble ourselves a great deal about the internal affairs of the Apollinean Institute. These schools are, in the nature of things, not so very unlike each other as to require a minute description for each particular one among them. They have all very much the same general features, pleasing and displeasing. All feeding-establishments have something odious about them,—from the wretched country-houses where paupers are farmed out to the lowest bidder, up to the commons-tables at colleges and even the fashionable boarding-house. A person's appetite should be at war with no other purse than his own. Young people, especially, who have a bone-factory at work in them, and have to feed the living looms of innumerable growing tissues, should be provided for, if possible, by those who love them like their own flesh and blood. Elsewhere their appetites will be sure to make them enemies, or, what are almost as bad, friends whose interests are at variance with the claims of their exacting necessities and demands.

Besides, all commercial transactions in regard to the most sacred interests of life are hateful even to those who profit by them. The clergyman, the physician, the teacher, must be paid; but each of them, if his duty be performed in the true spirit, can hardly help a shiver of disgust when money is counted out to him for administering the consolations of religion, for saving some precious life, for sowing the seeds of Christian civilization in young ingenuous souls.

And yet all these schools, with their provincial French and their mechanical accomplishments, with their cheap parade of diplomas and commencements and other public honors, have an ever fresh interest to all who see the task they are performing in our new social order. These girls are not being educated for governesses, or to be exported, with other manufactured articles, to colonies where there happens to be a surplus of males. Most of them will be wives, and every American-born husband is a possible President of these United States. Any one of these girls may be a four-years' queen. There is no sphere of human activity so exalted that she may not be called upon to fill it.

But there is another consideration of far higher interest. The education of our community to all that is beautiful is flowing in mainly through its women, and that to a considerable extent by the aid of these large establishments, the least perfect of which do something to stimulate the higher tastes and partially instruct them. Sometimes there is, perhaps, reason to fear that girls will be too highly educated for their own happiness, if they are lifted by their culture out of the range of the practical and every-day working youth by whom they are surrounded. But this is a risk we must take. Our young men come into active life so early, that, if our girls were not educated to something beyond mere practical duties, our material prosperity would outstrip our culture; as it often does in large places where money is made too rapidly. This is the meaning, therefore, of that somewhat ambitious programme common to most of these large institutions, at which we sometimes smile, perhaps unwisely or uncharitably.

We shall take it for granted that the routine of instruction went on at the Apollinean Institute much as it does in other schools of the same class. People, young or old, are wonderfully different, if we contrast extremes in pairs. They approach much nearer, if we take them in groups of twenty. Take two separate hundreds as they come, without choosing, and you get the gamut of human character in both so completely that you can strike many chords in each which shall be in perfect unison with corresponding ones in the other. If we go a step farther, and compare the population of two villages of the same race and region, there is such a regularly graduated distribution and parallelism of character, that it seems as if Nature must turn out human beings in sets like chessmen.

It must be confessed that the position in which Mr. Bernard now found himself had a pleasing danger about it which might well justify all the fears entertained on his account by more experienced friends, when they learned that he was engaged in a Young Ladies' Seminary. The school never went on more smoothly than during the first period of his administration, after he had arranged its duties, and taken his share, and even more than his share, upon himself. But human nature does not wait for the diploma of the Apollinean Institute to claim the exercise of its instincts and faculties. These young girls saw but little of the youth of the neighborhood. The mansion-house young men were off at college or in the cities, or making love to each other's sisters, or at any rate unavailable for some reason or other. There were a few "clerks,"—that is, young men who attended shops, commonly called "stores,"

—who were fond of walking by the Institute, when they were off duty, for the sake of exchanging a word or a glance with any one of the young ladies they might happen to know, if any such were stirring abroad: crude young men, mostly, with a great many "Sirs" and "Ma'ams" in their speech, and with that style of address sometimes acquired in the retail business, as if the salesman were recommending himself to a customer,—"First-rate family article, Ma'am; warranted to wear a lifetime; just one yard and three quarters in this pattern, Ma'am; sha'n't I have the pleasure?" and so forth. If there had been ever so many of them, and if they had been ever so fascinating, the quarantine of the Institute was too rigorous to allow any romantic infection to be introduced from without.

Anybody might see what would happen, with a good-looking, well-dressed, well-bred young man, who had the authority of a master, it is true, but the manners of a friend and equal, moving about among these young girls day after day, his eyes meeting theirs, his breath mingling with theirs, his voice growing familiar to them, never in any harsh tones, often soothing, encouraging, always sympathetic, with its male depth and breadth of sound among the chorus of trebles, as if it were a river in which a hundred of these little piping streamlets might lose themselves; anybody might see what would happen. Young girls wrote home to their parents that they enjoyed themselves much, this term, at the Institute, and thought they were making rapid progress in their studies. There was a great enthusiasm for the young master's reading-classes in English poetry. Some of the poor little things began to adorn themselves with an extra ribbon, or a bit of such jewelry as they had before kept for great occasions. Dear souls! they only half knew what they were doing it for. Does the bird know why its feathers grow more brilliant and its voice becomes musical in the pairing season?

And so, in the midst of this quiet inland town, where a mere accident had placed Mr. Bernard Langdon, there was a concentration of explosive materials which might at any time change its Arcadian and academic repose into a scene of dangerous commotion. What said Helen Darley, when she saw with her woman's glance that more than one girl, when she should be looking at her book, was looking over it toward the master's desk? Was her own heart warmed by any livelier feeling than gratitude, as its life began to flow with fuller pulses, and the morning sky again looked bright and the flowers recovered their lost fragrance? Was there any strange, mysterious affinity between the master and the dark girl who sat by herself? Could she call him at will by looking at him? Could it be that——? It made her shiver to think of it.—And who was that strange horseman who passed Mr. Bernard at dusk the other evening, looking so like Mephistopheles galloping hard to be in season at the witches' Sabbath-gathering? That must be the cousin of Elsie's who wants to marry her, they say. A dangerous-looking fellow for a rival, if one took a fancy to the dark girl! And who is she, and what?—by what demon is she haunted, by what taint is she blighted, by what curse is she followed, by what destiny is she marked, that her strange beauty has such a terror in it, and that hardly one shall dare to love her, and her eye glitters always, but warms for none?

Some of these questions are ours. Some were Helen Darley's. Some of them mingled with the dreams of Bernard Langdon, as he slept the night after meeting the strange horseman. In the morning he happened to be a little late in entering the school-room. There was something between the leaves of the Virgil which lay upon his desk. He opened it and saw a freshly gathered mountain-flower. He looked at Elsie, instinctively, involuntarily. She had another such flower on her breast.

A young girl's graceful compliment,—that is all,—no doubt,—no doubt. It was odd that the flower should have happened to be laid between the leaves of the Fourth Book of the "Æneid," and at this line,—

"Incipit effari, mediâque in voce resistit."

A remembrance of an ancient superstition flashed through the master's mind, and he determined to try the *Sortes Virgilianæ*. He shut the volume, and opened it again at a venture.—The story of Laocoön!

He read, with a strange feeling of unwilling fascination, from *"Horresco referens"* to *"Bis medium amplexi,"* and flung the book from him, as if its leaves had been steeped in the subtle poisons that princes die of.

CHAPTER XIII

CURIOSITY

People will talk. *Ciascun lo dice* is a tune that is played oftener than the national air of this country or any other.

"That's what they say. Means to marry her, if she *is* his cousin. Got money himself,—that's the story,—but wants to come and live in the old place, and get the Dudley property by-and-by."—"Mother's folks was wealthy."—"Twenty-three to twenty-five year old."—"He a'n't more'n twenty, or twenty-one at the outside."—"Looks as if he knew too much to be only twenty year old."—"Guess he's been through the mill,—don't look so green, anyhow,—hey? Did y' ever mind that cut over his left eyebrow?"

So they gossiped in Rockland. The young fellows could make nothing of Dick Venner. He was shy and proud with the few who made advances to him. The young ladies called him handsome and romantic, but he looked at them like a many-tailed pacha who was in the habit of ordering his wives by the dozen.

"What do you think of the young man over there at the Venners'?" said Miss Arabella Thornton to her father.

"Handsome," said the Judge, "but dangerous-looking. His face is indictable at common law. Do you know, my dear, I think there is a blank at the Sheriff's office, with a place for his name in it?"

The Judge paused and looked grave, as if he had just listened to the verdict of the jury and was going to pronounce sentence.

"Have you heard anything against him?" said the Judge's daughter.

"Nothing. But I don't like these mixed bloods and half-told stories. Besides, I have seen a good many desperate fellows at the bar, and I have a fancy they all have a look belonging to them. The worst one I ever sentenced looked a good deal like this fellow. A wicked mouth. All our other features are made for us; but a man makes his own mouth."

"Who was the person you sentenced?"

"He was a young fellow that undertook to garrote a man who had won his money at cards. The same slender shape, the same cunning, fierce look, smoothed over with a plausible air. Depend upon it, there is an expression in all the sort of people who live by their wits when they can, and by worse weapons when their wits fail them, that we old law-doctors know just as well as the medical counsellors know the marks of disease in a man's face. Dr. Kittredge looks at a man and says he is going to die; I look at another man and say he is going to be hanged, if nothing happens. I don't say so of this one, but I don't like his looks. I wonder Dudley Venner takes to him so kindly."

"It's all for Elsie's sake," said Miss Thornton. "I feel quite sure of that. He never does anything that is not meant for her in some way. I suppose it amuses her to have her cousin about the house. She rides a good deal since he has been here. Have you seen them galloping about together? He looks like my idea of a Spanish bandit on that wild horse of his."

"Possibly he has been one,—or is one," said the Judge,—smiling as men smile whose lips have often been freighted with the life and death of their fellow-creatures. "I met them riding the other day. Perhaps Dudley is right, if it pleases her to have a companion. What will happen, though, if he makes love to her? Will Elsie be easily taken with such a fellow? You young folks are supposed to know more about these matters than we middle-aged people."

"Nobody can tell. Elsie is not like anybody else. The girls who have seen most of her think she hates men, all but 'Dudley,' as she calls her father. Some of them doubt whether she loves him. They doubt whether she can love anything human, except perhaps the old black woman who has taken care of her since she was a baby. The village people have the strangest stories about her; you know what they call her?"

She whispered three words in her father's ear. The Judge changed color as she spoke, sighed deeply, and was silent as if lost in thought for a moment.

"I remember her mother," he said, "so well! A sweeter creature never lived. Elsie has something of her in her look, but those are not her mother's eyes. They were dark, but soft, as in all I ever saw of her race. Her father's are dark too, but mild, and even tender, I should say. I don't know what there is about Elsie's,—but do you know, my dear, I find myself curiously influenced by them? I have had to face a good many sharp eyes and hard ones,—murderers' eyes and pirates',—men who had to be watched in the bar, where they stood on trial, for fear they should spring on the prosecuting officers like tigers,—but I never saw such eyes as Elsie's; and yet they have a kind of drawing virtue or power about them,—I don't know what else to call it: have you never observed this?"

His daughter smiled in her turn.

"Never observed it? Why, of course, nobody could be with Elsie Venner and not observe it. There are a good many other strange things about her: did you ever notice how she dresses?"

"Why, handsomely enough, I should think," the Judge answered. "I suppose she dresses as she likes, and sends to the city for what she wants. What do you mean in particular? We men notice effects in dress, but not much in detail."

"You never noticed the colors and patterns of her dresses? You never remarked anything curious about her ornaments? Well! I don't believe you men know, half the time, whether a lady wears a ninepenny collar or a thread-lace cape worth a thousand dollars. I don't believe you know a silk dress from a bombazine one. I don't believe you can tell whether a woman is in black or in colors, unless you happen to know she is a widow. Elsie Venner has a strange taste in dress, let me tell you. She sends for the oddest patterns of stuffs, and picks out the most curious things at the jeweller's, whenever she goes to town with her father. They say the old Doctor tells him to let her have her way about all such matters. Afraid of her mind, if she is contradicted, I suppose.—You've heard about her going to school at that place,—the 'Instritoot,' as those people call it? They say she's bright enough in her way,—has studied at home, you know, with her father a good deal,—knows some modern languages and Latin, I believe: at any rate, she would have it so,—she must go to the 'Instritoot.' They have a very good female teacher there, I hear; and the new master, that young Mr. Langdon, looks and talks like a well-educated young man. I wonder what they'll make of Elsie, between them!"

So they talked at the Judge's, in the calm, judicial-looking mansion-house, in the grave, still library, with the troops of wan-hued law-books staring blindly out of their titles at them as they talked, like the ghosts of dead attorneys fixed motionless and speechless, each with a thin, golden film over his unwinking eyes.

In the mean time, everything went on quietly enough after Cousin Richard's return. A man of sense,—that is, a man who knows perfectly well that a cool head is worth a dozen warm hearts in carrying the fortress of a woman's affections, (not yours, "Astarte," nor yours, "Viola,")—who knows that men are rejected by women every day because they, the men, love them, and are accepted every day because they do not, and therefore can study the arts of pleasing,—a man of sense, when he finds he has established his second parallel too soon, retires quietly to his first, and begins working on his covered ways again. [The whole art of love may be read in any Encyclopædia under the title *Fortification*, where the terms just used are explained.] After the little adventure of the necklace, Dick retreated at once to his first parallel. Elsie loved riding,—and would go off with him on a gallop now and then. He was a master of all those strange Indian horseback-feats which shame the tricks of the circus-riders, and used to astonish and almost amuse her sometimes by disappearing from his saddle, like a phantom horseman, lying flat against the side of the bounding creature that bore him, as if he were a hunting leopard with his claws in the horse's flank and flattening himself out against his heaving ribs. Elsie knew a little Spanish too, which she had learned from the young person who had taught her dancing, and Dick enlarged her vocabulary with a few soft phrases, and would sing her a song sometimes, touching the air upon an ancient-looking guitar they had found with the ghostly things in the garret,—a quaint old instrument, marked E. M. on the back, and supposed to have belonged to a certain Elizabeth Mascarene, before mentioned in connection with a work of art,—a fair, dowerless lady, who smiled and sung and faded away, unwedded, a hundred years ago, as dowerless ladies, not a few, are smiling and singing and fading now,—God grant each of them His love,—and one human heart as its interpreter!

As for school, Elsie went or stayed away as she liked. Sometimes, when they thought she was at her desk in the great school-room, she would be on The Mountain,—alone always. Dick wanted to go with her, but she would never let him. Once, when she had followed the zigzag path a little way up, she looked back and caught a glimpse of him following her. She turned and passed him without a word, but giving him a look which seemed to make the scars on his wrist tingle, went to her room, where she locked herself up, and did not come out again till evening,—Old Sophy having brought her food, and set it down, not speaking, but looking into her eyes inquiringly, like a dumb beast trying to feel out his master's will in his face. The evening was clear and the moon shining. As Dick sat at his chamber-window, looking at the mountain-side, he saw a gray-dressed figure flit between the trees and steal along the narrow path which led upward. Elsie's pillow was unpressed that night, but she had not been missed by the household, —for Dick knew enough to keep his own counsel. The next morning she avoided him and went off early to school. It was the same morning that the young master found the flower between the leaves of his Virgil.

The girl got over her angry fit, and was pleasant enough with her cousin for a few days after this; but she shunned rather than sought him. She had taken a new interest in her books, and especially in certain poetical readings which the master conducted with the elder scholars. This gave

Master Langdon a good chance to study her ways when her eye was on her book, to notice the inflections of her voice, to watch for any expression of her sentiments; for, to tell the truth, he had a kind of fear that the girl had taken a fancy to him, and, though she interested him, he did not wish to study her heart from the inside.

The more he saw her, the more the sadness of her beauty wrought upon him. She looked as if she might hate, but could not love. She hardly smiled at anything, spoke rarely, but seemed to feel that her natural power of expression lay all in her bright eyes, the force of which so many had felt, but none perhaps had tried to explain to themselves. A person accustomed to watch the faces of those who were ailing in body or mind, and to search in every line and tint for some underlying source of disorder, could hardly help analyzing the impression such a face produced upon him. The light of those beautiful eyes was like the lustre of ice; in all her features there was nothing of that human warmth which shows that sympathy has reached the soul beneath the mask of flesh it wears. The look was that of remoteness, of utter isolation. There was in its stony apathy, it seemed to him, the pathos which we find in the blind who show no film or speck over the organs of sight; for Nature had meant her to be lovely, and left out nothing but love. And yet the master could not help feeling that some instinct was working in this girl which was in some way leading her to seek his presence. She did not lift her glittering eyes upon him as at first. It seemed strange that she did not, for they were surely her natural weapons of conquest. Her color did not come and go like that of young girls under excitement. She had a clear brunette complexion, a little sun-touched, it may be,—for the master noticed once, when her necklace was slightly displaced, that a faint ring or band of a little lighter shade than the rest of the surface encircled her neck. What was the slight peculiarity of her enunciation, when she read? Not a lisp, certainly, but the least possible imperfection in articulating some of the lingual sounds,—just enough to be noticed at first, and quite forgotten after being a few times heard.

Not a word about the flower on either side. It was not

uncommon for the school-girls to leave a rose or pink or wild flower on the teacher's desk. Finding it in the Virgil was nothing, after all; it was a little delicate flower, which looked as if it were made to press, and it was probably shut in by accident at the particular place where he found it. He took it into his head to examine it in a botanical point of view. He found it was not common,—that it grew only in certain localities,—and that one of these was among the rocks of the eastern spur of The Mountain.

It happened to come into his head how the Swiss youth climb the sides of the Alps to find the flower called the *Edelweiss* for the maidens whom they wish to please. It is a pretty fancy, that of scaling some dangerous height before the dawn, so as to gather the flower in its freshness, that the favored maiden may wear it to church on Sunday morning, a proof at once of her lover's devotion and his courage. Mr. Bernard determined to explore the region where this flower was said to grow, that he might see where the wild girl sought the blossoms of which Nature was so jealous.

It was on a warm, fair Saturday afternoon that he undertook his land-voyage of discovery. He had more curiosity, it may be, than he would have owned; for he had heard of the girl's wandering habits, and the guesses about her sylvan haunts, and was thinking what the chances were that he should meet her in some strange place, or come upon traces of her which would tell secrets she would not care to have known.

The woods are all alive to one who walks through them with his mind in an excited state, and his eyes and ears wide open. The trees are always talking, not merely whispering with their leaves, (for every tree talks to itself in that way, even when it stands alone in the middle of a pasture,) but grating their boughs against each other, as old horn-handed farmers press their dry, rustling palms together, dropping a nut or a leaf or a twig, clicking to the tap of a woodpecker, or rustling as a squirrel flashes along a branch. It was now the season of singing-birds, and the woods were haunted with mysterious, tender music. The voices of the birds which love the deeper shades of the forest are sadder than those of the open fields: these are the nuns who have taken the veil, the hermits that have hidden themselves away from the world and tell their griefs to the infinite listening Silences of the wilderness,— for the one deep inner silence that Nature breaks with her fitful superficial sounds becomes multiplied as the image of a star in ruffled waters. Strange! The woods at first convey the impression of profound repose, and yet, if you watch their ways with open ear, you find the life which is in them is restless and nervous as that of a woman: the little twigs are crossing and twining and separating like slender fingers that cannot be still; the stray leaf is to be flattened into its place like a truant curl; the limbs sway and twist, impatient of their constrained attitude; and the rounded masses of foliage swell upward and subside from time to time with long soft sighs, and, it may be, the falling of a few rain-drops which had lain hidden among the deeper shadows. I pray you, notice, in the sweet summer days which will soon see you among the mountains, this inward tranquillity that belongs to the heart of the woodland, with this nervousness, for I do not know what else to call it, of outer movement. One would say, that Nature, like untrained persons, could not sit still without nestling about or doing something with her limbs or features, and that high breeding was only to be looked for in trim gardens, where the soul of the trees is ill at ease perhaps, but their manners are unexceptionable, and a rustling branch or leaf falling out of season is an indecorum. The real forest is hardly still except in the Indian summer; then there is death in the house, and they are waiting for the sharp shrunken months to come with white raiment for the summer's burial.

There were many hemlocks in this neighborhood, the grandest and most solemn of all the forest-trees in the mountain regions. Up to a certain period of growth they are eminently beautiful, their boughs disposed in the most graceful pagoda-like series of close terraces, thick and dark with green crystalline leaflets. In spring the tender shoots come out of a paler green, finger-like, as if they were pointing to the violets at their feet. But when the trees have grown old, and their rough boles measure a yard and more through their diameter, they are no longer beautiful, but they have a sad solemnity all their own, too full of meaning to require the heart's comment to be framed in words. Below, all their earthward-looking branches are sapless and shattered, splintered by the weight of many winters' snows; above, they are still green and full of life, but their summits overtop all the deciduous trees around them, and in their companionship with heaven they are alone. On these the lightning loves to fall. One such Mr. Bernard saw,—or rather, what had been one such; for the bolt had torn the tree like an explosion from within, and the ground was strewed all around the broken stump with flakes of rough bark and strips and chips of shivered wood, into which the old tree had been rent by the bursting rocket from the thunder-cloud.

——The master had struck up The Mountain obliquely from the western side of the Dudley mansion-house. In this way he ascended until he reached a point many hundred feet above the level of the plain, and commanding all the country beneath and around. Almost at his feet he saw the mansion-house, the chimney standing out of the middle of the roof, or rather, like a black square hole in it,—the trees almost directly over their stems, the fences as lines, the whole nearly as an architect would draw a ground-plan of the house and the inclosures round it. It frightened him to see how the huge masses of rock and old forest-growths hung over the home below. As he descended a little and drew near the ledge of evil name, he was struck with the appearance of a long narrow fissure that ran parallel with it and above it for many rods, not seemingly of very old standing,—for there were many fibres of roots which had evidently been snapped asunder when the rent took place, and some of which were still succulent in both separated portions.

Mr. Bernard had made up his mind, when he set forth, not to come back before he had examined the dreaded ledge. He had half persuaded himself that it was scientific curiosity. He wished to examine the rocks, *to see what flowers grew there*, and perhaps pick up an adventure in the zoölogical line; for he had on a pair of high, stout boots, and he carried a stick in his hand, which was forked at one extremity, so as to be very convenient to hold down a *crotalus* with, if he should happen to encounter one. He knew the aspect of the ledge from a distance; for its bald and leprous-looking declivities stood out in their nakedness from the wooded sides of The Mountain, when this was viewed from certain points of the village. But the nearer aspect of the blasted region had something frightful in it. The cliffs were water-worn, as if they had been gnawed for thousands of years by hungry waves. In some places they overhung their base so as to look like leaning towers which might topple over at any minute. In other parts they were scooped into niches or caverns. Here and there they were cracked in deep fissures, some of them of such width that one might enter them, if he cared to run the risk of meeting the regular tenants, who might treat him as an intruder.

Parts of the ledge were cloven perpendicularly, with nothing but cracks or slightly projecting edges in which or on which a foot could find hold. High up on one of these precipitous walls of rock he saw some tufts of flowers, and knew them at once for the same that he had found between the leaves of his Virgil. Not there, surely! No woman would have clung against that steep, rough parapet to gather an idle blossom. And yet the master looked round everywhere, and even up the side of that rock, to see if there were no signs of a woman's footstep. He peered about curiously, as if his eye might fall on some of those fragments of dress which women leave after them, whenever they run against each other or against anything else,—in crowded ballrooms, in the brushwood after picnics, on the fences after rambles, scattered round over every place which has witnessed an act of violence, where rude hands have been laid upon them. Nothing. Stop, though, one moment. That stone is smooth and polished, as if it had been somewhat worn by the pressure of human feet. There is one twig broken among the stems of that clump of shrubs. He put his foot upon the stone and took hold of the close-clinging shrub. In this way he turned a sharp angle of the rock and found himself on a natural platform, which lay in front of one of the wider fissures,—whether the mouth of a cavern or not he could not yet tell. A flat stone made an easy seat, upon which he sat down, as he was very glad to do, and looked mechanically about him. A small fragment splintered from the rock was at his feet. He took it and threw it down the declivity a little below where he sat. He looked about for a stem or a straw of some kind to bite upon,—a country-instinct,—relic, no doubt, of the old vegetable-feeding habits of Eden. Is that a stem or a straw? He picked it up. It was a hair-pin.

To say that Mr. Langdon had a strange sort of thrill shoot through him at the sight of this harmless little implement would be a statement not at variance with the fact of the case. That smooth stone had been often trodden, and by what foot he could not doubt. He rose up from his seat to look round for other signs of a woman's visits. What if there is a cavern here, where she has a retreat, fitted up, perhaps, as anchorites fitted their cells,—nay, it may be, carpeted and mirrored, and with one of those tiger-skins for a couch, such as they say the girl loves to lie on? Let us look, at any rate.

Mr. Bernard walked to the mouth of the cavern or fissure and looked into it. His look was met by the glitter of two diamond eyes, small, sharp, cold, shining out of the darkness, but gliding with a smooth, steady motion towards the light, and himself. He stood fixed, struck dumb, staring back into them with dilating pupils and sudden numbness of fear that cannot move, as in the terror of dreams. The two sparks of light came forward until they grew to circles of flame, and all at once lifted themselves up as if in angry surprise. Then for the first time thrilled in Mr. Bernard's ears the dreadful sound that nothing which breathes, be it man or brute, can hear unmoved,—the long, loud, stinging whirr, as the huge, thick-bodied reptile shook his many-jointed rattle and adjusted his loops for the fatal stroke. His eyes were drawn as with magnets toward the circles of flame. His ears rung as in the overture to the swooning dream of chloroform. Nature was before man with her anæsthetics: the cat's first shake stupefies the mouse; the lion's first shake deadens the man's fear and feeling; and the *crotalus* paralyzes before he strikes. He waited as in a trance,—waited as one that longs to have the blow fall, and all over, as the man who shall be in two pieces in a second waits for the axe to drop. But while he looked straight into the flaming eyes, it seemed to him that they were losing their light and terror, that they were growing tame and dull; the charm was dissolving, the numbness was passing away, he could move once more. He heard a light breathing close to his ear, and, half turning, saw the face of Elsie Venner, looking motionless into the reptile's eyes, which had shrunk and faded under the stronger enchantment of her own.

CHAPTER XIV

FAMILY SECRETS

It was commonly understood in the town of Rockland that Dudley Venner had had a great deal of trouble with that daughter of his, so handsome, yet so peculiar, about whom there were so many strange stories. There was no end to the tales which were told of her extraordinary doings. Yet her name was never coupled with that of any youth or man, until this cousin had provoked remark by his visit; and even then it was oftener in the shape of wondering conjectures whether he would dare to make love to her, than in any pretended knowledge of their relations to each other, that the public tongue exercised its village-prerogative of tattle.

The more common version of the trouble at the mansion-house was this:—Elsie was not exactly in her right mind. Her temper was singular, her tastes were anomalous, her habits were lawless, her antipathies were many and intense, and she was liable to explosions of ungovernable anger. Some said that was not the worst of it. At nearly fifteen years old, when she was growing fast, and in an irritable state of mind and body, she had had a governess placed over her for whom she had conceived an aversion. It was whispered among a few who knew more of the family secrets than others, that, worried and exasperated by the presence and jealous oversight of this person, Elsie had attempted to get finally rid of her by unlawful means, such as young girls have been known to employ in their straits, and to which the sex at all ages has a certain instinctive tendency, in preference to more palpable instruments for the righting of its wrongs. At any rate, this governess had been taken suddenly ill, and the Doctor had been sent for at midnight. Old Sophy had taken her master into a room apart, and said a few words to him which turned him as white as a sheet. As soon as he recovered himself, he sent Sophy out, called in the old Doctor, and gave him some few hints, on which he acted at once, and had the satisfaction of seeing his patient out of danger before he left in the morning. It is proper to say, that, during the following days, the most thorough search was made in every nook and cranny of those parts of the house which Elsie chiefly haunted, but nothing was found which might be accused of having been the intentional cause of the probably accidental sudden illness of the governess. From this time forward her father was never easy. Should he keep her apart, or shut her up, for fear of risk to others, and so lose every chance of restoring her mind to its healthy tone by kindly influences and intercourse with wholesome natures? There was no proof, only presumption, as to the agency of Elsie in the matter referred to. But the doubt was worse, perhaps, than certainty would have been,—for then he would have known what to do.

He took the old Doctor as his adviser. The shrewd old man listened to the father's story, his explanations of possibilities, of probabilities, of dangers, of hopes. When he had got through, the Doctor looked him in the face steadily, as if he were saying, *Is that all?*

The father's eyes fell. This was *not* all. There was something at the bottom of his soul which he could not bear to speak of,—nay, which, as often as it reared itself through the dark waves of unworded consciousness into the breathing air of thought, he trod down as the ruined angels tread down a lost soul trying to come up out of the seething sea of torture. Only this one daughter! No! God never would have ordained such a thing. There was nothing ever heard of like it; it could not be; she was ill,—she would outgrow all these singularities; he had had an aunt who was peculiar; he had heard that hysteric girls showed the strangest forms of moral obliquity for a time, but came right at last. She would change all at once, when her health got more firmly settled in the course of her growth. Are there not rough buds that open into sweet flowers? Are there not fruits, which, while unripe, are not to be tasted or endured, which mature into the richest taste and fragrance? In God's good time she would come to her true nature; her eyes would lose that frightful, cold glitter; her lips would not feel so cold when she pressed them against his cheek; and that faint birth-mark, her mother swooned when she first saw, would fade wholly out,—it was less marked, surely, now than it used to be!

So Dudley Venner felt, and would have thought, if he had let his thoughts breathe the air of his soul. But the Doctor read through words and thoughts and all into the father's consciousness. There are states of mind which may be shared by two persons in presence of each other, which remain not only unworded, but *unthoughted*, if such a word may be coined for our special need. Such a mutually interpenetrative consciousness there was between the father and the old physician. By a common impulse, both of them rose in a mechanical way and went to the western window, where each started, as he saw the other's look directed towards the white stone which stood in the midst of the small plot of green turf.

The Doctor had, for a moment, forgotten himself, but he looked up at the clouds, which were angry, and said, as if speaking of the weather, "It is dark now, but we hope it will clear up by-and-by. There are a great many more clouds than rains, and more rains than strokes of lightning, and more strokes of lightning than there are people killed. We must let this girl of ours have her way, as far as it is safe. Send away this woman she hates, quietly. Get her a foreigner for a governess, if you can,—one that can dance and sing and will teach her. In the house old Sophy will watch her best. Out of it you must trust her, I am afraid,—for she will not be followed round, and she is in less danger than you think. If she wanders at night, find her, if you can; the woods are not absolutely safe. If she will be friendly with any young people, have them to see her,—young men, especially. She will not love any one easily, perhaps not at all; yet love would be more like to bring her right than anything else. If any young person seems in danger of falling in love with her, send him to me for counsel."

Dry, hard advice, but given from a kind heart, with a moist eye, and in tones which tried to be cheerful and were full of sympathy. This advice was the key to the more than indulgent treatment which, as we have seen, the girl had received from her father and all about her. The old Doctor often came in, in the kindest, most natural sort of way, got into pleasant relations with Elsie by always treating her in the same easy manner as at the great party, encouraging all her harmless fancies, and rarely reminding her that he was a professional adviser, except when she came out of her own accord, as in the talk they had at the party, telling him of some wild trick she had been playing.

"Let her go to the girls' school, by all means," said the Doctor, when she had begun to talk about it. "Possibly she may take to some of the girls or of the teachers. Anything to interest her. Friendship, love, religion,—whatever will set her nature at work. We must have headway on, or there will be no piloting her. Action first of all, and then we will see what to do with it."

So, when Cousin Richard came along, the Doctor, though he did not like his looks any too well, told her father to encourage his staying for a time. If she liked him, it was good; if she only tolerated him, it was better than nothing.

"You know something about that nephew of yours, during these last years, I suppose?" the Doctor said. "Looks as if he had seen life. Has a scar that was made by a sword-cut, and a white spot on the side of his neck that looks like a bullet-mark. I think he has been what folks call a 'hard customer.'"

Dudley Venner owned that he had heard little or nothing of him of late years. He had invited himself, and of course it would not be decent not to receive him as a relative. He thought Elsie rather liked having him about the house for a while. She was very capricious,—acted as if she fancied him one day and disliked him the next. He did not know,—but sometimes thought that this nephew of his might take a serious liking to Elsie. What should he do about it, if it turned out so?

The Doctor lifted his eyebrows a little. He thought there

was no fear. Elsie was naturally what they call a man-hater, and there was very little danger of any sudden passion springing up between two such young persons. Let him stay awhile; it gives her something to think about. So he stayed awhile, as we have seen.

The more Mr. Richard became acquainted with the family,—that is, with the two persons of whom it consisted,—the more favorably the idea of a permanent residence in the mansion-house seemed to impress him. The estate was large,—hundreds of acres, with woodlands and meadows of great value. The father and daughter had been living quietly, and there could not be a doubt that the property which came through the Dudleys must have largely increased of late years. It was evident enough that they had an abundant income, from the way in which Elsie's caprices were indulged. She had horses and carriages to suit herself; she sent to the great city for everything she wanted in the way of dress. Even her diamonds—and the young man knew something about these gems—must be of considerable value; and yet she wore them carelessly, as it pleased her fancy. She had precious old laces, too, almost worth their weight in diamonds,—laces which had been snatched from altars in ancient Spanish cathedrals during the wars, and which it would not be safe to leave a duchess alone with for ten minutes. The old house was fat with the deposits of rich generations which had gone before. The famous "golden" fire-set was a purchase of one of the family who had been in France during the Revolution, and must have come from a princely palace, if not from one of the royal residences. As for silver, the iron closet which had been made in the dining-room wall was running over with it: tea-kettles, coffee-pots, heavy-lidded tankards, chafing-dishes, punch-bowls, all that all the Dudleys had ever used, from the caudle-cup which used to be handed round the young mother's chamber, and the porringer from which children scooped their bread-and-milk with spoons as solid as ingots, to that ominous vessel, on the upper shelf, far back in the dark, with a spout like a slender italic S, out of which the sick and dying, all along the last century, and since, had taken the last drops that passed their lips. Without being much of a scholar, Dick could see well enough, too, that the books in the library had been ordered from the great London houses, whose imprint they bore, by persons who knew what was best and meant to have it. A man does not require much learning to feel pretty sure, when he takes one of those solid, smooth, velvet-leaved quartos, say a Baskerville Addison, for instance, bound in red morocco, with a margin of gold as rich as the embroidery of a prince's collar, as Vandyck drew it,—he need not know much to feel pretty sure that a score or two of shelves full of such books mean that it took a long purse, as well as a literary taste, to bring them together.

To all these attractions the mind of this thoughtful young gentleman may be said to have been fully open. He did not disguise from himself, however, that there were a number of drawbacks in the way of his becoming established as the heir of the Dudley mansion-house and fortune. In the first place, Cousin Elsie was, unquestionably, very piquant, very handsome, game as a hawk, and hard to please, which made her worth trying for. But then there was something about Cousin Elsie,—(the small, white scars began stinging, as he said this to himself, and he pushed his sleeve up to look at them,)—there was something about Cousin Elsie he couldn't make out. What was the matter with her eyes, that they sucked your life out of you in that strange way? What did she always wear a necklace for? Had she some such love-token on her neck as the old Don's revolver had left on his? How safe would anybody feel to live with her? Besides, her father would last forever, if he was left to himself. And he may take it into his head to marry again. That would be pleasant!

So talked Cousin Richard to himself, in the calm of the night and in the tranquillity of his own soul. There was much to be said on both sides. It was a balance to be struck after the two columns were added up. He struck the balance, and came to the conclusion that he would fall in love with Elsie Venner.

The intelligent reader will not confound this matured and serious intention of falling in love with the young lady with that mere impulse of the moment before mentioned as an instance of making love. On the contrary, the moment Mr. Richard had made up his mind that he should fall in love with Elsie, he began to be more reserved with her, and to try to make friends in other quarters. Sensible men, you know, care very little what a girl's present fancy is. The question is: Who manages her, and how can you get at that person or those persons? Her foolish little sentiments are all very well in their way; but business is business, and we can't stop for such trifles. The old political wire-pullers never go near the man they want to gain, if they can help it; they find out who his intimates and managers are, and work through them. Always handle any positively electrical body, whether it is charged with passion or power, with some non-conductor between you and it, not with your naked hands.—The above were some of the young gentleman's working axioms; and he proceeded to act in accordance with them.

He began by paying his court more assiduously to his uncle. It was not very hard to ingratiate himself in that quarter; for his manners were insinuating, and his precocious experience of life made him entertaining. The old neglected billiard-room was soon put in order, and Dick, who was a magnificent player, had a series of games with his uncle, in which, singularly enough, he was beaten, though his antagonist had been out of play for years. He evinced a profound interest in the family history, insisted on having the details of its early alliances, and professed a great pride in it, which he had inherited from his father, who, though he had allied himself with the daughter of an alien race, had yet chosen one with the real azure blood in her veins, as proud as if she had Castile and Aragon for her dower and the Cid for her grandpapa. He also asked a great deal of advice, such as inexperienced young persons are in need of, and listened to it with due reverence.

It is not very strange that Uncle Dudley took a kinder view of his nephew than the Judge, who thought he could read a questionable history in his face,—or the old Doctor, who knew men's temperaments and organizations pretty well, and had his prejudices about races, and could tell an old sword-cut and a bullet-mark in two seconds from a scar got by falling against the fender, or a mark left by king's evil. He could not be expected to share our own prejudices; for he had heard nothing of the wild youth's adventures, or his scamper over the Pampas at short notice. So, then, "Richard Venner, Esquire, guest of Dudley Venner, Esquire, at his elegant mansion," prolonged his visit until his presence became something like a matter of habit, and the neighbors began to think that the fine old house would be illuminated before long for a grand marriage.

He had done pretty well with the father: the next thing was to gain over the nurse. Old Sophy was as cunning as a red fox or a gray woodchuck. She had nothing in the world to do but to watch Elsie; she had nothing to care for but this girl and her father. She had never liked Dick too well; for he used to make faces at her and tease her when he was a boy, and now he was a man there was something about him—she could not tell what—that made her suspicious of him. It was no small matter to get her over to his side.

The jet-black Africans know that gold never looks so well as on the foil of their dark skins. Dick found in his trunk a string of gold beads, such as are manufactured in some of our cities, which he had brought from the gold region of Chili,—so he said,—for the express purpose of giving them to old Sophy. These Africans, too, have a perfect passion for gay-colored clothing; being condemned by Nature, as it were, to a perpetual mourning-suit, they love to enliven it with all sorts of variegated stuffs of sprightly patterns, aflame with red and yellow. The considerate young man had remembered this, too, and brought home for Sophy some handkerchiefs of rainbow hues, which had been strangely overlooked till now, at the bottom of one of his trunks. Old Sophy took his gifts, but kept her black eyes open and watched every movement of the young people all the more closely. It was through her that the father had always known most of the actions and tendencies of his daughter.

In the meantime the strange adventure on The Mountain had brought the young master into new relations with Elsie. She had led him out of danger; perhaps saved him from death by the strange power she exerted. He was grateful, and yet shuddered at the recollection of the whole scene. In his dreams he was pursued by the glare of cold glittering eyes,—whether they were in the head of a woman or of a reptile he could not always tell, the images had so run together. But he could not help seeing that the eyes of the young girl had been often, very often, turned upon him when he had been looking away, and fell as his own glance met them. Helen Darley told him very plainly that this girl was thinking about him more than about her book. Dick Venner found she was getting more constant in her attendance at school. He learned, on inquiry, that there was a new master, a handsome young man. The handsome young man would not have liked the look that came over Dick's face when he heard this fact mentioned.

In short, everything was getting tangled up together, and there would be no chance of disentangling the threads in this chapter.

CHAPTER XV

PHYSIOLOGICAL

If Master Bernard felt a natural gratitude to his young pupil for saving him from an imminent peril, he was in a state of infinite perplexity to know why he should have needed such aid. He, an active, muscular, courageous, adventurous young fellow, with a stick in his hand, ready to hold down the Old Serpent himself, if he had come in his way, to stand still, staring into those two eyes, until they came up close to him, and the strange, terrible sound seemed to freeze him stiff where he stood,—what was the meaning of it? Again, what was the influence this girl had seemingly exerted, under which the venomous creature had collapsed in such a sudden way? Whether he had been awake or dreaming he did not feel quite sure. He knew he had gone up The Mountain, at any rate; he knew he had come down The Mountain with the girl walking just before him;—there was no forgetting her figure, as she walked on in silence, her braided locks falling a little, for want of the lost hair-pin, perhaps, and looking like a wreathing coil of— Shame on such fancies!—to wrong that supreme crowning gift of abounding Nature, a rush of shining black hair, which, shaken loose, would cloud her all round, like Godiva, from brow to instep! He was sure he had sat down before the fissure or cave. He was sure that he was led softly away from the place, and that it was Elsie who had led him. There was the hair-pin to show that so far it was not a dream. But between these recollections came a strange confusion; and the more the master thought, the more he was perplexed to know whether she had waked him, sleeping, as he sat on the stone, from some frightful dream, such as may come in a very brief slumber, or whether she had bewitched him into a trance with those strange eyes of hers, or whether it was all true, and he must solve its problem as he best might.

There was another recollection connected with this mountain adventure. As they approached the mansion-house, they met a young man, whom Mr. Bernard remembered having seen once at least before, and whom he had heard of as a cousin of the young girl. As Cousin Richard Venner, the person in question, passed them, he took the measure, so to speak, of Mr. Bernard, with a look so piercing, so exhausting, so practised, so profoundly suspicious, that the young master felt in an instant that he had an enemy in this handsome youth,—an enemy, too, who was like to be subtle and dangerous.

Mr. Bernard had made up his mind, that, come what might, enemy or no enemy, live or die, he would solve the mystery of Elsie Venner, sooner or later. He was not a man to be frightened out of his resolution by a scowl, or a stiletto, or any unknown means of mischief, of which a whole armory was hinted at in that passing look Dick Venner had given him. Indeed, like most adventurous young persons, he found a kind of charm in feeling that there might be some dangers in the way of his investigations. Some rumors which had reached him about the supposed suitor of Elsie Venner, who was thought to be a desperate kind of fellow, and whom some believed to be an unscrupulous adventurer, added a curious, romantic kind of interest to the course of physiological and psychological inquiries he was about instituting.

The afternoon on The Mountain was still uppermost in his mind. Of course he knew the common stories about fascination. He had once been himself an eye-witness of the charming of a small bird by one of our common harmless serpents. Whether a human being could be reached by this subtle agency, he had been skeptical, notwithstanding the mysterious relation generally felt to exist between man and this creature, "cursed above all cattle and above every beast of the field,"—a relation which some interpret as the fruit of the curse, and others hold to be so instinctive that this animal has been for that reason adopted as the natural symbol of evil. There was another solution, however, supplied him by his professional reading. The curious work of Mr. Braid of Manchester had made him familiar with the phenomena of a state allied to that produced by animal magnetism, and called by that writer by the name of *hypnotism*. He found, by referring to his note-book, the statement was, that, by fixing the eyes on *a bright object* so placed as *to produce a strain* upon the eyes and eyelids, and to maintain *a steady fixed stare*, there comes on in a few seconds a very singular condition, characterized by *muscular rigidity* and *inability to move*, with a strange *exaltation of most of the senses*, and *generally* a closure of the eyelids,—this condition being followed by *torpor*.

Now this statement of Mr. Braid's, well known to the scientific world, and the truth of which had been confirmed by Mr. Bernard in certain experiments he had instituted, as it has been by many other experimenters, went far to explain the strange impressions, of which, waking or dreaming, he had certainly been the subject. His nervous system had been in a high state of exaltation at the time. He remembered how the little noises that made rings of sound in the silence of the woods, like pebbles dropped in still waters, had reached his inner consciousness. He remembered that singular sensation in the roots of the hair, when he came on the traces of the girl's presence, reminding him of a line in a certain poem which he had read lately with a new and peculiar interest. He even recalled a curious evidence of exalted sensibility and irritability, in the twitching of the minute muscles of the internal ear at every unexpected sound, producing an odd little snap in the middle of the head, which proved to him that he was getting very nervous.

The next thing was to find out whether it were possible that the venomous creature's eyes should have served the purpose of Mr. Braid's "bright object" held very close to the person experimented on, or whether they had any special power which could be made the subject of exact observation.

For this purpose Mr. Bernard considered it necessary to

get a live *crotalus* or two into his possession, if this were possible. On inquiry, he found that there was a certain family living far up the mountain-side, not a mile from the ledge, the members of which were said to have taken these creatures occasionally, and not to be in any danger, or at least in any fear, of being injured by them. He applied to these people, and offered a reward sufficient to set them at work to capture some of these animals, if such a thing were possible.

A few days after this, a dark, gypsy-looking woman presented herself at his door. She held up her apron as if it contained something precious in the bag she made with it.

"Y' wanted some rattlers," said the woman. "Here they be."

She opened her apron and showed a coil of rattlesnakes lying very peaceably in its fold. They lifted their heads up, as if they wanted to see what was going on, but showed no sign of anger.

"Are you crazy?" said Mr. Bernard. "You're dead in an hour, if one of those creatures strikes you!"

He drew back a little, as he spoke; it might be simple disgust; it might be fear; it might be what we call antipathy, which is different from either, and which will sometimes show itself in paleness, and even faintness, produced by objects perfectly harmless and not in themselves offensive to any sense.

"Lord bless you," said the woman, "rattlers never touches our folks. I'd jest 'z lieves handle them creatures as so many stripéd snakes."

So saying, she put their heads down with her hand, and packed them together in her apron as if they had been bits of cart-rope.

Mr. Bernard had never heard of the power, or, at least, the belief in the possession of a power by certain persons, which enables them to handle these frightful reptiles with perfect impunity. The fact, however, is well known to others, and more especially to a very distinguished Professor in one of the leading institutions of the great city of the land, whose experiences in the neighborhood of Graylock, as he will doubtless inform the curious, were very much like those of the young master.

Mr. Bernard had a wired cage ready for his formidable captives, and studied their habits and expression with a strange sort of interest. What did the Creator mean to signify, when he made such shapes of horror, and, as if he had doubly cursed this envenomed wretch, had set a mark upon him and sent him forth, the Cain of the brotherhood of serpents? It was a very curious fact that the first train of thoughts Mr. Bernard's small menagerie suggested to him was the grave, though somewhat worn, subject of the origin of evil. There is now to be seen in a tall glass jar, in the Museum of Comparative Anatomy at Cantabridge in the territory of the Massachusetts, a huge *crotalus*, of a species which grows to more frightful dimensions than our own, under the hotter skies of South America. Look at it, ye who would know what is the tolerance, the freedom from prejudice, which can suffer such an incarnation of all that is devilish to lie unharmed in the cradle of Nature! Learn, too, that there are many things in this world which we are warned to shun, and are even suffered to slay, if need be, but which we must not hate, unless we would hate what God loves and cares for.

Whatever fascination the creature might exercise in his native haunts, Mr. Bernard found himself not in the least nervous or affected in any way while looking at his caged reptiles. When their cage was shaken, they would lift their heads and spring their rattles; but the sound was by no means so formidable to listen to as when it reverberated among the chasms of the echoing rocks. The expression of the creatures was watchful, still, grave, passionless, fate-like, suggesting a cold malignity which seemed to be waiting for its opportunity. Their awful, deep-cut mouths were sternly closed over the long hollow fangs which rested their roots against the swollen poison-gland, where the venom had been hoarding up ever since the last stroke had emptied it. They never winked, for ophidians have no movable eyelids, but kept up that awful fixed stare which made the two *unwinking* gladiators the survivors of twenty pairs matched by one of the Roman Emperors, as Pliny tells us, in his

"Natural History." Their eyes did not flash, but shone with a cold still light. They were of a pale-golden or straw color, horrible to look into, with their stony calmness, their pitiless indifference, hardly enlivened by the almost imperceptible vertical slit of the pupil, through which Death seemed to be looking out like the archer behind the long narrow loop-hole in a blank turret-wall. On the whole, the caged reptiles, horrid as they were, hardly matched his recollections of what he had seen or dreamed he saw at the cavern. These looked dangerous enough, but yet quiet. A treacherous stillness, however,—as the unfortunate New York physician found, when he put his foot out to wake up the torpid creature, and instantly the fang flashed through his boot, carrying the poison into his blood, and death with it.

Mr. Bernard kept these strange creatures, and watched all their habits with a natural curiosity. In any collection of animals the venomous beasts are looked at with the greatest interest, just as the greatest villains are most run after by the unknown public. Nobody troubles himself for a common striped snake or a petty thief, but a *cobra* or a wife-killer is a centre of attraction to all eyes. These captives did very little to earn their living, but, on the other hand, their living was not expensive, their diet being nothing but air, *au naturel*. Months and months these creatures will live and seem to thrive well enough, as any showman who has them in his menagerie will testify, though they never touch anything to eat or drink.

In the mean time Mr. Bernard had become very curious about a class of subjects not treated of in any detail in those text-books accessible in most country-towns, to the exclusion of the more special treatises, and especially of the rare and ancient works found on the shelves of the larger city-libraries. He was on a visit to old Dr. Kittredge one day, having been asked by him to call in for a few moments as soon as convenient. The Doctor smiled good-humoredly when he asked him if he had an extensive collection of medical works.

"Why, no," said the old Doctor, "I haven't got a great many printed books; and what I have I don't read quite as often as I might, I'm afraid. I read and studied in the time of it, when I was in the midst of the young men who were all at work with their books; but it's a mighty hard matter, when you go off alone into the country, to keep up with all that's going on in the Societies and the Colleges. I'll tell you, though, Mr. Langdon, when a man that's once started right lives among sick folks for five-and-thirty years, as I've done, if he hasn't got a library of five-and-thirty volumes bound up in his head at the end of that time, he'd better stop driving round and sell his horse and sulky. I know the bigger part of the families within a dozen miles' ride. I know the families that have a way of living through everything, and I know the other set that have the trick of dying without any kind of reason for it. I know the years when the fevers and dysenteries are in earnest, and when they're only making believe. I know the folks that think they're dying as soon as they're sick, and the folks that never find out they're sick till they're dead. I don't want to undervalue your science, Mr. Langdon. There are things I never learned, because they came in after my day, and I am very glad to send my patients to those that do know them, when I am at fault; but I know these people about here, fathers and mothers, and children and grandchildren, so as all the science in the world can't know them, without it takes time about it, and sees them grow up and grow old, and how the wear and tear of life comes to them. You can't tell a horse by driving him once, Mr. Langdon, nor a patient by talking half an hour with him."

"Do you know much about the Venner family?" said Mr. Bernard, in a natural way enough, the Doctor's talk having suggested the question.

The Doctor lifted his head with his accustomed movement, so as to command the young man through his spectacles.

"I know all the families of this place and its neighborhood," he answered.

"We have the young lady studying with us at the Institute," said Mr. Bernard.

"I know it," the Doctor answered. "Is she a good scholar?"

All this time the Doctor's eyes were fixed steadily on Mr. Bernard, looking through the glasses.

"She is a good scholar enough, but I don't know what to make of her. Sometimes I think she is a little out of her head. Her father, I believe, is sensible enough;—what sort of a woman was her mother, Doctor?—I suppose, of course, you remember all about her?"

"Yes, I knew her mother. She was a very lovely young woman."—The Doctor put his hand to his forehead and drew a long breath.—"What is there you notice out of the way about Elsie Venner?"

"A good many things," the master answered. "She shuns all the other girls. She is getting a strange influence over my fellow-teacher, a young lady,—you know Miss Helen Darley, perhaps? I am afraid this girl will kill her. I never saw or heard of anything like it, in prose at least;—do you remember much of Coleridge's Poems, Doctor?"

The good old Doctor had to plead a negative.

"Well, no matter. Elsie would have been burned for a witch in old times. I have seen the girl look at Miss Darley when she had not the least idea of it, and all at once I would see her grow pale and moist, and sigh, and move round uneasily, and turn towards Elsie, and perhaps get up and go to her, or else have slight spasmodic movements that looked like hysterics;—do you believe in the evil eye, Doctor?"

"Mr. Langdon," the Doctor said, solemnly, "there are strange things about Elsie Venner,—very strange things. This was what I wanted to speak to you about. Let me advise you all to be very patient with the girl, but also very careful. Her love is not to be desired, and"—he spoke in a lower tone—"her hate is to be dreaded. Do you think she has any special fancy for anybody else in the school besides Miss Darley?"

Mr. Bernard could not stand the old Doctor's spectacled eyes without betraying a little of the feeling natural to a young man to whom a home question involving a possible sentiment is put suddenly.

"I have suspected," he said,—"I have had a kind of feeling—that she—— Well, come, Doctor,—I don't know that there's any use in disguising the matter,—I have thought

Elsie Venner had rather a fancy for somebody else,—I mean myself."

There was something so becoming in the blush with which the young man made this confession, and so manly, too, in the tone with which he spoke, so remote from any shallow vanity, such as young men who are incapable of love are apt to feel, when some loose tendril of a woman's fancy which a chance wind has blown against them twines about them for the want of anything better, that the old Doctor looked at him admiringly, and could not help thinking that it was no wonder any young girl should be pleased with him.

"You are a man of nerve, Mr. Langdon?" said the Doctor.

"I thought so till very lately," he replied. "I am not easily frightened, but I don't know but I might be bewitched or magnetized, or whatever it is when one is tied up and cannot move. I think I can find nerve enough, however, if there is any special use you want to put it to."

"Let me ask you one more question, Mr. Langdon. Do you find yourself disposed to take a special interest in Elsie, —to fall in love with her, in a word? Pardon me, for I do not ask from curiosity, but a much more serious motive."

"Elsie interests me," said the young man, "interests me strangely. She has a wild flavor in her character which is wholly different from that of any human creature I ever saw. She has marks of genius,—poetic or dramatic,—I hardly know which. She read a passage from Keats's 'Lamia' the other day, in the school-room, in such a way that I declare to you I thought some of the girls would faint or go into fits. Miss Darley got up and left the room, trembling all over. Then I pity her, she is so lonely. The girls are afraid of her, and she seems to have either a dislike or a fear of them. They have all sorts of painful stories about her. They give her a name which no human creature ought to bear. They say she hides a mark on her neck by always wearing a necklace. She is very graceful, you know, and they will have it that she can twist herself into all sorts of shapes, or tie herself in a knot, if she wants to. There is not one of them that will look her in the eyes. I pity the poor girl; but, Doctor, I do not love her. I would risk my life for her, if it would do her any good, but it would be in cold blood.

If her hand touches mine, it is not a thrill of passion I feel running through me, but a very different emotion. Oh, Doctor! there must be something in that creature's blood which has killed the humanity in her. God only knows the cause that has blighted such a soul in so beautiful a body! No, Doctor, I do not love the girl."

"Mr. Langdon," said the Doctor, "you are young, and I am old. Let me talk to you with an old man's privilege, as an adviser. You have come to this country-town without suspicion, and you are moving in the midst of perils. There are things which I must not tell you now; but I may warn you. Keep your eyes open and your heart shut. If, through pitying that girl, you ever come to love her, you are lost. If you deal carelessly with her, beware! This is not all. There are other eyes on you beside Elsie Venner's.—Do you go armed?"

"I do!" said Mr. Bernard,—and he "put his hands up" in the shape of fists, in such a way as to show that he was master of the natural weapons at any rate.

The Doctor could not help smiling. But his face fell in an instant.

"You may want something more than those tools to work with. Come with me into my sanctum."

The Doctor led Mr. Bernard into a small room opening out of the study. It was a place such as anybody but a medical man would shiver to enter. There was the usual tall box with its bleached, rattling tenant; there were jars in rows where "interesting cases" outlived the grief of widows and heirs in alcoholic immortality,—for your "preparation-jar" is the true "*monumentum ære perennius*"; there were various semipossibilities of minute dimensions and unpromising developments; there were shining instruments of evil aspect, and grim plates on the walls, and on one shelf by itself, accursed and apart, coiled in a long cylinder of spirit, a huge *crotalus*, rough-scaled, flat-headed, variegated with dull bands, one of which partially encircled the neck like a collar,—an awful wretch to look upon, with murder written all over him in horrid hieroglyphics. Mr. Bernard's look was riveted on this creature,—not fascinated certainly, for its eyes looked like white beads, being clouded by the action of the spirits in which it had been long kept,—but fixed by some indefinite sense of the renewal of a previous impression;—everybody knows the feeling, with its suggestion of some past state of existence. There was a scrap of paper on the jar, with something written on it. He was reaching up to read it when the Doctor touched him lightly.

"Look here, Mr. Langdon!" he said, with a certain vivacity of manner, as if wishing to call away his attention,—"this is my armory."

The Doctor threw open the door of a small cabinet, where were disposed in artistic patterns various weapons of offence and defence,—for he was a virtuoso in his way, and by the side of the implements of the art of healing had pleased himself with displaying a collection of those other instruments, the use of which renders the first necessary.

"See which of these weapons you would like best to carry about you," said the Doctor.

Mr. Bernard laughed, and looked at the Doctor as if he half doubted whether he was in earnest.

"This looks dangerous enough," he said,—"for the man who carries it, at least."

He took down one of the prohibited Spanish daggers or knives which a traveller may occasionally get hold of and smuggle out of the country. The blade was broad, trowel-like, but the point drawn out several inches, so as to look like a skewer.

"This must be a jealous bull-fighter's weapon," he said, and put it back in its place.

Then he took down an ancient-looking broad-bladed dagger, with a complex aspect about it, as if it had some kind of mechanism connected with it.

"Take care!" said the Doctor; "there is a trick to that dagger."

He took it and touched a spring. The dagger split suddenly into three blades, as when one separates the forefinger and the ring-finger from the middle one. The outside blades were sharp on their outer edge. The stab was to be made with the dagger shut, then the spring touched and the split blades withdrawn.

Mr. Bernard replaced it, saying, that it would have

served for side-arm to old Suwarrow, who told his men to work their bayonets back and forward when they pinned a Turk, but to wriggle them about in the wound when they stabbed a Frenchman.

"Here," said the Doctor, "this is the thing you want."

He took down a much more modern and familiar implement,—a small, beautifully finished revolver.

"I want you to carry this," he said; "and more than that, I want you to practise with it often, as for amusement, but so that it may be seen and understood that you are apt to have a pistol about you. Pistol-shooting is pleasant sport enough, and there is no reason why you should not practise it like other young fellows. And now," the Doctor said, "I have one other weapon to give you."

He took a small piece of parchment and shook a white powder into it from one of his medicine-jars. The jar was marked with the name of a mineral salt, of a nature to have been serviceable in case of sudden illness in the time of the Borgias. The Doctor folded the parchment carefully, and marked the Latin name of the powder upon it.

"Here," he said, handing it to Mr. Bernard,—"you see what it is, and you know what service it can render. Keep these two protectors about your person day and night; they will not harm you, and you may want one or the other or both before you think of it."

Mr. Bernard thought it was very odd, and not very old-gentlemanlike, to be fitting him out for treason, stratagem, and spoils, in this way. There was no harm, however, in carrying a doctor's powder in his pocket, or in amusing himself with shooting at a mark, as he had often done before. If the old gentleman had these fancies, it was as well to humor him. So he thanked old Doctor Kittredge, and shook his hand warmly as he left him.

"The fellow's hand did not tremble, nor his color change," the Doctor said, as he watched him walking away. "He is one of the right sort."

CHAPTER XVI

EPISTOLARY

Mr. Langdon to the Professor

MY DEAR PROFESSOR,—

You were kind enough to promise me that you would assist me in any professional or scientific investigations in which I might become engaged. I have of late become deeply interested in a class of subjects which present peculiar difficulty, and I must exercise the privilege of questioning you on some points upon which I desire information I cannot otherwise obtain. I would not trouble you, if I could find any person or books competent to enlighten me on some of these singular matters which have so excited me. The leading doctor here is a shrewd, sensible man, but not versed in the curiosities of medical literature.

I proceed, with your leave, to ask a considerable number of questions,—hoping to get answers to some of them, at least.

Is there any evidence that human beings can be infected or wrought upon by poisons, or otherwise, so that they shall manifest any of the peculiarities belonging to beings of a lower nature? Can such peculiarities be transmitted by inheritance? Is there anything to countenance the stories, long and widely current, about the "evil eye"? or is it a mere fancy that such a power belongs to any human being? Have you any personal experience as to the power of *fascination* said to be exercised by certain animals? What can you make of those circumstantial statements we have seen in the papers, of children forming mysterious friendships with ophidians of different species, sharing their food with them, and seeming to be under some subtle influence exercised by those creatures? Have you read, critically,

Coleridge's poem of "Christabel," and Keats's "Lamia"? If so, can you understand them, or find any physiological foundation for the story of either?

There is another set of questions of a different nature I should like to ask, but it is hardly fair to put so many on a single sheet. There is one, however, you must answer. Do you think there may be predispositions, inherited or ingrafted, but at any rate constitutional, which shall take out certain apparently voluntary determinations from the control of the will, and leave them as free from moral responsibility as the instincts of the lower animals? Do you not think there may be a *crime* which is not a *sin*?

Pardon me, my dear Sir, for troubling you with such a list of notes of interrogation. There are some *very strange* things going on here in this place, country-town as it is. Country-life is apt to be dull; but when it once gets going, it beats the city hollow, because it gives its whole mind to what it is about. These rural sinners make terrible work with the middle of the Decalogue, when they get started. However, I hope I shall live through my year's schoolkeeping without catastrophes, though there are queer doings about me which puzzle me and might scare some people. If anything *should* happen, you will be one of the first to hear of it, no doubt. But I trust not to help out the editors of the "Rockland Weekly Universe" with an obituary of the late lamented, who signed himself in life

Your friend and pupil,
BERNARD C. LANGDON

The Professor to Mr. Langdon

MY DEAR MR. LANGDON,—

I do not wonder that you find no answer from your country friends to the curious questions you put. They belong to that middle region between science and poetry which sensible men, as they are called, are very shy of meddling with. Some people think that truth and gold are always to be washed for; but the wiser sort are of opinion, that, unless there are so many grains to the peck of sand or nonsense respectively, it does not pay to wash for either, so long as one can find anything else to do. I don't doubt there is some truth in the phenomena of animal magnetism, for instance; but when you ask me to cradle for it, I tell you that the hysteric girls cheat so, and the professionals are such a set of pickpockets, that I can do something better than hunt for the grains of truth among their tricks and lies. Do you remember what I used to say in my lectures?—or were you asleep just then, or cutting your initials on the rail? (You see I can ask questions, my young friend.) *Leverage* is everything,—was what I used to say;—don't begin to pry till you have got the long arm on your side.

To please you, and satisfy your doubts as far as possible, I have looked into the old books,—into Schenckius and Turner and Kenelm Digby and the rest, where I have found plenty of curious stories which you must take for what they are worth.

Your first question I can answer in the affirmative upon pretty good authority. Mizaldus tells, in his "Memorabilia," the well-known story of the girl fed on poisons, who was sent by the king of the Indies to Alexander the Great. "When Aristotle saw her eyes *sparkling and snapping like those of serpents,* he said, 'Look out for yourself, Alexander! this is a dangerous companion for you!'"—and sure enough, the young lady proved to be a very unsafe person to her friends. Cardanus gets a story from Avicenna, of a certain man bit by a serpent, who recovered of his bite, the snake dying therefrom. This man afterwards had a daughter whom venomous serpents could not harm, though *she had a fatal power over them.*

I suppose you may remember the statements of old authors about *lycanthropy,* the disease in which men took on the nature and aspect of wolves. Aëtius and Paulus, both men of authority, describe it. Altomaris gives a horrid case; and Fincelius mentions one occurring as late as 1541, the subject of which was captured, still *insisting that he was a wolf,* only that the hair of his hide was turned in! *Versipelles,* it may be remembered, was the Latin name for these "were-wolves."

As for the cases where rabid persons have barked and bit like dogs, there are plenty of such on record.

More singular, or at least more rare, is the account given by Andreas Baccius, of a man who was struck in the hand by a cock, with his beak, and who died on the third day thereafter, looking for all the world *like a fighting-cock*, to the great horror of the spectators.

As to impressions transmitted *at a very early period of existence*, every one knows the story of King James's fear of a naked sword, and the way it is accounted for. Sir Kenelm Digby says,—"I remember when he dubbed me Knight, in the ceremony of putting the point of a naked sword upon my shoulder, he could not endure to look upon it, but turned his face another way, insomuch, that, in lieu of touching my shoulder, he had almost thrust the point into my eyes, had not the Duke of Buckingham guided his hand aright." It is he, too, who tells the story of the *mulberry mark* upon the neck of a certain lady of high condition, which "every year, in mulberry season, did swell, grow big, and itch." And Gaffarel mentions the case of a girl born with the figure of a *fish* on one of her limbs, of which the wonder was, that, when the girl did eat fish, this mark put her to sensible pain. But there is no end to cases of this kind, and I could give some of recent date, if necessary, lending a certain plausibility at least to the doctrine of transmitted impressions.

I never saw a distinct case of *evil eye*, though I have seen eyes so bad that they might produce strange effects on very sensitive natures. But the belief in it under various names, fascination, *jettatura*, etc., is so permanent and universal, from Egypt to Italy, and from the days of Solomon to those of Ferdinand of Naples, that there must be some *peculiarity*, to say the least, on which the opinion is based. There is very strong evidence that some such power is exercised by certain of the lower animals. Thus, it is stated on good authority that "almost every animal becomes panic-struck at the sight of the *rattlesnake*, and seems at once deprived of the power of motion, or the exercise of its usual instinct of self-preservation." Other serpents seem to share this power of fascination, as the *Cobra* and the *Bucephalus*

Capensis. Some think that it is nothing but fright; others attribute it to the

> "strange powers that lie
> Within the magic circle of the eye,"—

as Churchill said, speaking of Garrick.

You ask me about those mysterious and frightful intimacies between children and serpents, of which so many instances have been recorded. I am sure I cannot tell what to make of them. I have seen several such accounts in recent papers, but here is one published in the seventeenth century, which is as striking as any of the more modern ones:—

"Mr. *Herbert Jones* of *Monmouth*, when he was a little Boy, was used to eat his Milk in a Garden in the Morning, and was no sooner there, but a large Snake always came, and eat out of the Dish with him, and did so for a considerable time, till one Morning, he striking the Snake on the Head, it hissed at him. Upon which he told his Mother that the Baby (for so he call'd it) cry'd *Hiss* at him. His Mother had it kill'd, which occasioned him a great *Fit of Sickness*, and 'twas thought would have dy'd, but did recover."

There was likewise one "*William Writtle*, condemned at *Maidston Assizes* for a double murder, told a Minister that was with him after he was condemned, that his mother told him, that when he was a Child, there crept always to him a Snake, wherever she laid him. Sometimes she would convey him up Stairs, and leave him never so little, she should be sure to find a Snake in the Cradle with him, but never perceived it did him any harm."

One of the most striking alleged facts connected with the mysterious relation existing between the serpent and the human species is the influence which the poison of the *Crotalus*, taken internally, seemed to produce over the *moral faculties*, in the experiments instituted by Dr. Hering at Surinam. There is something frightful in the disposition of certain ophidians, as the whipsnake, which darts at the eyes of cattle without any apparent provocation or other motive. It is natural enough that the evil principle should have been represented in the form of a serpent, but it is strange to think of introducing it into a human being like cow-pox by vaccination.

You know all about the *Psylli*, or ancient serpent-tamers, I suppose. Savary gives an account of the modern serpent-tamers in his "Letters on Egypt." These modern jugglers are in the habit of making the venomous *Naja* counterfeit death, lying out straight and stiff, *changing it into a rod*, as the ancient magicians did with their serpents, (probably the same animal,) in the time of Moses.

I am afraid I cannot throw much light on "Christabel" or "Lamia" by any criticism I can offer. Geraldine, in the former, seems to be simply a malignant witch-woman with the *evil eye*, but with no absolute ophidian relationship. Lamia is a serpent transformed by magic into a woman. The idea of both is mythological, and not in any sense physiological. Some women unquestionably suggest the image of serpents; men rarely or never. I have been struck, like many others, with the ophidian head and eye of the famous Rachel.

Your question about inherited predispositions, as limiting the sphere of the will, and, consequently, of moral accountability, opens a very wide range of speculation. I can give you only a brief abstract of my own opinions on this delicate and difficult subject. Crime and sin, being the *preserves* of two great organized interests, have been guarded against all reforming poachers with as great jealousy as the Royal Forests. It is so easy to hang a troublesome fellow! It is so much simpler to consign a soul to perdition, or say masses, for money, to save it, than to take the blame on ourselves for letting it grow up in neglect and run to ruin for want of humanizing influences! They hung poor, crazy Bellingham for shooting Mr. Perceval. The ordinary of Newgate preached to women who were to swing at Tyburn for a petty theft as if they were worse than other people, —just as though he would not have been a pickpocket or shoplifter, himself, if he had been born in a den of thieves and bred up to steal or starve! The English law never began to get hold of the idea that a crime was not necessarily a sin, till Hadfield, who thought he was the Saviour of mankind, was tried for shooting at George the Third;—lucky for him that he did not hit his Majesty!

It is very singular that we recognize all the bodily defects that unfit a man for military service, and all the intellectual ones that limit his range of thought, but always talk at him as if all his moral powers were perfect. I suppose we must punish evil-doers as we extirpate vermin; but I don't know that we have any more right to judge them than we have to judge rats and mice, which are just as good as cats and weasels, though we think it necessary to treat them as criminals.

The limitations of human responsibility have never been properly studied, unless it be by the phrenologists. You know from my lectures that I consider phrenology, as taught, a pseudo-science, and not a branch of positive knowledge; but, for all that, we owe it an immense debt. It has melted the world's conscience in its crucible, and cast it in a new mould, with features less like those of Moloch and more like those of humanity. If it has failed to demonstrate its system of special correspondences, it has proved that there are fixed relations between organization and mind and character. It has brought out that great doctrine of moral insanity, which has done more to make men charitable and soften legal and theological barbarism than any one doctrine that I can think of since the message of peace and good-will to men.

Automatic action in the moral world; the *reflex movement* which *seems* to be self-determination, and has been hanged and howled at as such (metaphorically) for nobody knows how many centuries: until somebody shall study this as Marshall Hall has studied reflex nervous action in the bodily system, I would not give much for men's judgments of each others' characters. Shut up the robber and the defaulter, we must. But what if your oldest boy had been stolen from his cradle and bred in a North-Street cellar? What if you are drinking a little too much wine and smoking a little too much tobacco, and your son takes after you, and so your poor grandson's brain being a little injured in physical texture, he loses the fine moral sense on which you pride yourself, and doesn't see the difference between signing another man's name to a draft and his own?

I suppose the study of automatic action in the moral world (you see what I mean through the apparent contradiction of terms) may be a dangerous one in the view of many people. It is liable to abuse, no doubt. People are always glad to get hold of anything which limits their responsibility. But remember that our moral estimates come down to us from ancestors who hanged children for stealing forty shillings' worth, and sent their souls to perdition for the sin of being born,—who punished the unfortunate families of suicides, and in their eagerness for justice executed one innocent person every three years, on the average, as Sir James Mackintosh tells us.

I do not know in what shape the practical question may present itself to you; but I will tell you my rule in life, and I think you will find it a good one. *Treat bad men exactly as if they were insane.* They are *in-sane*, out of health, morally. Reason, which is food to sound minds, is not tolerated, still less assimilated, unless administered with the greatest caution; perhaps, not at all. Avoid collision with them, so far as you honorably can; keep your temper, if you can,—for one angry man is as good as another; restrain them from violence, promptly, completely, and with the least possible injury, just as in the case of maniacs,—and when you have got rid of them, or got them tied hand and foot so that they can do no mischief, sit down and contemplate them charitably, remembering that nine tenths of their perversity comes from outside influences, drunken ancestors, abuse in childhood, bad company, from which you have happily been preserved, and for some of which you, as a member of society, may be fractionally responsible. I think also that there are *special influences* which *work in the blood like ferments*, and I have a suspicion that some of those curious old stories I cited may have more recent parallels. Have you ever met with any cases which admitted of a solution like that which I have mentioned?

Yours very truly,

Bernard Langdon to Philip Staples

MY DEAR PHILIP,—

I have been for some months established in this place, turning the main crank of the machinery for the manufactory of accomplishments superintended by, or rather worked to the profit of, a certain Mr. Silas Peckham. He is a poor wretch, with a little thin fishy blood in his body, lean and flat, long-armed and large-handed, thick-jointed and thin-muscled,—you know those unwholesome, weak-eyed, half-fed creatures, that look not fit to be round among live folks, and yet not quite dead enough to bury. If you ever hear of my being in court to answer to a charge of assault and battery, you may guess that I have been giving him a thrashing to settle off old scores; for he is a tyrant, and has come pretty near killing his principal lady-assistant with overworking her and keeping her out of all decent privileges.

Helen Darley is this lady's name,—twenty-two or -three years old, I should think,—a very sweet, pale woman,—daughter of the usual country-clergyman,—thrown on her own resources from an early age, and the rest: a common story, but an uncommon person,—very. All conscience and sensibility, I should say,—a cruel worker,—no kind of regard for herself,—seems as fragile and supple as a young willow-shoot, but try her and you find she has the spring in her of a steel cross-bow. I am glad I happened to come to this place, if it were only for her sake. I have saved that girl's life; I am as sure of it as if I had pulled her out of the fire or water.

Of course I'm in love with her, you say,—we always love those whom we have benefited; "saved her life,—her love was the reward of his devotion," etc., etc., as in a regular set novel. In love, Philip? Well, about that,—I love Helen Darley—very much: there is hardly anybody I love so well. What a noble creature she is! One of those that just go right on, do their own work and everybody else's, killing themselves inch by inch without ever thinking about it,—singing and dancing at their toil when they begin, worn and saddened after a while, but pressing steadily on, tottering by-and-by, and catching at the rail by the way-side to help them lift one foot before the other, and at last falling, face down, arms stretched forward——

Philip, my boy, do you know I am the sort of man that locks his door sometimes and cries his heart out of his eyes, —that can sob like a woman and not be ashamed of it? I come of fighting-blood on one side, you know; I think I could be savage on occasion. But I am tender,—more and more tender as I come into my fulness of manhood. I don't like to strike a man, (laugh, if you like,—I know I hit hard when I do strike,)—but what I can't stand is the sight of these poor, patient, toiling women, who never find out in this life how good they are, and never know what it is to be told they are angels while they still wear the pleasing incumbrances of humanity. I don't know what to make of these cases. To think that a woman is never to be a woman again, whatever she may come to as an unsexed angel,— and that she should die unloved! Why does not somebody come and carry off this noble woman, waiting here all ready to make a man happy? Philip, do you know the pathos there is in the eyes of unsought women, oppressed with the burden of an inner life unshared? I can see into them now as I could not in those earlier days. I sometimes think their pupils dilate on purpose to let my consciousness glide through them; indeed, I dread them, I come so close to the nerve of the soul itself in these momentary intimacies. You used to tell me I was a Turk,—that my heart was full of pigeon-holes, with accommodations inside for a whole flock of doves. I don't know but I am still as Youngish as ever in my ways,—Brigham-Youngish, I mean; at any rate, I always want to give a little love to all the poor things that cannot have a whole man to themselves. If they would only be contented with a little!

Here now are two girls in this school where I am teaching. One of them, Rosa M., is not more than sixteen years old, I think they say; but Nature has forced her into a tropical luxuriance of beauty, as if it were July with her, instead of May. I suppose it is all natural enough that this girl should like a young man's attention, even if he were a grave schoolmaster; but the eloquence of this young thing's look is unmistakable,—and yet she does not know the language it is talking,—they none of them do; and there is where a good many poor creatures of our good-for-nothing sex are mistaken. There is no danger of my being rash, but I think this girl will cost somebody his life yet. She is one of those women men make a quarrel about and fight to the death for,—the old feral instinct, you know.

Pray, don't think I am lost in conceit, but there is another girl here who I begin to think looks with a certain kindness on me. Her name is Elsie V., and she is the only daughter and heiress of an old family in this place. She is a portentous and almost fearful creature. If I should tell you all I know and half of what I fancy about her, you would tell me to get my life insured at once. Yet she is the most painfully interesting being,—so handsome! so lonely! —for she has no friends among the girls, and sits apart from them,—with black hair like the flow of a mountain-brook after a thaw, with a low-browed, scowling beauty of face, and such eyes as were never seen before, I really believe, in any human creature.

Philip, I don't know what to say about this Elsie. There is something about her I have not fathomed. I have conjectures which I could not utter to any living soul. I dare not even hint the possibilities which have suggested themselves to me. This I will say,—that I do take the most intense interest in this young person, an interest much more like pity than love in its common sense. If what I guess at is true, of all the tragedies of existence I ever knew this is the saddest, and yet so full of meaning! Do not ask me any questions,—I have said more than I meant to already; but I am involved in strange doubts and perplexities,—in dangers too, very possibly,—and it is a relief just to speak ever so guardedly of them to an early and faithful friend.

Yours ever,

BERNARD

P.S. I remember you had a copy of Fortunius Licetus' "De Monstris" among your old books. Can't you lend it to me for a while? I am curious, and it will amuse me.

CHAPTER XVII

OLD SOPHY CALLS ON THE REVEREND DOCTOR

The two meeting-houses which faced each other like a pair of fighting-cocks had not flapped their wings or crowed at each other for a considerable time. The Reverend Mr. Fairweather had been dyspeptic and low-spirited of late, and was too languid for controversy. The Reverend Doctor Honeywood had been very busy with his benevolent associations, and had discoursed chiefly on practical matters, to the neglect of special doctrinal subjects. His senior deacon ventured to say to him that some of his people required to be reminded of the great fundamental doctrine of the worthlessness of all human efforts and motives. Some of them were altogether too much pleased with the success of the Temperance Society and the Association for the Relief of the Poor. There was a pestilent heresy about, concerning the satisfaction to be derived from a good conscience,—as if anybody ever did anything which was not to be hated, loathed, despised, and condemned.

The old minister listened gravely, with an inward smile, and told his deacon that he would attend to his suggestion. After the deacon had gone, he tumbled over his manuscripts, until at length he came upon his first-rate old sermon on "Human Nature." He had read a great deal of hard theology, and had at last reached that curious state which is so common in good ministers,—that, namely, in which they contrive to switch off their logical faculties on the narrow side-track of their technical dogmas, while the great freight-train of their substantial human qualities keeps in the main highway of common-sense, in which kindly souls are always found by all who approach them by their human side.

The Doctor read his sermon with a pleasant, paternal interest: it was well argued from his premises. Here and there he dashed his pen through a harsh expression. Now and then he added an explanation or qualified a broad statement. But his mind was on the logical side-track, and he followed the chain of reasoning without fairly perceiving where it would lead him, if he carried it into real life.

He was just touching up the final proposition, when his granddaughter, Letty, once before referred to, came into the room with her smiling face and lively movement. Miss Letty or Letitia Forrester was a city-bred girl of some fifteen or sixteen years old, who was passing the summer with her grandfather for the sake of country air and quiet. It was a sensible arrangement; for, having the promise of figuring as a belle by-and-by, and being a little given to dancing, and having a voice which drew a pretty dense circle around the piano when she sat down to play and sing, it was hard to keep her from being carried into society before her time, by the mere force of mutual attraction. Fortunately, she had some quiet as well as some social tastes, and was willing enough to pass two or three of the summer months in the country, where she was much better bestowed than she would have been at one of those watering-places where so many half-formed girls get prematurely hardened in the vice of self-consciousness.

Miss Letty was altogether too wholesome, hearty, and high-strung a young girl to be a model, according to the flat-chested and cachectic pattern which is the classical type of certain excellent young females, often the subjects of biographical memoirs. But the old minister was proud of his granddaughter for all that. She was so full of life, so graceful, so generous, so vivacious, so ready always to do all she could for him and for everybody, so perfectly frank in her avowed delight in the pleasures which this miserable world offered her in the shape of natural beauty, of poetry, of music, of companionship, of books, of cheerful coöperation in the tasks of those about her, that the Reverend Doctor could not find it in his heart to condemn her because she was deficient in those particular graces and that signal other-worldliness he had sometimes noticed in feeble young persons suffering from various chronic diseases which impaired their vivacity and removed them from the range of temptation.

When Letty, therefore, came bounding into the old minister's study, he glanced up from his manuscript, and, as his eye fell upon her, it flashed across him that there was nothing so very monstrous and unnatural about the specimen of congenital perversion he was looking at, with his features opening into their pleasantest sunshine. Technically, according to the fifth proposition of the sermon on Human Nature, very bad, no doubt. Practically, according to the fact before him, a very pretty piece of the Creator's handiwork, body and soul. Was it not a conceivable thing that the divine grace might show itself in different forms in a fresh young girl like Letitia, and in that poor thing he had visited yesterday, half-grown, half-colored, in bed for the last year with hip-disease? Was it to be supposed that this healthy young girl, with life throbbing all over her, *could*, without a miracle, be good according to the invalid pattern and formula?

And yet there were mysteries in human nature which pointed to some tremendous perversion of its tendencies, —to some profound, radical vice of moral constitution, native or transmitted, as you will have it, but positive, at any rate, as the leprosy, breaking out in the blood of races, guard them ever so carefully. Did he not know the case of a young lady in Rockland, daughter of one of the first families in the place, a very beautiful and noble creature to look at, for whose bringing-up nothing had been spared, —a girl who had had governesses to teach her at the house, who had been indulged almost too kindly,—a girl whose father had given himself up to her, he being himself a pure and high-souled man?—and yet this girl was accused in whispers of having been on the very verge of committing a fatal crime; she was an object of fear to all who knew the dark hints which had been let fall about her, and there were some that believed—— Why, what was this but an instance of the total obliquity and degeneration of the moral principle? and to what could it be owing, but to an innate organic tendency?

"Busy, grandpapa?" said Letty, and without waiting for an answer kissed his cheek with a pair of lips made on purpose for that little function,—fine, but richly turned out, the corners tucked in with a finish of pretty dimples, the rose-bud lips of girlhood's June.

The old gentleman looked at his granddaughter. Nature swelled up from his heart in a wave that sent a glow to his cheek and a sparkle to his eye. But it is very hard to be interrupted just as we are winding up a string of propositions with the grand conclusion which is the statement in brief of all that has gone before: our own starting-point, into which we have been trying to back our reader or listener as one backs a horse into the shafts.

"*Video meliora, proboque,*—I see the better, and approve it; *deteriora sequor*, I follow after the worse; 'tis that natural dislike to what is good, pure, holy, and true, that inrooted selfishness, totally insensible to the claims of"——

Here the worthy man was interrupted by Miss Letty.

"Do come, if you can, grandpapa," said the young girl; "here is a poor old black woman wants to see you so much!"

The good minister was as kind-hearted as if he had never groped in the dust and ashes of those cruel old abstractions which have killed out so much of the world's life and happiness. "With the heart man believeth unto righteousness"; a man's love is the measure of his fitness for good or bad company here or elsewhere. Men are tattooed with their special beliefs like so many South-Sea Islanders; but a real human heart, with Divine love in it, beats with the same glow under all the patterns of all earth's thousand tribes!

The Doctor sighed, and folded the sermon, and laid the Quarto Cruden on it. He rose from his desk, and, looking once more at the young girl's face, forgot his logical conclusions, and said to himself that she was a little angel, —which was in violent contradiction to the leading doctrine of his sermon on Human Nature. And so he followed her out of the study into the wide entry of the old-fashioned country-house.

An old black woman sat on the plain oaken settle which humble visitors waiting to see the minister were wont to occupy. She was old, but how old it would be very hard to guess. She might be seventy. She might be ninety. One could not swear she was not a hundred. Black women remain at a stationary age (to the eyes of *white* people, at least) for thirty years. They do not appear to change during this period any more than so many Trenton trilobites. Bent up, wrinkled, yellow-eyed, with long upper-lip, projecting jaws, retreating chin, still meek features, long arms, large flat hands with uncolored palms and slightly webbed fingers, it was impossible not to see in this old creature a hint of the gradations by which life climbs up through the lower natures to the highest human developments. We cannot tell such old women's ages because we do not understand the physiognomy of a race so unlike our own. No doubt they see a great deal in each other's faces that we cannot, —changes of color and expression as real as our own, blushes and sudden betrayals of feeling,—just as these two canaries know what their single notes and short sentences and full song with this or that variation mean, though it is a mystery to us unplumed mortals.

This particular old black woman was a striking specimen of her class. Old as she looked, her eye was bright and knowing. She wore a red-and-yellow turban, which set off her complexion well, and hoops of gold in her ears, and beads of gold about her neck, and an old funeral ring upon her finger. She had that touching stillness about her which belongs to animals that wait to be spoken to and then look up with a kind of sad humility.

"Why, Sophy!" said the good minister, "is this you?"

She looked up with the still expression on her face. "It's ol' Sophy," she said.

"Why," said the Doctor, "I did not believe you could walk so far as this to save the Union. Bring Sophy a glass of wine, Letty. Wine's good for old folks like Sophy and me, after walking a good way, or preaching a good while."

The young girl stepped into the back-parlor, where she found the great pewter flagon in which the wine that was left after each communion-service was brought to the minister's house. With much toil she managed to tip it so as to get a couple of glasses filled. The minister tasted his, and made old Sophy finish hers.

"I wan' to see you 'n' talk wi' you all alone," she said presently.

The minister got up and led the way towards his study. "To be sure," he said; he had only waited for her to rest a moment before he asked her into the library. The young girl took her gently by the arm, and helped her feeble steps along the passage. When they reached the study, she smoothed the cushion of a rocking-chair, and made the old woman sit down in it. Then she tripped lightly away, and left her alone with the minister.

Old Sophy was a member of the Reverend Doctor Honeywood's church. She had been put through the necessary confessions in a tolerably satisfactory manner. To be sure, as her grandfather had been a cannibal chief, according to the common story, and, at any rate, a terrible wild savage, and as her mother retained to the last some of the prejudices of her early education, there was a heathen flavor in her Christianity which had often scandalized the elder of the minister's two deacons. But the good minister had smoothed matters over: had explained that allowances were to be made for those who had been long sitting without the gate of Zion,—that, no doubt, a part of the curse which descended to the children of Ham consisted in "having the understanding darkened," as well as the skin,—and so had brought his suspicious senior deacon to tolerate old Sophy as one of the communion of fellow-sinners.

——Poor things! How little we know the simple notions with which these rudiments of souls are nourished by the Divine Goodness! Did not Mrs. Professor come home this very blessed morning with a story of one of her old black women?

"And how do you feel to-day, Mrs. Robinson?"

"Oh, my dear, I have this singing in my head all the time." (What doctors call *tinnitus aurium*.)

"She's got a cold in the head," said old Mrs. Rider.

"Oh, no, my dear! Whatever I'm thinking about, it's all this singing, this music. When I'm thinking of the dear Redeemer, it all turns into this singing and music. When the clark came to see me, I asked him if he couldn't cure me, and he said, No,—it was the Holy Spirit in me, singing to me; and all the time I hear this beautiful music, and it's the Holy Spirit a-singing to me."——

The good man waited for Sophy to speak; but she did not open her lips as yet.

"I hope you are not troubled in mind or body," he said to her at length, finding she did not speak.

The poor old woman took out a white handkerchief, and lifted it to her black face. She could not say a word for her tears and sobs.

The minister would have consoled her; he was used to tears, and could in most cases withstand their contagion manfully; but something choked his voice suddenly, and when he called upon it, he got no answer, but a tremulous movement of the muscles, which was worse than silence.

At last she spoke.

"Oh, no, no, no! It's my poor girl, my darling, my beauty, my baby, that's grown up to be a woman; she will come to a bad end; she will do something that will make them kill her or shut her up all her life. Oh, Doctor, Doctor, save her, pray for her! It a'n't her fault. It a'n't her fault. If they knew all that I know, they wouldn' blame that poor child. I must tell you, Doctor: if I should die, perhaps nobody else would tell you. Massa Venner can't talk about it. Doctor Kittredge won't talk about it. Nobody but old Sophy to tell you, Doctor; and old Sophy can't die without telling you."

The kind minister soothed the poor old soul with those gentle, quieting tones which had carried peace and comfort to so many chambers of sickness and sorrow, to so many hearts overburdened by the trials laid upon them.

Old Sophy became quiet in a few minutes, and proceeded to tell her story. She told it in the low half-whisper which is the natural voice of lips oppressed with grief and fears; with quick glances around the apartment from time to time, as if she dreaded lest the dim portraits on the walls and the dark folios on the shelves might overhear her words.

It was not one of those conversations which a third person can report minutely, unless by that miracle of clairvoyance known to the readers of stories made out of authors' brains. Yet its main character can be imparted in a much briefer space than the old black woman took to give all its details.

She went far back to the time when Dudley Venner was born,—she being then a middle-aged woman. The heir and hope of a family which had been narrowing down as if doomed to extinction, he had been surrounded with every care and trained by the best education he could have in New England. He had left college, and was studying the profession which gentlemen of leisure most affect, when he fell in love with a young girl left in the world almost alone, as he was. The old woman told the story of his young love and his joyous bridal with a tenderness which had something more, even, than her family sympathies to account for it. Had she not hanging over her bed a paper-cutting of a profile—jet black, but not blacker than the face it represented—of one who would have been her own husband in the small years of this century, if the vessel in which he went to sea, like Jamie in the ballad, had not sailed away and never come back to land? Had she not her bits of furniture stowed away which had been got ready for her own wedding,—*two* rocking-chairs, one worn with long use, one kept for him so long that it had grown a superstition with her never to sit in it,—and might he not come back yet, after all? Had she not her chest of linen ready for her humble house-keeping, with store of serviceable huckaback and piles of neatly folded kerchiefs, wherefrom this one that showed so white against her black face was taken, for that she knew her eyes would betray her in "the presence"?

All the first part of the story the old woman told tenderly, and yet dwelling upon every incident with a loving pleasure. How happy this young couple had been, what plans and projects of improvement they had formed, how they lived in each other, always together, so young and fresh and beautiful as she remembered them in that one early summer when they walked arm in arm through the wilderness of roses that ran riot in the garden,—she told of this as loath to leave it and come to the woe that lay beneath.

She told the whole story;—shall I repeat it? Not now. If, in the course of relating the incidents I have undertaken to report, *it tells itself,* perhaps this will be better than to run the risk of producing a painful impression on some of those susceptible readers whom it would be ill-advised to disturb or excite, when they rather require to be amused and soothed. In our pictures of life, we must show the flowering-out of terrible growths which have their roots deep, deep underground. Just how far we shall lay bare the unseemly roots themselves is a matter of discretion and taste, in which none of us are infallible.

The old woman told the whole story of Elsie, of her birth, of her peculiarities of person and disposition, of the passionate fears and hopes with which her father had watched the course of her development. She recounted all her strange ways, from the hour when she first tried to crawl across the carpet, and her father's look as she worked her way towards him. With the memory of Juliet's nurse she told the story of her teething, and how, the woman to whose breast she had clung dying suddenly about that time, they had to struggle hard with the child before she would learn the accomplishment of feeding with a spoon. And so of her fierce plays and fiercer disputes with that boy who had been her companion, and the whole scene of the quarrel when she struck him with those sharp white teeth, frightening her, old Sophy, almost to death; for, as she said, the boy would have died, if it hadn't been for the old Doctor's galloping over as fast as he could gallop and burning the places right out of his arm. Then came the story of that other incident, sufficiently alluded to already, which had produced such an ecstasy of fright and left such a nightmare of apprehension in the household. And so the old woman came down to this present time. That boy she never loved nor trusted was grown to a dark, dangerous-looking man, and he was under their roof. He wanted to marry our poor Elsie, and Elsie hated him, and sometimes she would look at him over her shoulder just as she used to look at that woman she hated; and she, old Sophy, couldn't sleep for thinking she should hear a scream from the white chamber some night and find him in spasms such as that woman came so near dying with. And then there was something about Elsie she did not know what to make of: she would sit and hang her head sometimes, and look as if she were dreaming; and she brought home books they said a young gentleman up at the great school lent her; and once she heard her whisper in her sleep, and she talked as young girls do to themselves when they're thinking about somebody they have a liking for and think nobody knows it.

She finished her long story at last. The minister had listened to it in perfect silence. He sat still even when she had done speaking,—still, and lost in thought. It was a very awkward matter for him to have a hand in. Old Sophy was his parishioner, but the Venners had a pew in the Reverend Mr. Fairweather's meeting-house. It would seem that he, Mr. Fairweather, was the natural adviser of the parties most interested. Had he sense and spirit enough to deal with such people? Was there enough capital of humanity in his somewhat limited nature to furnish sympathy and unshrinking service for his friends in an emergency? or was he too busy with his own attacks of spiritual neuralgia, and too much occupied with taking account of stock of his own thin-blooded offences, to forget himself and his personal interests on the small scale and the large, and run a risk of his life, if need were, at any rate give himself up without reserve to the dangerous task of guiding and counselling these distressed and imperilled fellow-creatures?

The good minister thought the best thing to do would be to call and talk over some of these matters with Brother Fairweather,—or so he would call him at times, especially if his senior deacon were not within earshot. Having settled this point, he comforted Sophy with a few words of counsel and a promise of coming to see her very soon. He then called his man to put the old white horse into the chaise and drive Sophy back to the mansion-house.

When the Doctor sat down to his sermon again, it looked very differently from the way it had looked at the moment he left it. When he came to think of it, he did not feel quite so sure *practically* about that matter of the utter natural selfishness of everybody. There was Letty, now, seemed to take a very *un*selfish interest in that old black woman, and indeed in poor people generally; perhaps it would not be too much to say that she was always thinking of other people. He thought he had seen other young persons naturally unselfish, thoughtful for others; it seemed to be a family trait in some he had known.

But most of all he was exercised about this poor girl whose story Sophy had been telling. If what the old woman believed was true,—and it had too much semblance of probability,—what became of his theory of ingrained moral obliquity applied to such a case? If by the visitation of God a person receives any injury which impairs the intellect or the moral perceptions, is it not monstrous to judge such a person by our common working standards of right and wrong? Certainly, everybody will answer, in cases where there is a palpable organic change brought about, as when a blow on the head produces insanity. Fools! How long will it be before we shall learn that for every wound which betrays itself to the sight by a scar, there are a thousand unseen mutilations that cripple, each of them, some one or more of our highest faculties? If what Sophy told and believed was the real truth, what prayers could be agonizing enough, what tenderness could be deep enough, for this poor, lost, blighted, hapless, blameless child of misfortune, struck by such a doom as perhaps no living creature in all the sisterhood of humanity shared with her?

The minister thought these matters over until his mind was bewildered with doubts and tossed to and fro on that stormy deep of thought heaving forever beneath the conflict of windy dogmas. He laid by his old sermon. He put back a pile of old commentators with their eyes and mouths and hearts full of the dust of the schools. Then he opened the book of Genesis at the eighteenth chapter and read that remarkable argument of Abraham's with his Maker in which he boldly appeals to first principles. He took as his text, "Shall not the Judge of all the earth do right?" and began to write his sermon, afterwards so famous,—"On the Obligations of an Infinite Creator to a Finite Creature."

It astonished the good people, who had been accustomed so long to repeat mechanically their Oriental hyperboles of self-abasement, to hear their worthy minister maintaining that the dignified attitude of the old Patriarch, insisting on what was reasonable and fair with reference to his fellow-creatures, was really much more respectful to his Maker, and a great deal manlier and more to his credit, than if he had yielded the whole matter, and pretended that men had not rights as well as duties. The same logic which had carried him to certain conclusions with reference to human nature, this same irresistible logic carried him straight on from his text until he arrived at those other results, which not only astonished his people, as was said, but surprised himself. He went so far in defence of the rights of man, that he put his foot into several heresies, for which men had been burned so often, it was time, if ever it could be, to acknowledge the demonstration of the *argumentum ad ignem*. He did not believe in the responsibility of idiots. He did not believe a new-born infant was morally answerable for other people's acts. He thought a man with a crooked spine would never be called to account for not walking erect. He thought if the crook was in his brain, instead of his back, he could not fairly be blamed for any consequence of this natural defect, whatever lawyers or divines might call it. He argued, that, if a person inherited a perfect mind, body, and disposition, and had perfect teaching from infancy, that person could do nothing more than keep the moral law perfectly. But supposing that the Creator allows a person to be born with an hereditary or ingrafted organic tendency, and then puts this person into the hands of teachers incompetent or positively bad, is not what is called *sin* or transgression of the law necessarily involved in the premises? Is not a Creator bound to guard his children against the ruin which inherited ignorance might entail on them? Would it be fair for a parent to put into a child's hands the title-deeds to all its future possessions, and a bunch of matches? And are not men children, nay, babes, in the eye of Omniscience?—The minister grew bold in his questions. Had not he as good right to ask questions as Abraham?

This was the dangerous vein of speculation in which the Reverend Doctor Honeywood found himself involved, as a consequence of the suggestions forced upon him by old

Sophy's communication. The truth was, the good man had got so humanized by mixing up with other people in various benevolent schemes, that, the very moment he could escape from his old scholastic abstractions, he took the side of humanity instinctively, just as the Father of the Faithful did,—all honor be to the noble old Patriarch for insisting on the worth of an honest man, and making the best terms he could for a very ill-conditioned metropolis, which might possibly, however, have contained ten righteous people, for whose sake it should be spared!

The consequence of all this was, that he was in a singular and seemingly self-contradictory state of mind when he took his hat and cane and went forth to call on his heretical brother. The old minister took it for granted that the Reverend Mr. Fairweather knew the private history of his parishioner's family. He did not reflect that there are griefs men *never* put into words,—that there are fears which must not be spoken,—intimate matters of consciousness which must be carried, as bullets which have been driven deep into the living tissues are sometimes carried, for a whole lifetime,—*encysted* griefs, if we may borrow the chirurgeon's term, never to be reached, never to be seen, never to be thrown out, but to go into the dust with the frame that bore them about with it, during long years of anguish, known only to the sufferer and his Maker. Dudley Venner had talked with his minister about this child of his. But he had talked cautiously, feeling his way for sympathy, looking out for those indications of tact and judgment which would warrant him in some partial communication, at least, of the origin of his doubts and fears, and never finding them.

There was something about the Reverend Mr. Fairweather which repressed all attempts at confidential intercourse. What this something was, Dudley Venner could hardly say; but he felt it distinctly, and it sealed his lips. He never got beyond certain generalities connected with education and religious instruction. The minister could not help discovering, however, that there were difficulties connected with this girl's management, and he heard enough outside of the family to convince him that she had manifested tendencies, from an early age, at variance with the theoretical opinions he was in the habit of preaching, and in a dim way of holding for truth, as to the natural dispositions of the human being.

About this terrible fact of congenital obliquity his new beliefs began to cluster as a centre, and to take form as a crystal around its nucleus. Still, he might perhaps have struggled against them, had it not been for the little Roman Catholic chapel he passed every Sunday, on his way to the meeting-house. Such a crowd of worshippers, swarming into the pews like bees, filling all the aisles, running over at the door like berries heaped too full in the measure,—some kneeling on the steps, some standing on the side-walk, hats off, heads down, lips moving, some looking on devoutly from the other side of the street! Oh, could he have followed his own Bridget, maid of all work, into the heart of that steaming throng, and bowed his head while the priests intoned their Latin prayers! could he have snuffed up the cloud of frankincense, and felt that he was in the great ark which holds the better half of the Christian world, while all around it are wretched creatures, some struggling against the waves in leaky boats, and some on ill-connected rafts, and some with their heads just above water, thinking to ride out the flood which is to sweep the earth clean of sinners, upon their own private, individual life-preservers!

Such was the present state of mind of the Reverend Chauncy Fairweather, when his clerical brother called upon him to talk over the questions to which old Sophy had called his attention.

CHAPTER XVIII

THE REVEREND DOCTOR CALLS ON BROTHER FAIRWEATHER

For the last few months, while all these various matters were going on in Rockland, the Reverend Chauncy Fairweather had been busy with the records of ancient councils and the writings of the early fathers. The more he read, the more discontented he became with the platform upon which he and his people were standing. They and he were clearly in a minority, and his deep inward longing to be with the majority was growing into an engrossing passion. He yearned especially towards the good old unquestioning, authoritative Mother Church, with her articles of faith which took away the necessity for private judgment, with her traditional forms and ceremonies, and her whole apparatus of stimulants and anodynes.

About this time he procured a breviary and kept it in his desk under the loose papers. He sent to a Catholic bookstore and obtained a small crucifix suspended from a string of beads. He ordered his new coat to be cut very narrow in the collar and to be made single-breasted. He began an informal series of religious conversations with Miss O'Brien, the young person of Irish extraction already referred to as Bridget, maid of all work. These not proving very satisfactory, he managed to fall in with Father McShane, the Catholic priest of the Rockland church. Father McShane encouraged his nibble very scientifically. It would be such a fine thing to bring over one of those Protestant heretics, and a "liberal" one too!—not that there was any real difference between them, but it sounded better, to say that one of these rationalizing free-and-equal religionists had been made a convert than any of those half-way Protestants who were the slaves of catechisms instead of councils, and of commentators instead of popes. The subtle priest played his disciple with his finest tackle. It was hardly necessary: when anything or anybody wishes to be caught, a bare hook and a coarse line are all that is needed.

If a man has a genuine, sincere, hearty wish to get rid of his liberty, if he is really bent upon becoming a slave, nothing can stop him. And the temptation is to some natures a very great one. Liberty is often a heavy burden on a man. It involves that necessity for perpetual choice which is the kind of labor men have always dreaded. In common life we shirk it by forming *habits*, which take the place of self-determination. In politics party-organization saves us the pains of much thinking before deciding how to cast our vote. In religious matters there are great multitudes watching us perpetually, each propagandist ready with his bundle of finalities, which having accepted we may be at peace. The more absolute the submission demanded, the stronger the temptation becomes to those who have been long tossed among doubts and conflicts.

So it is that in all the quiet bays which indent the shores of the great ocean of thought, at every sinking wharf, we see moored the hulks and the razees of enslaved or half-enslaved intelligences. They rock peacefully as children in their cradles on the subdued swell which comes feebly in over the bar at the harbor's mouth, slowly crusting with barnacles, pulling at their iron cables as if they really wanted to be free, but better contented to remain bound as they are. For these no more the round unwalled horizon of the open sea, the joyous breeze aloft, the furrow, the foam, the sparkle, that track the rushing keel! They have escaped the dangers of the wave, and lie still henceforth, evermore. Happiest of souls, if lethargy is bliss, and palsy the chief beatitude!

America owes its political freedom to religious Protestantism. But political freedom is reacting on religious prescription with still mightier force. We wonder, therefore, when we find a soul which was born to a full sense of individual liberty, an unchallenged right of self-determination on every new alleged truth offered to its intelligence, voluntarily surrendering any portion of its liberty to a spiritual dictatorship which always proves to rest, in the last analysis, on *a majority vote*, nothing more nor less, commonly an old one, passed in those barbarous times when men cursed and murdered each other for differences of opinion, and of course were not in a condition to settle the beliefs of a comparatively civilized community.

In our disgust, we are liable to be intolerant. We forget that weakness is not in itself a sin. We forget that even cowardice may call for our most lenient judgment, if it spring from innate infirmity. Who of us does not look with great tenderness on the young chieftain in the "Fair Maid of Perth," when he confesses his want of courage? All of us love companionship and sympathy; some of us may love them too much. All of us are more or less imaginative in our theology. Some of us may find the aid of material symbols a comfort, if not a necessity. The boldest thinker may have his moments of languor and discouragement, when he feels as if he could willingly exchange faiths with the old beldame crossing herself at the cathedral-door,—nay, that, if he could drop all coherent thought, and lie in the flowery meadow with the brown-eyed solemnly unthinking cattle, looking up to the sky, and all their simple consciousness staining itself blue, then down to the grass, and life turning to a mere greenness, blended with confused scents of herbs,—no individual mind-movement such as men are teased with, but the great calm cattle-sense of all time and all places that know the milky smell of herds,—if he could be like these, he would be content to be driven home by the cow-boy, and share the grassy banquet of the king of ancient Babylon. Let us be very generous, then, in our judgment of those who leave the front ranks of thought for the company of the meek non-combatants who follow with the baggage and provisions. Age, illness, too much wear and tear, a half-formed paralysis, may bring any of us to this pass. But while we can think and maintain the rights of our own individuality against every human combination, let us not forget to caution all who are disposed to waver that there is a cowardice which is criminal, and a longing for rest which it is baseness to indulge. God help him, over whose dead soul in his living body must be uttered the sad supplication, *Requiescat in pace!*

A knock at the Reverend Mr. Fairweather's study-door called his eyes from the book on which they were intent. He looked up, as if expecting a welcome guest.

The Reverend Pierrepont Honeywood, D.D., entered the study of the Reverend Chauncy Fairweather. He was not the expected guest. Mr. Fairweather slipped the book he was reading into a half-open drawer, and pushed in the drawer. He slid something which rattled under a paper lying on the table. He rose with a slight change of color, and welcomed, a little awkwardly, his unusual visitor.

"Good evening, Brother Fairweather!" said the Reverend Doctor, in a very cordial, good-humored way. "I hope I am not spoiling one of those eloquent sermons I never have a chance to hear."

"Not at all, not at all," the younger clergyman answered, in a languid tone, with a kind of habitual half-querulousness which belonged to it,—the vocal expression which we meet with now and then, and which says as plainly as so many words could say it, "I am a suffering individual. I am persistently undervalued, wronged, and imposed upon by mankind and the powers of the universe generally. But I endure all. I endure *you*. Speak. I listen. It is a burden to me, but I even approve. I sacrifice myself. Behold this movement of my lips! It is a smile."

The Reverend Doctor knew this forlorn way of Mr. Fairweather's, and was not troubled by it. He proceeded to relate the circumstances of his visit from the old black woman, and the fear she was in about the young girl, who being a parishioner of Mr. Fairweather's, he had thought it best to come over and speak to him about old Sophy's fears and fancies.

In telling the old woman's story, he alluded only vaguely to those peculiar circumstances to which she had attributed so much importance, taking it for granted that the other minister must be familiar with the whole series of incidents she had related. The old minister was mistaken, as we have before seen. Mr. Fairweather had been settled in the place only about ten years, and, if he had heard a strange hint now and then about Elsie, had never considered it as anything more than idle and ignorant, if not malicious, village-gossip. All that he fully understood was that this had been a perverse and unmanageable child, and that the extraordinary care which had been bestowed on her had been so far thrown away that she was a dangerous, self-willed girl, whom all feared and almost all shunned, as if she carried with her some malignant influence.

He replied, therefore, after hearing the story, that Elsie had always given trouble. There seemed to be a kind of natural obliquity about her. Perfectly unaccountable. A very dark case. Never amenable to good influences. Had sent her good books from the Sunday-school library. Remembered that she tore out the frontispiece of one of them, and kept it, and flung the book out of the window. It was a picture of Eve's temptation; and he recollected her saying that Eve was a good woman,—and she'd have done just so, if she'd been there. A very sad child,—very sad; bad from infancy.—He had talked himself bold, and said all at once,—

"Doctor, do you know I am almost ready to accept your doctrine of the congenital sinfulness of human nature? I am afraid that is the only thing which goes to the bottom of the difficulty."

The old minister's face did not open so approvingly as Mr. Fairweather had expected.

"Why, yes,—well,—many find comfort in it,—I believe;—there is much to be said,—there are many bad people,—and bad children,—I can't be so sure about bad babies,—though they cry very malignantly at times,—especially if they have the stomach-ache. But I really don't know how to condemn this poor Elsie; she may have impulses that act in her like instincts in the lower animals, and so not come under the bearing of our ordinary rules of judgment."

"But this depraved tendency, Doctor,—this unaccountable perverseness. My dear Sir, I am afraid your school is in the right about human nature. Oh, those words of the Psalmist, 'shapen in iniquity,' and the rest! What are we to do with them,—we who teach that the soul of a child is an unstained white tablet?"

"King David was very subject to fits of humility, and much given to self-reproaches," said the Doctor, in a rather dry way. "We owe you and your friends a good deal for calling attention to the natural graces, which, after all, may, perhaps, be considered as another form of manifestation of the divine influence. Some of our writers have pressed rather too hard on the tendencies of the human soul toward evil as such. It may be questioned whether these views have not interfered with the sound training of certain young persons, sons of clergymen and others. I am nearer of your mind about the possibility of educating children so that they shall become good Christians without any violent transition. That is what I should hope for from bringing them up 'in the nurture and admonition of the Lord.'"

The younger minister looked puzzled, but presently answered,—

"Possibly we may have called attention to some neglected truths; but, after all, I fear we must go to the old school, if we want to get at the root of the matter. I know there is an outward amiability about many young persons, some young girls especially, that seems like genuine goodness; but I have been disposed of late to lean toward your view, that these human affections, as we see them in our children,—ours, I say, though I have not the fearful responsibility of training any of my own,—are only a kind of disguised and sinful selfishness."

The old minister groaned in spirit. His heart had been softened by the sweet influences of children and grandchildren. He thought of a half-sized grave in the burial-ground, and the fine, brave, noble-hearted boy he laid in it thirty years before,—the sweet, cheerful child who had made his home all sunshine until the day when he was brought into it, his long curls dripping, his fresh lips purpled in death,—foolish dear little blessed creature to throw himself into the deep water to save the drowning boy, who clung about him and carried him under! Disguised selfishness! And his granddaughter too, whose disguised selfishness was the light of his household!

"Don't call it my view!" he said. "Abstractly, perhaps, all natures may be considered vitiated; but practically, as I see it in life, the divine grace keeps pace with the perverted instincts from infancy in many natures. Besides, this perversion itself may often be disease, bad habits transmitted, like drunkenness, or some hereditary misfortune, as with this Elsie we were talking about."

The younger minister was completely mystified. At every step he made towards the Doctor's recognized theological position, the Doctor took just one step towards his. They would cross each other soon at this rate, and might as well exchange pulpits,—as Colonel Sprowle once wished they would, it may be remembered.

The doctor, though a much clearer-headed man, was almost equally puzzled. He turned the conversation again upon Elsie, and endeavored to make her minister feel the importance of bringing every friendly influence to bear upon her at this critical period of her life. His sympathies did not seem so lively as the Doctor could have wished. Perhaps he had vastly more important objects of solicitude in his own spiritual interests.

A knock at the door interrupted them. The Reverend Mr. Fairweather rose and went towards it. As he passed the table, his coat caught something, which came rattling to the floor. It was a crucifix with a string of beads attached. As he opened the door, the Milesian features of Father McShane presented themselves, and from their centre proceeded the clerical benediction in Irish-sounding Latin, *Pax vobiscum!*

The Reverend Doctor Honeywood rose and left the priest and his disciple together.

CHAPTER XIX

THE SPIDER ON HIS THREAD

There was nobody, then, to counsel poor Elsie except her father, who had learned to let her have her own way so as not to disturb such relations as they had together, and the old black woman, who had a real, though limited influence over the girl. Perhaps she did not need counsel. To look upon her, one might well suppose that she was competent to defend herself against any enemy she was like to have. That glittering, piercing eye was not to be softened by a few smooth words spoken in low tones, charged with the common sentiments which win their way to maidens' hearts. That round, lithe, sinuous figure was as full of dangerous life as ever lay under the slender flanks and clean-shaped limbs of a panther.

There were particular times when Elsie was in such a mood that it must have been a bold person who would have intruded upon her with reproof or counsel. "This is one of her days," old Sophy would say quietly to her father, and he would, as far as possible, leave her to herself. These days were more frequent, as old Sophy's keen, concentrated watchfulness had taught her, at certain periods of the year. It was in the heats of summer that they were most common and most strongly characterized. In winter, on the other hand, she was less excitable, and even at times heavy and as if chilled and dulled in her sensibilities. It was a strange, paroxysmal kind of life that belonged to her. It seemed to come and go with the sunlight. All winter long she would be comparatively quiet, easy to manage, listless, slow in her motions; her eye would lose something of its strange lustre; and the old nurse would feel so little anxiety, that her whole expression and aspect would show the change, and people would say to her, "Why, Sophy, how young you're looking!"

As the spring came on, Elsie would leave the fireside, have her tiger-skin spread in the empty southern chamber next the wall, and lie there basking for whole hours in the sunshine. As the season warmed, the light would kindle afresh in her eyes, and the old woman's sleep would grow restless again,—for she knew, that, so long as the glitter was fierce in the girl's eyes, there was no trusting her impulses or movements.

At last, when the veins of the summer were hot and swollen, and the juices of all the poison-plants and the blood of all the creatures that feed upon them had grown thick and strong,—about the time when the second mowing was in hand, and the brown, wet-faced men were following up the scythes as they chased the falling waves of grass, (falling as the waves fall on sickle-curved beaches; the foam-flowers dropping as the grass-flowers drop,—with sharp semivowel consonantal sounds,—*frsh*,—for that is the way the sea talks, and leaves all pure vowel-sounds for the winds to breathe over it, and all mutes to the unyielding earth,)— about this time of over-ripe midsummer, the life of Elsie seemed fullest of it malign and restless instincts. This was the period of the year when the Rockland people were most cautious of wandering in the leafier coverts which skirted the base of The Mountain, and the farmers liked to wear thick, long boots, whenever they went into the bushes. But Elsie was never so much given to roaming over The Mountain as at this season; and as she had grown more absolute and uncontrollable, she was as like to take the night as the day for her rambles.

At this season, too, all her peculiar tastes in dress and ornament came out in a more striking way than at other times. She was never so superb as then, and never so threatening in her scowling beauty. The barred skirts she always fancied showed sharply beneath her diaphanous muslins; the diamonds often glittered on her breast as if for her own pleasure rather than to dazzle others; the asp-like bracelet hardly left her arm. She was never seen without some necklace,—either the golden cord she wore at the great party, or a chain of mosaics, or simply a ring of golden scales. Some said that Elsie always slept in a necklace, and that when she died she was to be buried in one. It was a fancy of hers,—but many thought there was a reason for it.

Nobody watched Elsie with a more searching eye than her cousin, Dick Venner. He had kept more out of her way of late, it is true, but there was not a movement she made which he did not carefully observe just so far as he could without exciting her suspicion. It was plain enough to him that the road to fortune was before him, and that the first thing was to marry Elsie. What course he should take with her, or with others interested, after marrying her, need not be decided in a hurry.

He had now done all he could expect to do at present in the way of conciliating the other members of the household. The girl's father tolerated him, if he did not even like him. Whether he suspected his project or not Dick did not feel sure; but it was something to have got a foothold in the house, and to have overcome any prepossession against him which his uncle might have entertained. To be a good listener and a bad billiard-player was not a very great sacrifice to effect this object. Then old Sophy could hardly help feeling well-disposed towards him, after the gifts he had bestowed on her and the court he had payed her. These were the only persons on the place of much importance to gain over. The people employed about the house and farm-lands had little to do with Elsie, except to obey her without questioning her commands.

Mr. Richard began to think of reopening his second parallel. But he had lost something of the coolness with which he had begun his system of operations. The more he had reflected upon the matter, the more he had convinced himself that this was his one great chance in life. If he suffered this girl to escape him, such an opportunity could hardly, in the nature of things, present itself a second time. Only one life between Elsie and her fortune,—and lives are so uncertain! The girl might not suit him as a wife. Possibly. Time enough to find out after he had got her. In short, he must have the property, and Elsie Venner, as she was to go with it,—and then, if he found it convenient and agreeable to lead a virtuous life, he would settle down and raise children and vegetables; but if he found it inconvenient and disagreeable, so much the worse for those who made it so. Like many other persons, he was not principled against virtue, provided virtue were a better investment than its opposite; but he knew that there might be contingencies in which the property would be better without its incumbrances, and he contemplated this conceivable problem in the light of all its possible solutions.

One thing Mr. Richard could not conceal from himself: Elsie had some new cause of indifference, at least, if not of aversion to him. With the acuteness which persons who make a sole business of their own interest gain by practice, so that fortune-hunters are often shrewd where real lovers are terribly simple, he fixed at once on the young man up at the school where the girl had been going of late, as probably at the bottom of it.

"Cousin Elsie in love!" so he communed with himself upon his lonely pillow. "In love with a Yankee schoolmaster! What else can it be? Let him look out for himself! He'll stand but a bad chance between us. What makes you think she's in love with him? Met her walking with him. Don't like her looks and ways;—she's thinking about *something*, anyhow. Where does she get those books she is reading so often? Not out of our library, that's certain. If I could have ten minutes' peep into her chamber now, I would find out where she got them, and what mischief she was up to."

At that instant, as if some tributary demon had heard his wish, a shape which could be none but Elsie's flitted through a gleam of moonlight into the shadow of the trees. She was setting out on one of her midnight rambles.

Dick felt his heart stir in its place, and presently his cheeks flushed with the old longing for an adventure. It was not much to invade a young girl's deserted chamber, but it would amuse a wakeful hour, and tell him some little matters he wanted to know. The chamber he slept in was over the room which Elsie chiefly occupied at this season. There was no great risk of his being seen or heard, if he ventured down-stairs to her apartment.

Mr. Richard Venner, in the pursuit of his interesting project, arose and lighted a lamp. He wrapped himself in a dressing-gown and thrust his feet into a pair of cloth slippers. He stole carefully down the stair, and arrived safely at the door of Elsie's room. The young lady had taken the natural precaution to leave it fastened, carrying the key with her, no doubt,—unless, indeed, she had got out by the window, which was not far from the ground. Dick could get in at this window easily enough, but he did not like the idea of leaving his footprints in the flower-bed just under it. He returned to his own chamber, and held a council of war with himself.

He put his head out of his own window and looked at that beneath. It was open. He then went to one of his trunks, which he unlocked, and began carefully removing its contents. What these were we need not stop to mention,—only remarking that there were dresses of various patterns, which might afford an agreeable series of changes, and in certain contingencies prove eminently useful. After removing a few of these, he thrust his hand to the very bottom of the remaining pile and drew out a coiled strip of leather many yards in length, ending in a noose,—a tough, well-seasoned *lasso*, looking as if it had seen service and was none the worse for it. He uncoiled a few yards of this and fastened it to the knob of a door. Then he threw the loose end out of the window so that it should hang by the open casement of Elsie's room. By this he let himself down opposite her window, and with a slight effort swung himself inside the room. He lighted a match, found a candle, and, having lighted that, looked curiously about him, as Clodius might have done when he smuggled himself in among the Vestals.

Elsie's room was almost as peculiar as her dress and ornaments. It was a kind of museum of objects, such as the woods are full of to those who have eyes to see them, but many of them such as only few could hope to reach, even if they knew where to look for them. Crows' nests, which are never found but in the tall trees, commonly enough in the forks of ancient hemlocks, eggs of rare birds, which must have taken a quick eye and a hard climb to find and get hold of, mosses and ferns of unusual aspect, and quaint monstrosities of vegetable growth, such as Nature delights in, showed that Elsie had her tastes and fancies like any naturalist or poet.

Nature, when left to her own freaks in the forest, is grotesque and fanciful to the verge of license, and beyond it. The foliage of trees does not always require clipping to make it look like an image of life. From those windows at Canoe Meadow, among the mountains, we could see all summer long a lion rampant, a Shanghai chicken, and General Jackson on horseback, done by Nature in green leaves, each with a single tree. But to Nature's tricks with boughs and roots and smaller vegetable growths there is no end. Her fancy is infinite, and her humor not always refined. There is a perpetual reminiscence of animal life in her rude caricatures, which sometimes actually reach the point of imitating the complete human figure, as in that extraordinary specimen which nobody will believe to be genuine, except the men of science, and of which the discreet reader may have a glimpse by application in the proper quarter.

Elsie had gathered so many of these sculpture-like monstrosities, that one might have thought she had robbed old Sophy's grandfather of his fetishes. They helped to give her room a kind of enchanted look, as if a witch had her home in it. Over the fireplace was a long, staff-like branch, strangled in the spiral coils of one of those vines which strain the smaller trees in their clinging embraces, sinking into the bark until the parasite becomes almost identified with its support. With these sylvan curiosities were blended objects of art, some of them not less singular, but others showing a love for the beautiful in form and color, such as a girl of fine organization and nice culture might naturally be expected to feel and to indulge, in adorning her apartment.

All these objects, pictures, bronzes, vases, and the rest, did not detain Mr. Richard Venner very long, whatever may have been his sensibilities to art. He was more curious about books and papers. A copy of Keats lay on the table. He opened it and read the name of *Bernard C. Langdon* on the blank leaf. An envelope was on the table with Elsie's name written in a similar hand; but the envelope was empty, and he could not find the note it contained. Her desk was locked, and it would not be safe to tamper with it. He had seen enough; the girl received books and notes from this fellow up at the school,—this usher, this Yankee quill-driver;—*he* was aspiring to become the lord of the Dudley domain, then, was he?

Elsie had been reasonably careful. She had locked up her papers, whatever they might be. There was little else that promised to reward his curiosity, but he cast his eye on everything. There was a clasp-Bible among her books. Dick wondered if she ever unclasped it. There was a book of hymns; it had her name in it, and looked as if it might have been often read;—what the *diablo* had Elsie to do with hymns?

Mr. Richard Venner was in an observing and analytical state of mind, it will be noticed, or he might perhaps have been touched with the innocent betrayals of the poor girl's chamber. Had she, after all, some human tenderness in her heart? That was not the way he put the question,—but whether she would take seriously to this schoolmaster, and if she did, what would be the neatest and surest and quickest way of putting a stop to all that nonsense. All this, however, he could think over more safely in his own quarters. So he stole softly to the window, and, catching the end of the leathern thong, regained his own chamber and drew in the lasso.

It needs only a little jealousy to set a man on who is doubtful in love or wooing, or to make him take hold of his courting in earnest. As soon as Dick had satisfied himself that the young schoolmaster was his rival in Elsie's good graces, his whole thoughts concentrated themselves more than ever on accomplishing his great design of securing her for himself. There was no time to be lost. He must come into closer relations with her, so as to withdraw her thoughts from this fellow, and to find out more exactly what was the state of her affections, if she had any. So he began to court her company again, to propose riding with her, to sing to her, to join her whenever she was strolling about the grounds, to make himself agreeable, according to the ordinary understanding of that phrase, in every way which seemed to promise a chance for succeeding in that amiable effort.

The girl treated him more capriciously than ever. She would be sullen and silent, or she would draw back fiercely at some harmless word or gesture, or she would look at him with her eyes narrowed in such a strange way and with such a wicked light in them that Dick swore to himself they were too much for him, and would leave her for the moment. Yet she tolerated him, almost as a matter of necessity, and sometimes seemed to take a kind of pleasure in trying her power upon him. This he soon found out, and humored her in the fancy that she could exercise a kind of fascination over him,—though there were times in which he actually felt an influence he could not understand, an effect of some peculiar expression about her, perhaps, but still centring in those diamond eyes of hers which it made one feel so curiously to look into.

Whether Elsie saw into his object or not was more than he could tell. His idea was, after having conciliated the good-will of all about her as far as possible, to make himself first a habit and then a necessity with the girl,—not to spring any trap of a declaration upon her until tolerance had grown into such a degree of inclination as her nature was like to admit. He had succeeded in the first part of his plan. He was at liberty to prolong his visit at his own pleasure. This was not strange; these three persons, Dudley Venner, his daughter, and his nephew, represented all that remained of an old and honorable family. Had Elsie been like other girls, her father might have been less willing to entertain a young fellow like Dick as an inmate; but he had long outgrown all the slighter apprehensions which he might have had in common with all parents, and followed rather than led the imperious instincts of his daughter. It was not a question of sentiment, but of life and death, or more than that,—some dark ending, perhaps, which would close the history of his race with disaster and evil report upon the lips of all coming generations.

As to the thought of his nephew's making love to his daughter, it had almost passed from his mind. He had been so long in the habit of looking at Elsie as outside of all common influences and exceptional in the law of her nature, that it was difficult for him to think of her as a girl to be fallen in love with. Many persons are surprised, when others court their female relatives; they know them as good young or old women enough,—aunts, sisters, nieces, daughters, whatever they may be,—but never think of anybody's falling in love with them, any more than of their being struck by lightning. But in this case there were special reasons, in addition to the common family delusion,—reasons which seemed to make it impossible that she should attract a suitor. Who would *dare* to marry Elsie? No, let her have the pleasure, if it was one, at any rate the wholesome excitement, of companionship; it might save her from lapsing into melancholy or a worse form of madness. Dudley Venner had a kind of superstition, too, that, if Elsie could only outlive three septenaries, twenty-one years, so that, according to the prevalent idea, her whole frame would have been thrice made over, counting from her birth, she would revert to the natural standard of health of mind and feelings from which she had been so long perverted. The thought of any other motive than love being sufficient to induce Richard to become her suitor had not occurred to him. He had married early, at that happy period when interested motives are least apt to influence the choice; and his single idea of marriage was, that it was the union of persons naturally drawn towards each other by some mutual attraction. Very simple, perhaps; but he had lived lonely for many years since his wife's death, and judged the hearts of others, most of all of his brother's son, by his own. He had often thought whether, in case of Elsie's dying or being necessarily doomed to seclusion, he might not adopt this nephew and make him his heir; but it had not occurred to him that Richard might wish to become his son-in-law for the sake of his property.

It is very easy to criticise other people's modes of dealing with their children. Outside observers see results; parents see processes. They notice the trivial movements and accents which betray the blood of this or that ancestor; they can detect the irrepressible movement of hereditary impulse in looks and acts which mean nothing to the common observer. To be a parent is almost to be a fatalist. This boy sits with legs crossed, just as his uncle used to whom he never saw; his grandfathers both died before he was born, but he has the movement of the eyebrows which we remember in one of them, and the gusty temper of the other.

These are things parents can see, and which they must take account of in education, but which few except parents can be expected to really understand. Here and there a sagacious person, old, or of middle age, who has *triangulated* a race, that is, taken three or more observations from the several standing-places of three different generations, can tell pretty nearly the range of possibilities and the limitations of a child, actual or potential, of a given stock,—errors excepted always, because children of the same stock are not bred just alike, because the traits of some less known ancestor are liable to break out at any time, and because each human being has, after all, a small fraction of individuality about him which gives him a flavor, so that he is distinguishable from others by his friends or in a court of justice, and which occasionally makes a genius or a saint or a criminal of him. It is well that young persons cannot read these fatal oracles of Nature. Blind impulse is her highest wisdom, after all. We make our great jump, and then she takes the bandage off our eyes. That is the way the broad sea-level of average is maintained, and the physiological democracy is enabled to fight against the principle of selection which would disinherit all the weaker children. The magnificent constituency of mediocrities of which the world is made up,—the people without biographies, whose lives have made a clear solution in the fluid menstruum of time, instead of being precipitated in the opaque sediment of history——

But this is a narrative, and not a disquisition.

CHAPTER XX

FROM WITHOUT AND FROM WITHIN

There were not wanting people who accused Dudley Venner of weakness and bad judgment in his treatment of his daughter. Some were of opinion that the great mistake was in not "breaking her will" when she was a little child. There was nothing the matter with her, they said, but that she had been spoiled by indulgence. If *they* had had the charge of her, they'd have brought her down. She'd got the upperhand of her father now; but if he'd only taken hold of her in season! There are people who think that everything may be done, if the doer, be he educator or physician, be only called "in season." No doubt,—but *in season* would often be a hundred or two years before the child was born; and people never send so early as that.

The father of Elsie Venner knew his duties and his difficulties too well to trouble himself about anything others might think or say. So soon as he found that he could not govern his child, he gave his life up to following her and protecting her as far as he could. It was a stern and terrible trial for a man of acute sensibility, and not without force of intellect and will, and the manly ambition for himself and his family-name which belonged to his endowments and his position. Passive endurance is the hardest trial to persons of such a nature.

What made it still more a long martyrdom was the necessity for bearing his cross in utter loneliness. He could not tell his griefs. He could not talk of them even with those who knew their secret spring. His minister had the unsympathetic nature which is common in the meaner sort of devotees,—persons who mistake spiritual selfishness for sanctity, and grab at the infinite prize of the great Future and Elsewhere with the egotism they excommunicate in its hardly more odious forms of avarice and self-indulgence. How could he speak with the old physician and the old black woman about a sorrow and a terror which but to name was to strike dumb the lips of Consolation?

In the dawn of his manhood he had found that second consciousness for which young men and young women go about looking into each other's faces, with their sweet, artless aim playing in every feature, and making them beautiful to each other, as to all of us. He had found his other self early, before he had grown weary in the search and wasted his freshness in vain longings: the lot of many, perhaps we may say of most, who infringe the patent of our social order by intruding themselves into a life already upon half allowance of the necessary luxuries of existence. The life he had led for a brief space was not only beautiful in outward circumstance, as old Sophy had described it to the Reverend Doctor. It was that delicious process of the tuning of two souls to each other, string by string, not without little half-pleasing discords now and then when some chord in one or the other proves to be over-strained or over-lax, but always approaching nearer and nearer to harmony, until they become at last as two instruments with a single voice. Something more than a year of this blissful doubled consciousness had passed over him when he found himself once more alone,—alone, save for the little diamond-eyed child lying in the old black woman's arms, with the coral necklace round her throat and the rattle in her hand.

He would not die by his own act. It was the way in his family. There may have been other, perhaps better reasons, but this was enough; he did not come of suicidal stock. He must live for this child's sake, at any rate; and yet,—oh, yet, who could tell with what thoughts he looked upon her? Sometimes her little features would look placid, and something like a smile would steal over them; then all his tender feelings would rush up into his eyes, and he would put his arms out to take her from the old woman,—but all at once her eyes would narrow and she would throw her head back, and a shudder would seize him as he stooped over his child,—he could not look upon her,—he could not touch his lips to her cheek; nay, there would sometimes come into his soul such frightful suggestions that he would hurry from the room lest the hinted thought should become a momentary madness and he should lift his hand against the hapless infant which owed him life.

In those miserable days he used to wander all over The Mountain in his restless endeavor to seek some relief for inward suffering in outward action. He had no thought of throwing himself from the summit of any of the broken cliffs, but he clambered over them recklessly, as having no particular care for his life. Sometimes he would go into the accursed district where the venomous reptiles were always to be dreaded, and court their worst haunts, and kill all he could come near with a kind of blind fury which was strange in a person of his gentle nature.

One overhanging cliff was a favorite haunt of his. It frowned upon his home beneath in a very menacing way; he noticed slight seams and fissures that looked ominous; —what would happen, if it broke off some time or other and came crashing down on the fields and roofs below? He thought of such a possible catastrophe with a singular indifference, in fact with a feeling almost like pleasure. It would be such a swift and thorough solution of this great problem of life he was working out in ever-recurring daily anguish! The remote possibility of such a catastrophe had frightened some timid dwellers beneath The Mountain to other places of residence; here the danger was most imminent, and yet he loved to dwell upon the chances of its occurrence. Danger is often the best *counterirritant* in cases of mental suffering; he found a solace in careless exposure of his life, and learned to endure the trials of each day better by dwelling in imagination on the possibility that it might be the last for him and the home that was his.

Time, the great consoler, helped these influences, and he gradually fell into more easy and less dangerous habits of life. He ceased from his more perilous rambles. He thought less of the danger from the great overhanging rocks and forests; they had hung there for centuries; it was not very likely they would crash or slide in his time. He became accustomed to all Elsie's strange looks and ways. Old Sophy dressed her with ruffles round her neck, and hunted up the red coral branch with silver bells which the little toothless Dudleys had bitten upon for a hundred years. By an infinite effort, her father forced himself to become the companion of this child, for whom he had such a mingled feeling, but whose presence was always a trial to him, and often a terror.

At a cost which no human being could estimate, he had done his duty, and in some degree reaped his reward. Elsie grew up with a kind of filial feeling for him, such as her nature was capable of. She never would obey him; that was not to be looked for. Commands, threats, punishments, were out of the question with her; the mere physical effects of crossing her will betrayed themselves in such changes of expression and manner that it would have been senseless to attempt to govern her in any such way. Leaving her mainly to herself, she could be to some extent indirectly influenced,—not otherwise. She called her father "Dudley," as if he had been her brother. She ordered everybody and would be ordered by none.

Who could know all these things, except the few people of the household? What wonder, therefore, that ignorant and shallow persons laid the blame on her father of those peculiarities which were freely talked about,—of those darker tendencies which were hinted of in whispers? To all this talk, so far as it reached him, he was supremely indifferent, not only with the indifference which all gentlemen feel to the gossip of their inferiors, but with a charitable calmness which did not wonder or blame. He knew that his position was not simply a difficult, but an impossible one, and schooled himself to bear his destiny as well as he might, and report himself only at Headquarters.

He had grown gentle under this discipline. His hair was just beginning to be touched with silver, and his expression was that of habitual sadness and anxiety. He had no counsellor, as we have seen, to turn to, who did not know either too much or too little. He had no heart to rest upon and into which he might unburden himself of the secrets and the sorrows that were aching in his own breast. Yet he had not allowed himself to run to waste in the long time since he was left alone to his trials and fears. He had resisted the seductions which always beset solitary men with restless brains overwrought by depressing agencies. He disguised no misery to himself with the lying delusion of wine. He sought no sleep from narcotics, though he lay with throbbing, wide-open eyes through all the weary hours of the night.

It was understood between Dudley Venner and old Doctor Kittredge that Elsie was a subject of occasional medical observation, on account of certain mental peculiarities which might end in a permanent affection of her reason. Beyond this nothing was said, whatever may have been in the mind of either. But Dudley Venner had studied Elsie's case in the light of all the books he could find which might do anything towards explaining it. As in all cases where men meddle with medical science for a special purpose, having no previous acquaintance with it, his imagination found what it wanted in the books he read, and adjusted it to the facts before him. So it was he came to cherish those two fancies before alluded to: that the ominous birthmark she had carried from infancy might fade and become obliterated, and that the age of complete maturity might be signalized by an entire change in her physical and mental state. He held these vague hopes as all of us nurse our only half-believed illusions. Not for the world would he have questioned his sagacious old medical friend as to the probability or possibility of their being true. We are very shy of asking questions of those who know enough to destroy with one word the hopes we live on.

In this life of comparative seclusion to which the father had doomed himself for the sake of his child, he had found time for large and varied reading. The learned Judge Thornton confessed himself surprised at the extent of Dudley Venner's information. Doctor Kittredge found that he was in advance of him in the knowledge of recent physiological discoveries. He had taken pains to become acquainted with agricultural chemistry; and the neighboring farmers owed him some useful hints about the management of their land. He renewed his old acquaintance with the classic authors. He loved to warm his pulses with Homer and calm them down with Horace. He received all manner of new books and periodicals, and gradually gained an interest in the events of the passing time. Yet he remained almost a hermit, not absolutely refusing to see his neighbors, nor ever churlish towards them, but on the other hand not cultivating any intimate relations with them.

He had retired from the world a young man, little more than a youth, indeed, with sentiments and aspirations all of them suddenly extinguished. The first had bequeathed him a single huge sorrow, the second a single trying duty. In due time the anguish had lost something of its poignancy, the light of earlier and happier memories had begun to struggle with and to soften its thick darkness, and even that duty which he had confronted with such an effort had become an endurable habit.

At a period of life when many have been living on the capital of their acquired knowledge and their youthful stock of sensibilities until their intellects are really shallower and their hearts emptier than they were at twenty, Dudley Venner was stronger in thought and tenderer in soul than in the first freshness of his youth, when he counted but half his present years. He had entered that period which marks the decline of men who have ceased growing in knowledge and strength: from forty to fifty a man must move upward, or the natural falling off in the vigor of life will carry him rapidly downward. At this time his inward nature was richer and deeper than in any earlier period of his life. If he could only be summoned to action, he was capable of noble service. If his sympathies could only find an outlet, he was never so capable of love as now; for his natural affections had been gathering in the course of all these years, and the traces of that ineffaceable calamity of his life were softened and partially hidden by new growths of thought and feeling, as the wreck left by a mountain-slide is covered over by the gentle intrusion of the soft-stemmed herbs which will prepare it for the stronger vegetation that will bring it once more into harmony with the peaceful slopes around it.

Perhaps Dudley Venner had not gained so much in

worldly wisdom as if he had been more in society and less in his study. The indulgence with which he treated his nephew was, no doubt, imprudent. A man more in the habit of dealing with men would have been more guarded with a person with Dick's questionable story and unquestionable physiognomy. But he was singularly unsuspicious, and his natural kindness was an additional motive to the wish for introducing some variety into the routine of Elsie's life.

If Dudley Venner did not know just what he wanted at this period of his life, there were a great many people in the town of Rockland who thought they did know. He had been a widower long enough,—nigh twenty year, wa'n't it? He'd been aout to Spraowles's party,—there wa'n't anything to hender him why he shouldn't stir raound l'k other folks. What was the reason he didn't go abaout to taown-meetin's 'n' Sahbath-meetin's, 'n' lýceums, 'n' school 'xaminations, 'n' s'prise-parties, 'n' funerals,—and other entertainments where the still-faced two-story folks were in the habit of looking round to see if any of the mansion-house gentry were present?—Fac' was, he was livin' too lonesome daown there at the mansion-haouse. Why shouldn't he make up to the Jedge's daughter? She was genteel enough for him, and—let's see, haow old was she? Seven-'n'-twenty, —no, six-'n'-twenty,—born the same year we buried aour little Anny Marí'.

There was no possible objection to this arrangement, if the parties interested had seen fit to make it or even to think of it. But "Portia," as some of the mansion-house people called her, did not happen to awaken the elective affinities of the lonely widower. He met her once in a while, and said to himself that she was a good specimen of the grand style of woman; and then the image came back to him of a woman not quite so large, not quite so imperial in her port, not quite so incisive in her speech, not quite so judicial in her opinions, but with two or three more joints in her frame, and two or three soft inflections in her voice, which for some absurd reason or other drew him to her side and so bewitched him that he told her half his secrets and looked into her eyes all that he could not tell, in less time than it would have taken him to discuss the champion paper of the last Quarterly with the admirable "Portia." *Heu, quanto minus!* How much more was that lost image to him than all it left on earth!

The study of love is very much like that of meteorology. We know that just about so much rain will fall in a season; but on what particular day it will shower is more than we can tell. We know that just about so much love will be made every year in a given population; but who will rain his young affections upon the heart of whom is not known except to the astrologers and fortune-tellers. And why rain falls as it does, and why love is made just as it is, are equally puzzling questions.

The woman a man loves is always his own daughter, far more his daughter than the female children born to him by the common law of life. It is not the outside woman, who takes his name, that he loves: before her image has reached the centre of his consciousness, it has passed through fifty many-layered nerve-strainers, been churned over by ten thousand pulse-beats, and reacted upon by millions of lateral impulses which bandy it about through the mental spaces as a reflection is sent back and forward in a saloon lined with mirrors. With this altered image of the woman before him, his preëxisting ideal becomes blended. The object of his love is in part the offspring of her legal parents, but more of her lover's brain. The difference between the real and the ideal objects of love must not exceed a fixed maximum. The heart's vision cannot unite them stereoscopically into a single image, if the divergence passes certain limits. A formidable analogy, much in the nature of a proof, with very serious consequences, which moralists and match-makers would do well to remember! Double vision with the eyes of the heart is a dangerous physiological state, and may lead to missteps and serious falls.

Whether Dudley Venner would ever find a breathing image near enough to his ideal one, to fill the desolate chamber of his heart, or not, was very doubtful. Some gracious and gentle woman, whose influence would steal upon him as the first low words of prayer after that interval of silent mental supplication known to one of our simpler forms of public worship, gliding into his consciousness without hurting its old griefs, herself knowing the chastening of sorrow, and subdued into sweet acquiescence with the Divine will,—some such woman as this, if Heaven should send him such, might call him back to the world of happiness, from which he seemed forever exiled. He could never again be the young lover who walked through the garden-alleys all red with roses in the old dead and buried June of long ago. He could never forget the bride of his youth, whose image, growing phantom-like with the lapse of years, hovered over him like a dream while waking and like a reality in dreams. But if it might be in God's good providence that this desolate life should come under the influence of human affections once more, what an ecstasy of renewed existence was in store for him! His life had not all been buried under that narrow ridge of turf with the white stone at its head. It seemed so for a while; but it was not and could not and ought not to be so. His first passion had been a true and pure one; there was no spot or stain upon it. With all his grief there blended no cruel recollection of any word or look he would have wished to forget. All those little differences, such as young married people with any individual flavor in their characters must have, if they are tolerably mated, had only added to the music of existence, as the lesser discords admitted into some perfect symphony, fitly resolved, add richness and strength to the whole harmonious movement. It was a deep wound that Fate had inflicted on him; nay, it seemed like a mortal one; but the weapon was clean, and its edge was smooth. Such wounds must heal with time in healthy natures, whatever a false sentiment may say, by the wise and beneficent law of our being. The recollection of a deep and true affection is rather a divine nourishment for a life to grow strong upon than a poison to destroy it.

Dudley Venner's habitual sadness could not be laid wholly to his early bereavement. It was partly the result of the long struggle between natural affection and duty, on one side, and the involuntary tendencies these had to overcome, on the other,—between hope and fear, so long in conflict that despair itself would have been like an anodyne, and he would have slept upon some final catastrophe with the heavy sleep of a bankrupt after his failure is proclaimed. Alas! some new affection might perhaps rekindle the fires of youth in his heart; but what power could calm that haggard terror of the parent which rose with every morning's sun and watched with every evening star,—what power save alone that of him who comes bearing the inverted torch, and leaving after him only the ashes printed with his footsteps?

CHAPTER XXI

THE WIDOW ROWENS GIVES A TEA-PARTY

There was a good deal of interest felt, as has been said, in the lonely condition of Dudley Venner in that fine mansion-house of his, and with that strange daughter, who would never be married, as many people thought, in spite of all the stories. The feelings expressed by the good folks who dated from the time when they "buried aour little Anny Marí'," and others of that homespun stripe, were founded in reason, after all. And so it was natural enough that they should be shared by various ladies, who, having conjugated the verb *to live* as far as the preterpluperfect tense, were ready to change one of its vowels and begin with it in the present indicative. Unfortunately, there was very little chance of showing sympathy in its active form for a gentleman who kept himself so much out of the way as the master of the Dudley Mansion.

Various attempts had been made, from time to time, of late years, to get him out of his study, which had, for the most part, proved failures. It was a surprise, therefore, when he was seen at the Great Party at the Colonel's. But it was an encouragement to try him again, and the consequence had been that he had received a number of notes inviting him to various smaller entertainments, which, as neither he nor Elsie had any fancy for them, he had politely declined.

Such was the state of things when he received an invitation to take tea *sociably*, with *a few friends*, at Hyacinth Cottage, the residence of the Widow Rowens, relict of the late Beeri Rowens, Esquire, better known as Major Rowens. Major Rowens was at the time of his decease a promising officer in the militia, in the direct line of promotion, as his waistband was getting tighter every year; and, as all the world knows, the militia-officer who splits off most buttons and fills the largest sword-belt stands the best chance of rising, or, perhaps we might say, spreading, to be General.

Major Rowens united in his person certain other traits which help a man to eminence in the branch of public service referred to. He ran to high colors, to wide whiskers, to open pores; he had the saddle-leather skin common in Englishmen, rarer in Americans,—never found in the Brahmin caste, oftener in the military and the commodores: observing people know what is meant; blow the seed-arrows from the white-kid-looking button which holds them on a dandelion-stalk, and the pricked-pincushion surface shows you what to look for. He had the loud gruff voice which implies the right to command. He had the thick hand, stubbed fingers, with bristled pads between their joints, square, broad thumb-nails, and sturdy limbs, which mark a constitution made to use in rough out-door work. He had the never-failing predilection for showy switch-tailed horses that step high, and sidle about, and act as if they were going to do something fearful the next minute, in the face of awed and admiring multitudes gathered at mighty musters or imposing cattle-shows. He had no objection, either, to holding the reins in a wagon behind another kind of horse,—a slouching, listless beast, with a strong slant to his shoulder and a notable depth to his quarter and an emphatic angle at the hock, who commonly walked or lounged along in a lazy trot of five or six miles an hour; but, if a lively colt happened to come rattling up alongside, or a brandy-faced old horse-jockey took the road to show off a fast nag, and threw his dust into the Major's face, would pick his legs up all at once, and straighten his body out, and swing off into a three-minute gait, in a way that "Old Blue" himself need not have been ashamed of.

For some reason which must be left to the next generation of professors to find out, the men who are knowing in horse-flesh have an eye also for, —— let a long dash separate the brute creation from the angelic being now to be named, —for lovely woman. Of this fact there can be no possible doubt; and therefore you shall notice, that, if a fast horse trots before two, one of the twain is apt to be a pretty bit of muliebrity, with shapes to her, and eyes flying about in all directions.

Major Rowens, at that time Lieutenant of the Rockland Fusileers, had driven and "traded" horses not a few before he turned his acquired skill as a judge of physical advantages in another direction. He knew a neat, snug hoof, a delicate pastern, a broad haunch, a deep chest, a close ribbed-up barrel, as well as any other man in the town. He was not to be taken in by your thick-jointed, heavy-headed cattle, without any go to them, that suit a country-parson, nor yet by the "gaänted-up," long-legged animals, with all their constitutions bred out of them, such as rich greenhorns buy and cover up with their plated trappings.

Whether his equine experience was of any use to him in the selection of the mate with whom he was to go in double harness so long as they both should live, we need not stop to question. At any rate, nobody could find fault with the points of Miss Marilla Van Deusen, to whom he offered the privilege of becoming Mrs. Rowens. The *Van* must have been crossed out of her blood, for she was an out-and-out brunette, with hair and eyes black enough for a Mohawk's daughter. A fine style of woman, with very striking tints and outlines,—an excellent match for the Lieutenant, except for one thing. She was marked by Nature for a widow. She was evidently got up for mourning, and never looked so well as in deep black, with jet ornaments.

The man who should dare to marry her would doom himself; for how could she become the widow she was bound to be, unless he would retire and give her a chance? The Lieutenant lived, however, as we have seen, to become Captain and then Major, with prospects of further advancement. But Mrs. Rowens often said she should never look well in colors. At last her destiny fulfilled itself, and the justice of Nature was vindicated. Major Rowens got overheated galloping about the field on the day of the Great Muster, and had a rush of blood to the head, according to the common report,—at any rate, something which stopped him short in his career of expansion and promotion, and established Mrs. Rowens in her normal condition of widowhood.

The Widow Rowens was now in the full bloom of ornamental sorrow. A very shallow crape bonnet, frilled and froth-like, allowed the parted raven hair to show its glossy smoothness. A jet pin heaved upon her bosom with every sigh of memory, or emotion of unknown origin. Jet bracelets shone with every movement of her slender hands, cased in close-fitting black gloves. Her sable dress was ridged with manifold flounces, from beneath which a small foot showed itself from time to time, clad in the same hue of mourning. Everything about her was dark, except the whites of her eyes and the enamel of her teeth. The effect was complete. Gray's Elegy was not a more perfect composition.

Much as the Widow was pleased with the costume belonging to her condition, she did not disguise from herself that under certain circumstances she might be willing to change her name again. Thus, for instance, if a gentleman not too far gone in maturity, of dignified exterior, with an ample fortune, and of unexceptionable character, should happen to set his heart upon her, and the only way to make him happy was to give up her weeds and go into those unbecoming colors again for his sake,—why, she felt that it was in her nature to make the sacrifice. By a singular coincidence it happened that a gentleman was now living in Rockland who united in himself all these advantages. Who he was, the sagacious reader may very probably have divined. Just to see how it looked, one day, having bolted her door, and drawn the curtains close, and glanced under the sofa, and listened at the keyhole to be sure there was nobody in the entry,—just to see how it looked, she had taken out an envelope and written on the back of it *Mrs. Marilla Venner*. It made her head swim and her knees tremble. What if she should faint, or die, or have a stroke of palsy, and they should break into the room and find that name written! How she caught it up and tore it into little shreds, and then could not be easy until she had burned the small heap of pieces! But these are things which every honorable reader will consider imparted in strict confidence.

The Widow Rowens, though not of the mansion-house

set, was among the most genteel of the two-story circle, and was in the habit of visiting some of the great people. In one of these visits she met a dashing young fellow with an olive complexion at the house of a professional gentleman who had married one of the white necks and pairs of fat arms from a distinguished family before referred to. The professional gentleman himself was out, but the lady introduced the olive-complexioned young man as Mr. Richard Venner.

The Widow was particularly pleased with this accidental meeting. Had heard Mr. Venner's name frequently mentioned. Hoped his uncle was well, and his charming cousin, —was she as original as ever? Had often admired that charming creature he rode: *we* had had some fine horses. Had never got over her taste for riding, but could find nobody that liked a good long gallop since——well—she couldn't help wishing she was alongside of him, the other day, when she saw him dashing by, just at twilight.

The Widow paused; lifted a flimsy handkerchief with a very deep black border so as to play the jet bracelet; pushed the tip of her slender foot beyond the lowest of her black flounces; looked up; looked down; looked at Mr. Richard, the very picture of artless simplicity,—as represented in well-played genteel comedy.

"A good bit of stuff," Dick said to himself,—"and something of it left yet; *caramba!*" The Major had not studied points for nothing, and the Widow was one of the right sort. The young man had been a little restless of late, and was willing to vary his routine by picking up an acquaintance here and there. So he took the Widow's hint. He should like to have a scamper of half a dozen miles with her some fine morning.

The Widow was infinitely obliged; was not sure that she could find any horse in the village to suit her; but it was *so* kind in him! Would he not call at Hyacinth Cottage, and let her thank him again there?

Thus began an acquaintance which the Widow made the most of, and on the strength of which she determined to give a tea-party and invite a number of persons of whom we know something already. She took a half-sheet of note-paper and made out her list as carefully as a country "merchant's" "clerk" adds up two and threepence (New-England nomenclature) and twelve and a half cents, figure by figure, and fraction by fraction, before he can be sure they will make half a dollar, without cheating somebody. After much consideration the list reduced itself to the following names: Mr. Richard Venner and Mrs. Blanche Creamer, the lady at whose house she had met him,—mansion-house breed,—but will come,—soft on Dick; Dudley Venner,—take care of him herself; Elsie,—Dick will see to her,—won't it fidget the Creamer woman to see him round her? the old Doctor,—he's always handy; and there's that young master there, up at the school,—know him well enough to ask him,—oh, yes, he'll come. One, two, three, four, five, six,—seven; not room enough, without the leaf in the table; one place empty, if the leaf's in. Let's see,—Helen Darley,—she'll do well enough to fill it up,—why, yes, just the thing,—light brown hair, blue eyes,—won't my pattern show off well against her? Put her down,—she's worth her tea and toast ten times over,—nobody knows what a "thunder-and-lightning woman," as poor Major used to have it, is, till she gets alongside of one of those old-maidish girls, with hair the color of brown sugar, and eyes like the blue of a teacup.

The Widow smiled with a feeling of triumph at having overcome her difficulties and arranged her party,—arose and stood before her glass, three-quarters front, one-quarter profile, so as to show the whites of the eyes and the down of the upper lip. "Splendid!" said the Widow—and to tell the truth, she was not far out of the way, and with Helen Darley as a foil anybody would know she must be foudroyant and pyramidal,—if these French adjectives may be naturalized for this one particular exigency.

So the Widow sent out her notes. The black grief which had filled her heart and overflowed in surges of crape around her person had left a deposit half an inch wide at the margin of her note-paper. Her seal was a small youth with an inverted torch, the same on which Mrs. Blanche Creamer made her spiteful remark, that she expected to see that boy of the Widow's standing on his head yet;

meaning, as Dick supposed, that she would get the torch right-side up as soon as she had a chance. That was after Dick had made the Widow's acquaintance, and Mrs. Creamer had got it into her foolish head that she would marry that young fellow, if she could catch him. How could he ever come to fancy such a quadroon-looking thing as that, she should like to know?

It is easy enough to ask seven people to a party; but whether they will come or not is an open question, as it was in the case of the spirits of the vasty deep. If the note issues from a three-story mansion-house, and goes to two-story acquaintances, they will all be in an excellent state of health, and have much pleasure in accepting this very polite invitation. If the note is from the lady of a two-story family to three-story ones, the former highly respectable person will very probably find that an endemic complaint is prevalent, not represented in the weekly bills of mortality, which occasions numerous regrets in the bosoms of eminently desirable parties that they *cannot* have the pleasure of and-so-forthing.

In this case there was room for doubt,—mainly as to whether Elsie would take a fancy to come or not. If she should come, her father would certainly be with her. Dick had promised, and thought he could bring Elsie. Of course the young schoolmaster will come, and that poor tired-out looking Helen,—if only to get out of sight of those horrid Peckham wretches. They don't get such invitations every day. The others she felt sure of,—all but the old Doctor,—he might have some horrid patient or other to visit; tell him Elsie Venner's going to be there,—he always likes to have an eye on her, they say,—oh, he'd come fast enough, without any more coaxing.

She wanted the Doctor, particularly. It was odd, but she was afraid of Elsie. She felt as if she should be safe enough, if the old Doctor were there to see to the girl; and then she should have leisure to devote herself more freely to the young lady's father, for whom all her sympathies were in a state of lively excitement.

It was a long time since the Widow had seen so many persons round her table as she had now invited. Better have the plates set and see how they will fill it up with the leaf in.—A little too scattering with only eight plates set: if she could find two more people, now, that would bring the chairs a little closer,—snug, you know,—which makes the company sociable. The Widow thought over her acquaintances. Why! how stupid! there was her good minister, the same who had married her, and might—might—bury her for aught she knew, and his granddaughter staying with him,—nice little girl, pretty, and not old enough to be dangerous;—for the Widow had no notion of making a tea-party and asking people to it that would be like to stand between her and any little project she might happen to have on anybody's heart,—not she! It was all right now;—Blanche was married and so forth; Letty was a child; Elsie was his daughter; Helen Darley was a nice, worthy drudge, —poor thing!—faded, faded,—colors wouldn't wash,—just what she wanted to show off against. Now, if the Dudley mansion-house people would only come,—that was the great point.

"Here's a note for us, Elsie," said her father, as they sat round the breakfast-table. "Mrs. Rowens wants us all to come to tea."

It was one of "Elsie's days," as Old Sophy called them. The light in her eyes was still, but very bright. She looked up so full of perverse and wilful impulses, that Dick knew he could make her go with him and her father. He had his own motives for bringing her to this determination,— and his own way of setting about it.

"I don't want to go," he said. "What do you say, Uncle?"

"To tell the truth, Richard, I don't much fancy the Major's widow. I don't like to see her weeds flowering out quite so strong. I suppose you don't care about going, Elsie?"

Elsie looked up in her father's face with an expression which he knew but too well. She was just in the state which the plain sort of people call "contrary," when they have to deal with it in animals. She would insist on going to that tea-party; he knew it just as well before she spoke as after she had spoken. If Dick had said he wanted to go and her father had seconded his wishes, she would have insisted on staying at home. It was no great matter, her father said to himself, after all; very likely it would amuse her; the Widow was a lively woman enough,—perhaps a little *comme il ne faut pas* socially, compared with the Thorntons and some other families; but what did he care for these petty village distinctions?

Elsie spoke.

"I mean to go. You must go with me, Dudley. You may do as you like, Dick."

That settled the Dudley-mansion business, of course. They all three accepted, as fortunately did all the others who had been invited.

Hyacinth Cottage was a pretty place enough, a little too much choked round with bushes, and too much overrun with climbing-roses, which, in the season of slugs and rosebugs, were apt to show so brown about the leaves and so coleopterous about the flowers, that it might be questioned whether their buds and blossoms made up for these unpleasant animal combinations,—especially as the smell of whale-oil soap was very commonly in the ascendant over that of the roses. It had its patch of grass called "the lawn," and its glazed closet known as "the conservatory," according to that system of harmless fictions characteristic of the rural imagination and shown in the names applied to many familiar objects. The interior of the cottage was more tasteful and ambitious than that of the ordinary two-story dwellings. In place of the prevailing hair-cloth covered furniture, the visitor had the satisfaction of seating himself upon a chair covered with some of the Widow's embroidery, or a sofa luxurious with soft caressing plush. The sporting tastes of the late Major showed in various prints on the wall: Herring's "Plenipotentiary," the "red bullock" of the '34 Derby; "Cadland" and "The Colonel"; "Crucifix"; "West-Australian," fastest of modern racers; and among native celebrities, ugly, game old "Boston," with his straight neck and ragged hips; and gray "Lady Suffolk," queen, in her day, not of the turf but of the track, "extending" herself till she measured a rod, more or less, skimming along within a yard of the ground, her legs opening and shutting under her with a snap, like the four blades of a compound jack-knife.

These pictures were much more refreshing than those dreary fancy death-bed scenes, common in two-story country-houses, in which Washington and other distinguished personages are represented as obligingly devoting their last moments to taking a prominent part in a *tableau*, in which weeping relatives, attached servants, professional assistants, and celebrated personages who might by a stretch of imagination be supposed present, are grouped in the most approved style of arrangement about the chief actor's pillow.

A single glazed bookcase held the family library, which was hidden from vulgar eyes by green silk curtains behind the glass. It would have been instructive to get a look at it, as it always is to peep into one's neighbor's book-shelves. From other sources and opportunities a partial idea of it has been obtained. The Widow had inherited some books from her mother, who was something of a reader: Young's "Night-Thoughts"; "The Preceptor"; "The Task, a Poem," by William Cowper; Hervey's "Meditations"; "Alonzo and Melissa"; "Buccaneers of America"; "The Triumphs of Temper"; "La Belle Assemblée"; Thomson's "Seasons"; and a few others. The Major had brought in "Tom Jones" and "Peregrine Pickle"; various works by Mr. Pierce Egan; "Boxiana"; "The Racing Calendar"; and a "Book of Lively Songs and Jests." The Widow had added the Poems of Lord Byron and T. Moore; "Eugene Aram"; "The Tower of London," by Harrison Ainsworth; some of Scott's Novels; "The Pickwick Papers"; a volume of Plays, by W. Shakspeare; "Proverbial Philosophy"; "Pilgrim's Progress"; "The Whole Duty of Man" (a present when she was married); with two celebrated religious works, one by William Law and the other by Philip Doddridge, which were sent her after her husband's death, and which she had tried to read, but found that they did not agree with her. Of course the bookcase held a few school manuals and compendiums, and one of Mr. Webster's Dictionaries. But the gilt-edged Bible always lay on the centre-table, next to the magazine with the fashion-plates and the scrap-book with pictures from old annuals and illustrated papers.

The reader need not apprehend the recital, at full length, of such formidable preparations for the Widow's tea-party as were required in the case of Colonel Sprowle's Social Entertainment. A tea-party, even in the country, is a comparatively simple and economical piece of business. As soon as the Widow found that all her company were coming, she set to work, with the aid of her "smart" maid-servant and a daughter of her own, who was beginning to stretch and spread at a fearful rate, but whom she treated as a small child, to make the necessary preparations. The silver had to be rubbed; also the grand plated urn,—her mother's before hers,—style of the Empire,—looking as if it might have been made to hold the Major's ashes. Then came the making and baking of cake and gingerbread, the smell whereof reached even as far as the sidewalk in front of the cottage, so that small boys returning from school snuffed it in the breeze, and discoursed with each other on its suggestions; so that the Widow Leech, who happened to pass, remembered she hadn't called on Marilly Raowens for a consid'ble spell, and turned in at the gate and rang three times with long intervals,—but all in vain, the inside Widow having "spotted" the outside one through the blinds, and whispered to her aides-de-camp to let the old thing ring away till she pulled the bell out by the roots, but not to stir to open the door.

Widow Rowens was what they called a real smart, capable woman, not very great on books, perhaps, but knew what was what and who was who as well as another,—knew how to make the little cottage look pretty, how to set out a tea-table, and, what a good many women never can find out, knew her own style and "got herself up tip-top," as our young friend Master Geordie, Colonel Sprowle's heir-apparent, remarked to his friend from one of the fresh-water colleges. Flowers were abundant now, and she had dressed her rooms tastefully with them. The centre-table had two or three gilt-edged books lying carelessly about on it, and some prints and a stereoscope with stereographs to match, chiefly groups of picnics, weddings, etc., in which the same somewhat fatigued-looking ladies of fashion and brides received the attentions of the same unpleasant-looking young men, easily identified under their different disguises, consisting of fashionable raiment such as gentlemen are supposed to wear habitually. With these, however, were some pretty English scenes,—pretty except for the old fellow with the hanging under-lip who infests every one of that interesting series; and a statue or two, especially that famous one commonly called the Lahcóon, so as to rhyme with moon and spoon, and representing an old man with his two sons in the embraces of two monstrous serpents.

There is no denying that it was a very dashing achievement of the Widow's to bring together so considerable a number of desirable guests. She felt proud of her feat; but as to the triumph of getting Dudley Venner to come out for a visit to Hyacinth Cottage, she was surprised and almost frightened at her own success. So much *might* depend on the impressions of that evening!

The next thing was to be sure that everybody should be in the right place at the tea-table, and this the Widow thought she could manage by a few words to the older guests and a little shuffling about and shifting when they got to the table. To settle everything the Widow made out a diagram, which the reader should have a chance of inspecting in an authentic copy, if these pages were allowed under any circumstances to be the vehicle of illustrations. If, however, he or she really wishes to see the way the pieces stood as they were placed at the beginning of the game, (the Widow's gambit,) he or she had better at once take a sheet of paper, draw an oval, and arrange the characters according to the following schedule.

At the head of the table, the Hostess, Widow Marilla Rowens. Opposite her, at the other end, Rev. Dr. Honeywood. At the *right* of the Hostess, Dudley Venner, next him Helen Darley, next her Dr. Kittredge, next him Mrs. Blanche Creamer, then the Reverend Doctor. At the *left* of the Hostess, Bernard Langdon, next him Letty Forrester, next Letty Mr. Richard Venner, next him Elsie, and so to the Reverend Doctor again.

The company came together a little before the early hour at which it was customary to take tea in Rockland. The Widow knew everybody, of course: who was there in Rockland she did not know? But some of them had to be introduced: Mr. Richard Venner to Mr. Bernard, Mr. Bernard to Miss Letty, Dudley Venner to Miss Helen Darley, and so on. The two young men looked each other straight in the eyes,—both full of youthful life, but one of frank and fearless aspect, the other with a dangerous feline beauty alien to the New England half of his blood.

The guests talked, turned over the prints, looked at the flowers, opened the "Proverbial Philosophy" with gilt edges, and the volume of Plays by W. Shakspeare, examined the horse-pictures on the walls, and so passed away the time until tea was announced, when they paired off for the room where it was in readiness. The Widow had managed it well; everything was just as she wanted it. Dudley Venner was between herself and the poor tired-looking school-mistress with her faded colors. Blanche Creamer, a lax, tumble-to-pieces, *Greuze*-ish looking blonde, whom the Widow hated because the men took to her, was purgatoried between the two old Doctors, and could see all the looks that passed between Dick Venner and his cousin. The young school-master could talk to Miss Letty: it was his business to know how to talk to school-girls. Dick would amuse himself with his cousin Elsie. The old Doctors only wanted to be well fed and they would do well enough.

It would be very pleasant to describe the tea-table; but in reality, it did not pretend to offer a plethoric banquet to the guests. The Widow had not visited at the mansion-houses for nothing, and she had learned there that an overloaded tea-table may do well enough for farm-hands when they come in at evening from their work and sit down unwashed in their shirt-sleeves, but that for decently bred people such an insult to the memory of a dinner not yet half-assimilated is wholly inadmissible. Everything was delicate, and almost everything of fair complexion: white bread and biscuits, frosted and sponge cake, cream, honey, straw-colored butter; only a shadow here and there, where the fire had crisped and browned the surfaces of a stack of dry toast, or where a preserve had brought away some of the red sunshine of the last year's summer. The Widow shall have the credit of her well-ordered tea-table, also of her bountiful cream-pitchers; for it is well known that city-people find cream a very scarce luxury in a good many country-houses of more pretensions than Hyacinth Cottage. There are no better maxims for ladies who give tea-parties than these:—

Cream is thicker than water.

Large heart never loved little cream-pot.

There is a common feeling in genteel families that the third meal of the day is not so essential a part of the daily bread as to require any especial acknowledgment to the Providence which bestows it. Very devout people, who would never sit down to a breakfast or a dinner without the grace before meat which honors the Giver of it, feel as if they thanked Heaven enough for their tea and toast by partaking of them cheerfully without audible petition or ascription. But the Widow was not exactly mansion-house-bred, and so thought it necessary to give the Reverend Doctor a peculiar look which he understood at once as inviting his professional services. He, therefore, uttered a few simple words of gratitude, very quietly,—much to the satisfaction of some of the guests, who had expected one of those elaborate effusions, with rolling up of the eyes and rhetorical accents, so frequent with eloquent divines when they address their Maker in genteel company.

Everybody began talking with the person sitting next at hand. Mr. Bernard naturally enough turned his attention first to the Widow; but somehow or other the right side of the Widow seemed to be more wide awake than the left side, next him, and he resigned her to the courtesies of Mr. Dudley Venner, directing himself, not very unwillingly, to the young girl next him on the other side. Miss Letty Forrester, the granddaughter of the Reverend Doctor, was city-bred, as anybody might see, and city-dressed, as any woman would know at sight; a man might only feel the general effect of clear, well-matched colors, of harmonious proportions, of the cut which makes everything cling like a bather's sleeve where a natural outline is to be kept, and ruffle itself up like the hackle of a pitted fighting-cock where art has a right to luxuriate in silken exuberance. How this city-bred and city-dressed girl came to be in Rockland Mr. Bernard did not know, but he knew at any rate that she was his next neighbor and entitled to his courtesies. She was handsome, too, when he came to look, very handsome when he came to look again,—endowed with that city beauty which is like the beauty of wall-fruit, something finer in certain respects than can be reared off the pavement.

The miserable routinists who keep repeating invidiously Cowper's

"God made the country and man made the town,"

as if the town were a place to kill out the race in, do not know what they are talking about. Where could they raise such Saint-Michael pears, such Saint-Germains, such Brown Beurrés, as we had until within a few years growing within the walls of our old city-gardens? Is the dark and damp cavern where a ragged beggar hides himself better than a town-mansion which fronts the sunshine and backs on its own cool shadow, with gas and water and all appliances to suit all needs? God made the *cavern* and man made the *house!* What then?

There is no doubt that the pavement keeps a deal of mischief from coming up out of the earth, and, with a dash off of it in summer, just to cool the soles of the feet when it gets too hot, is the best place for many constitutions, as some few practical people have already discovered. And just so these beauties that grow and ripen against the citywalls, these young fellows with cheeks like peaches and young girls with cheeks like nectarines, show that the most perfect forms of artificial life can do as much for the human product as garden-culture for strawberries and blackberries.

If Mr. Bernard had philosophized or prosed in this way, with so pretty, nay, so lovely a neighbor as Miss Letty Forrester waiting for him to speak to her, he would have to be dropped from this narrative as a person unworthy of his good-fortune, and not deserving the kind reader's further notice. On the contrary, he no sooner set his eyes fairly on her than he said to himself that she was charming, and that he wished she were one of his scholars at the Institute. So he began talking with her in an easy way; for he knew something of young girls by this time, and, of course, could adapt himself to a young lady who looked as if she might be not more than fifteen or sixteen years old, and therefore could hardly be a match in intellectual resources for the seventeen and eighteen year-old first-class scholars of the Apollinean Institute. But city-wall-fruit ripens early, and he soon found that this girl's training had so sharpened her wits and stored her memory, that he need not be at the trouble to stoop painfully in order to come down to her level.

The beauty of good-breeding is that it adjusts itself to all relations without effort, true to itself always, however the manners of those around it may change. Self-respect and respect for others,—the sensitive consciousness poises itself in these as the compass in the ship's binnacle balances itself and maintains its true level within the two concentric rings which suspend it on their pivots. This thorough-bred school-girl quite enchanted Mr. Bernard. He could not understand where she got her style, her way of dress, her enunciation, her easy manners. The minister was a most worthy gentleman, but this was not the Rockland native-born manner; some new element had come in between the good, plain, worthy man and this young girl, fit to be a Crown Prince's partner where there were a thousand to choose from.

He looked across to Helen Darley, for he knew she would understand the glance of admiration with which he called her attention to the young beauty at his side; and Helen knew what a young girl could be, as compared with what too many a one is, as well as anybody.

This poor, dear Helen of ours! How admirable the contrast between her and the Widow on the other side of Dudley Venner! But, what was very odd, that gentleman apparently thought the contrast was to the advantage of this poor, dear Helen. At any rate, instead of devoting himself solely to the Widow, he happened to be just at that moment talking in a very interested and, apparently, not uninteresting way to his right-hand neighbor, who, on her part, never looked more charmingly,—as Mr. Bernard could not help saying to himself,—but, to be sure, he had just been looking at the young girl next him, so that his eyes were brimful of beauty, and may have spilled some of it on the first comer: for you know M. Becquerel has been showing us lately how everything is phosphorescent; that it soaks itself with light in an instant's exposure, so that it is wet with liquid sunbeams, or, if you will, tremulous with luminous vibrations, when first plunged into the negative bath of darkness, and betrays itself by the light which escapes from its surface.

Whatever were the reason, this poor, dear Helen never looked so sweetly. Her plainly parted brown hair, her meek, blue eyes, her cheek just a little tinged with color, the almost sad simplicity of her dress, and that look he knew so well,—so full of cheerful patience, so sincere, that he had trusted her from the first moment as the believers of the larger half of Christendom trust the Blessed Virgin,—Mr. Bernard took this all in at a glance, and felt as pleased as if it had been his own sister Dorothea Elizabeth that he was looking at. As for Dudley Venner, Mr. Bernard could not help being struck by the animated expression of his countenance. It certainly showed great kindness, on his part, to pay so much attention to this quiet girl, when he had the thunder-and-lightning Widow on the other side of him.

Mrs. Marilla Rowens did not know what to make of it. She had made her tea-party expressly for Mr. Dudley Venner. She had placed him just as she wanted, between herself and a meek, delicate woman who dressed in gray, wore a plain breastpin with hair in it, who taught a pack of girls up there at the school, and looked as if she were born for a teacher,—the very best foil that she could have chosen; and here was this man, polite enough to herself, to be sure, but turning round to that very undistinguished young person, as if he rather preferred her conversation of the two!

The truth was that Dudley Venner and Helen Darley met as two travellers might meet in the desert, wearied, both of them, with their long journey, one having food, but no water, the other water, but no food. Each saw that the other had been in long conflict with some trial; for their voices were low and tender, as patiently borne sorrow and humbly uttered prayers make every human voice. Through these tones, more than by what they said, they came into natural sympathetic relations with each other. Nothing could be more unstudied. As for Dudley Venner, no beauty in all the world could have so soothed and magnetized him as the very repose and subdued gentleness which the Widow had thought would make the best possible background for her own more salient and effective attractions. No doubt, Helen, on her side, was almost too readily pleased with the confidence this new acquaintance she was making seemed to show her from the very first. She knew so few men of any condition! Mr. Silas Peckham: he was her employer, and she ought to think of him as well as she could; but every time she thought of him it was with a shiver of disgust. Mr. Bernard Langdon: a noble young man, a true friend, like a brother to her,—God bless him, and send him some young heart as fresh as his own! But this gentleman produced a new impression upon her, quite different from any to which she was accustomed. His rich, low tones had the strangest significance to her; she felt sure he must have lived through long experiences, sorrowful like her own. Elsie's father! She looked into his dark eyes, as she listened to him, to see if they had any glimmer of that peculiar light, diamond-bright, but cold and still, which she knew so well in Elsie's. Anything but that! Never was there more tenderness, it seemed to her, than in the whole look and expression of Elsie's father. She must have been a great trial to him; yet his face was that of one who had been saddened, not soured, by his discipline. Knowing what Elsie must be to him, how hard she must make any parent's life, Helen could not but be struck with the interest Mr. Dudley Venner showed in her as his daughter's instructress. He was too kind to her; again and again she meekly turned from him, so as to leave him free to talk to the showy lady at his other side, who was looking all the while

"like the night
Of cloudless realms and starry skies";

but still Mr. Dudley Venner, after a few courteous words, came back to the blue eyes and brown hair; still he kept his look fixed upon her, and his tones grew sweeter and lower as he became more interested in talk, until this poor, dear Helen, what with surprise, and the bashfulness natural to one who had seen little of the gay world, and the stirring of deep, confused sympathies with this suffering father, whose heart seemed so full of kindness, felt her cheeks glowing with unwonted flame, and betrayed the pleasing trouble of her situation by looking so sweetly as to arrest Mr. Bernard's eye for a moment, when he looked away from the young beauty sitting next him.

Elsie meantime had been silent, with that singular, still, watchful look which those who knew her well had learned to fear. Her head just a little inclined on one side, perfectly motionless for whole minutes, her eyes seeming to grow small and bright, as always when she was under her evil influence, she was looking obliquely at the young girl on the other side of her cousin Dick and next to Bernard Langdon. As for Dick himself, she seemed to be paying very little attention to him. Sometimes her eyes would wander off to Mr. Bernard, and their expression, as old Dr. Kittredge, who watched her for a while pretty keenly, noticed, would change perceptibly. One would have said that she looked with a kind of dull hatred at the girl, but with a half-relenting reproachful anger at Mr. Bernard.

Miss Letty Forrester, at whom Elsie had been looking from time to time in this fixed way, was conscious meanwhile of some unusual influence. First it was a feeling of constraint,—then, as it were, a diminished power over the muscles, as if an invisible elastic cobweb were spinning round her,—then a tendency to turn away from Mr. Bernard, who was making himself very agreeable, and look straight into those eyes which would not leave her, and which seemed to be drawing her towards them, while at the same time they chilled the blood in all her veins.

Mr. Bernard saw this influence coming over her. All at once he noticed that she sighed, and that some little points of moisture began to glisten on her forehead. But she did not grow pale perceptibly; she had no involuntary or hysteric movements; she still listened to him and smiled naturally enough. Perhaps she was only nervous at being stared at. At any rate, she was coming under some unpleasant influence or other, and Mr. Bernard had seen enough of the strange impression Elsie sometimes produced to wish this young girl to be relieved from it, whatever it was. He turned toward Elsie and looked at her in such a way as to draw her eyes upon him. Then he looked steadily and calmly into them. It was a great effort, for some perfectly inexplicable reason. At one instant he thought he could not sit where he was; he must go and speak to Elsie. Then he wanted to take his eyes away from hers; there was something intolerable in the light that came from them. But he was determined to look her down, and he believed he could do it, for he had seen her countenance change more than once when he had caught her gaze steadily fixed on him. All this took not minutes, but seconds. Presently she changed color slightly,—lifted her head, which was inclined a little to one side,—shut and opened her eyes two or three times, as if they had been pained or wearied,—and turned away baffled, and shamed, as it would seem, and shorn for the time of her singular and formidable or at least evil-natured power of swaying the impulses of those around her.

It takes too long to describe these scenes where a good deal of life is concentrated into a few silent seconds. Mr. Richard Venner had sat quietly through it all, although this short pantomime had taken place literally before his face. He saw what was going on well enough, and understood it all perfectly well. Of course the school-master had been trying to make Elsie jealous, and had succeeded. The little school-girl was a decoy-duck,—that was all. Estates like the Dudley property were not to be had every day, and no doubt the Yankee usher was willing to take some pains to make sure of Elsie. Doesn't Elsie look savage? Dick involuntarily moved his chair a little away from her, and thought he felt a pricking in the small white scars on his wrist. A dare-devil fellow, but somehow or other this girl had taken strange hold of his imagination, and he often swore to himself, that, when he married her, he would carry a loaded revolver with him to his bridal chamber.

Mrs. Blanche Creamer raged inwardly at first to find herself between the two old gentlemen of the party. It very soon gave her great comfort, however, to see that Marilla Rowens had just missed it in her calculations, and she chuckled immensely to find Dudley Venner devoting himself chiefly to Helen Darley. If the Rowens woman should hook Dudley, she felt as if she should gnaw all her nails off for spite. To think of seeing her barouching about Rockland behind a pair of long-tailed bays and a coachman with a band on his hat, while she, Blanche Creamer, was driving herself about in a one-horse "carriage"! Recovering her spirits by degrees, she began playing her surfaces off at the two old Doctors, just by way of practice. First she heaved up a glaring white shoulder, the right one, so that the Reverend Doctor should be stunned by it, if such a thing might be. The Reverend Doctor was human, as the Apostle was not ashamed to confess himself. Half-devoutly and half-mischievously he repeated inwardly, "Resist the Devil and he will flee from you." As the Reverend Doctor did not show any lively susceptibility, she thought she would try the left shoulder on old Dr. Kittredge. That worthy and experienced student of science was not at all displeased with the manœuvre, and lifted his head so as to command the exhibition through his glasses. "Blanche is good for half a dozen years or so, if she is careful," the Doctor said to himself, "and then she must take to her prayer-book." After this spasmodic failure of Mrs. Blanche Creamer's to stir up the old Doctors, she returned again to the pleasing task of watching the Widow in her evident discomfiture. But dark as the Widow looked in her half-concealed pet, she was but as a pale shadow, compared to Elsie in her silent concentration of shame and anger.

"Well, there is one good thing," said Mrs. Blanche Creamer; "Dick doesn't get much out of that cousin of his this evening! Doesn't he look handsome, though?"

So Mrs. Blanche, being now a good deal taken up with her observations of those friends of hers and ours, began to be rather careless of her two old Doctors, who naturally enough fell into conversation with each other across the white surfaces of that lady,—perhaps not very politely, but, under the circumstances, almost as a matter of necessity.

When a minister and a doctor get talking together, they

always have a great deal to say; and so it happened that the company left the table just as the two Doctors were beginning to get at each other's ideas about various interesting matters. If we follow them into the other parlor, we can, perhaps, pick up something of their conversation.

CHAPTER XXII

WHY DOCTORS DIFFER

The company rearranged itself with some changes after leaving the tea-table. Dudley Venner was very polite to the Widow; but that lady having been called off for a few moments for some domestic arrangement, he slid back to the side of Helen Darley, his daughter's faithful teacher. Elsie had got away by herself, and was taken up in studying the stereoscopic Laocoön. Dick, being thus set free, had been seized upon by Mrs. Blanche Creamer, who had diffused herself over three-quarters of a sofa and beckoned him to the remaining fourth. Mr. Bernard and Miss Letty were having a snug *tête-à-tête* in the recess of a bay-window. The two Doctors had taken two arm-chairs and sat squared off against each other. Their conversation is perhaps as well worth reporting as that of the rest of the company, and, as it was carried on in a louder tone, was of course more easy to gather and put on record.

It was a curious sight enough to see those two representatives of two great professions brought face to face to talk over the subjects they had been looking at all their lives from such different points of view. Both were old; old enough to have been moulded by their habits of thought and life; old enough to have all their beliefs "fretted in," as vintners say,—thoroughly worked up with their characters. Each of them looked his calling. The Reverend Doctor had lived a good deal among books in his study; the Doctor, as we will call the medical gentleman, had been riding about the country for between thirty and forty years. His face looked tough and weather-worn; while the Reverend Doctor's, hearty as it appeared, was of finer texture.

The Doctor's was the graver of the two; there was something of grimness about it,—partly owing to the northeasters he had faced for so many years, partly to long companionship with that stern personage who never deals in sentiment or pleasantry. His speech was apt to be brief and peremptory; it was a way he had got by ordering patients; but he could discourse somewhat, on occasion, as the reader may find out. The Reverend Doctor had an open, smiling expression, a cheery voice, a hearty laugh, and a cordial way with him which some thought too lively for his cloth, but which children, who are good judges of such matters, delighted in, so that he was the favorite of all the little rogues about town. But he had the clerical art of sobering down in a moment, when asked to say grace while somebody was in the middle of some particularly funny story; and though his voice was so cheery in common talk, in the pulpit, like almost all preachers, he had a wholly different and peculiar way of speaking, supposed to be more acceptable to the Creator than the natural manner. In point of fact, most of our anti-papal and anti-prelatical clergymen do really *intone* their prayers, without suspecting in the least that they have fallen into such a Romish practice.

This is the way the conversation between the Doctor of Divinity and the Doctor of Medicine was going on at the point where these notes take it up.

"*Ubi tres medici, duo athei*, you know, Doctor. Your profession has always had the credit of being lax in doctrine,—though pretty stringent in *practice*, ha! ha!"

"Some priest said that," the Doctor answered, dryly. "They always talked Latin when they had a bigger lie than common to get rid of."

"Good!" said the Reverend Doctor; "I'm afraid they would lie a little sometimes. But isn't there some truth in it, Doctor? Don't you think your profession is apt to see 'Nature' in the place of the God of Nature,—to lose sight of the great First Cause in their daily study of secondary causes?"

"I've thought about that," the Doctor answered, "and

I've talked about it and read about it, and I've come to the conclusion that nobody believes in God and trusts in God quite so much as the doctors; only it isn't just the sort of Deity that some of your profession have wanted them to take up with. There was a student of mine wrote a dissertation on the Natural Theology of Health and Disease, and took that old lying proverb for his motto. He knew a good deal more about books than ever I did, and had studied in other countries. I'll tell you what he said about it. He said the old Heathen Doctor, Galen, praised God for his handiwork in the human body, just as if he had been a Christian, or the Psalmist himself. He said they had this sentence set up in large letters in the great lecture-room in Paris where he attended: *I dressed his wound and God healed him.* That was an old surgeon's saying. And he gave a long list of doctors who were not only Christians, but famous ones. I grant you, though, ministers and doctors are very apt to see differently in spiritual matters."

"That's it," said the Reverend Doctor; "you are apt to see 'Nature' where we see God, and appeal to 'Science' where we are contented with Revelation."

"We don't separate God and Nature, perhaps, as you do," the Doctor answered. "When we say that God is omnipresent and omnipotent and omniscient, we are a little more apt to mean it than your folks are. We think, when a wound heals, that God's *presence* and *power* and *knowledge* are there, healing it, just as that old surgeon did. We think a good many theologians, working among their books, don't see the facts of the world they live in. When we tell 'em of these facts, they are apt to call us materialists and atheists and infidels, and all that. We can't help seeing the facts, and we don't think it's wicked to mention 'em."

"Do tell me," the Reverend Doctor said, "some of these facts we are in the habit of overlooking, and which your profession thinks it can see and understand."

"That's very easy," the Doctor replied. "For instance: you don't understand or don't allow for idiosyncrasies as we learn to. We know that food and physic act differently with different people; but you think the same kind of truth is going to suit, or ought to suit, all minds. We don't fight with a patient because he can't take magnesia or opium; but you are all the time quarrelling over your beliefs, as if belief did not depend very much on race and constitution, to say nothing of early training."

"Do you mean to say that every man is not absolutely free to choose his beliefs?"

"The men you write about in your studies are, but not the men we see in the real world. There is some apparently congenital defect in the Indians, for instance, that keeps them from choosing civilization and Christianity. So with the Gypsies, very likely. Everybody knows that Catholicism or Protestantism is a good deal a matter of race. Constitution has more to do with belief than people think for. I went to a Universalist church, when I was in the city one day, to hear a famous man whom all the world knows, and I never saw such pews-full of broad shoulders and florid faces, and substantial, wholesome-looking persons, male and female, in all my life. Why, it was astonishing. Either their creed made them healthy, or they chose it because they were healthy. Your folks have never got the hang of human nature."

"I am afraid this would be considered a degrading and dangerous view of human beliefs and responsibility for them," the Reverend Doctor replied. "Prove to a man that his will is governed by something outside of himself, and you have lost all hold on his moral and religious nature. There is nothing bad men want to believe so much as that they are governed by necessity. Now that which is at once degrading and dangerous cannot be true."

"No doubt," the Doctor replied, "all large views of mankind limit our estimate of the absolute freedom of the will. But I don't think it degrades or endangers us, for this reason, that, while it makes us charitable to the rest of mankind, our own sense of freedom, whatever it is, is never affected by argument. *Conscience won't be reasoned with.* We feel that *we* can practically do this or that, and if we choose the wrong, we know we are responsible; but observation teaches us that this or that other race or individual has not the same practical freedom of choice. I don't see how we can avoid this conclusion in the instance of the

American Indians. The science of Ethnology has upset a good many theoretical notions about human nature."

"Science!" said the Reverend Doctor, "science! that was a word the Apostle Paul did not seem to think much of, if we may judge by the Epistle to Timothy: 'Oppositions of science falsely so called.' I own that I am jealous of that word and the pretensions that go with it. Science has seemed to me to be very often only the handmaid of skepticism."

"Doctor!" the physician said, emphatically, "science is knowledge. Nothing that is not *known* properly belongs to science. Whenever knowledge obliges us to doubt, we are always safe in doubting. Astronomers foretell eclipses, say how long comets are to stay with us, point out where a new planet is to be found. We see they *know* what they assert, and the poor old Roman Catholic Church has at last to knock under. So Geology *proves* a certain succession of events, and the best Christian in the world must make the earth's history square with it. Besides, I don't think you remember what great revelations of himself the Creator has made in the minds of the men who have built up science. You seem to me to hold his human masterpieces very cheap. Don't you think the 'inspiration of the Almighty' gave Newton and Cuvier 'understanding'?"

The Reverend Doctor was not arguing for victory. In fact, what he wanted was to call out the opinions of the old physician by a show of opposition, being already predisposed to agree with many of them. He was rather trying the common arguments, as one tries tricks of fence merely to learn the way of parrying. But just here he saw a tempting opening, and could not resist giving a home-thrust.

"Yes; but you surely would not consider it inspiration of the same kind as that of the writers of the Old Testament?"

That cornered the Doctor, and he paused a moment before he replied. Then he raised his head, so as to command the Reverend Doctor's face through his spectacles, and said,—

"I did not say that. You are clear, I suppose, that the

Omniscient spoke through Solomon, but that Shakspeare wrote without his help?"

The Reverend Doctor looked very grave. It was a bold, blunt way of putting the question. He turned it aside with the remark, that Shakspeare seemed to him at times to come as near inspiration as any human being not included among the sacred writers.

"Doctor," the physician began, as from a sudden suggestion, "you won't quarrel with me, if I tell you some of my real thoughts, will you?"

"Say on, my dear Sir, say on," the minister answered, with his most genial smile; "your real thoughts are just what I want to get at. A man's real thoughts are a great rarity. If I don't agree with you, I shall like to hear you."

The Doctor began; and in order to give his thoughts more connectedly, we will omit the conversational breaks, the questions and comments of the clergyman, and all accidental interruptions.

"When the old ecclesiastics said that where there were three doctors there were two atheists, they lied, of course. They called everybody who differed from them atheists, until they found out that not believing in God wasn't nearly so ugly a crime as not believing in some particular dogma; then they called them *heretics*, until so many good people had been burned under that name that it began to smell too strong of roasting flesh,—and after that *infidels*, which properly means people without faith, of whom there are not a great many in any place or time. But then, of course, there was some reason why doctors shouldn't think about religion exactly as ministers did, or they never would have made that proverb. It's very likely that something of the same kind is true now; whether it is so or not, I am going to tell you the reasons why it would not be strange, if doctors should take rather different views from clergymen about some matters of belief. I don't, of course, mean all doctors nor all clergymen. Some doctors go as far as any old New-England divine, and some clergymen agree very well with the doctors that think least according to rule.

"To begin with their ideas of the Creator himself. They

always see him trying to help his creatures out of their troubles. A man no sooner gets a cut, than the Great Physician, whose agency we often call *Nature*, goes to work, first to stop the blood, and then to heal the wound, and then to make the scar as small as possible. If a man's pain exceeds a certain amount, he faints, and so gets relief. If it lasts too long, habit comes in to make it tolerable. If it is altogether too bad, he dies. That is the best thing to be done under the circumstances. So you see, the doctor is constantly in presence of a benevolent agency working against a settled order of things, of which pain and disease are the accidents, so to speak. Well, no doubt they find it harder than clergymen to believe that there can be any world or state from which this benevolent agency is wholly excluded. This may be very wrong; but it is not unnatural. They can hardly conceive of a permanent state of being in which cuts would never try to heal, nor habit render suffering endurable. This is one effect of their training.

"Then, again, their attention is very much called to human limitations. Ministers work out the machinery of responsibility in an abstract kind of way; they have a sort of algebra of human nature, in which *friction* and *strength* (or *weakness*) *of material* are left out. You see, a doctor is in the way of studying children from the moment of birth upwards. For the first year or so he sees that they are just as much pupils of their Maker as the young of any other animals. Well, their Maker trains them to *pure selfishness*. Why? In order that they may be sure to take care of themselves. So you see, when a child comes to be, we will say a year and a day old, and makes his first choice between right and wrong, he is at a disadvantage; for he has that *vis a tergo*, as we doctors call it, that force from behind, of a whole year's life of selfishness, for which he is no more to blame than a calf is to blame for having lived in the same way, purely to gratify his natural appetites. Then we see that baby grow up to a child, and, if he is fat and stout and red and lively, we expect to find him troublesome and noisy, and, perhaps, sometimes disobedient more or less; that's the way each new generation breaks its egg-shell; but if he is very weak and thin, and is one of the kind that may be expected to die early, he will very likely sit in the house all day and read good books about other little sharp-faced children just like himself, who died early, having always been perfectly indifferent to all the out-door amusements of the wicked little red-cheeked children. Some of the little folks we watch grow up to be young women, and occasionally one of them gets nervous, what we call hysterical, and then that girl will begin to play all sorts of pranks,—to lie and cheat, perhaps, in the most unaccountable way, so that she might seem to a minister a good example of total depravity. We don't see her in that light. We give her iron and valerian, and get her on horseback, if we can, and so expect to make her will come all right again. By-and-by we are called in to see an old baby, threescore years and ten or more old. We find this old baby has never got rid of that first year's teaching which led him to fill his stomach with all he could pump into it, and his hands with everything he could grab. People call him a miser. We are sorry for him; but we can't help remembering his first year's training, and the natural effect of money on the great majority of those that have it. So while the ministers say he 'shall hardly enter into the kingdom of heaven,' we like to remind them that 'with God all things are possible.'

"Once more, we see all kinds of monomania and insanity. We learn from them to recognize all sorts of queer tendencies in minds supposed to be sane, so that we have nothing but compassion for a large class of persons condemned as sinners by theologians, but considered by us as invalids. We have constant reasons for noticing the transmission of qualities from parents to offspring, and we find it hard to hold a child accountable in any moral point of view for inherited bad temper or tendency to drunkenness,—as hard as we should to blame him for inheriting gout or asthma. I suppose we are more lenient with human nature than theologians generally are. We know that the spirits of men and their views of the present and the future go up and down with the barometer, and that a permanent depression of one inch in the mercurial column would affect the whole theology of Christendom.

"Ministers talk about the human will as if it stood on a high look-out, with plenty of light, and elbow-room reaching to the horizon. Doctors are constantly noticing how it is tied up and darkened by inferior organization, by disease, and all sorts of crowding interferences, until they get to look upon Hottentots and Indians—and a good many of their own race—as a kind of self-conscious blood-clocks with very limited power of self-determination. That's the *tendency*, I say, of a doctor's experience. But the people to whom they address their statements of the results of their observation belong to the thinking class of the highest races, and *they* are conscious of a great deal of liberty of will. So in the face of the fact that civilization with all it offers has proved a dead failure with the aboriginal races of this country,—on the whole, I say, a dead failure,—they talk as if they knew from their own will all about that of a Digger Indian! We are more apt to go by observation of the facts in the case. We are constantly seeing weakness where you see depravity. I don't say we're *right*; I only tell what you must often find to be the fact, right or wrong, in talking with doctors. You see, too, our notions of bodily and moral disease, or sin, are apt to go together. We used to be as hard on sickness as you were on sin. We know better now. We don't look at sickness as we used to, and try to poison it with everything that is offensive,—burnt toads and earthworms and viper-broth, and worse things than these. We know that disease has something back of it which the body isn't to blame for, at least in most cases, and which very often it is trying to get rid of. Just so with sin. I will agree to take a hundred new-born babes of a certain stock and return seventy-five of them in a dozen years true and honest, if not 'pious' children. And I will take another hundred, of a different stock, and put them in the hands of certain Ann-Street or Five-Points teachers, and seventy-five of them will be thieves and liars at the end of the same dozen years. I have heard of an old character, Colonel Jaques, I believe it was, a famous cattle-breeder, who used to say he could breed to pretty much any pattern he wanted to. Well, we doctors see so much of families, how the tricks of the blood keep breaking out, just as much in character as they do in looks, that we can't help feeling as if a great many people hadn't a fair chance to be what is called 'good,' and that there isn't a text in the Bible better worth keeping always in mind than that one, 'Judge not, that ye be not judged.'

"As for our getting any quarter at the hands of theologians, we don't expect it, and have no right to. You don't give each other any quarter. I have had two religious books sent me by friends within a week or two. One is Mr. Brownson's; he is as fair and square as Euclid; a real honest, strong thinker, and one that knows what he is talking about, —for he has tried all sorts of religions, pretty much. He tells us that the Roman Catholic Church is the one 'through which alone we can hope for heaven.' The other is by a worthy Episcopal rector, who appears to write as if he were in earnest, and he calls the Papacy the 'Devil's Masterpiece,' and talks about the 'Satanic scheme' of that very Church 'through which alone,' as Mr. Brownson tells us, 'we can hope for heaven'! What's the use in *our* caring about hard words after this,—'atheists,' heretics, infidels, and the like? They're after all, only the cinders picked up out of those heaps of ashes round the stumps of the old stakes where they used to burn men, women, and children for not thinking just like other folks. They'll 'crock' your fingers, but they can't burn us.

"Doctors are the best-natured people in the world, except when they get fighting with each other. And they have some advantages over you. You inherit your notions from a set of priests that had no wives and no children, or none to speak of, and so let their humanity die out of them. It didn't seem much to them to condemn a few thousand millions of people to purgatory or worse for a mistake of judgment. They didn't know what it was to have a child look up in their faces and say 'Father!' It will take you a hundred or two more years to get decently humanized, after so many centuries of *de*-humanizing celibacy.

"Besides, though our libraries are, perhaps, not commonly quite so big as yours, God opens one book to physicians that a good many of you don't know much about, —the Book of Life. That is none of your dusty folios with black letters between pasteboard and leather, but it is printed in bright red type, and the binding of it is warm and tender to every touch. They reverence that book as one of the Almighty's infallible revelations. They will insist on reading you lessons out of it, whether you call them names or not. These will always be lessons of charity. No doubt, nothing can be more provoking to listen to. But do beg your folks to remember that the Smithfield fires are all out, and that the cinders are very dirty and not in the least dangerous. They'd a great deal better be civil, and not be throwing old proverbs in the doctors' faces, when they say that the man of the old monkish notions is one thing and the man they watch from his cradle to his coffin is something very different."

It has cost a good deal of trouble to work the Doctor's talk up into this formal shape. Some of his sentences have been rounded off for him, and the whole brought into a more rhetorical form than it could have pretended to, if taken as it fell from his lips. But the exact course of his remarks has been followed, and as far as possible his expressions have been retained. Though given in the form of a discourse, it must be remembered that this was a conversation, much more fragmentary and colloquial than it seems as just read.

The Reverend Doctor was very far from taking offense at the old physician's freedom of speech. He knew him to be honest, kind, charitable, self-denying, wherever any sorrow was to be alleviated, always reverential, with a cheerful trust in the great Father of all mankind. To be sure, his senior deacon, old Deacon Shearer,—who seemed to have got his Scripture-teachings out of the "Vinegar Bible," (the one where *Vineyard* is misprinted *Vinegar*, which a good many people seem to have adopted as the true reading,) —his senior deacon had called Dr. Kittredge an "infidel." But the Reverend Doctor could not help feeling, that, unless the text, "By their fruits ye shall know them," were an interpolation, the Doctor was the better Christian of the two. Whatever his senior deacon might think about it, he said to himself that he shouldn't be surprised if he met the Doctor in heaven yet, inquiring anxiously after old Deacon Shearer.

He was on the point of expressing himself very frankly to the Doctor, with that benevolent smile on his face which had sometimes come near giving offence to the readers of the "Vinegar" edition, but he saw that the physician's attention had been arrested by Elsie. He looked in the same direction himself, and could not help being struck by her attitude and expression. There was something singularly graceful in the curves of her neck and the rest of her figure, but she was so perfectly still that it seemed as if she were hardly breathing. Her eyes were fixed on the young girl with whom Mr. Bernard was talking. He had often noticed their brilliancy, but now it seemed to him that they appeared dull, and the look on her features was as of some passion which had missed its stroke. Mr. Bernard's companion seemed unconscious that she was the object of this attention, and was listening to the young master as if he had succeeded in making himself very agreeable.

Of course Dick Venner had not mistaken the game that was going on. The school-master meant to make Elsie jealous,—and he had done it. That's it: get her savage first, and then come wheedling round her,—a sure trick, if he isn't headed off somehow. But Dick saw well enough that he had better let Elsie alone just now, and thought the best way of killing the evening would be to amuse himself in a little lively talk with Mrs. Blanche Creamer, and incidentally to show Elsie that he could make himself acceptable to other women, if not to herself.

The Doctor presently went up to Elsie, determined to engage her in conversation and get her out of her thoughts, which he saw, by her look, were dangerous. Her father had been on the point of leaving Helen Darley to go to her, but felt easy enough when he saw the old Doctor at her side, and so went on talking. The Reverend Doctor, being now left alone, engaged the Widow Rowens, who put the best face on her vexation she could, but was devoting herself to all the underground deities for having been such a fool as to ask that pale-faced thing from the Institute to fill up her party.

There is no space left to report the rest of the conversation. If there was anything of any significance in it, it will turn up by-and-by, no doubt. At ten o'clock the Reverend Doctor called Miss Letty, who had no idea it was so late; Mr. Bernard gave his arm to Helen; Mr. Richard saw to Mrs. Blanche Creamer; the Doctor gave Elsie a cautioning look, and went off alone, thoughtful; Dudley Venner and his daughter got into their carriage and were whirled away. The Widow's gambit was played, and she had not won the game.

CHAPTER XXIII

THE WILD HUNTSMAN

The young master had not forgotten the old Doctor's cautions. Without attributing any great importance to the warning he had given him, Mr. Bernard had so far complied with his advice that he was becoming a pretty good shot with the pistol. It was an amusement as good as many others to practise, and he had taken a fancy to it after the first few days.

The popping of a pistol at odd hours in the back-yard of the Institute was a phenomenon more than sufficiently remarkable to be talked about in Rockland. The viscous intelligence of a country-village is not easily stirred by the winds which ripple the fluent thought of great cities, but it holds every straw and entangles every insect that lights upon it. It soon became rumored in the town that the young master was a wonderful shot with the pistol. Some said he could hit a fo'pence-ha'penny at three rod; some, that he had shot a swallow, flying, with a single ball; some, that he snuffed a candle five times out of six at ten paces, and that he could hit any button in a man's coat he wanted to. In other words, as in all such cases, all the common feats were ascribed to him, as the current jokes of the day are laid at the door of any noted wit, however innocent he may be of them.

In the natural course of things, Mr. Richard Venner, who had by this time made some acquaintances, as we have seen, among that class of the population least likely to allow a live cinder of gossip to go out for want of air, had heard incidentally that the master up there at the Institute was all the time practising with a pistol, that they say he can snuff a candle at ten rods, (that was Mrs. Blanche Creamer's version,) and that he could hit anybody he wanted to right in the eye, as far as he could see the white of it.

Dick did not like the sound of all this any too well. Without believing more than half of it, there was enough to make the Yankee school-master too unsafe to be trifled with. However, shooting at a mark was pleasant work enough; he had no particular objection to it himself. Only he did not care so much for those little popgun affairs that a man carries in his pocket, and with which you couldn't shoot a fellow,—a robber, say,—without getting the muzzle under his nose. Pistols for boys; long-range rifles for men. There was such a gun lying in a closet with the fowling-pieces. He would go out into the fields and see what he could do as a marksman.

The nature of the mark which Dick chose for experimenting upon was singular. He had found some panes of glass which had been removed from an old sash, and he placed these successively before his target, arranging them at different angles. He found that a bullet would go through the glass without glancing or having its force materially abated. It was an interesting fact in physics, and might prove of some practical significance hereafter. Nobody knows what may turn up to render these out-of-the-way facts useful. All this was done in a quiet way in one of the bare spots high up the side of The Mountain. He was very thoughtful in taking the precaution to get so far away; rifle-bullets are apt to glance and come whizzing about people's ears, if they are fired in the neighborhood of houses. Dick satisfied himself that he could be tolerably sure of hitting a pane of glass at a distance of thirty rods, more or less, and that, if there happened to be anything behind it, the glass would not materially alter the force or direction of the bullet.

About this time it occurred to him also that there was an old accomplishment of his which he would be in danger of losing for want of practice, if he did not take some opportunity to try his hand and regain its cunning, if it had begun to be diminished by disuse. For his first trial, he chose an evening when the moon was shining, and after the hour when the Rockland people were like to be stirring abroad. He was so far established now that he could do much as he pleased without exciting remark.

The prairie horse he rode, the mustang of the Pampas, wild as he was, had been trained to take part in at least one exercise. This was the accomplishment in which Mr. Richard now proposed to try himself. For this purpose he sought the implement of which, as it may be remembered, he had once made an incidental use,—the *lasso*, or long strip of hide with a slip-noose at the end of it. He had been accustomed to playing with such a thong from his boyhood, and had become expert in its use in capturing wild cattle in the course of his adventures. Unfortunately, there were no wild bulls likely to be met with in the neighborhood, to become the subjects of his skill. A stray cow in the road, an ox or a horse in a pasture, must serve his turn,—dull beasts, but moving marks to aim at, at any rate.

Never, since he had galloped in the chase over the Pampas, had Dick Venner felt such a sense of life and power as when he struck the long spurs into his wild horse's flanks, and dashed along the road with the lasso lying like a coiled snake at the saddle-bow. In skilful hands, the silent, bloodless noose, flying like an arrow, but not like that leaving a wound behind it,—sudden as a pistol-shot, but without the tell-tale explosion,—is one of the most fearful and mysterious weapons that arm the hand of man. The old Romans knew how formidable, even in contest with a gladiator equipped with sword, helmet, and shield, was the almost naked *retiarius*, with his net in one hand and his three-pronged javelin in the other. Once get a net over a man's head, or a cord round his neck, or, what is more frequently done nowadays, *bonnet* him by knocking his hat down over his eyes, and he is at the mercy of his opponent. Our soldiers who served against the Mexicans found this out too well. Many a poor fellow has been lassoed by the fierce riders from the plains, and fallen an easy victim to the captor who had snared him in the fatal noose.

But, imposing as the sight of the wild huntsmen of the Pampas might have been, Dick could not help laughing at the mock sublimity of his situation, as he tried his first experiment on an unhappy milky mother who had strayed from her herd and was wandering disconsolately along the road, laying the dust, as she went, with thready streams from her swollen, swinging udders. "Here goes the Don at the windmill!" said Dick, and tilted full speed at her, whirling the lasso round his head as he rode. The creature swerved to one side of the way, as the wild horse and his rider came rushing down upon her, and presently turned and ran, as only cows and——it wouldn't be safe to say it—can run. Just before he passed,—at twenty or thirty feet from her,—the lasso shot from his hand, uncoiling as it flew, and in an instant its loop was round her horns. "Well cast!" said Dick, as he galloped up to her side and dexterously disengaged the lasso. "Now for a horse on the run!"

He had the good luck to find one, presently, grazing in a pasture at the road-side. Taking down the rails of the fence at one point, he drove the horse into the road and gave chase. It was a lively young animal enough, and was easily roused to a pretty fast pace. As his gallop grew more and more rapid, Dick gave the reins to the mustang, until the two horses stretched themselves out in their longest strides. If the first feat looked like play, the one he was now to attempt had a good deal of the appearance of real work. He touched the mustang with the spur, and in a few fierce leaps found himself nearly abreast of the frightened animal he was chasing. Once more he whirled the lasso round and round over his head, and then shot it forth, as the rattlesnake shoots his head from the loops against which it rests. The noose was round the horse's neck, and in another instant was tightened so as almost to stop his breath. The prairie horse knew the trick of the cord, and leaned away from the captive, so as to keep the thong tensely stretched between his neck and the peak of the saddle to which it was fastened. Struggling was of no use with a halter round his windpipe, and he very soon began to tremble and stagger,—blind, no doubt, and with a roaring in his ears as of a thousand battle-trumpets,—at any rate, subdued and helpless. That was enough. Dick loosened his lasso, wound it up again, laid it like a pet snake in a coil at his saddle-bow, turned his horse, and rode slowly along towards the mansion-house.

The place had never looked more stately and beautiful to him than as he now saw it in the moonlight. The undulations of the land,—the grand mountain-screen which sheltered the mansion from the northern blasts, rising with all its hanging forests and parapets of naked rock high towards the heavens,—the ancient mansion, with its square chimneys, and body-guard of old trees, and cincture of low walls with marble-pillared gateways,—the fields, with their various coverings,—the beds of flowers,—the plots of turf, one with a gray column in its centre bearing a sun-dial on which the rays of the moon were idly shining, another with a white stone and a narrow ridge of turf,—over all these objects, harmonized with all their infinite details into one fair whole by the moonlight, the prospective heir, as he deemed himself, looked with admiring eyes.

But while he looked, the thought rose up in his mind like waters from a poisoned fountain, that there was a deep plot laid to cheat him of the inheritance which by a double claim he meant to call his own. Every day this ice-cold beauty, this dangerous, handsome cousin of his, went up to that place,—that usher's girl-trap. Every day,—regularly now,—it used to be different. Did she go only to get out of his, her cousin's, reach? Was she not rather becoming more and more involved in the toils of this plotting Yankee?

If Mr. Bernard had shown himself at that moment a few rods in advance, the chances are that in less than one minute he would have found himself with a noose round his neck, at the heels of a mounted horseman. Providence spared him for the present. Mr. Richard rode his horse quietly round to the stable, put him up, and proceeded towards the house. He got to his bed without disturbing the family, but could not sleep. The idea had fully taken possession of his mind that a deep intrigue was going on which would end by bringing Elsie and the school-master into relations fatal to all his own hopes. With that ingenuity which always accompanies jealousy, he tortured every circumstance of the last few weeks so as to make it square with this belief. From this vein of thought he naturally passed to a consideration of every possible method by which the issue he feared might be avoided.

Mr. Richard talked very plain language with himself in all these inward colloquies. Supposing it came to the worst, what could be done then? First, an accident might happen to the school-master which should put a complete and final check upon his projects and contrivances. The particular accident which might interrupt his career must, evidently, be determined by circumstances; but it must be of a nature to explain itself without the necessity of any particular person's becoming involved in the matter. It would be unpleasant to go into particulars; but everybody knows well enough that men sometimes get in the way of a stray bullet, and that young persons occasionally do violence to themselves in various modes,—by fire-arms, suspension, and other means,—in consequence of disappointment in love, perhaps, oftener than from other motives. There was still another kind of accident which might serve his purpose. If anything should happen to Elsie, it would be the most natural thing in the world that his uncle should adopt him, his nephew and only near relation, as his heir. Unless, indeed, Uncle Dudley should take it into his head to marry again. In that case, where would he, Dick, be? This was the most detestable complication which he could conceive of. And yet he had noticed—he could not help noticing—that his uncle had been very attentive to, and, as it seemed, very much pleased with, that young woman from the school. What did that mean? Was it possible that he was going to take a fancy to her?

It made him wild to think of all the several contingencies which might defraud him of that good-fortune which seemed but just now within his grasp. He glared in the darkness at imaginary faces: sometimes at that of the handsome, treacherous school-master; sometimes at that of the meek-looking, but, no doubt, scheming, lady-teacher; sometimes at that of the dark girl whom he was ready to make his wife; sometimes at that of his much respected uncle, who, of course, could not be allowed to peril the fortunes of his relatives by forming a new connection. It was a frightful perplexity in which he found himself, because there was no one single life an accident to which would be sufficient to insure the fitting and natural course of descent to the great Dudley property. If it had been a simple question of helping forward a casualty to any one person, there was nothing in Dick's habits of thought and living to make that a serious difficulty. He had been so much with lawless people, that a life between his wish and his object seemed only as an obstacle to be removed, provided the object were worth the risk and trouble. But if there were two or three lives in the way, manifestly that altered the case.

His Southern blood was getting impatient. There was enough of the New-Englander about him to make him calculate his chances before he struck; but his plans were liable to be defeated at any moment by a passionate impulse such as the dark-hued races of Southern Europe and their descendants are liable to. He lay in his bed, sometimes arranging plans to meet the various difficulties already mentioned, sometimes getting into a paroxysm of blind rage in the perplexity of considering what object he should select as the one most clearly in his way. On the whole, there could be no doubt where the most threatening of all his embarrassments lay. It was in the probable growing relation between Elsie and the school-master. If it should prove, as it seemed likely, that there was springing up a serious attachment tending to a union between them, he knew what he should do, if he was not quite so sure how he should do it.

There was one thing at least which might favor his projects, and which, at any rate, would serve to amuse him. He could, by a little quiet observation, find out what were the school-master's habits of life: whether he had any routine which could be calculated upon; and under what circumstances a strictly private interview of a few minutes with him might be reckoned on, in case it should be desirable. He could also very probably learn some facts about Elsie: whether the young man was in the habit of attending her on her way home from school; whether she stayed about the school-room after the other girls had gone; and any incidental matters of interest which might present themselves.

He was getting more and more restless for want of some excitement. A mad gallop, a visit to Mrs. Blanche Creamer, who had taken such a fancy to him, or a chat with the Widow Rowens, who was very lively in her talk, for all her sombre colors, and reminded him a good deal of some of his earlier friends, the *señoritas*,—all these were distractions, to be sure, but not enough to keep his fiery spirit from fretting itself in longings for more dangerous excitements. The thought of getting a knowledge of all Mr. Bernard's ways, so that he would be in his power at any moment, was a happy one.

For some days after this he followed Elsie at a long distance behind, to watch her until she got to the school-house. One day he saw Mr. Bernard join her: a mere accident, very probably, for it was only once this happened. She came on her homeward way alone,—quite apart from the groups of girls who strolled out of the school-house yard in company. Sometimes she was behind them all,—which was suggestive. Could she have stayed to meet the schoolmaster?

If he could have smuggled himself into the school, he would have liked to watch her there, and see if there was not some understanding between her and the master which betrayed itself by look or word. But this was beyond the limits of his audacity, and he had to content himself with such cautious observations as could be made at a distance. With the aid of a pocket-glass he could make out persons without the risk of being observed himself.

Mr. Silas Peckham's corps of instructors was not expected to be off duty or to stand at ease for any considerable length of time. Sometimes Mr. Bernard, who had more freedom than the rest, would go out for a ramble in the daytime, but more frequently it would be in the evening, after the hour of "retiring," as bedtime was elegantly termed by the young ladies of the Apollinean Institute. He would then not unfrequently walk out alone in the common roads, or climb up the sides of The Mountain, which seemed to be one of his favorite resorts. Here, of course, it was impossible to follow him with the eye at a distance. Dick had a hideous, gnawing suspicion that somewhere in these deep shades the school-master might meet Elsie, whose evening wanderings he knew so well. But of this he was not able to assure himself. Secrecy was necessary to his present plans, and he could not compromise himself by over-eager curiosity. One thing he learned with certainty. The master returned, after his walk one evening, and entered the building where his room was situated. Presently a light betrayed the window of his apartment. From a wooded bank, some thirty or forty rods from this building, Dick Venner could see the interior of the chamber, and watch the master as he sat at his desk, the light falling strongly upon his face, intent upon the book or manuscript before him. Dick contemplated him very long in this attitude. The sense of watching his every motion, himself meanwhile utterly unseen, was delicious. How little the master was thinking what eyes were on him!

Well,—there were two things quite certain. One was, that, if he chose, he could meet the school-master alone, either in the road or in a more solitary place, if he preferred to watch his chance for an evening or two. The other was, that he commanded his position, as he sat at his desk in the evening, in such a way that there would be very little difficulty,—so far as that went; of course, however, silence is always preferable to noise, and there is a great difference in the marks left by different casualties. Very likely nothing would come of all this espionage; but, at any rate, the first thing to be done with a man you want to have in your power is to learn his habits.

Since the tea-party at the Widow Rowens's, Elsie had been more fitful and moody than ever. Dick understood all this well enough, you know. It was the working of her jealousy against that young school-girl to whom the master had devoted himself for the sake of piquing the heiress of the Dudley mansion. Was it possible, in any way, to exasperate her irritable nature against him, and in this way to render her more accessible to his own advances? It was difficult to influence her at all. She endured his company without seeming to enjoy it. She watched him with that strange look of hers, sometimes as if she were on her guard against him, sometimes as if she would like to strike at him as in that fit of childish passion. She ordered him about with a haughty indifference which reminded him of his own way with the dark-eyed women whom he had known so well of old. All this added a secret pleasure to the other motives he had for worrying her with jealous suspicions. He knew she brooded silently on any grief that poisoned her comfort,—that she fed on it, as it were, until it ran with every drop of blood in her veins,—and that, except in some paroxysm of rage, of which he himself was not likely the second time to be the object, or in some deadly vengeance wrought secretly, against which he would keep a sharp lookout, so far as he was concerned, she had no outlet for her dangerous, smouldering passions.

Beware of the woman who cannot find free utterance for all her stormy inner life either in words or song! So long as a woman can talk, there is nothing she cannot bear. If she cannot have a companion to listen to her woes, and has no musical utterance, vocal or instrumental,—then, if she is of the real woman sort, and has a few heartfuls of wild blood in her, and you have done her a wrong,—double-bolt the door which she may enter on noiseless slipper at midnight, —look twice before you taste of any cup whose draught the shadow of her hand may have darkened!

But let her talk, and, above all, cry, or, if she is one of the coarser-grained tribe, give her the run of all the red-hot expletives in the language and let her blister her lips with them until she is tired, she will sleep like a lamb after it, and you may take a cup of coffee from her without stirring it up to look for its sediment.

So, if she can sing, or play on any musical instrument, all her wickedness will run off through her throat or the tips of her fingers. How many tragedies find their peaceful catastrophe in fierce roulades and strenuous bravuras! How many murders are executed in double-quick time upon the keys which stab the air with their dagger-strokes of sound! What would our civilization be without the piano? Are not Erard and Broadwood and Chickering the true humanizers of our time? Therefore do I love to hear the all-pervading *tum tum* jarring the walls of little parlors in houses with double door-plates on their portals, looking out on streets and courts which to know is to be unknown, and where to exist is not to live, according to any true definition of living. Therefore complain I not of modern degeneracy, when, even from the open window of the small unlovely farmhouse, tenanted by the hard-handed man of bovine flavors and the flat-patterned woman of broken-down countenance, issue the same familiar sounds. For who knows that Almira, but for these keys, which throb away her wild impulses in harmless discords, would not have been floating, dead, in the brown stream which slides through the meadows by her father's door,—or living, with that other current which runs beneath the gas-lights over the slimy pavement, choking with wretched weeds that were once in spotless flower?

Poor Elsie! She never sang nor played. She never shaped her inner life in words: such utterance was as much denied to her nature as common articulate speech to the deaf mute. Her only language must be in action. Watch her well by day and by night, Old Sophy! watch her well! or the long line of her honored name may close in shame, and the stately mansion of the Dudleys remain a hissing and a reproach till its roof is buried in its cellar!

CHAPTER XXIV

ON HIS TRACKS

"Abel!" said the old Doctor, one morning, "after you've harnessed Caustic, come into the study a few minutes, will you?"

Abel nodded. He was a man of few words, and he knew that the "will you" did not require an answer, being the true New-England way of rounding the corners of an employer's order,—a tribute to the personal independence of an American citizen.

The hired man came into the study in the course of a few minutes. His face was perfectly still, and he waited to be spoken to; but the Doctor's eye detected a certain meaning in his expression, which looked as if he had something to communicate.

"Well?" said the Doctor.

"He's up to mischief o' some kind, I guess," said Abel. "I jest happened daown by the mansion-haouse last night, 'n' he come aout o' the gate on that queer-lookin' creatur' o' his. I watched him, 'n' he rid, very slow, all raoun' by the Institoot, 'n' acted as ef he was spyin' abaout. He looks to me like a man that's calc'latin' to do some kind of ill-turn to somebody. I shouldn't like to have him raoun' me, 'f there wa'n't a pitchfork or an eel-spear or some sech weep'n within reach. He may be all right; but I don't like his looks, 'n' I don't see what he's lurkin' raoun' the Institoot for, after folks is abed."

"Have you watched him pretty close for the last few days?" said the Doctor.

"W'll, yes,—I've had my eye on him consid'ble o' the time. I haf to be pooty shy abaout it, or he'll find aout th't

I'm on his tracks. I don' want him to get a spite ag'inst me, 'f I c'n help it; he looks to me like one o' them kind that kerries what they call slung-shot, 'n' hits ye on the side o' th' head with 'em so suddin y' never know what hurts ye."

"Why," said the Doctor, sharply,—"have you ever seen him with any such weapon about him?"

"W'll, no,—I caän't say that I hev," Abel answered. "On'y he looks kin' o' dangerous. Maybe he's all jest 'z he ought to be,—I caän't say that he a'n't,—but he's aout late nights, 'n' lurkin' raoun' jest 'z ef he wus spyin' somebody, 'n' somehaow I caän't help mistrustin' them Portagee-lookin' fellahs. I caän't keep the run o' this chap all the time; but I've a notion that old black woman daown 't the mansion-haouse knows 'z much abaout him 'z anybody."

The Doctor paused a moment, after hearing this report from his private detective, and then got into his chaise, and turned Caustic's head in the direction of the Dudley mansion. He had been suspicious of Dick from the first. He did not like his mixed blood, nor his looks, nor his ways. He had formed a conjecture about his projects early. He had made a shrewd guess as to the probable jealousy Dick would feel of the school-master, had found out something of his movements, and had cautioned Mr. Bernard,—as we have seen. He felt an interest in the young man,—a student of his own profession, an intelligent and ingenuously unsuspecting young fellow, who had been thrown by accident into the companionship or the neighborhood of two persons, one of whom he knew to be dangerous, and the other he believed instinctively might be capable of crime.

The Doctor rode down to the Dudley mansion solely for the sake of seeing Old Sophy. He was lucky enough to find her alone in her kitchen. He began talking with her as a physician; he wanted to know how her rheumatism had been. The shrewd old woman saw through all that with her little beady black eyes. It was something quite different he had come for, and Old Sophy answered very briefly for her aches and ails.

"Old folks' bones a'n't like young folks'," she said. "It's the Lord's doin's, 'n' 't a'n't much matter. I sha'n' be long roun' this kitchen. It's the young Missis, Doctor,—it's our

Elsie,—it's the baby, as we use' t' call her,—don' you remember, Doctor? Seventeen year ago, 'n' her poor mother cryin' for her,—'Where is she? where is she? Let me see her!'—'n' how I run up-stairs,—I could run then,—'n' got the coral necklace 'n' put it round her little neck, 'n' then showed her to her mother,—'n' how her mother looked at her, 'n' looked, 'n' then put out her poor thin fingers 'n' lifted the necklace,—'n' fell right back on her piller, as white as though she was laid out to bury?"

The Doctor answered her by silence and a look of grave assent. He had never chosen to let Old Sophy dwell upon these matters, for obvious reasons. The girl must not grow up haunted by perpetual fears and prophecies, if it were possible to prevent it.

"Well, how has Elsie seemed of late?" he said, after this brief pause.

The old woman shook her head. Then she looked up at the Doctor so steadily and searchingly that the diamond eyes of Elsie herself could hardly have pierced more deeply.

The Doctor raised his head, by his habitual movement, and met the old woman's look with his own calm and scrutinizing gaze, sharpened by the glasses through which he now saw her.

Sophy spoke presently in an awed tone, as if telling a vision.

"We shall be havin' trouble before long. The' 's somethin' comin' from the Lord. I've had dreams, Doctor. It's many a year I've been a-dreamin', but now they're comin' over 'n' over the same thing. Three times I've dreamed one thing, Doctor,—one thing!"

"And what was that?" the Doctor said, with that shade of curiosity in his tone which a metaphysician would probably say is an index of a certain tendency to belief in the superstition to which the question refers.

"I ca'n' jestly tell y' what it was, Doctor," the old woman answered, as if bewildered and trying to clear up her recollections; "but it was somethin' fearful, with a great noise 'n' a great cryin' o' people,—like the Las' Day, Doctor! The Lord have mercy on my poor chil', 'n' take care of her, if anything happens! But I's feared she'll never live to see the Las' Day, 'f 't don' come pooty quick."

Poor Sophy, only the third generation from cannibalism, was, not unnaturally, somewhat confused in her theological notions. Some of the Second-Advent preachers had been about, and circulated their predictions among the kitchen-population of Rockland. This was the way in which it happened that she mingled her fears in such a strange manner with their doctrines.

The Doctor answered solemnly, that of the day and hour we knew not, but it became us to be always ready.—"Is there anything going on in the household different from common?"

Old Sophy's wrinkled face looked as full of life and intelligence, when she turned it full upon the Doctor, as if she had slipped off her infirmities and years like an outer garment. All those fine instincts of observation which came straight to her from her savage grandfather looked out of her little eyes. She had a kind of faith that the Doctor was a mighty conjurer, who, if he would, could bewitch any of them. She had relieved her feelings by her long talk with the minister, but the Doctor was the immediate adviser of the family, and had watched them through all their troubles. Perhaps he could tell them what to do. She had but one real object of affection in the world,—this child that she had tended from infancy to womanhood. Troubles were gathering thick round her; how soon they would break upon her, and blight or destroy her, no one could tell; but there was nothing in all the catalogue of terrors which might not come upon the household at any moment. Her own wits had sharpened themselves in keeping watch by day and night, and her face had forgotten its age in the excitement which gave life to its features.

"Doctor," Old Sophy said, "there's strange things goin' on here by night and by day. I don' like that man,—that Dick,—I never liked him. He giv' me some o' these things I' got on; I take 'em 'cos I know it make him mad, if I no take 'em; I wear 'em, so that he needn' feel as if I didn' like him; but, Doctor, I hate him,—jes' as much as a member o' the church has the Lord's leave to hate anybody."

Her eyes sparkled with the old savage light, as if her ill-will to Mr. Richard Venner might perhaps go a little farther than the Christian limit she had assigned. But remember that her grandfather was in the habit of inviting his friends to dine with him upon the last enemy he had bagged, and that her grandmother's teeth were filed down to points, so that they were as sharp as a shark's.

"What is that you have seen about Mr. Richard Venner that gives you such a spite against him, Sophy?" asked the Doctor.

"What I' seen 'bout Dick Venner?" she replied, fiercely. "I'll tell y' what I' seen. Dick wan's to marry our Elsie,—that's what he wan's; 'n' he don' love her, Doctor,—he hates her, Doctor, as bad as I hate him! He wan's to marry our Elsie, 'n' live here in the big house, 'n' have nothin' to do but jes' lay still 'n' watch Massa Venner 'n' see how long 't 'll take him to die, 'n' 'f he don' die fas' 'nuff, help him some way t' die fasser!—Come close up t' me, Doctor! I wan' t' tell you somethin' I tol' th' minister t' other day. Th' minister, he come down 'n' prayed 'n' talked good,—he's a good man, that Doctor Honeywood, 'n' I tol' him all 'bout our Elsie,—but he didn' tell nobody what to do to stop all what I been dreamin' about happenin'. Come close up to me, Doctor!"

The Doctor drew his chair close up to that of the old woman.

"Doctor, nobody mus'n' never marry our Elsie 's long 's she lives! Nobody mus'n' never live with Elsie but Ol' Sophy; 'n' Ol' Sophy won't never die 's long 's Elsie 's alive to be took care of. But I's feared, Doctor, I's greatly feared Elsie wan' to marry somebody. The' 's a young gen'l'm'n up at that school where she go,—so some of 'em tells me,—'n' she loves t' see him 'n' talk wi' him, 'n' she talks about him when she's asleep sometimes. She mus'n' never marry nobody, Doctor! If she do, he die, certain!"

"If she has a fancy for the young man up at the school there," the Doctor said, "I shouldn't think there would be much danger from Dick."

"Doctor, nobody know nothin' 'bout Elsie but Ol' Sophy. She no like any other creatur' th't ever drawed the bref o' life. If she ca'n' marry one man 'cos she love him, she marry another man 'cos she hate him."

"Marry a man because she hates him, Sophy? No woman ever did such a thing as that, or ever will do it."

"Who tol' you Elsie was a woman, Doctor?" said Old Sophy, with a flash of strange intelligence in her eyes.

The Doctor's face showed that he was startled. The old woman could not know much about Elsie that he did not know; but what strange superstition had got into her head, he was puzzled to guess. He had better follow Sophy's lead and find out what she meant.

"I should call Elsie a woman, and a very handsome one," he said. "You don't mean that she has any mark about her, except—you know—under the necklace?"

The old woman resented the thought of any deformity about her darling.

"I didn' say she had nothin'—but jes' that—you know. My beauty have anything ugly? She's the beautifullest-shaped lady that ever had a shinin' silk gown drawed over her shoulders. On'y she a'n't like no other woman in none of her ways. She don't cry 'n' laugh like other women. An' she ha'n' got the same kind o' feelin's as other women.— Do you know that young gen'l'm'n up at the school, Doctor?"

"Yes, Sophy, I've met him sometimes. He's a very nice sort of young man, handsome, too, and I don't much wonder Elsie takes to him. Tell me, Sophy, what do you think would happen, if he should chance to fall in love with Elsie, and she with him, and he should marry her?"

"Put your ear close to my lips, Doctor, dear!" She whispered a little to the Doctor, then added aloud, "He die,—that's all."

"But surely, Sophy, you a'n't afraid to have Dick marry her, if she would have him for any reason, are you? He can take care of himself, if anybody can."

"Doctor!" Sophy answered, "nobody can take care of his-self that live wi' Elsie! Nobody never in all this worl' mus' live wi' Elsie but Ol' Sophy, I tell you. You don' think I care for Dick? What do I care, if Dick Venner die? He wan's to marry our Elsie so 's to live in the big house 'n' get all the money 'n' all the silver things 'n' all the chists full o' linen 'n' beautiful clothes. That's what Dick wan's. An' he hates Elsie 'cos she don' like him. But if he marry Elsie, she'll make him die some wrong way or other, 'n' they'll take her 'n' hang her, or he'll get mad with her 'n' choke her.—Oh, I know his chokin' tricks!—he don' leave his keys roun' for nothin'!"

"What's that you say, Sophy? Tell me what you mean by all that."

So poor Sophy had to explain certain facts not in all respects to her credit. She had taken the opportunity of his absence to look about his chamber, and, having found a key in one of his drawers, had applied it to a trunk, and, finding that it opened the trunk, had made a kind of inspection for contraband articles, and, seeing the end of a leather thong, had followed it up until she saw that it finished with a noose, which, from certain appearances, she inferred to have seen service of at least doubtful nature. An unauthorized search; but Old Sophy considered that a game of life and death was going on in the household, and that she was bound to look out for her darling.

The Doctor paused a moment to think over this odd piece of information. Without sharing Sophy's belief as to the kind of use this mischievous-looking piece of property had been put to, it was certainly very odd that Dick should have such a thing at the bottom of his trunk. The Doctor remembered reading or hearing something about the *lasso* and the *lariat* and the *bolas*, and had an indistinct idea that they had been sometimes used as weapons of warfare or private revenge; but they were essentially a huntsman's implements, after all, and it was not very strange that this young man had brought one of them with him. Not strange, perhaps, but worth noting.

"Do you really think Dick means mischief to anybody, that he has such dangerous-looking things?" the Doctor said, presently.

"I tell you, Doctor. Dick means to have Elsie. If he ca'n' get her, he never let nobody else have her. Oh, Dick's a dark man, Doctor! I know him! I 'member him when he was little boy,—he always cunnin'. I think he mean mischief to somebody. He come home late nights,—come in softly,—oh, I hear him! I lay awake, 'n' got sharp ears,—I hear the cats walkin' over the roofs,—'n' I hear Dick Venner, when he comes up in his stockin'-feet as still as a cat. I think he mean mischief to somebody. I no like his looks these las' days.—Is that a very pooty gen'l'm'n up at the school-house, Doctor?"

"I told you he was good-looking. What if he is?"

"I should like to see him, Doctor,—I should like to see the pooty gen'l'm'n that my poor Elsie loves. She mus'n' never marry nobody,—but, oh, Doctor, I should like to see him, 'n' jes' think a little how it would ha' been, if the Lord hadn' been so hard on Elsie."

She wept and wrung her hands. The kind Doctor was touched, and left her a moment to her thoughts.

"And how does Mr. Dudley Venner take all this?" he said, by way of changing the subject a little.

"Oh, Massa Venner, he good man, but he don' know nothin' 'bout Elsie, as Ol' Sophy do. I keep close by her; I help her when she go to bed, 'n' set by her sometime when she 'sleep; I come to her in th' mornin' 'n' help her put on her things."—Then, in a whisper,—"Doctor, Elsie lets Ol' Sophy take off that necklace for her. What you think she do, 'f anybody else tech it?"

"I don't know, I'm sure, Sophy,—strike the person, perhaps."

"Oh, yes, strike 'em! but not with her han's, Doctor!"—The old woman's significant pantomime must be guessed at.

"But you haven't told me, Sophy, what Mr. Dudley Venner thinks of his nephew, nor whether he has any notion that Dick wants to marry Elsie."

"I tell you, Massa Venner, he good man, but he no see nothin' 'bout what goes on here in the house. He sort o' broken-hearted, you know,—sort o' giv' up,—don' know what to do wi' Elsie, 'xcep' say 'Yes, yes.' Dick always look smilin' 'n' behave well before him. One time I thought Massa Venner b'lieve Dick was goin' to take to Elsie; but now he don' seem to take much notice,—he kin' o' stupid-like 'bout sech things. It's trouble, Doctor; 'cos Massa

Venner bright man naterally,—'n' he's got a great heap o' books. I don' think Massa Venner never been jes' heself sence Elsie's born. He done all he know how,—but, Doctor, that wa'n' a great deal. You men-folks don' know nothin' 'bout these young gals; 'n' 'f you knowed all the young gals that ever lived, y' wouldn' know nothin' 'bout our Elsie."

"No,—but, Sophy, what I want to know is, whether you think Mr. Venner has any kind of suspicion about his nephew,—whether he has any notion that he's a dangerous sort of fellow,—or whether he feels safe to have him about, or has even taken a sort of fancy to him."

"Lor' bless you, Doctor, Massa Venner no more idee 'f any mischief 'bout Dick than he has 'bout you or me. Y' see, he very fond o' the Cap'n,—that Dick's father,—'n' he live so long alone here, 'long wi' us, that he kin' o' like to see mos' anybody 't 's got any o' th' ol' family-blood in 'em. He ha'n't got no more suspicions 'n a baby,—y' never see sech a man 'n y'r life. I kin' o' think he don' care for nothin' in this world 'xcep' jes' t' do what Elsie wan's him to. The fus' year after young Madam die he do nothin' but jes' set at the window 'n' look out at her grave, 'n' then come up 'n' look at the baby's neck 'n' say, '*It's fadin', Sophy, d'n't it?*' 'n' then go down in the study 'n' walk 'n' walk, 'n' then kneel down 'n' pray. Doctor, there was two places in the old carpet that was all threadbare, where his knees had worn 'em. An' sometimes,—you remember 'bout all that,—he'd go off up into The Mountain, 'n' be gone all day, 'n' kill all the Ugly Things he could find up there.— Oh, Doctor, I don' like to think o' them days!—An' by-'n'-by he grew kin' o' still, 'n' begun to read a little, 'n' 't las' he got 's quiet 's a lamb, 'n' that's the way he is now. I think he's got religion, Doctor; but he a'n't so bright about what's goin' on, 'n' I don' believe he never suspec' nothin' till somethin' happens;—for the' 's somethin' goin' to happen, Doctor, if the Las' Day doesn' come to stop it; 'n' you mus' tell us what to do, 'n' save my poor Elsie, my baby that the Lord hasn' took care of like all his other childer."

The Doctor assured the old woman that he was thinking a great deal about them all, and that there were other eyes on Dick besides her own. Let her watch him closely about the house, and he would keep a look-out elsewhere. If there was anything new, she must let him know at once. Send up one of the men-servants, and he would come down at a moment's warning.

There was really nothing definite against this young man; but the Doctor was sure that he was meditating some evil design or other. He rode straight up to the Institute. There he saw Mr. Bernard, and had a brief conversation with him, principally on matters relating to his personal interests.

That evening, for some unknown reason, Mr. Bernard changed the place of his desk and drew down the shades of his windows. Late that night Mr. Richard Venner drew the charge of a rifle, and put the gun back among the fowling-pieces, swearing that a leather halter was worth a dozen of it.

CHAPTER XXV

THE PERILOUS HOUR

Up to this time Dick Venner had not decided on the particular mode and the precise period of relieving himself from the unwarrantable interference which threatened to defeat his plans. The luxury of feeling that he had his man in his power was its own reward. One who watches in the dark, outside, while his enemy, in utter unconsciousness, is illuminating his apartment and himself so that every movement of his head and every button on his coat can be seen and counted, experiences a peculiar kind of pleasure, if he holds a loaded rifle in his hand, which he naturally hates to bring to its climax by testing his skill as a marksman upon the object of his attention.

Besides, Dick had two sides in his nature, almost as distinct as we sometimes observe in those persons who are the subjects of the condition known as *double consciousness.* On his New-England side he was cunning and calculating, always cautious, measuring his distance before he risked his stroke, as nicely as if he were throwing his lasso. But he was liable to intercurrent fits of jealousy and rage, such as the light-hued races are hardly capable of conceiving,— blinding paroxysms of passion, which for the time overmastered him, and which, if they found no ready outlet, transformed themselves into the more dangerous forces that worked through the instrumentality of his cool craftiness.

He had failed as yet in getting any positive evidence that there was any relation between Elsie and the school-master other than such as might exist unsuspected and unblamed between a teacher and his pupil. A book, or a note, even, did not prove the existence of any sentiment. At one time he would be devoured by suspicions, at another he would try to laugh himself out of them. And in the mean while he followed Elsie's tastes as closely as he could, determined to make some impression upon her,—to become a habit, a convenience, a necessity,—whatever might aid him in the attainment of the one end which was now the aim of his life.

It was to humor one of her tastes already known to the reader, that he said to her one morning,—"Come, Elsie, take your castanets, and let us have a dance."

He had struck the right vein in the girl's fancy, for she was in the mood for this exercise, and very willingly led the way into one of the more empty apartments. What there was in this particular kind of dance which excited her it might not be easy to guess; but those who looked in with the old Doctor, on a former occasion, and saw her, will remember that she was strangely carried away by it, and became almost fearful in the vehemence of her passion. The sound of the castanets seemed to make her alive all over. Dick knew well enough what the exhibition would be, and was almost afraid of her at these moments; for it was like the dancing mania of Eastern devotees, more than the ordinary light amusement of joyous youth,—a convulsion of the body and the mind, rather than a series of voluntary modulated motions.

Elsie rattled out the triple measure of a saraband. Her eyes began to glitter more brilliantly, and her shape to undulate in freer curves. Presently she noticed that Dick's look was fixed upon her necklace. His face betrayed his curiosity; he was intent on solving the question, why she always wore something about her neck. The chain of mosaics she had on at that moment displaced itself at every step, and he was peering with malignant, searching eagerness to see if an unsunned ring of fairer hue than the rest of the surface, or any less easily explained peculiarity, were hidden by her ornaments.

She stopped suddenly, caught the chain of mosaics and settled it hastily in its place, flung down her castanets, drew herself back, and stood looking at him, with her head a little on one side, and her eyes narrowing in the way he had known so long and well.

"What is the matter, Cousin Elsie? What do you stop for?" he said.

Elsie did not answer, but kept her eyes on him, full of malicious light. The jealousy which lay covered up under his surface-thoughts took this opportunity to break out.

"You wouldn't act so, if you were dancing with Mr. Langdon,—would you, Elsie?" he asked.

It was with some effort that he looked steadily at her to see the effect of his question.

Elsie *colored*,—not much, but still perceptibly. Dick could not remember that he had ever seen her show this mark of emotion before, in all his experience of her fitful changes of mood. It had a singular depth of significance, therefore, for him; he knew how hardly her color came. Blushing means nothing, in some persons; in others, it betrays a profound inward agitation,—a perturbation of the feelings far more trying than the passions which with many easily moved persons break forth in tears. All who have observed much are aware that some men, who have seen a good deal of life in its less chastened aspects and are anything but modest, will blush often and easily, while there are delicate and sensitive women who can faint, or go into fits, if necessary, but are very rarely seen to betray their feelings in their cheeks, even when their expression shows that their inmost soul is blushing scarlet.

Presently she answered, abruptly and scornfully,—

"Mr. Langdon is a gentleman, and would not vex me as you do."

"A gentleman!" Dick answered, with the most insulting accent,—"a gentleman! Come, Elsie, you've got the Dudley blood in your veins, and it doesn't do for you to call this poor, sneaking school-master a gentleman!"

He stopped short. Elsie's bosom was heaving, the faint flush on her cheek was becoming a vivid glow. Whether it were shame or wrath, he saw that he had reached some deep-lying centre of emotion. There was no longer any doubt in his mind. With another girl these signs of confusion might mean little or nothing; with her they were decisive and final. Elsie Venner loved Bernard Langdon.

The sudden conviction, absolute, overwhelming, which rushed upon him, had well-nigh led to an explosion of wrath, and perhaps some terrible scene which might have fulfilled some of Old Sophy's predictions. This, however, would never do. Dick's face whitened with his thoughts, but he kept still until he could speak calmly.

"I've nothing against the young fellow," he said; "only I don't think there's anything quite good enough to keep the company of people that have the Dudley blood in them. You a'n't as proud as I am. I can't quite make up my mind to call a school-master a gentleman, though this one may be well enough. I've nothing against him, at any rate."

Elsie made no answer, but glided out of the room and slid away to her own apartment. She bolted the door and drew her curtains close. Then she threw herself on the floor, and fell into a dull, slow ache of passion, without tears, without words, almost without thoughts. So she remained, perhaps, for a half-hour, at the end of which time it seemed that her passion had become a sullen purpose. She arose, and, looking cautiously round, went to the hearth, which was ornamented with curious old Dutch tiles, with pictures of Scripture subjects. One of these represented the lifting of a brazen serpent. She took a hair-pin from one of her braids, and, insinuating its points under the edge of the tile, raised it from its place. A small leaden box lay under the tile, which she opened, and, taking from it a little white powder, which she folded in a scrap of paper, replaced the box and the tile over it.

Whether Dick had by any means got a knowledge of this proceeding, or whether he only suspected some unmentionable design on her part, there is no sufficient means of determining. At any rate, when they met, an hour or two after these occurrences, he could not help noticing how easily she seemed to have got over her excitement. She was very pleasant with him,—too pleasant, Dick thought. It was not Elsie's way to come out of a fit of anger so easily as that. She had contrived some way of letting off her spite; that was certain. Dick was pretty cunning, as Old Sophy had said, and, whether or not he had any means of knowing Elsie's private intentions, watched her closely, and was on his guard against accidents.

For the first time, he took certain precautions with reference to his diet, such as were quite alien to his common habits. On coming to the dinner-table, that day, he complained of headache, took but little food, and refused the cup of coffee which Elsie offered him, saying that it did not agree with him when he had these attacks.

Here was a new complication. Obviously enough, he could not live in this way, suspecting everything but plain bread and water, and hardly feeling safe in meddling with them. Not only had this school-keeping wretch come between him and the scheme by which he was to secure his future fortune, but his image had so infected his cousin's mind that she was ready to try on him some of those tricks which, as he had heard hinted in the village, she had once before put in practice upon a person who had become odious to her.

Something must be done, and at once, to meet the double necessities of this case. Every day, while the young girl was in these relations with the young man, was only making matters worse. They could exchange words and looks, they could arrange private interviews, they would be stooping together over the same book, her hair touching his cheek, her breath mingling with his, all the magnetic attractions drawing them together with strange, invisible effluences. As her passion for the school-master increased, her dislike to him, her cousin, would grow with it, and all his dangers would be multiplied. It was a fearful point he had reached. He was tempted at one moment to give up all his plans and to disappear suddenly from the place, leaving with the school-master, who had come between him and his object, an anonymous token of his personal sentiments which would be remembered a good while in the history of the town of Rockland. This was but a momentary thought; the great Dudley property could not be given up in that way.

Something must happen at once to break up all this order of things. He could think of but one Providential event adequate to the emergency,—an event foreshadowed by various recent circumstances, but hitherto floating in his mind only as a possibility. Its occurrence would at once change the course of Elsie's feelings, providing her with something to think of besides mischief, and remove the accursed obstacle which was thwarting all his own projects. Every possible motive, then,—his interest, his jealousy, his longing for revenge, and now his fears for his own safety,— urged him to regard the happening of a certain casualty as a matter of simple necessity. This was the self-destruction of Mr. Bernard Langdon.

Such an event, though it might be surprising to many people, would not be incredible, nor without many parallel cases. He was poor, a miserable fag, under the control of that mean wretch up there at the school, who looked as if he had sour buttermilk in his veins instead of blood. He was in love with a girl above his station, rich, and of old family, but strange in all her ways, and it was conceivable that he should become suddenly jealous of her. Or she might have frightened him with some display of her peculiarities which had filled him with a sudden repugnance in the place of love. Any of these things were credible, and would make a probable story enough,—so thought Dick over to himself with the New-England half of his mind.

Unfortunately, men will not always take themselves out of the way when, so far as their neighbors are concerned, it would be altogether the most appropriate and graceful and acceptable service they could render. There was at this particular moment no special reason for believing that the school-master meditated any violence to his own person. On the contrary, there was good evidence that he was taking some care of himself. He was looking well and in good spirits, and in the habit of amusing himself and exercising, as if to keep up his standard of health, especially of taking certain evening-walks, before referred to, at an hour when most of the Rockland people had "retired," or, in vulgar language, "gone to bed."

Dick Venner settled it, however, in his own mind, that Mr. Bernard Langdon must lay violent hands upon himself. He even went so far as to determine the precise hour, and the method in which the "rash act," as it would undoubtedly be called in the next issue of "The Rockland Weekly Universe," should be committed. Time,—*this evening*. Method,—asphyxia, by suspension. It was, unquestionably, taking a great liberty with a man to decide that he should become *felo de se* without his own consent. Such, however, was the decision of Mr. Richard Venner with regard to Mr. Bernard Langdon.

If everything went right, then, there would be a coroner's inquest to-morrow upon what remained of that gentleman, found suspended to the branch of a tree somewhere within a mile of the Apollinean Institute. The "Weekly Universe" would have a startling paragraph announcing a "SAD EVENT!!!" which had "thrown the town into an intense state of excitement. Mr. Barnard Langden, a well-known teacher at the Appolinian Institute, was found, etc., etc. The vital spark was extinct. The motive to the rash act can only be conjectured, but is supposed to be disapointed affection. The name of an accomplished young lady of *the highest respectability* and great beauty is mentioned in connection with this melencholy occurence."

Dick Venner was at the tea-table that evening, as usual. —No, he would take green tea, if she pleased,—the same that her father drank. It would suit his headache better.— Nothing,—he was much obliged to her. He would help himself,—which he did in a little different way from common, naturally enough, on account of his headache. He noticed that Elsie seemed a little nervous while she was rinsing some of the teacups before their removal.

"There's something going on in that witch's head," he said to himself. "I know her,—she'd be savage now, if she hadn't got some trick in hand. Let's see how she looks to-morrow!"

Dick announced that he should go to bed early that evening, on account of this confounded headache which had been troubling him so much. In fact, he went up early, and locked his door after him, with as much noise as he could make. He then changed some part of his dress, so that it should be dark throughout, slipped off his boots, drew the lasso out from the bottom of the contents of his trunk, and, carrying that and his boots in his hand, opened his door softly, locked it after him, and stole down the back-stairs, so as to get out of the house unnoticed. He went straight to the stable and saddled the mustang. He took a rope from the stable with him, mounted his horse, and set forth in the direction of the Institute.

Mr. Bernard, as we have seen, had not been very profoundly impressed by the old Doctor's cautions,—enough, however, to follow out some of his hints which were not troublesome to attend to. He laughed at the idea of carrying a loaded pistol about with him; but still it seemed only fair, as the old Doctor thought so much of the matter, to humor him about it. As for not going about when and where he liked, for fear he might have some lurking enemy, that was a thing not to be listened to nor thought of. There was nothing to be ashamed of or troubled about in any of his relations with the school-girls. Elsie, no doubt, showed a kind of attraction towards him, as did perhaps some others; but he had been perfectly discreet, and no father or brother or lover had any just cause of quarrel with him. To be sure, that dark young man at the Dudley mansion-house looked as if he were his enemy, when he had met him; but certainly there was nothing in their relations to each other, or in his own to Elsie, that would be like to stir such malice in his mind as would lead him to play any of his wild Southern tricks at his, Mr. Bernard's, expense. Yet he had a vague feeling that this young man was dangerous, and he had been given to understand that one of the risks he ran was from that quarter.

On this particular evening, he had a strange, unusual sense of some impending peril. His recent interview with the Doctor, certain remarks which had been dropped in his hearing, but above all an unaccountable impression upon his spirits, all combined to fill his mind with a foreboding conviction that he was very near some overshadowing danger. It was as the chill of the ice-mountain toward which the ship is steering under full sail. He felt a strong impulse to see Helen Darley and talk with her. She was in the common parlor, and, fortunately, alone.

"Helen," he said,—for they were almost like brother and

sister now,—"I have been thinking what you would do, if I should have to leave the school at short notice, or be taken away suddenly by any accident."

"Do?" she said, her cheek growing paler than its natural delicate hue,—"why, I do not know how I could possibly consent to live here, if you left us. Since you came, my life has been almost easy; before, it was getting intolerable. You must not talk about going, my dear friend; you have spoiled me for my place. Who is there here that I can have any true society with, but you? You would not leave us for another school, would you?"

"No, no, my dear Helen," Mr. Bernard said, "if it depends on myself, I shall stay out my full time, and enjoy your company and friendship. But everything is uncertain in this world. I have been thinking that I might be wanted elsewhere, and called when I did not think of it;—it was a fancy, perhaps,—but I can't keep it out of my mind this evening. If any of my fancies should come true, Helen, there are two or three messages I want to leave with you. I have marked a book or two with a cross in pencil on the fly-leaf;—these are for you. There is a little hymn-book I should like to have you give to Elsie from me;—it may be a kind of comfort to the poor girl."

Helen's eyes glistened as she interrupted him,—

"What do you mean? You must not talk so, Mr. Langdon. Why, you never looked better in your life. Tell me now, you are not in earnest, are you, but only trying a little sentiment on me?"

Mr. Bernard smiled, but rather sadly.

"About half in earnest," he said. "I have had some fancies in my head,—superstitions, I suppose,—at any rate, it does no harm to tell you what I should like to have done, if anything should happen,—very likely nothing ever will. Send the rest of the books home, if you please, and write a letter to my mother. And, Helen, you will find one small volume in my desk enveloped and directed, you will see to whom; —give this with your own hands; it is a keepsake."

The tears gathered in her eyes; she could not speak at first. Presently,—

"Why, Bernard, my dear friend, my brother, it cannot

be that you are in danger? Tell me what it is, and, if I can share it with you, or counsel you in any way, it will only be paying back the great debt I owe you. No, no,—it can't be true,—you are tired and worried, and your spirits have got depressed. I know what that is;—I was sure, one winter, that I should die before spring; but I lived to see the dandelions and buttercups go to seed. Come, tell me it was nothing but your imagination."

She felt a tear upon her cheek, but would not turn her face away from him; it was the tear of a sister.

"I am really in earnest, Helen," he said. "I don't know that there is the least reason in the world for these fancies. If they all go off and nothing comes of them, you may laugh at me, if you like. But if there should be any occasion, remember my requests. You don't believe in presentiments, do you?"

"Oh, don't ask me, I beg you," Helen answered. "I have had a good many frights for every one real misfortune I have suffered. Sometimes I have thought I was warned beforehand of coming trouble, just as many people are of changes in the weather, by some unaccountable feeling,— but not often, and I don't like to talk about such things. I wouldn't think about these fancies of yours. I don't believe you have exercised enough;—don't you think it's confinement in the school has made you nervous?"

"Perhaps it has; but it happens that I have thought more of exercise lately, and have taken regu'ar evening walks, besides playing my old gymnastic tricks every day."

They talked on many subjects, but through all he said Helen perceived a pervading tone of sadness, and an expression as of a dreamy foreboding of unknown evil. They parted at the usual hour, and went to their several rooms. The sadness of Mr. Bernard had sunk into the heart of Helen, and she mingled many tears with her prayers that evening, earnestly entreating that he might be comforted in his days of trial and protected in his hour of danger.

Mr. Bernard stayed in his room a short time before setting out for his evening walk. His eye fell upon the Bible his mother had given him when he left home, and he opened it in the New Testament at a venture. It happened that the first words he read were these,—"*Lest, coming suddenly, he find you sleeping.*" In the state of mind in which he was at the moment, the text startled him. It was like a supernatural warning. He was not going to expose himself to any particular danger this evening; a walk in a quiet village was as free from risk as Helen Darley or his own mother could ask; yet he had an unaccountable feeling of apprehension, without any definite object. At this moment he remembered the old Doctor's counsel, which he had sometimes neglected, and, blushing at the feeling which led him to do it, he took the pistol his suspicious old friend had forced upon him, which he had put away loaded, and, thrusting it into his pocket, set out upon his walk.

The moon was shining at intervals, for the night was partially clouded. There seemed to be nobody stirring, though his attention was unusually awake, and he could hear the whirr of the bats overhead, and the pulsating croak of the frogs in the distant pools and marshes. Presently he detected the sound of hoofs at some distance, and, looking forward, saw a horseman coming in his direction. The moon was under a cloud at the moment, and he could only observe that the horse and his rider looked like a single dark object, and that they were moving along at an easy pace. Mr. Bernard was really ashamed of himself, when he found his hand on the butt of his pistol. When the horseman was within a hundred and fifty yards of him, the moon shone out suddenly and revealed each of them to the other. The rider paused for a moment, as if carefully surveying the pedestrian, then suddenly put his horse to the full gallop, and dashed towards him, rising at the same instant in his stirrups and swinging something round his head,—what, Mr. Bernard could not make out. It was a strange manœuvre,—so strange and threatening in aspect that the young man forgot his nervousness in an instant, cocked his pistol, and waited to see what mischief all this meant. He did not wait long. As the rider came rushing towards him, he made a rapid motion and something leaped five-and-twenty feet through the air, in Mr. Bernard's direction. In an instant he felt a ring, as of a rope or thong, settle upon his shoulders. There was no time to think,—he would be lost in another second. He raised his pistol and fired,—not at the rider, but at the horse. His aim was true; the mustang gave one bound and fell lifeless, shot through the head. The lasso was fastened to his saddle, and his last bound threw Mr. Bernard violently to the earth, where he lay motionless, as if stunned.

In the mean time, Dick Venner, who had been dashed down with his horse, was trying to extricate himself,—one of his legs being held fast under the animal, the long spur on his boot having caught in the saddle-cloth. He found, however, that he could do nothing with his right arm, his shoulder having been in some way injured in his fall. But his Southern blood was up, and, as he saw Mr. Bernard move as if he were coming to his senses, he struggled violently to free himself.

"I'll have the dog, yet," he said,—"only let me get at him with the knife!"

He had just succeeded in extricating his imprisoned leg, and was ready to spring to his feet, when he was caught firmly by the throat, and looking up, saw a clumsy barbed weapon, commonly known as a hay-fork, within an inch of his breast.

"Hold on there! What 'n thunder 'r' y' abaout, y' darned Portagee?" said a voice, with a decided nasal tone in it, but sharp and resolute.

Dick looked from the weapon to the person who held it, and saw a sturdy, plain man standing over him, with his teeth clinched, and his aspect that of one all ready for mischief.

"Lay still, naow!" said Abel Stebbins, the Doctor's man; "'f y' don't, I'll stick ye, 'z sure 'z y' 'r' alive! I been aäfter ye f'r a week, 'n' I got y' naow! I knowed I'd ketch ye at some darned trick or 'nother 'fore I'd done 'ith ye!"

Dick lay perfectly still, feeling that he was crippled and helpless, thinking all the time with the Yankee half of his mind what to do about it. He saw Mr. Bernard lift his head and look around him. He would get his senses again in a few minutes, very probably, and then he, Mr. Richard Venner, would be done for.

"Let me up! let me up!" he cried, in a low, hurried voice,

—"I'll give you a hundred dollars in gold to let me go. The man a'n't hurt,—don't you see him stirring? He'll come to himself in two minutes. Let me up! I'll give you a hundred and fifty dollars in gold, now, here on the spot,—and the watch out of my pocket; take it yourself, with your own hands!"

"I'll see y' darned fust! Ketch me lett'n' go!" was Abel's emphatic answer. "Yeou lay still, 'n' wait t'll that man comes tew."

He kept the hay-fork ready for action at the slightest sign of resistance.

Mr. Bernard, in the mean time, had been getting, first his senses, and then some few of his scattered wits, a little together.

"What is it?"—he said. "Who's hurt? What's happened?"

"Come along here 'z quick 'z y' ken," Abel answered, "'n' haälp me fix this fellah. Y' been hurt, y'rself, 'n' the' 's murder come pooty nigh happenin'."

Mr. Bernard heard the answer, but presently stared about and asked again, *"Who's hurt? What's happened?"*

"Y' 'r' hurt, y'rself, I tell ye," said Abel; "'n' the' 's been a murder, pooty nigh."

Mr. Bernard felt something about his neck, and, putting his hands up, found the loop of the lasso, which he loosened, but did not think to slip over his head, in the confusion of his perceptions and thoughts. It was a wonder that it had not choked him, but he had fallen forward so as to slacken it.

By this time he was getting some notion of what he was about, and presently began looking round for his pistol, which had fallen. He found it lying near him, cocked it mechanically, and walked, somewhat unsteadily, towards the two men, who were keeping their position as still as if they were performing in a *tableau*.

"Quick, naow!" said Abel, who had heard the click of cocking the pistol, and saw that he held it in his hand, as he came towards him. "Gi' me that pistil, and yeou fetch that 'ere rope layin' there. I'll have this here fellah fixed 'n less 'n two minutes."

Mr. Bernard did as Abel said,—stupidly and mechanically, for he was but half right as yet. Abel pointed the pistol at Dick's head.

"Naow hold up y'r hands, yeou fellah," he said, "'n' keep 'em up, while this man puts the rope raound y'r wrists."

Dick felt himself helpless, and, rather than have his disabled arm roughly dealt with, held up his hands. Mr. Bernard did as Abel said; he was in a purely passive state, and obeyed orders like a child. Abel then secured the rope in a most thorough and satisfactory complication of twists and knots.

"Naow get up, will ye?" he said; and the unfortunate Dick rose to his feet.

"*Who's hurt? What's happened?*" asked poor Mr. Bernard again, his memory having been completely jarred out of him for the time.

"Come, look here naow, yeou, don' stan' aäskin' questions over 'n' over;—'t beats all! ha'n't I tol' y' a dozen times?"

As Abel spoke, he turned and looked at Mr. Bernard.

"Hullo! What 'n thunder's that 'ere raoun' y'r neck? Ketched ye 'ith a slippernoose, hey? Wal, if that a'n't the craowner! Hol' on a minute, Cap'n, 'n' I'll show ye what that 'ere halter's good for."

Abel slipped the noose over Mr. Bernard's head, and put it round the neck of the miserable Dick Venner, who made no sign of resistance,—whether on account of the pain he was in, or from mere helplessness, or because he was waiting for some unguarded moment to escape,—since resistance seemed of no use.

"I'm go'n' to kerry y' home," said Abel; "th' ol' Doctor, he's got a gre't cur'osity t' see ye. Jes' step along naow,— off that way, will ye?—'n' I'll hol' on t' th' bridle, f' fear y' sh'd run away."

He took hold of the leather thong, but found that it was fastened at the other end to the saddle. This was too much for Abel.

"Wal, naow, yeou *be* a pooty chap to hev raound! A fellah's neck in a slippernoose at one eend of a halter, 'n' a hoss on th' full spring at t'other eend!"

He looked at him from head to foot as a naturalist inspects a new specimen. His clothes had suffered in his fall, especially on the leg which had been caught under the horse.

"Hullo! look o' there, naow! What's that 'ere stickin' aout o' y'r boot?"

It was nothing but the handle of an ugly knife, which Able instantly relieved him of.

The party now took up the line of march for old Doctor Kittredge's house, Abel carrying the pistol and knife, and Mr. Bernard walking in silence, still half-stunned, holding the hay-fork, which Abel had thrust into his hand. It was all a dream to him as yet. He remembered the horseman riding at him, and his firing the pistol; but whether he was alive, and these walls around him belonged to the village of Rockland, or whether he had passed the dark river, and was in a suburb of the New Jerusalem, he could not as yet have told.

They were in the street where the Doctor's house was situated.

"I guess I'll fire off one o' these here berrils," said Abel. He fired.

Presently there was a noise of opening windows, and the nocturnal head-dresses of Rockland flowered out of them like so many developments of the Night-blooming Cereus. White cotton caps and red bandanna handkerchiefs were the prevailing forms of efflorescence. The main point was that the village was waked up. The old Doctor always waked easily, from long habit, and was the first among those who looked out to see what had happened.

"Why, Abel!" he called out, "what have you got there? and what's all this noise about?"

"We've ketched the Portagee!" Abel answered, as laconically as the hero of Lake Erie, in his famous dispatch. "Go in there, you fellah!"

The prisoner was marched into the house, and the Doctor, who had bewitched his clothes upon him in a way that would have been miraculous in anybody but a physician, was down in presentable form as soon as if it had been a child in a fit that he was sent for.

"Richard Venner!" the Doctor exclaimed. "What is the

meaning of all this? Mr. Langdon, has anything happened to you?"

Mr. Bernard put his hand to his head.

"My mind is confused," he said. "I've had a fall.—Oh, yes!—wait a minute and it will all come back to me."

"Sit down, sit down," the Doctor said. "Abel will tell me about it. Slight concussion of the brain. Can't remember very well for an hour or two,—will come right by to-morrow."

"Been stunded," Abel said. "He can't tell nothin'."

Abel then proceeded to give a Napoleonic bulletin of the recent combat of cavalry and infantry and its results, —none slain, one captured.

The Doctor looked at the prisoner through his spectacles.

"What's the matter with your shoulder, Venner?"

Dick answered sullenly, that he didn't know,—fell on it when his horse came down. The Doctor examined it as carefully as he could through his clothes.

"Out of joint. Untie his hands, Abel."

By this time a small alarm had spread among the neighbors, and there was a circle around Dick, who glared about on the assembled honest people like a hawk with a broken wing.

When the Doctor said, "Untie his hands," the circle widened perceptibly.

"Isn't it a leetle rash to give him the use of his hands? I see there's females and children standin' near."

This was the remark of our old friend, Deacon Soper, who retired from the front row, as he spoke, behind a respectable-looking, but somewhat hastily dressed person of the defenceless sex, the female help of a neighboring household, accompanied by a boy, whose unsmoothed shock of hair looked like a last-year's crow's-nest.

But Abel untied his hands, in spite of the Deacon's considerate remonstrance.

"Now," said the Doctor, "the first thing is to put the joint back."

"Stop," said Deacon Soper,—"stop a minute. Don't you think it will be safer—for the women-folks—jest to wait till mornin', afore you put that j'int into the socket?"

Colonel Sprowle, who had been called by a special messenger, spoke up at this moment.

"Let the women-folks and the deacons go home, if they're scared, and put the fellah's j'int in as quick as you like. I'll resk him, j'int in or out."

"I want one of you to go straight down to Dudley Venner's with a message," the Doctor said. "I will have the young man's shoulder in quick enough."

"Don't send that message!" said Dick, in a hoarse voice; —"do what you like with my arm, but don't send that message! Let me go,—I can walk, and I'll be off from this place. There's nobody hurt but myself. Damn the shoulder! —let me go! You shall never hear of me again!"

Mr. Bernard came forward.

"My friends," he said, "I am not injured,—seriously, at least. Nobody need complain against this man, if I don't. The Doctor will treat him like a human being, at any rate; and then, if he will go, let him. There are too many witnesses against him here for him to want to stay."

The Doctor, in the mean time, without saying a word to all this, had got a towel round the shoulder and chest and another round the arm, and had the bone replaced in a very few minutes.

"Abel, put Cassia into the new chaise," he said, quietly. "My friends and neighbors, leave this young man to me."

"Colonel Sprowle, you're a justice of the peace," said Deacon Soper, "and you know what the law says in cases like this. It a'n't so clear that it won't have to come afore the Grand Jury, whether we will or no."

"I guess we'll set that j'int to-morrow mornin'," said Colonel Sprowle,—which made a laugh at the Deacon's expense, and virtually settled the question.

"Now trust this young man in my care," said the old Doctor, "and go home and finish your naps. I knew him when he was a boy and I'll answer for it, he won't trouble you any more. The Dudley blood makes folks proud, I can tell you, whatever else they are."

The good people so respected and believed in the Doctor that they left the prisoner with him.

Presently, Cassia, the fast Morgan mare, came up to the

front-door, with the wheels of the new, light chaise flashing behind her in the moonlight. The Doctor drove Dick forty miles at a stretch that night, out of the limits of the State.

"Do you want money?" he said, before he left him.

Dick told him the secret of his golden belt.

"Where shall I send your trunk after you from your uncle's?"

Dick gave him a direction to a seaport town to which he himself was going, to take passage for a port in South America.

"Good-bye, Richard," said the Doctor. "Try to learn something from to-night's lesson."

The Southern impulses in Dick's wild blood overcame him, and he kissed the old Doctor on both cheeks, crying as only the children of the sun can cry, after the first hours in the dewy morning of life. So Dick Venner disappears from this story. An hour after dawn, Cassia pointed her fine ears homeward, and struck into her square, honest trot, as if she had not been doing anything more than her duty during her four hours' stretch of the last night.

Abel was not in the habit of questioning the Doctor's decisions.

"It's all right," he said to Mr. Bernard. "The fellah's Squire Venner's relation, anyhaow. Don't you want to wait here, jest a little while, till I come back? The' 's a consid'-able nice saddle 'n' bridle on a dead hoss that's layin' daown there in the road 'n' I guess the' a'n't no use in lettin' on 'em spile,—so I'll jest step aout 'n' fetch 'em along. I kind o' calc'late 't won't pay to take the cretur's shoes 'n' hide off to-night,—'n' the' won't be much iron on that hoss's huffs an haour after daylight, I'll bate ye a quarter."

"I'll walk along with you," said Mr. Bernard;—"I feel as if I could get along well enough now."

So they set off together. There was a little crowd round the dead mustang already, principally consisting of neighbors who had adjourned from the Doctor's house to see the scene of the late adventure. In addition to these, however, the assembly was honored by the presence of Mr. Principal Silas Peckham, who had been called from his slumbers by a message that Master Langdon was shot through the head by a highway-robber, but had learned a true version of the story by this time. His voice was at that moment heard above the rest,—sharp, but thin, like bad cider-vinegar.

"I take charge of that property, I say. Master Langdon's actin' under my orders, and I claim that hoss and all that's on him. Hiram! jest slip off that saddle and bridle, and carry 'em up to the Institoot, and bring down a pair of pinchers and a file,—and—stop—fetch a pair of shears, too; there's hoss-hair enough in that mane and tail to stuff a bolster with."

"You let that hoss alone!" spoke up Colonel Sprowle. "When a fellah goes out huntin' and shoots a squirrel, do you think he's go'n' to let another fellah pick him up and kerry him off? Not if he's got a double-berril gun, and t'other berril ha'n't been fired off yet! I should like to see the mahn that'll take off that seddle 'n' bridle, excep' the one th't hez a fair right to the whole concern!"

Hiram was from one of the lean streaks in New Hampshire, and, not being overfed in Mr. Silas Peckham's kitchen, was somewhat wanting in stamina, as well as in stomach, for so doubtful an enterprise as undertaking to carry out his employer's orders in the face of the Colonel's defiance.

Just then Mr. Bernard and Abel came up together.

"Here they be," said the Colonel. "Stan' beck, gentlemen!"

Mr. Bernard, who was pale and still a little confused, but gradually becoming more like himself, stood and looked in silence for a moment.

All his thoughts seemed to be clearing themselves in this interval. He took in the whole series of incidents: his own frightful risk; the strange, instinctive, nay, Providential impulse which had led him so suddenly to do the one only thing which could possibly have saved him; the sudden appearance of the Doctor's man, but for which he might yet have been lost; and the discomfiture and capture of his dangerous enemy.

It was all past now, and a feeling of pity rose in Mr. Bernard's heart.

"He loved that horse, no doubt," he said,—"and no wonder. A beautiful, wild-looking creature! Take off those things that are on him, Abel, and have them carried to Mr. Dudley Venner's. If he does not want them, you may keep them yourself, for all that I have to say. One thing more. I hope nobody will lift his hand against this noble creature to mutilate him in any way. After you have taken off the saddle and bridle, Abel, bury him just as he is. Under that old beech-tree will be a good place. You'll see to it,—won't you, Abel?"

Abel nodded assent, and Mr. Bernard returned to the Institute, threw himself in his clothes on the bed, and slept like one who is heavy with wine.

Following Mr. Bernard's wishes, Abel at once took off the high-peaked saddle and the richly ornamented bridle from the mustang. Then, with the aid of two or three others, he removed him to the place indicated. Spades and shovels were soon procured, and before the moon had set, the wild horse of the Pampas was at rest under the turf at the way-side, in the far village among the hills of New England.

CHAPTER XXVI

THE NEWS REACHES THE DUDLEY MANSION

Early the next morning Abel Stebbins made his appearance at Dudley Venner's, and requested to see the maän o' the haouse abaout somethin' o' consequence. Mr. Venner sent word that the messenger should wait below, and presently appeared in the study, where Abel was making himself at home, as is the wont of the republican citizen, when he hides the purple of empire beneath the apron of domestic service.

"Good mornin', Squire!" said Abel, as Mr. Venner entered. "My name's Stebbins, 'n' I'm stoppin' f'r a spell 'ith ol' Doctor Kittredge."

"Well, Stebbins," said Mr. Dudley Venner, "have you brought any special message from the Doctor?"

"Y' ha'n't heerd nothin' abaout it, Squire, d' ye mean t' say?" said Abel,—beginning to suspect that he was the first to bring the news of last evening's events.

"About what?" asked Mr. Venner, with some interest.

"Dew tell, naow! Waäl, that beats all! Why, that 'ere Portagee relation o' yourn 'z been tryin' t' ketch a fellah 'n a slippernoose, 'n' got ketched himself,—that's all. Y' ha'n't heerd noth'n' abaout it?"

"Sit down," said Mr. Dudley Venner, calmly, "and tell me all you have to say."

So Abel sat down and gave him an account of the events of the last evening. It was a strange and terrible surprise to Dudley Venner to find that his nephew, who had been an inmate of his house and the companion of his daughter, was to all intents and purposes guilty of the gravest of crimes. But the first shock was no sooner over than he began to think what effect the news would have on Elsie. He imagined that there was a kind of friendly feeling between them, and he feared some crisis would be provoked in his daughter's mental condition by the discovery. He would wait, however, until she came from her chamber, before disturbing her with the evil tidings.

Abel did not forget his message with reference to the equipments of the dead mustang.

"The' was some things on the hoss, Squire, that the man he ketched said he didn' care no gre't abaout; but perhaps you'd like to have 'em fetched to the mansion-haouse. Ef y' *didn'* care abaout 'em, though, I shouldn' min' keepin' on 'em; they might come handy some time or 'nother: they say, holt on t' anything for ten year 'n' there'll be some kin' o' use for 't."

"Keep everything," said Dudley Venner. "I don't want to see anything belonging to that young man."

So Abel nodded to Mr. Venner, and left the study to find some of the men about the stable to tell and talk over with them the events of the last evening. He presently came upon Elbridge, chief of the equine department, and driver of the family-coach.

"Good mornin', Abe," said Elbridge. "What's fetched y' daown here so all-fired airly?"

"You're a darned pooty lot daown here, you be!" Abel answered. "Better keep your Portagees t' home nex' time, ketchin' folks 'ith slippernooses raoun' their necks, 'n' kerryin' knives 'n their boots!"

"What 'r' you jawin' abaout?" Elbridge said, looking up to see if he was in earnest, and what he meant.

"*Jawin'* abaout? You'll find aout 'z soon 'z y' go into that 'ere stable o' yourn! Y' won't curry that 'ere long-tailed black hoss no more; 'n' y' won't set y'r eyes on the fellah that rid him, ag'in, in a hurry!"

Elbridge walked straight to the stable, without saying a word, found the door unlocked, and went in.

"Th' critter's gone, sure enough!" he said. "Glad on 't! The darndest, kickin'est, bitin'est beast th't ever I see, 'r ever wan' t' see ag'in! Good reddance! Don' wan' no snappin'-turkles in my stable! Whar's the man gone th't brought the critter?"

"Whar he 's gone? Guess y' better go 'n aäsk my ol' man; he kerried him off laäs' night; 'n' when he comes back, mebbe he'll tell ye whar he's gone tew!"

By this time Elbridge had found out that Abel was in earnest, and had something to tell. He looked at the litter in the mustang's stall, then at the crib.

"Ha'n't ēat b't haälf his feed. Ha'n't been daown on his straw. Must ha' been took aout somewhere abaout ten 'r 'leven o'clock. I know that 'ere critter's ways. The fellah's had him aout nights afore; b't I never thought nothin' o' no mischief. He's a kin' o' haälf Injin. What is 't the chap 's been a-doin' on? Tell 's all abaout it."

Abel sat down on a meal-chest, picked up a straw and put it into his mouth. Elbridge sat down at the other end, pulled out his jack-knife, opened the penknife-blade, and began sticking it into the lid of the meal-chest. The Doctor's man had a story to tell, and he meant to get all the enjoyment out of it. So he told it with every luxury of circumstance. Mr. Venner's man heard it all with open mouth. No listener in the gardens of Stamboul could have found more rapture in a tale heard amidst the perfume of roses and the voices of birds and tinkling of fountains than Elbridge in following Abel's narrative, as they sat there in the aromatic ammoniacal atmosphere of the stable, the grinding of the horses' jaws keeping evenly on through it all, with now and then the interruption of a stamping hoof, and at intervals a ringing crow from the barn-yard.

Elbridge stopped a minute to think, after Abel had finished.

"Who's took care o' them things that was on the hoss?" he said, gravely.

"Waäl, Langden, he seemed to kin' o' think I'd ought to have 'em,—'n' the Squire, he didn' seem to have no 'bjection; 'n' so,—waäl, I calc'late I sh'll jes' holt on to 'em myself; they a'n't good f'r much, but they're cur'ous t' keep t' look at."

Mr. Venner's man did not appear much gratified by this arrangement, especially as he had a shrewd suspicion that some of the ornaments of the bridle were of precious metal, having made occasional examinations of them with the edge of a file. But he did not see exactly what to do about it, except to get them from Abel in the way of bargain.

"Waäl, no,—they *d'n't* good for much 'xcep' to look at. 'F y' ever rid on that seddle once, y' wouldn' try it ag'in, very spry,—not 'f y' c'd haälp y'rsaälf. I tried it,—darned 'f I sot daown f'r th' nex' week,—ēat all my victuals stan'in'. I sh'd like t' hev them things wal enough to heng up 'n the stable; 'f y' want t' trade some day, fetch 'em along daown."

Abel rather expected that Elbridge would have laid claim to the saddle and bridle on the strength of some promise or other presumptive title, and thought himself lucky to get off with only offering to think abaout tradin'.

When Elbridge returned to the house, he found the family in a state of great excitement. Mr. Venner had told Old Sophy, and she had informed the other servants. Everybody knew what had happened, excepting Elsie. Her father had charged them all to say nothing about it to her; he would tell her, when she came down.

He heard her step at last,—a light, gliding step,—so light that her coming was often unheard, except by those who perceived the faint rustle that went with it. She was paler than common this morning, as she came into her father's study.

After a few words of salutation, he said quietly,—

"Elsie, my dear, your cousin Richard has left us."

She grew still paler, as she asked,—

"*Is he dead?*"

Dudley Venner started to see the expression with which Elsie put this question.

"He is living,—but dead to us from this day forward," said her father.

He proceeded to tell her, in a general way, the story he had just heard from Abel. There could be no doubting it;— he remembered him as the Doctor's man; and as Abel had seen all with his own eyes,—as Dick's chamber, when unlocked with a spare key, was found empty, and his bed had not been slept in, he accepted the whole account as true.

When he told of Dick's attempt on the young school-master, ("You know Mr. Langdon very well, Elsie,—a perfectly inoffensive young man, as I understand,") Elsie turned her face away and slid along by the wall to the window which looked out on the little grass-plot with the white stone standing in it. Her father could not see her face, but he knew by her movements that her dangerous mood was on her. When she heard the sequel of the story, the discomfiture and capture of Dick, she turned round for an instant, with a look of contempt and of something like triumph upon her face. Her father saw that her cousin had become odious to her. He knew well, by every change of her countenance, by her movements, by every varying curve of her graceful figure, the transitions from passion to repose, from fierce excitement to the dull languor which often succeeded her threatening paroxysms.

She remained looking out at the window. A group of white fan-tailed pigeons had lighted on the green plot before it and clustered about one of their companions who lay on his back, fluttering in a strange way, with outspread wings and twitching feet. Elsie uttered a faint cry; these were her special favorites and often fed from her hand. She threw open the long window, sprang out, caught up the white fan-tail, and held it to her bosom. The bird stretched himself out, and then lay still, with open eyes, lifeless. She looked at him a moment, and, sliding in through the open window and through the study, sought her own apartment, where she locked herself in, and began to sob and moan like those that weep. But the gracious solace of tears seemed to be denied her, and her grief, like her anger, was a dull ache, longing, like that, to finish itself with a fierce paroxysm, but wanting its natural outlet.

This seemingly trifling incident of the death of her favorite appeared to change all the current of her thought. Whether it were the sight of the dying bird, or the thought that her own agency might have been concerned in it, or some deeper grief, which took this occasion to declare itself,—some dark remorse or hopeless longing,—whatever it might be, there was an unwonted tumult in her soul. To whom should she go in her vague misery? Only to Him who knows all His creatures' sorrows, and listens to the faintest human cry. She knelt, as she had been taught to kneel from her childhood, and tried to pray. But her thoughts refused to flow in the language of supplication. She could not plead for herself as other women plead in their hours of anguish. She rose like one who should stoop to drink, and find dust in the place of water. Partly from restlessness, partly from an attraction she hardly avowed to herself, she followed her usual habit and strolled listlessly along to the school.

Of course everybody at the Institute was full of the terrible adventure of the preceding evening. Mr. Bernard felt poorly enough; but he had made it a point to show himself the next morning, as if nothing had happened. Helen Darley knew nothing of it all until she had risen, when the gossipy matron of the establishment made her acquainted with all its details, embellished with such additional ornamental appendages as it had caught up in transmission from lip to lip. She did not love to betray her sensibilities, but she was pale and tremulous and very nearly tearful when Mr. Bernard entered the sitting-room, showing on his features traces of the violent shock he had received and the heavy slumber from which he had risen with throbbing brows. What the poor girl's impulse was, on seeing him, we need not inquire too curiously. If he had been her own brother, she would have kissed him and cried on his neck; but something held her back. There is no galvanism in kiss-your-brother; it is copper against copper: but alien bloods develop strange currents, when they flow close to each other, with only the films that cover lip and cheek between them. Mr. Bernard, as some of us may remember, violated the proprieties and laid himself open to reproach by his enterprise with a bouncing village-girl, to whose rosy cheek an honest smack was not probably an absolute novelty. He made it all up by his discretion and good behavior now. He saw by Helen's moist eye and trembling lip that her woman's heart was off its guard, and he knew, by the infallible instinct of sex, that he should be forgiven, if he thanked her for her sisterly sympathies in the most natural way,— expressive, and at the same time economical of breath and utterance. He would not give a false look to their friendship by any such demonstration. Helen was a little older than himself, but the aureole of young womanhood had not yet begun to fade from around her. She was surrounded by that enchanted atmosphere into which the girl walks with dreamy eyes, and out of which the woman passes with a story written on her forehead. Some people think very little of these refinements; they have not studied magnetism and the law of the square of the distance.

So Mr. Bernard thanked Helen for her interest without the aid of the twenty-seventh letter of the alphabet,—the love labial,—the limping consonant which it takes two to speak plain. Indeed, he scarcely let her say a word, at first; for he saw that it was hard for her to conceal her emotion. No wonder; he had come within a hair's-breadth of losing his life, and he had been a very kind friend and a very dear companion to her.

There were some curious spiritual experiences connected with his last evening's adventure which were working very strongly in his mind. It was borne in upon him irresistibly that he had been *dead* since he had seen Helen,—as dead as the son of the Widow of Nain before the bier was touched and he sat up and began to speak. There was an interval between two conscious moments which appeared to him like a temporary annihilation, and the thoughts it suggested were worrying him with strange perplexities.

He remembered seeing the dark figure on horseback rise in the saddle and something leap from its hand. He remembered the thrill he felt as the coil settled on his shoulders, and the sudden impulse which led him to fire as he did. With the report of the pistol all became blank, until he found himself in a strange, bewildered state, groping about for the weapon, which he had a vague consciousness of having dropped. But, according to Abel's account, there must have been an interval of some minutes between these recollections, and he could not help asking, Where was the mind, the soul, the thinking principle, all this time?

A man is stunned by a blow with a stick on the head. He becomes unconscious. Another man gets a harder blow on the head from a bigger stick, and it kills him. Does he become unconscious, too? If so, *when does he come to his consciousness?* The man who has had a slight or moderate blow comes to himself when the immediate shock passes off and the organs begin to work again, or when a bit of the skull is pried up, if that happens to be broken. Suppose the blow is hard enough to spoil the brain and stop the play of the organs, what happens then?

A British captain was struck by a cannon-ball on the head, just as he was giving an order, at the Battle of the Nile. Fifteen months afterwards he was trephined at Greenwich Hospital, having been insensible all that time. Immediately after the operation his consciousness returned, and he at once began carrying out the order he was giving when the shot struck him. Suppose he had never been trephined, when would his consciousness have returned? When his breath ceased and his heart stopped beating?

When Mr. Bernard said to Helen, "I have been dead since I saw you," it startled her not a little; for his expression was that of perfect good faith, and she feared that his mind was disordered. When he explained, not as has been done just now, at length, but in a hurried, imperfect way, the meaning of his strange assertion, and the fearful Sadduceeisms which it had suggested to his mind, she looked troubled at first, and then thoughtful. She did not feel able to answer all the difficulties he raised, but she met them with that faith which is the strength as well as the weakness of women,—which makes them weak in the hands of man, but strong in the presence of the Unseen.

"It is a strange experience," she said; "but I once had something like it. I fainted, and lost some five or ten minutes out of my life, as much as if I had been dead. But when I came to myself, I was the same person every way, in my recollections and character. So I suppose that loss of consciousness is not death. And if I was born out of unconsciousness into infancy with many *family*-traits of mind and body, I can believe, from my own reason, even without help from Revelation, that I shall be born again out of the unconsciousness of death with my *individual*-traits of mind and body. If death is, as it should seem to be, a loss of consciousness, that does not shake my faith; for I have been put into a body once already to fit me for living here, and I hope to be in some way fitted after this life to enjoy a better one. But it is all trust in God and in his Word. These are enough for me; I hope they are for you."

Helen was a minister's daughter, and familiar from her childhood with this class of questions, especially with all the doubts and perplexities which are sure to assail every thinking child bred in any inorganic or not thoroughly vitalized faith,—as is too often the case with the children of professional theologians. The kind of discipline they are subjected to is like that of the Flat-Head Indian pappooses. At five or ten or fifteen years old they put their hands up to their foreheads and ask, What are they strapping down my brains in this way for? So they tear off the sacred bandages of the great Flat-Head tribe, and there follows a mighty rush of blood to the long-compressed region. This accounts, in the most lucid manner, for those sudden freaks with which certain children of this class astonish their worthy parents at the period of life when they are growing fast, and, the frontal pressure beginning to be felt as something intolerable, they tear off the holy compresses.

The hour for school came, and they went to the great hall for study. It would not have occurred to Mr. Silas Peckham to ask his assistant whether he felt well enough to attend to his duties; and Mr. Bernard chose to be at his post. A little headache and confusion were all that remained of his symptoms.

Later, in the course of the forenoon, Elsie Venner came and took her place. The girls all stared at her,—naturally enough; for it was hardly to have been expected that she would show herself, after such an event in the household to which she belonged. Her expression was somewhat peculiar, and, of course, was attributed to the shock her feelings had undergone on hearing of the crime attempted by her cousin and daily companion. When she was looking on her book, or on any indifferent object, her countenance betrayed some inward disturbance, which knitted her dark brows, and seemed to throw a deeper shadow over her features. But, from time to time, she would lift her eyes toward Mr. Bernard, and let them rest upon him, without a thought, seemingly, that she herself was the subject of observation or remark. Then they seemed to lose their cold glitter, and soften into a strange, dreamy tenderness. The deep instincts of womanhood were striving to grope their way to the surface of her being through all the alien influences which overlaid them. She could be secret and cunning in working out any of her dangerous impulses, but she did not know how to mask the unwonted feeling which fixed her eyes and her thoughts upon the only person who had ever reached the spring of her hidden sympathies.

The girls all looked at Elsie, whenever they could steal a glance unperceived, and many of them were struck with this singular expression her features wore. They had long whispered it around among each other that she had a liking for the master; but there were too many of them of whom something like this could be said, to make it very remarkable. Now, however, when so many little hearts were fluttering at the thought of the peril through which the handsome young master had so recently passed, they were more alive than ever to the supposed relation between him and the dark school-girl. Some had supposed there was a mutual attachment between them; there was a story that they were secretly betrothed, in accordance with the rumor which had been current in the village. At any rate, some conflict was going on in that still, remote, clouded soul, and all the girls who looked upon her face were impressed and awed as they had never been before by the shadows that passed over it.

One of these girls was more strongly arrested by Elsie's look than the others. This was a delicate, pallid creature, with a high forehead, and wide-open pupils, which looked as if they could take in all the shapes that flit in what, to common eyes, is darkness,—a girl said to be *clairvoyant* under certain influences. In the *recess*, as it was called, or interval of suspended studies in the middle of the forenoon, this girl carried her autograph-book,—for she had one of those indispensable appendages of the boarding-school miss of every degree,—and asked Elsie to write her name in it. She had an irresistible feeling, that, sooner or later, and perhaps very soon, there would attach an unusual interest to this autograph. Elsie took the pen and wrote, in her sharp Italian hand,

Elsie Venner, Infelix.

It was a remembrance, doubtless, of the forlorn queen of the "Æneid"; but its coming to her thought in this way confirmed the sensitive school-girl in her fears for Elsie, and she let fall a tear upon the page before she closed it.

Of course, the keen and practised observation of Helen Darley could not fail to notice the change of Elsie's manner and expression. She had long seen that she was attracted to the young master, and had thought, as the old Doctor did, that any impression which acted upon her affections might be the means of awakening a new life in her singularly isolated nature. Now, however, the concentration of the poor girl's thoughts upon the one object which had had power to reach her deeper sensibilities was so painfully revealed in her features, that Helen began to fear once more, lest Mr. Bernard, in escaping the treacherous violence of an assassin, had been left to the equally dangerous consequences of a violent, engrossing passion in the breast of a young creature whose love it would be ruin to admit and might be deadly to reject. She knew her own heart too well to fear that any jealousy might mingle with her new apprehensions. It was understood between Bernard and Helen that they were too good friends to tamper with the silences and edging proximities of love-making. She knew, too, the simply human, not masculine, interest which Mr. Bernard took in Elsie; he had been frank with Helen, and more than satisfied her that with all the pity and sympathy which overflowed his soul, when he thought of the stricken girl, there mingled not one drop of such love as a youth may feel for a maiden.

It may help the reader to gain some understanding of the anomalous nature of Elsie Venner, if we look with Helen into Mr. Bernard's opinions and feelings with reference to her, as they had shaped themselves in his consciousness at the period of which we are speaking.

At first he had been impressed by her wild beauty, and the contrast of all her looks and ways with those of the girls around her. Presently a sense of some ill-defined personal element, which half attracted and half repelled those who looked upon her, and especially those on whom she looked, began to make itself obvious to him, as he soon found it was painfully sensible to his more susceptible companion, the lady-teacher. It was not merely in the cold light of her diamond eyes, but in all her movements, in her graceful postures as she sat, in her costume, and, he sometimes thought, even in her speech, that this obscure and exceptional character betrayed itself. When Helen had said, that, if they were living in times when human beings were subject to *possession*, she should have thought there was something not human about Elsie, it struck an unsuspected vein of thought in his own mind, which he hated to put in words, but which was continually trying to articulate itself among the dumb thoughts which lie under the perpetual stream of mental whispers.

Mr. Bernard's professional training had made him slow to accept marvellous stories and many forms of superstition. Yet, as a man of science, he well knew that just on the verge of the demonstrable facts of physics and physiology there is a nebulous border-land which what is called "common sense" perhaps does wisely not to enter, but which uncommon sense, or the fine apprehension of privileged intelligences, may cautiously explore, and in so doing find itself behind the scenes which make up for the gazing world the show which is called Nature.

It was with something of this finer perception, perhaps with some degree of imaginative exaltation, that he set himself to solving the problem of Elsie's influence to attract and repel those around her. His letter already submitted to the reader hints in what direction his thoughts were disposed to turn. Here was a magnificent organization, superb in vigorous womanhood, with a beauty such as never comes but after generations of culture; yet through all this rich nature there ran some alien current of influence, sinuous and dark, as when a clouded streak seams the white marble of a perfect statue.

It would be needless to repeat the particular suggestions which had come into his mind, as they must probably have come into that of the reader who has noted the singularities of Elsie's tastes and personal traits. The images which certain poets had dreamed of seemed to have become a reality before his own eyes. Then came that unexplained adventure of The Mountain,—almost like a dream in recollection, yet assuredly real in some of its main incidents,—with all that it revealed or hinted. This girl did not fear to visit the dreaded region, where danger lurked in every nook and beneath every tuft of leaves. Did the tenants of the fatal ledge recognize some mysterious affinity which made them tributary to the cold glitter of her diamond eyes? Was she from her birth one of those frightful children, such as he had read about, and the Professor had told him of, who form unnatural friendships with cold, writhing ophidians? There was no need of so unwelcome a thought as this; she had drawn him away from the dark opening in the rock at the moment when he seemed to be threatened by one of its malignant denizens; that was all he could be sure of; the counter-fascination might have been a dream, a fancy, a coincidence. All wonderful things soon grow doubtful in our own minds, as do even common events, if great interests prove suddenly to attach to their truth or falsehood.

——I, who am telling of these occurrences, saw a friend in the great city, on the morning of a most memorable disaster, hours after the time when the train which carried its victims to their doom had left. I talked with him, and was for some minutes, at least, in his company. When I reached home, I found that the story had gone before that he was among the lost, and I alone could contradict it to his weeping friends and relatives. I did contradict it; but, alas! I began soon to doubt myself, penetrated by the contagion of their solicitude; my recollection began to question itself; the order of events became dislocated; and when I heard that he had reached home in safety, the relief was almost as great to me as to those who had expected to see their own brother's face no more.

Mr. Bernard was disposed, then, not to accept the thought of any odious personal relationship of the kind which had suggested itself to him when he wrote the letter referred to. That the girl had something of the feral nature, her wild, lawless rambles in forbidden and blasted regions of The Mountain at all hours, her familiarity with the lonely haunts where any other human foot was so rarely seen, proved clearly enough. But the more he thought of all her strange instincts and modes of being, the more he became convinced that whatever alien impulse swayed her will and modulated or diverted or displaced her affections came from some impression that reached far back into the past, before the days when the faithful Old Sophy had rocked her in the cradle. He believed that she had brought her ruling tendency, whatever it was, into the world with her.

When the school was over and the girls had all gone, Helen lingered in the school-room to speak with Mr. Bernard.

"Did you remark Elsie's ways this forenoon?" she said.

"No, not particularly; I have not noticed anything as sharply as I commonly do; my head has been a little queer, and I have been thinking over what we were talking about, and how near I came to solving the great problem which every day makes clear to such multitudes of people. What about Elsie?"

"Bernard, her liking for you is growing into a passion. I have studied girls for a long while, and I know the difference between their passing fancies and their real emotions. I told you, you remember, that Rosa would have to leave us; we barely missed a scene, I think, if not a whole tragedy, by her going at the right moment. But Elsie is infinitely more dangerous to herself and others. Women's love is fierce enough, if it once gets the mastery of them, always; but this poor girl does not know what to do with a passion."

Mr. Bernard had never told Helen the story of the flower in his Virgil, or that other adventure which he would have felt awkwardly to refer to; but it had been perfectly understood between them that Elsie showed in her own singular way a well-marked partiality for the young master.

"Why don't they take her away from the school, if she is in such a strange, excitable state?" said Mr. Bernard.

"I believe they are afraid of her," Helen answered. "It is

just one of those cases that are ten thousand thousand times worse than insanity. I don't think, from what I hear, that her father has ever given up hoping that she will outgrow her peculiarities. Oh, these peculiar children for whom parents go on hoping every morning and despairing every night! If I could tell you half that mothers have told me, you would feel that the worst of all diseases of the moral sense and the will are those which all the Bedlams turn away from their doors as not being cases of insanity!"

"Do you think her father has treated her judiciously?" said Mr. Bernard.

"I think," said Helen, with a little hesitation, which Mr. Bernard did not happen to notice,—"I think he has been very kind and indulgent, and I do not know that he could have treated her otherwise with a better chance of success."

"He must of course be fond of her," Mr. Bernard said; "there is nothing else in the world for him to love."

Helen dropped a book she held in her hand, and, stooping to pick it up, the blood rushed into her cheeks.

"It is getting late," she said; "you must not stay any longer in this close school-room. Pray, go and get a little fresh air before dinner-time."

CHAPTER XXVII

A SOUL IN DISTRESS

The events told in the last two chapters had taken place toward the close of the week. On Saturday evening the Reverend Chauncy Fairweather received a note which was left at his door by an unknown person who departed without saying a word. Its words were these:—

"One who is in distress of mind requests the prayers of this congregation that God would be pleased to look in mercy upon the soul that he has afflicted."

There was nothing to show from whom the note came, or the sex or age or special source of spiritual discomfort or anxiety of the writer. The handwriting was delicate and might well be a woman's. The clergyman was not aware of any particular affliction among his parishioners which was likely to be made the subject of a request of this kind. Surely neither of the Venners would advertise the attempted crime of their relative in this way. But who else was there? The more he thought about it, the more it puzzled him, and as he did not like to pray in the dark, without knowing for whom he was praying, he could think of nothing better than to step into old Doctor Kittredge's and see what he had to say about it.

The old Doctor was sitting alone in his study when the Reverend Mr. Fairweather was ushered in. He received his visitor very pleasantly, expecting, as a matter of course, that he would begin with some new grievance, dyspeptic, neuralgic, bronchitic, or other. The minister, however, began with questioning the old Doctor about the sequel of the other night's adventure; for he was already getting a little Jesuitical, and kept back the object of his visit until it should come up as if accidentally in the course of conversation.

"It was a pretty bold thing to go off alone with that reprobate, as you did," said the minister.

"I don't know what there was bold about it," the Doctor answered. "All he wanted was to get away. He was not quite a reprobate, you see; he didn't like the thought of disgracing his family or facing his uncle. I think he was ashamed to see his cousin, too, after what he had done."

"Did he talk with you on the way?"

"Not much. For half an hour or so he didn't speak a word. Then he asked where I was driving him. I told him, and he seemed to be surprised into a sort of grateful feeling. Bad enough, no doubt,—but might be worse. Has some humanity left in him yet. Let him go. God can judge him,— I can't."

"You are too charitable, Doctor," the minister said. "I condemn him just as if he had carried out his project, which, they say, was to make it appear as if the school-master had committed suicide. That's what people think the rope found by him was for. He has saved his neck,—but his soul is a lost one, I am afraid, beyond question."

"I can't judge men's souls," the Doctor said. "I can judge their acts, and hold them responsible for those,—but I don't know much about their souls. If you or I had found our soul in a half-breed body, and been turned loose to run among the Indians, we might have been playing just such tricks as this fellow has been trying. What if you or I had inherited all the tendencies that were born with his cousin Elsie?"

"Oh, that reminds me,"—the minister said, in a sudden way,—"I have received a note, which I am requested to read from the pulpit to-morrow. I wish you would just have the kindness to look at it and see where you think it came from."

The Doctor examined it carefully. It was a woman's or girl's note, he thought. Might come from one of the schoolgirls who was anxious about her spiritual condition. Handwriting was disguised; looked a little like Elsie Venner's, but not characteristic enough to make it certain. It would be a new thing, if she had asked public prayers for herself, and a very favorable indication of a change in her singular moral nature. It was just possible Elsie might have sent that note. Nobody could foretell her actions. It would be well to see the girl and find out whether any unusual impression had been produced on her mind by the recent occurrence or by any other cause.

The Reverend Mr. Fairweather folded the note and put it into his pocket.

"I have been a good deal exercised in mind lately, myself," he said.

The old Doctor looked at him through his spectacles, and said, in his usual professional tone,—

"Put out your tongue."

The minister obeyed him in that feeble way common with persons of weak character,—for people differ as much in their mode of performing this trifling act as Gideon's soldiers in their way of drinking at the brook. The Doctor took his hand and placed a finger mechanically on his wrist.

"It is more spiritual, I think, than bodily," said the Reverend Mr. Fairweather.

"Is your appetite as good as usual?" the Doctor asked.

"Pretty good," the minister answered; "but my sleep, my sleep, Doctor,—I am greatly troubled at night with lying awake and thinking of my future,—I am not at ease in mind."

He looked round at all the doors, to be sure they were shut, and moved his chair up close to the Doctor's.

"You do not know the mental trials I have been going through for the last few months."

"I think I do," the old Doctor said. "You want to get out of the new church into the old one, don't you?"

The minister blushed deeply; he thought he had been going on in a very quiet way, and that nobody suspected his secret. As the old Doctor was his counsellor in sickness, and almost everybody's confidant in trouble, he had intended to impart cautiously to him some hints of the change of sentiments through which he had been passing. He was too late with his information, it appeared, and there was nothing to be done but to throw himself on the Doctor's good sense and kindness, which everybody knew, and get what hints he could from him as to the practical course he should pursue. He began, after an awkward pause,—

"You would not have me stay in a communion which I feel to be alien to the true church, would you?"

"Have you stay, my friend?" said the Doctor, with a pleasant, friendly look,—"have you stay? Not a month, nor a week, nor a day, if I could help it. You have got into the wrong pulpit, and I have known it from the first. The sooner you go where you belong, the better. And I'm very glad you don't mean to stop half-way. Don't you know you've always come to me when you've been dyspeptic or sick anyhow, and wanted to put yourself wholly into my hands, so that I might order you like a child just what to do and what to take? That's exactly what you want in religion. I don't blame you for it. You never liked to take the responsibility of your own body; I don't see why you should want to have the charge of your own soul. But I'm glad you're going to the Old Mother of all. You wouldn't have been contented short of that."

The Reverend Mr. Fairweather breathed with more freedom. The Doctor saw into his soul through those awful spectacles of his,—into it and beyond it, as one sees through a thin fog. But it was with a real human kindness, after all. He felt like a child before a strong man; but the strong man looked on him with a father's indulgence. Many and many a time, when he had come desponding and bemoaning himself on account of some contemptible bodily infirmity, the old Doctor had looked at him through his spectacles, listened patiently while he told his ailments, and then, in his large parental way, given him a few words of wholesome advice, and cheered him up so that he went off with a light heart, thinking that the heaven he was so much afraid of was not so very near, after all. It was the same thing now. He felt, as feeble natures always do in the presence of strong ones, overmastered, circumscribed, shut in, humbled; but yet it seemed as if the old Doctor did not despise him any more for what he considered weakness of mind than he used to despise him when he complained of his nerves or his digestion.

Men who see *into* their neighbors are very apt to be contemptuous; but men who see *through* them find something lying behind every human soul which it is not for them to sit in judgment on, or to attempt to sneer out of the order of God's manifold universe.

Little as the Doctor had said out of which comfort could be extracted, his genial manner had something grateful in it. A film of gratitude came over the poor man's cloudy, uncertain eye, and a look of tremulous relief and satisfaction played about his weak mouth. He was gravitating to the majority, where he hoped to find "rest"; but he was dreadfully sensitive to the opinions of the minority he was on the point of leaving.

The old Doctor saw plainly enough what was going on in his mind.

"I sha'n't quarrel with you," he said,—"you know that very well; but you mustn't quarrel with me, if I talk honestly with you; it isn't everybody that will take the trouble. You flatter yourself that you will make a good many enemies by leaving your old communion. Not so many as you think. This is the way the common sort of people will talk:—'You have got your ticket to the feast of life, as much as any other man that ever lived. Protestantism says,—"Help yourself; here's a clean plate, and a knife and fork of your own, and plenty of fresh dishes to choose from." The Old Mother says,—"Give me your ticket, my dear, and I'll feed you with my gold spoon off these beautiful old wooden trenchers. Such nice bits as those good old gentlemen have left for you!" There is no quarrelling with a man who prefers broken victuals.' That's what the rougher sort will say; and then, where one scolds, ten will laugh. But, mind you, I don't either scold or laugh. I don't feel sure that you could very well have helped doing what you will soon do. You know you were never easy without some medicine to take when you felt ill in body. I'm afraid I've given you trashy stuff sometimes, just to keep you quiet. Now, let me tell you, there is just the same difference in spiritual patients that there is in bodily ones. One set believes in wholesome ways of living, and another must have a great list of specifics for all the soul's complaints. You belong with the last, and got accidentally shuffled in with the others."

The minister smiled faintly, but did not reply. Of course, he considered that way of talking as the result of the Doctor's professional training. It would not have been worth while to take offence at his plain speech, if he had been so disposed; for he might wish to consult him the next day as to "what he should take" for his dyspepsia or his neuralgia.

He left the Doctor with a hollow feeling at the bottom of his soul, as if a good piece of his manhood had been scooped out of him. His hollow aching did not explain itself in words, but it grumbled and worried down among the unshaped thoughts which lie beneath them. He knew that he had been trying to reason himself out of his birthright of reason. He knew that the inspiration which gave him understanding was losing its throne in his intelligence, and the almighty Majority-Vote was proclaiming itself in its stead. He knew that the great primal truths, which each successive revelation only confirmed, were fast becoming hidden beneath the mechanical forms of thought, which, as with all new converts, engrossed so large a share of his attention. The "peace," the "rest," which he had purchased were dearly bought to one who had been trained to the arms of thought, and whose noble privilege it might have been to live in perpetual warfare for the advancing truth which the next generation will claim as the legacy of the present.

The Reverend Mr. Fairweather was getting careless about his sermons. He must wait the fitting moment to declare himself; and in the mean time he was preaching to heretics. It did not matter much what he preached, under such circumstances. He pulled out two old yellow sermons from a heap of such, and began looking over that for the forenoon. Naturally enough, he fell asleep over it, and, sleeping, he began to dream.

He dreamed that he was under the high arches of an old cathedral, amidst a throng of worshippers. The light streamed in through vast windows, dark with the purple robes of royal saints, or blazing with yellow glories around the heads of earthly martyrs and heavenly messengers. The billows of the great organ roared among the clustered columns, as the sea breaks amidst the basaltic pillars which crowd the stormy cavern of the Hebrides. The voice of the alternate choirs of singing boys swung back and forward, as the silver censer swung in the hands of the white-robed children. The sweet cloud of incense rose in soft, fleecy mists, full of penetrating suggestions of the East and its perfumed altars. The knees of twenty generations had worn the pavement; their feet had hollowed the steps; their shoulders had smoothed the columns. Dead bishops and abbots lay under the marble of the floor in their crumbled vestments; dead warriors, in rusted armor, were stretched beneath their sculptured effigies. And all at once all the buried multitudes who had ever worshipped there came thronging in through the aisles. They choked every space, they swarmed into all the chapels, they hung in clusters over the parapets of the galleries, they clung to the images in every niche, and still the vast throng kept flowing and flowing in, until the living were lost in the rush of the returning dead who had reclaimed their own. Then, as his dream became more fantastic, the huge cathedral itself seemed to change into the wreck of some mighty antediluvian vertebrate; its flying-buttresses arched round like ribs, its piers shaped themselves into limbs, and the sound of the organ-blast changed to the wind whistling through its thousand-jointed skeleton.

And presently the sound lulled, and softened and softened, until it was as the murmur of a distant swarm of bees. A procession of monks wound along through an old street, chanting, as they walked. In his dream he glided in among them and bore his part in the burden of their song. He entered with the long train under a low arch, and presently he was kneeling in a narrow cell before an image of the Blessed Maiden holding the Divine Child in her arms, and his lips seemed to whisper,—

Sancta Maria, ora pro nobis!

He turned to the crucifix, and, prostrating himself before the spare, agonizing shape of the Holy Sufferer, fell into a long passion of tears and broken prayers. He rose and flung himself, worn-out, upon his hard pallet, and, seeming to slumber, dreamed again within his dream. Once more in the vast cathedral, with throngs of the living choking its aisles, amidst jubilant peals from the cavernous depths of the great organ, and choral melodies ringing from the fluty throats of the singing boys. A day of great rejoicings,—for a prelate was to be consecrated, and the bones of the mighty skeleton-minster were shaking with anthems, as if there were life of its own within its buttressed ribs. He looked down at his feet; the folds of the sacred robe were flowing about them: he put his hand to his head; it was crowned with the holy mitre. A long sigh, as of perfect content in the consummation of all his earthly hopes, breathed through the dreamer's lips, and shaped itself, as it escaped, into the blissful murmur,—

Ego sum Episcopus!

One grinning gargoyle looked in from beneath the roof through an opening in a stained window. It was the face of a mocking fiend, such as the old builders loved to place under the eaves to spout the rain through their open mouths. It looked at him, as he sat in his mitred chair, with its hideous grin growing broader and broader, until it laughed out aloud,—such a hard, stony, mocking laugh, that he awoke out of his second dream through his first into his common consciousness, and shivered, as he turned to the two yellow sermons which he was to pick over and weed of the little thought they might contain, for the next day's service.

The Reverend Chauncy Fairweather was too much taken up with his own bodily and spiritual condition to be deeply mindful of others. He carried the note requesting the prayers of the congregation in his pocket all day; and the soul in distress, which a single tender petition might have soothed, and perhaps have saved from despair or fatal error, found no voice in the temple to plead for it before the Throne of Mercy!

CHAPTER XXVIII

THE SECRET IS WHISPERED

The Reverend Chauncy Fairweather's congregation was not large, but select. The lines of social cleavage run through religious creeds as if they were of a piece with position and fortune. It is expected of persons of a certain breeding, in some parts of New England, that they shall be either Episcopalians or Unitarians. The mansion-house gentry of Rockland were pretty fairly divided between the little chapel, with the stained window and the trained rector and the meeting-house where the Reverend Mr. Fairweather officiated.

It was in the latter that Dudley Venner worshipped, when he attended service anywhere,—which depended very much on the caprice of Elsie. He saw plainly enough that a generous and liberally cultivated nature might find a refuge and congenial souls in either of these two persuasions, but he objected to some points of the formal creed of the older church, and especially to the mechanism which renders it hard to get free from its outworn and offensive formulæ, —remembering how Archbishop Tillotson wished in vain that it could be "well rid of" the Athanasian Creed. This, and the fact that the meeting-house was nearer than the chapel, determined him, when the new rector, who was not quite up to his mark in education, was appointed, to take a pew in the "liberal" worshippers' edifice.

Elsie was very uncertain in her feeling about going to church. In summer, she loved rather to stroll over The Mountain, on Sundays. There was even a story, that she had one of the caves before mentioned fitted up as an oratory, and that she had her own wild way of worshipping the God whom she sought in the dark chasms of the dreaded cliffs. Mere fables, doubtless; but they showed the common belief, that Elsie, with all her strange and dangerous elements of character, had yet strong religious feeling mingled with them. The hymn-book which Dick had found, in his midnight invasion of her chamber, opened to favorite hymns, especially some of the Methodist and Quietist character. Many had noticed, that certain tunes, as sung by the choir, seemed to impress her deeply; and some said, that at such times her whole expression would change, and her stormy look would soften so as to remind them of her poor, sweet mother.

On the Sunday morning after the talk recorded in the last chapter, Elsie made herself ready to go to meeting. She was dressed much as usual, excepting that she wore a thick veil, turned aside, but ready to conceal her features. It was natural enough that she should not wish to be looked in the face by curious persons who would be staring to see what effect the occurrence of the past week had had on her spirits. Her father attended her willingly; and they took their seats in the pew, somewhat to the surprise of many, who had hardly expected to see them, after so humiliating a family development as the attempted crime of their kinsman had just been furnishing for the astonishment of the public.

The Reverend Mr. Fairweather was now in his coldest mood. He had passed through the period of feverish excitement which marks a change of religious opinion. At first, when he had begun to doubt his own theological positions, he had defended them against himself with more ingenuity and interest, perhaps, than he could have done against another; because men rarely take the trouble to understand anybody's difficulties in a question but their own. After this, as he began to draw off from different points of his old belief, the cautious disentangling of himself from one mesh after another gave sharpness to his intellect, and the tremulous eagerness with which he seized upon the doctrine which, piece by piece, under various pretexts and with various disguises, he was appropriating, gave interest and something like passion to his words. But when he had gradually accustomed his people to his new phraseology, and was really adjusting his sermons and his service to disguise his thoughts, he lost at once all his intellectual acuteness and all his spiritual fervor.

Elsie sat quietly through the first part of the service, which was conducted in the cold, mechanical way to be expected. Her face was hidden by her veil; but her father knew her state of feeling, as well by her movements and attitudes as by the expression of her features. The hymn had been sung, the short prayer offered, the Bible read, and the long prayer was about to begin. This was the time at which the "notes" of any who were in affliction from loss of friends, the sick who were doubtful of recovery, those who had cause to be grateful for preservation of life or other signal blessing, were wont to be read.

Just then it was that Dudley Venner noticed that his daughter was trembling,—a thing so rare, so unaccountable, indeed, under the circumstances, that he watched her closely, and began to fear that some nervous paroxysm, or other malady, might have just begun to show itself in this way upon her.

The minister had in his pocket two notes. One, in the handwriting of Deacon Soper, was from a member of this congregation, returning thanks for his preservation through a season of great peril,—supposed to be the exposure which he had shared with others, when standing in the circle around Dick Venner. The other was the anonymous one, in a female hand, which he had received the evening before. He forgot them both. His thoughts were altogether too much taken up with more important matters. He prayed through all the frozen petitions of his expurgated form of supplication, and not a single heart was soothed or lifted, or reminded that its sorrows were struggling their way up to heaven, borne on the breath from a human soul that was warm with love.

The people sat down as if relieved when the dreary prayer was finished. Elsie alone remained standing until her father touched her. Then she sat down, lifted her veil, and looked at him with a blank, sad look, as if she had suffered some pain or wrong, but could not give any name or expression to her vague trouble. She did not tremble any longer, but remained ominously still, as if she had been frozen where she sat.

——Can a man love his own soul too well? Who, on the whole, constitute the nobler class of human beings? those who have lived mainly to make sure of their own personal welfare in another and future condition of existence, or they who have worked with all their might for their race, for their country, for the advancement of the kingdom of God, and left all personal arrangements concerning themselves to the sole charge of Him who made them and is responsible to Himself for their safe-keeping? Is an anchorite who has worn the stone floor of his cell into basins with his knees bent in prayer, more acceptable than the soldier who gives his life for the maintenance of any sacred right or truth, without thinking what will specially become of him in a world where there are two or three million colonists a month, from this one planet, to be cared for? These are grave questions, which must suggest themselves to those who know that there are many profoundly selfish persons who are sincerely devout and perpetually occupied with their own future, while there are others who are perfectly ready to sacrifice themselves for any worthy object in this world, but are really too little occupied with their exclusive personality to think so much as many do about what is to become of them in another.

The Reverend Chauncy Fairweather did not, most certainly, belong to this latter class. There are several kinds of believers, whose history we find among the early converts to Christianity.

There was the magistrate, whose social position was such that he preferred a private interview in the evening with the Teacher to following him with the street-crowd. He had seen extraordinary facts which had satisfied him that the young Galilean had a divine commission. But still he cross-questioned the Teacher himself. He was not ready to accept statements without explanation. That was the right kind of man. See how he stood up for the legal rights of his Master, when the people were for laying hands on him!

And again, there was the government official, intrusted with public money, which, in those days, implied that he was supposed to be honest. A single look of that heavenly countenance, and two words of gentle command, were enough for him. Neither of these men, the early disciple, nor the evangelist, seems to have been thinking primarily about his own personal safety.

But now look at the poor, miserable turnkey, whose occupation shows what he was like to be, and who had just been thrusting two respectable strangers, taken from the hands of a mob, covered with stripes and stripped of clothing, into the inner prison, and making their feet fast in the stocks. His thought, in the moment of terror, is for himself: first, suicide; then, what he shall do,—not to save his household,—not to fulfil his duty to his office,—not to repair the outrage he has been committing,—but to secure his own personal safety. Truly, character shows itself as much in a man's way of becoming a Christian as in any other!

——Elsie sat, statue-like, through the sermon. It would not be fair to the reader to give an abstract of that. When a man who has been bred to free thought and free speech suddenly finds himself stepping about, like a dancer amidst his eggs, among the old addled majority-votes which he must not tread upon, he is a spectacle for men and angels. Submission to intellectual precedent and authority does very well for those who have been bred to it; we know that the underground courses of their minds are laid in the Roman cement of tradition, and that stately and splendid structures may be reared on such a foundation. But to see one laying a platform over heretical quicksands, thirty or forty or fifty years deep, and then beginning to build upon it, is a sorry sight. A new convert from the reformed to the ancient faith may be very strong in the arms, but he will always have weak legs and shaky knees. He may use his hands well, and hit hard with his fists, but he will never stand on his legs in the way the man does who inherits his belief.

The services were over at last, and Dudley Venner and his daughter walked home together in silence. He always respected her moods, and saw clearly enough that some inward trouble was weighing upon her. There was nothing to be said in such cases, for Elsie could never talk of her griefs.

An hour, or a day, or a week of brooding, with perhaps a sudden flash of violence: this was the way in which the impressions which make other women weep, and tell their griefs by word or letter, showed their effects in her mind and acts.

She wandered off up into the remoter parts of The Mountain, that day, after their return. No one saw just where she went,—indeed, no one knew its forest-recesses and rocky fastnesses as she did. She was gone until late at night; and when Old Sophy, who had watched for her, bound up her long hair for her sleep, it was damp with the cold dews.

The old black woman looked at her without speaking, but questioning her with every feature as to the sorrow that was weighing on her.

Suddenly she turned to Old Sophy.

"You want to know what there is troubling me," she said. "Nobody loves me. I cannot love anybody. What is love, Sophy?"

"It's what poor Ol' Sophy's got for her Elsie," the old woman answered. "Tell me, darlin',—don' you love somebody?—don' you love——? you know,—oh, tell me, darlin', don' you love to see the gen'l'man that keeps up at the school where you go? They say he's the pootiest gen'l'man that was ever in the town here. Don' be 'fraid of poor Ol' Sophy, darlin',—she loved a man once,—see here! Oh, I've showed you this often enough!"

She took from her pocket a half of one of the old Spanish silver coins, such as were current in the earlier part of this century. The other half of it had been lying in the deep seasand for more than fifty years.

Elsie looked her in the face, but did not answer in words. What strange intelligence was that which passed between them through the diamond eyes and the little beady black ones?—what subtle intercommunication, penetrating so much deeper than articulate speech? This was the nearest approach to sympathetic relations that Elsie ever had: a kind of dumb intercourse of feeling, such as one sees in the eyes of brute mothers looking on their young. But, subtle as it was, it was narrow and individual; whereas an emotion which can shape itself in language opens the gate for itself into the great community of human affections; for every word we speak is the medal of a dead thought or feeling, struck in the die of some human experience, worn smooth by innumerable contacts, and always transferred warm from one to another. By words we share the common consciousness of the race, which has shaped itself in these symbols. By music we reach those special states of consciousness which, being without *form*, cannot be shaped with the mosaics of the vocabulary. The language of the eyes runs deeper into the personal nature, but it is purely individual, and perishes in the expression. If we consider them all as growing out of the consciousness as their root, language is the leaf, music is the flower; but when the eyes meet and search each other, it is the uncovering of the blanched stem through which the whole life runs, but which has never taken color or form from the sunlight.

For three days Elsie did not return to the school. Much of the time she was among the woods and rocks. The season was now beginning to wane, and the forest to put on its autumnal glory. The dreamy haze was beginning to soften the landscape, and the most delicious days of the year were lending their attraction to the scenery of The Mountain. It was not very singular that Elsie should be lingering in her old haunts, from which the change of season must soon drive her. But Old Sophy saw clearly enough that some internal conflict was going on, and knew very well that it must have its own way and work itself out as it best could. As much as looks could tell Elsie had told her. She had said in words, to be sure, that she could not love. Something warped and thwarted the emotion which would have been love in another, no doubt; but that such an emotion was striving with her against all malign influences which interfered with it the old woman had a perfect certainty in her own mind.

Everybody who has observed the working of emotions in persons of various temperaments knows well enough that they have periods of *incubation*, which differ with the individual, and with the particular cause and degree of excitement, yet evidently go through a strictly self-limited series of evolutions, at the end of which, their result—an act of violence, a paroxysm of tears, a gradual subsidence into repose, or whatever it may be—declares itself, like the last stage of an attack of fever and ague. No one can observe children without noticing that there is a *personal equation*, to use the astronomer's language, in their tempers, so that one sulks an hour over an offence which makes another a fury for five minutes, and leaves him or her an angel when it is over.

At the end of three days, Elsie braided her long, glossy, black hair, and shot a golden arrow through it. She dressed herself with more than usual care, and came down in the morning superb in her stormy beauty. The brooding paroxysm was over, or at least her passion had changed its phase. Her father saw it with great relief; he had always many fears for her in her hours and days of gloom, but, for reasons before assigned, had felt that she must be trusted to herself, without appealing to actual restraint, or any other supervision than such as Old Sophy could exercise without offence.

She went off at the accustomed hour to the school. All the girls had their eyes on her. None so keen as these young misses to know an inward movement by an outward sign of adornment: if they have not as many signals as the ships that sail the great seas, there is not an end of ribbon or a turn of a ringlet which is not a hieroglyphic with a hidden meaning to these little cruisers over the ocean of sentiment.

The girls all looked at Elsie with a new thought; for she was more sumptuously arrayed than perhaps ever before at the school; and they said to themselves that she had come meaning to draw the young master's eyes upon her. That was it; what else could it be? The beautiful cold girl with the diamond eyes meant to dazzle the handsome young gentleman. He would be afraid to love her; it couldn't be true, that which some people had said in the village; she wasn't the kind of young lady to make Mr. Langdon happy. Those dark people are never safe: so one of the young blondes said to herself. Elsie was not literary enough for such a scholar: so thought Miss Charlotte Ann Wood, the young poetess. She couldn't have a good temper, with those scowling eyebrows: this was the opinion of several broad-faced, smiling girls, who thought, each in her own snug little mental *sanctum*, that, if, etc., etc., she could make him *so* happy!

Elsie had none of the still, wicked light in her eyes, that morning. She looked gentle, but dreamy; played with her books; did not trouble herself with any of the exercises,— which in itself was not very remarkable, as she was always allowed, under some pretext or other, to have her own way.

The school-hours were over at length. The girls went out, but she lingered to the last. She then came up to Mr. Bernard, with a book in her hand, as if to ask a question.

"Will you walk towards my home with me to-day?" she said, in a very low voice, little more than a whisper.

Mr. Bernard was startled by the request, put in such a way. He had a presentiment of some painful scene or other. But there was nothing to be done but to assure her that it would give him great pleasure.

So they walked along together on their way toward the Dudley mansion.

"I have no friend," Elsie said, all at once. "Nothing loves me but one old woman. I cannot love anybody. They tell me there is something in my eyes that draws people to me and makes them faint. Look into them, will you?"

She turned her face toward him. It was very pale, and the diamond eyes were glittering with a film, such as beneath other lids would have rounded into a tear.

"Beautiful eyes, Elsie," he said,—"sometimes very piercing,—but soft now, and looking as if there were something beneath them that friendship might draw out. I am your friend, Elsie. Tell me what I can do to render your life happier."

"*Love me!*" said Elsie Venner.

What shall a man do, when a woman makes such a demand, involving such an avowal? It was the tenderest, cruellest, humblest moment of Mr. Bernard's life. He turned pale, he trembled almost, as if he had been a woman listening to her lover's declaration.

"Elsie," he said, presently, "I so long to be of some use to you, to have your confidence and sympathy, that I must not let you say or do anything to put us in false relations. I do love you, Elsie, as a suffering sister with sorrows of her own,—as one whom I would save at the risk of my happiness and life,—as one who needs a true friend more than any of all the young girls I have known. More than this you would not ask me to say. You have been through excitement and trouble lately, and it has made you feel such a need more than ever. Give me your hand, dear Elsie, and trust me that I will be as true a friend to you as if we were children of the same mother."

Elsie gave him her hand mechanically. It seemed to him that a cold *aura* shot from it along his arm and chilled the blood running through his heart. He pressed it gently, looked at her with a face full of grave kindness and sad interest, then softly relinquished it.

It was all over with poor Elsie. They walked almost in silence the rest of the way. Mr. Bernard left her at the gate of the mansion-house, and returned with sad forebodings. Elsie went at once to her own room, and did not come from it at the usual hours. At last Old Sophy began to be alarmed about her, went to her apartment, and, finding the door unlocked, entered cautiously. She found Elsie lying on her bed, her brows strongly contracted, her eyes dull, her whole look that of great suffering. Her first thought was that she had been doing herself a harm by some deadly means or other. But Elsie saw her fear, and reassured her.

"No," she said, "there is nothing wrong, such as you are thinking of; I am not dying. You may send for the Doctor; perhaps he can take the pain from my head. That is all I want him to do. There is no use in the pain, that I know of; if he can stop it, let him."

So they sent for the old Doctor. It was not long before the solid trot of Caustic, the old bay horse, and the crashing of the gravel under the wheels, gave notice that the physician was driving up the avenue.

The old Doctor was a model for visiting practitioners. He always came into the sick-room with a quiet, cheerful look, as if he had a consciousness that he was bringing some sure relief with him. The way a patient snatches his first look at his doctor's face, to see whether he is doomed, whether he is reprieved, whether he is unconditionally pardoned, has really something terrible about it. It is only to be met by an imperturbable mask of serenity, proof against anything and everything in a patient's aspect. The physician whose face reflects his patient's condition like a mirror may do well enough to examine people for a life-insurance office, but does not belong to the sick-room. The old Doctor did not keep people waiting in dread suspense, while he stayed talking about the case,—the patient all the time thinking that he and the friends are discussing some alarming symptom or formidable operation which he himself is by-and-by to hear of.

He was in Elsie's room almost before she knew he was in the house. He came to her bedside in such a natural, quiet way, that it seemed as if he were only a friend who had dropped in for a moment to say a pleasant word. Yet he was very uneasy about Elsie until he had seen her; he never knew what might happen to her or those about her, and came prepared for the worst.

"Sick, my child?" he said, in a very soft, low voice.

Elsie nodded, without speaking.

The Doctor took her hand,—whether with professional views, or only in a friendly way, it would have been hard to tell. So he sat a few minutes, looking at her all the time with a kind of fatherly interest, but with it all noting how she lay, how she breathed, her color, her expression, all that teaches the practised eye so much without a single question being asked. He saw she was in suffering, and said presently,—

"You have pain somewhere; where is it?"

She put her hand to her head.

As she was not disposed to talk, he watched her for a while, questioned Old Sophy shrewdly a few minutes, and so made up his mind as to the probable cause of disturbance and the proper remedies to be used.

Some very silly people thought the old Doctor did not believe in medicine, because he gave less than certain poor half-taught creatures in the smaller neighboring towns, who took advantage of people's sickness to disgust and disturb them with all manner of ill-smelling and ill-behaving drugs. In truth, he hated to give anything noxious or loathsome to those who were uncomfortable enough already, unless he was very sure it would do good,—in which case, he never played with drugs, but gave good, honest, efficient doses. Sometimes he lost a family of the more boorish sort, because they did not think they got their money's worth out of him, unless they had something more than a taste of everything he carried in his saddle-bags.

He ordered some remedies which he thought would relieve Elsie, and left her, saying he would call the next day, hoping to find her better. But the next day came, and the next, and still Elsie was on her bed,—feverish, restless, wakeful, silent. At night she tossed about and wandered, and it became at length apparent that there was a settled attack, something like what they called, formerly, a "nervous fever."

On the fourth day she was more restless than common. One of the women of the house came in to help to take care of her; but she showed an aversion to her presence.

"Send me Helen Darley," she said, at last.

The old Doctor told them, that, if possible, they must indulge this fancy of hers. The caprices of sick people were never to be despised, least of all of such persons as Elsie, when rendered irritable and exacting by pain and weakness.

So a message was sent to Mr. Silas Peckham at the Apollinean Institute, to know if he could not spare Miss Helen Darley for a few days, if required, to give her attention to a young lady who attended his school and who was now lying ill,—no other person than the daughter of Dudley Venner.

A mean man never agrees to anything without deliberately turning it over, so that he may see its dirty side, and, if he can, sweating the coin he pays for it. If an archangel should offer to save his soul for sixpence, he would try to find a sixpence with a hole in it. A gentleman says yes to a great many things without stopping to think: a shabby fellow is known by his caution in answering questions, for fear of compromising his pocket or himself.

Mr. Silas Peckham looked very grave at the request. The dooties of Miss Darley at the Institoot were important, very important. He paid her large sums of money for her time,—more than she could expect to get in any other institootion for the edoocation of female youth. A deduction from her selary would be necessary, in case she should retire from the sphere of her dooties for a season. He should be put to extry expense, and have to perform additional labors himself. He would consider of the matter. If any arrangement could be made, he would send word to Squire Venner's folks.

"Miss Darley," said Silas Peckham, "the' 's a message from Squire Venner's that his daughter wants you down at the mansion-house to see her. She's got a fever, so they inform me. If it's any kind of ketchin' fever, of course you won't think of goin' near the mansion-house. If Doctor Kittredge says it's safe, perfec'ly safe, I can't object to your goin', on sech conditions as seem to be fair to all concerned. You will give up your pay for the whole time you are absent,—portions of days to be caounted as whole days. You will be charged with board the same as if you ēat your victuals with the household. The victuals are of no use after they're cooked but to be ēat, and your bein' away is no savin' to our folks. I shall charge you a reasonable compensation for the demage to the school by the absence of a teacher. If Miss Crabs undertakes any dooties belongin' to your department of instruction, she will look to you for sech pecooniary considerations as you may agree upon between you. On these conditions I am willin' to give my consent to your temporary absence from the post of dooty. I will step down to Doctor Kittredge's, myself, and make inquiries as to the natur' of the complaint."

Mr. Peckham took up a rusty and very narrow-brimmed hat, which he cocked upon one side of his head, with an air peculiar to the rural gentry. It was the hour when the Doctor expected to be in his office, unless he had some special call which kept him from home.

He found the Reverend Chauncy Fairweather just taking leave of the Doctor. His hand was on the pit of his stomach, and his countenance was expressive of inward uneasiness.

"Shake it before using," said the Doctor; "and the sooner you make up your mind to speak right out, the better it will be for your digestion."

"Oh, Mr. Peckham! Walk in, Mr. Peckham! Nobody sick up at the school, I hope?"

"The haälth of the school is fust-rate," replied Mr. Peckham. "The sitooation is uncommonly favorable to saloobrity." (These last words were from the Annual Report of the past year.) "Providence has spared our female youth in a remarkable measure. I've come with reference to another consideration. Doctor Kittredge, is there any ketchin' complaint goin' about in the village?"

"Well, yes," said the Doctor, "I should say there was something of that sort. Measles. Mumps. And Sin,—that's always catching."

The old Doctor's eye twinkled; once in a while he had his little touch of humor.

Silas Peckham slanted his eye up suspiciously at the Doctor, as if he was getting some kind of advantage over him. That is the way people of his constitution are apt to take a bit of pleasantry.

"I don't mean sech things, Doctor; I mean fevers. Is there any ketchin' fevers—bilious, or nervous, or typus, or whatever you call 'em—now goin' round this village? That's what I want to ascertain, if there's no impropriety."

The old Doctor looked at Silas through his spectacles.

"Hard and sour as a green cider-apple," he thought to himself. "No," he said,—"I don't know any such cases."

"What's the matter with Elsie Venner?" asked Silas, sharply, as if he expected to have him this time.

"A mild feverish attack, I should call it in anybody else; but she has a peculiar constitution, and I never feel so safe about her as I should about most people."

"Anything ketchin' about it?" Silas asked, cunningly.

"No, indeed!" said the Doctor,—"catching?—no,—what put that into your head, Mr. Peckham?"

"Well, Doctor," the conscientious Principal answered,

"I naterally feel a graät responsibility, a very graäät responsibility, for the noomerous and lovely young ladies committed to my charge. It has been a question, whether one of my assistants should go, accordin' to request, to stop with Miss Venner for a season. Nothin' restrains my givin' my full and free consent to her goin' but the fear lest contagious maladies should be introdooced among those lovely female youth. I shall abide by your opinion,—I understan' you to say distinc'ly, her complaint is not ketchin'?—and urge upon Miss Darley to fulfil her dooties to a sufferin' fellow-creature at any cost to myself and my establishment. We shall miss her very much; but it is a good cause, and she shall go,—and I shall trust that Providence will enable us to spare her without permanent demage to the interests of the Institootion."

Saying this, the excellent Principal departed, with his rusty narrow-brimmed hat leaning over, as if it had a six-knot breeze abeam, and its gunwale (so to speak) was dipping into his coat-collar. He announced the result of his inquiries to Helen, who had received a brief note in the mean time from a poor relation of Elsie's mother, then at the mansion-house, informing her of the critical situation of Elsie and of her urgent desire that Helen should be with her. She could not hesitate. She blushed as she thought of the comments that might be made; but what were such considerations in a matter of life and death? She could not stop to make terms with Silas Peckham. She must go. He might fleece her, if he would; she would not complain,—not even to Bernard, who, she knew, would bring the Principal to terms, if she gave the least hint of his intended extortions.

So Helen made up her bundle of clothes to be sent after her, took a book or two with her to help her pass the time, and departed for the Dudley mansion. It was with a great inward effort that she undertook the sisterly task which was thus forced upon her. She had a kind of terror of Elsie; and the thought of having charge of her, of being alone with her, of coming under the full influence of those diamond eyes, —if, indeed, their light were not dimmed by suffering and weariness,—was one she shrank from. But what could she do? It might be a turning-point in the life of the poor girl; and she must overcome all her fears, all her repugnance, and go to her rescue.

"Is Helen come?" said Elsie, when she heard, with her fine sense quickened by the irritability of sickness, a light footfall on the stair, with a cadence unlike that of any inmate of the house.

"It's a strange woman's step," said Old Sophy, who, with her exclusive love for Elsie, was naturally disposed to jealousy of a new-comer. "Let Ol' Sophy set at th' foot o' th' bed, if th' young missis sets by th' piller,—won' y', darlin'? The' 's nobody that's white can love y' as th' ol' black woman does;—don' sen' her away, now, there's a dear soul!"

Elsie motioned her to sit in the place she had pointed to, and Helen at that moment entered the room. Dudley Venner followed her.

"She is your patient," he said, "except while the Doctor is here. She has been longing to have you with her, and we shall expect you to make her well in a few days."

So Helen Darley found herself established in the most unexpected manner as an inmate of the Dudley mansion. She sat with Elsie most of the time, by day and by night, soothing her, and trying to enter into her confidence and affections, if it should prove that this strange creature was really capable of truly sympathetic emotions.

What was this unexplained something which came between her soul and that of every other human being with whom she was in relations? Helen perceived, or rather felt, that she had, folded up in the depths of her being, a true womanly nature. Through the cloud that darkened her aspect, now and then a ray would steal forth, which, like the smile of stern and solemn people, was all the more impressive from its contrast with the expression she wore habitually. It might well be that pain and fatigue had changed her aspect; but, at any rate, Helen looked into her eyes without that nervous agitation which their cold glitter had produced on her when they were full of their natural light. She felt sure that her mother must have been a lovely, gentle woman. There were gleams of a beautiful nature shining through some ill-defined medium which disturbed and made them flicker and waver, as distant images do when seen through the rippling upward currents of heated air. She loved, in her own way, the old black woman, and seemed to keep up a kind of silent communication with her, as if they did not require the use of speech. She appeared to be tranquillized by the presence of Helen, and loved to have her seated at the bedside. Yet something, whatever it was, prevented her from opening her heart to her kind companion; and even now there were times when she would lie looking at her, with such a still, watchful, almost dangerous expression, that Helen would sigh, and change her place, as persons do whose breath some cunning orator has been sucking out of them with his spongy eloquence, so that, when he stops, they must get some air and stir about, or they feel as if they should be half smothered and palsied.

It was too much to keep guessing what was the meaning of all this. Helen determined to ask Old Sophy some questions which might probably throw light upon her doubts. She took the opportunity one evening when Elsie was lying asleep and they were both sitting at some distance from her bed.

"Tell me, Sophy," she said, "was Elsie always as shy as she seems to be now, in talking with those to whom she is friendly?"

"Always jes' so, Miss Darlin', ever sence she was little chil'. When she was five, six year old, she lisp some,—call me *Thophy*; that make her kin' o' 'shamed, perhaps: after she grow up, she never lisp, but she kin' o' got the way o' not talkin' much. Fac' is, she don' like talkin' as common gals do, 'xcep' jes' once in a while wi' some partic'lar folks, —'n' then not much."

"How old is Elsie?"

"Eighteen year this las' September."

"How long ago did her mother die?" Helen asked, with a little trembling in her voice.

"Eighteen year ago this October," said Old Sophy.

Helen was silent for a moment. Then she whispered, almost inaudibly,—for her voice appeared to fail her,—

"What did her mother die of, Sophy?"

The old woman's small eyes dilated until a ring of white showed round their beady centres. She caught Helen by the hand and clung to it, as if in fear. She looked round at Elsie, who lay sleeping, as if she might be listening. Then she drew Helen towards her and led her softly out of the room.

"'Sh!—'sh!" she said, as soon as they were outside the door. "Don' never speak in this house 'bout what Elsie's mother died of!" she said. "Nobody never says nothin' 'bout it. Oh, God has made Ugly Things wi' death in their mouths, Miss Darlin', an' He knows what they're for; but my poor Elsie!—to have her blood changed in her before—— It was in July Mistress got her death, but she liv' till three week after my poor Elsie was born."

She could speak no more. She had said enough. Helen remembered the stories she had heard on coming to the village, and among them one referred to in an early chapter of this narrative. All the unaccountable looks and tastes and ways of Elsie came back to her in the light of an antenatal impression which had mingled an alien element in her nature. She knew the secret of the fascination which looked out of her cold, glittering eyes. She knew the significance of the strange repulsion which she felt in her own intimate consciousness underlying the inexplicable attraction which drew her towards the young girl in spite of this repugnance. She began to look with new feelings on the contradictions in her moral nature,—the longing for sympathy, as shown by her wishing for Helen's company, and the impossibility of passing beyond the cold circle of isolation within which she had her being. The fearful truth of that instinctive feeling of hers, that there was something not human looking out of Elsie's eyes, came upon her with a sudden flash of penetrating conviction. There were two warring principles in that superb organization and proud soul. One made her a woman, with all a woman's powers and longings. The other chilled all the currents of outlet for her emotions. It made her tearless and mute, when another woman would have wept and pleaded. And it infused into her soul something—it was cruel now to call it malice—which was still and watchful and dangerous,—

which waited its opportunity, and then shot like an arrow from its bow out of the coil of brooding premeditation. Even those who had never seen the white scars on Dick Venner's wrist, or heard the half-told story of her supposed attempt to do a graver mischief, knew well enough by looking at her that she was one of the creatures not to be tampered with,—silent in anger and swift in vengeance.

Helen could not return to the bedside at once after this communication. It was with altered eyes that she must look on the poor girl, the victim of such an unheard-of fatality. All was explained to her now. But it opened such depths of solemn thought in her awakened consciousness, that it seemed as if the whole mystery of human life were coming up again before her for trial and judgment. "Oh," she thought, "if, while the will lies sealed in its fountain, it may be poisoned at its very source, so that it shall flow dark and deadly through its whole course, who are we that we should judge our fellow-creatures by ourselves?" Then came the terrible question, how far the elements themselves are capable of perverting the moral nature: if valor, and justice, and truth, the strength of man and the virtue of woman, may not be poisoned out of a race by the food of the Australian in his forest,—by the foul air and darkness of the Christians cooped up in the "tenement-houses" close by those who live in the palaces of the great cities?

She walked out into the garden, lost in thought upon these dark and deep matters. Presently she heard a step behind her, and Elsie's father came up and joined her. Since his introduction to Helen at the distinguished tea-party given by the Widow Rowens, and before her coming to sit with Elsie, Mr. Dudley Venner had in the most accidental way in the world met her on several occasions: once after church, when she happened to be caught in a slight shower and he insisted on holding his umbrella over her on her way home;—once at a small party at one of the mansion-houses, where the quick-eyed lady of the house had a wonderful knack of bringing people together who liked to see each other;—perhaps at other times and places; but of this there is no certain evidence.

They naturally spoke of Elsie, her illness, and the aspect

it had taken. But Helen noticed in all that Dudley Venner said about his daughter a morbid sensitiveness, as it seemed to her, an aversion to saying much about her physical condition or her peculiarities,—a wish to feel and speak as a parent should, and yet a shrinking, as if there were something about Elsie which he could not bear to dwell upon. She thought she saw through all this, and she could interpret it all charitably. There were circumstances about his daughter which recalled the great sorrow of his life; it was not strange that this perpetual reminder should in some degree have modified his feelings as a father. But what a life he must have been leading for so many years, with this perpetual source of distress which he could not name! Helen knew well enough, now, the meaning of the sadness which had left such traces in his features and tones, and it made her feel very kindly and compassionate towards him.

So they walked over the crackling leaves in the garden, between the lines of box breathing its fragrance of eternity; —for this is one of the odors which carry us out of time into the abysses of the unbeginning past; if we ever lived on another ball of stone than this, it must be that there was box growing on it. So they walked, finding their way softly to each other's sorrows and sympathies, each matching some counterpart to the other's experience of life, and startled to see how the different, yet parallel, lessons they had been taught by suffering had led them step by step to the same serene acquiescence in the orderings of that Supreme Wisdom which they both devoutly recognized.

Old Sophy was at the window and saw them walking up and down the garden-alleys. She watched them as her grandfather the savage watched the figures that moved among the trees when a hostile tribe was lurking about his mountain.

"There'll be a weddin' in the ol' house," she said, "before there's roses on them bushes ag'in. But it won' be my poor Elsie's weddin', 'n' Ol' Sophy won' be there."

When Helen prayed in the silence of her soul that evening, it was not that Elsie's life might be spared. She dared not ask that as a favor of Heaven. What could life be to her but a perpetual anguish, and to those about her an ever-present terror? Might she but be so influenced by divine grace, that what in her was most truly human, most purely woman-like, should overcome the dark, cold, unmentionable instinct which had pervaded her being like a subtle poison: that was all she could ask, and the rest she left to a higher wisdom and tenderer love than her own.

CHAPTER XXIX

THE WHITE ASH

When Helen returned to Elsie's bedside, it was with a new and still deeper feeling of sympathy, such as the story told by Old Sophy might well awaken. She understood, as never before, the singular fascination and as singular repulsion which she had long felt in Elsie's presence. It had not been without a great effort that she had forced herself to become the almost constant attendant of the sick girl; and now she was learning, but not for the first time, the blessed truth which so many good women have found out for themselves, that the hardest duty bravely performed soon becomes a habit, and tends in due time to transform itself into a pleasure.

The old Doctor was beginning to look graver, in spite of himself. The fever, if such it was, went gently forward, wasting the young girl's powers of resistance from day to day; yet she showed no disposition to take nourishment, and seemed literally to be living on air. It was remarkable that with all this her look was almost natural, and her features were hardly sharpened so as to suggest that her life was burning away. He did not like this, nor various other unobtrusive signs of danger which his practised eye detected. A very small matter might turn the balance which held life and death poised against each other. He surrounded her with precautions, that Nature might have every opportunity of cunningly shifting the weights from the scale of death to the scale of life, as she will often do if not rudely disturbed or interfered with.

Little tokens of good-will and kind remembrance were constantly coming to her from the girls in the school and the good people in the village. Some of the mansion-house people obtained rare flowers which they sent her, and her table was covered with fruits which tempted her in vain. Several of the school-girls wished to make her a basket of their own handiwork, and, filling it with autumnal flowers, to send it as a joint offering. Mr. Bernard found out their project accidentally, and, wishing to have his share in it, brought home from one of his long walks some boughs full of variously tinted leaves, such as were still clinging to the stricken trees. With these he brought also some of the already fallen leaflets of the white ash, remarkable for their rich olive-purple color, forming a beautiful contrast with some of the lighter-hued leaves. It so happened that this particular tree, the white ash, did not grow upon The Mountain, and the leaflets were more welcome for their comparative rarity. So the girls made their basket, and the floor of it they covered with the rich olive-purple leaflets. Such late flowers as they could lay their hands upon served to fill it, and with many kindly messages they sent it to Miss Elsie Venner at the Dudley mansion-house.

Elsie was sitting up in her bed when it came, languid, but tranquil, and Helen was by her, as usual, holding her hand, which was strangely cold, Helen thought, for one who was said to have some kind of fever. The school-girls' basket was brought in with its messages of love and hopes for speedy recovery. Old Sophy was delighted to see that it pleased Elsie, and laid it on the bed before her. Elsie began looking at the flowers, and taking them from the basket, that she might see the leaves. All at once she appeared to be agitated; she looked at the basket,—then around, as if there were some fearful presence about her which she was searching for with her eager glances. She took out the flowers, one by one, her breathing growing hurried, her eyes staring, her hands trembling,—till, as she came near the bottom of the basket, she flung out all the rest with a hasty movement, looked upon the olive-purple leaflets as if paralyzed for a moment, shrunk up, as it were, into herself in a curdling terror, dashed the basket from her, and fell back senseless, with a faint cry which chilled the blood of the startled listeners at her bedside.

"Take it away!—take it away!—quick!" said Old Sophy, as she hastened to her mistress's pillow. "It's the leaves of the tree that was always death to her,—take it away! She can't live wi' it in the room!"

The poor old woman began chafing Elsie's hands, and Helen to try to rouse her with hartshorn, while a third frightened attendant gathered up the flowers and the basket and carried them out of the apartment. She came to herself after a time, but exhausted and then wandering. In her delirium she talked constantly as if she were in a cave, with such exactness of circumstance that Helen could not doubt at all that she had some such retreat among the rocks of The Mountain, probably fitted up in her own fantastic way, where she sometimes hid herself from all human eyes, and of the entrance to which she alone possessed the secret.

All this passed away, and left her, of course, weaker than before. But this was not the only influence the unexplained paroxysm had left behind it. From this time forward there was a change in her whole expression and her manner. The shadows ceased flitting over her features, and the old woman, who watched her from day to day and from hour to hour as a mother watches her child, saw the likeness she bore to her mother coming forth more and more, as the cold glitter died out of the diamond eyes, and the stormy scowl disappeared from the dark brows and low forehead.

With all the kindness and indulgence her father had bestowed upon her, Elsie had never felt that he loved her. The reader knows well enough what fatal recollections and associations had frozen up the springs of natural affection in his breast. There was nothing in the world he would not do for Elsie. He had sacrificed his whole life to her. His very seeming carelessness about restraining her was all calculated; he knew that restraint would produce nothing but utter alienation. Just so far as she allowed him, he shared her studies, her few pleasures, her thoughts; but she was essentially solitary and uncommunicative. No person, as was said long ago, could judge him,—because his task was not merely difficult, but simply impracticable to human powers. A nature like Elsie's had necessarily to be studied by itself, and to be followed in its laws where it could not be led.

Every day, at different hours, during the whole of his daughter's illness, Dudley Venner had sat by her, doing all he could to soothe and please her. Always the same thin film of some emotional non-conductor between them; always that kind of habitual regard and family-interest, mingled with the deepest pity on one side and a sort of respect on the other, which never warmed into outward evidences of affection.

It was after this occasion, when she had been so profoundly agitated by a seemingly insignificant cause, that her father and Old Sophy were sitting, one at one side of her bed and one at the other. She had fallen into a light slumber. As they were looking at her, the same thought came into both their minds at the same moment. Old Sophy spoke for both, as she said, in a low voice,—

"It's her mother's look,—it's her mother's own face right over again,—she never look' so before,—the Lord's hand is on her! His will be done!"

When Elsie woke and lifted her languid eyes upon her father's face, she saw in it a tenderness, a depth of affection, such as she remembered at rare moments of her childhood, when she had won him to her by some unusual gleam of sunshine in her fitful temper.

"Elsie, dear," he said, "we were thinking how much your expression was sometimes like that of your sweet mother. If you could but have seen her, so as to remember her!"

The tender look and tone, the yearning of the daughter's heart for the mother she had never seen, save only with the unfixed, undistinguishing eyes of earliest infancy, perhaps the under-thought that she might soon rejoin her in another state of being,—all came upon her with a sudden overflow of feeling which broke through all the barriers between her heart and her eyes, and Elsie wept. It seemed to her father as if the malign influence—evil spirit it might almost be called—which had pervaded her being, had at last been driven forth or exorcised, and that these tears were at once the sign and the pledge of her redeemed nature. But now she was to be soothed, and not excited. After her tears she slept again, and the look her face wore was peaceful as never before.

Old Sophy met the Doctor at the door and told him all the circumstances connected with the extraordinary attack from which Elsie had suffered. It was the purple leaves, she said. She remembered that Dick once brought home a branch of a tree with some of the same leaves on it, and Elsie screamed and almost fainted then. She, Sophy, had asked her, after she had got quiet, what it was in the leaves that made her feel so bad. Elsie couldn't tell her,— didn't like to speak about it,—shuddered whenever Sophy mentioned it.

This did not sound so strangely to the old Doctor as it does to some who listen to this narrative. He had known some curious examples of antipathies, and remembered reading of others still more singular. He had known those who could not bear the presence of a cat, and recollected the story, often told, of a person's hiding one in a chest when one of these sensitive individuals came into the room, so as not to disturb him; but he presently began to sweat and turn pale, and cried out that there must be a cat hid somewhere. He knew people who were poisoned by strawberries, by honey, by different meats,—many who could not endure cheese,—some who could not bear the smell of roses. If he had known all the stories in the old books, he would have found that some have swooned and become as dead men at the smell of a rose,—that a stout soldier has been known to turn and run at the sight or smell of rue,—that cassia and even olive-oil have produced deadly faintings in certain individuals,—in short, that almost everything has seemed to be a poison to somebody.

"Bring me that basket, Sophy," said the old Doctor, "if you can find it."

Sophy brought it to him,—for he had not yet entered Elsie's apartment.

"These purple leaves are from the white ash," he said.

"You don't know the notion that people commonly have about that tree, Sophy?"

"I know they say the Ugly Things never go where the white ash grows," Sophy answered. "Oh, Doctor dear, what I'm thinkin' of a'n't true, is it?"

The Doctor smiled sadly, but did not answer. He went directly to Elsie's room. Nobody would have known by his manner that he saw any special change in his patient. He spoke with her as usual, made some slight alteration in his prescriptions, and left the room with a kind, cheerful look. He met her father on the stairs.

"Is it as I thought?" said Dudley Venner.

"There is everything to fear," the Doctor said, "and not much, I am afraid, to hope. Does not her face recall to you one that you remember, as never before?"

"Yes," her father answered,—"oh, yes! What is the meaning of this change which has come over her features, and her voice, her temper, her whole being? Tell me, oh, tell me, what is it? Can it be that the curse is passing away, and my daughter is to be restored to me,—such as her mother would have had her,—such as her mother was?"

"Walk out with me into the garden," the Doctor said, "and I will tell you all I know and all I think about this great mystery of Elsie's life."

They walked out together, and the Doctor began:—

"She has lived a double being, as it were,—the consequence of the blight which fell upon her in the dim period before consciousness. You can see what she might have been but for this. You know that for these eighteen years her whole existence has taken its character from that influence which we need not name. But you will remember that few of the lower forms of life last as human beings do; and thus it might have been hoped and trusted with some show of reason, as I have always suspected you hoped and trusted, perhaps more confidently than myself, that the lower nature which had become engrafted on the higher would die out and leave the real woman's life she inherited to outlive this accidental principle which had so poisoned her childhood and youth. I believe it is so dying out; but I am afraid,

—yes, I must say it, I fear it has involved the centres of life in its own decay. There is hardly any pulse at Elsie's wrist; no stimulants seem to rouse her; and it looks as if life were slowly retreating inwards, so that by-and-by she will sleep as those who lie down in the cold and never wake."

Strange as it may seem, her father heard all this not without deep sorrow, and such marks of it as his thoughtful and tranquil nature, long schooled by suffering, claimed or permitted, but with a resignation itself the measure of his past trials. Dear as his daughter might become to him, all he dared to ask of Heaven was that she might be restored to that truer self which lay beneath her false and adventitious being. If he could once see that the icy lustre in her eyes had become a soft, calm light,—that her soul was at peace with all about her and with Him above,—this crumb from the children's table was enough for him, as it was for the Syro-Phœnician woman who asked that the dark spirit might go out from her daughter.

There was little change the next day, until all at once she said in a clear voice that she should like to see her master at the school, Mr. Langdon. He came accordingly, and took the place of Helen at her bedside. It seemed as if Elsie had forgotten the last scene with him. Might it be that pride had come in, and she had sent for him only to show how superior she had grown to the weakness which had betrayed her into that extraordinary request, so contrary to the instincts and usages of her sex? Or was it that the singular change which had come over her had involved her passionate fancy for him and swept it away with her other habits of thought and feeling? Or could it be that she felt that all earthly interests were becoming of little account to her, and wished to place herself right with one to whom she had displayed a wayward movement of her unbalanced imagination? She welcomed Mr. Bernard as quietly as she had received Helen Darley. He colored at the recollection of that last scene, when he came into her presence; but she smiled with perfect tranquillity. She did not speak to him of any apprehension; but he saw that she looked upon herself as doomed. So friendly, yet so calm did she seem through all their interview, that Mr. Bernard could only look back upon her manifestation of feeling towards him on their walk from the school as a vagary of a mind laboring under some unnatural excitement, and wholly at variance with the true character of Elsie Venner as he saw her before him in her subdued, yet singular beauty. He looked with almost scientific closeness of observation into the diamond eyes; but that peculiar light which he knew so well was not there. She was the same in one sense as on that first day when he had seen her coiling and uncoiling her golden chain; yet how different in every aspect which revealed her state of mind and emotion! Something of tenderness there was, perhaps, in her tone towards him; she would not have sent for him, had she not felt more than an ordinary interest in him. But through the whole of his visit she never lost her gracious self-possession. The Dudley race might well be proud of the last of its daughters, as she lay dying, but unconquered by the feeling of the present or the fear of the future.

As for Mr. Bernard, he found it very hard to look upon her, and listen to her unmoved. There was nothing that reminded him of the stormy-browed, almost savage girl he remembered in her fierce loveliness,—nothing of all her singularities of air and of costume. Nothing? Yes, one thing. Weak and suffering as she was, she had never parted with one particular ornament, such as a sick person would naturally, as it might be supposed, get rid of at once. The golden cord which she wore round her neck at the great party was still there. A bracelet was lying by her pillow; she had unclasped it from her wrist.

Before Mr. Bernard left her, she said,—

"I shall never see you again. Some time or other, perhaps, you will mention my name to one whom you love. Give her this from your scholar and friend Elsie."

He took the bracelet, raised her hand to his lips, then turned his face away; in that moment he was the weaker of the two.

"Good-bye," she said; "thank you for coming."

His voice died away in his throat, as he tried to answer her. She followed him with her eyes as he passed from her sight through the door, and when it closed after him sobbed tremulously once or twice,—but stilled herself, and met Helen, as she entered, with a composed countenance.

"I have had a very pleasant visit from Mr. Langdon," Elsie said. "Sit by me, Helen, awhile without speaking; I should like to sleep, if I can,—and to dream."

CHAPTER XXX

THE GOLDEN CORD IS LOOSED

The Reverend Chauncy Fairweather, hearing that his parishioner's daughter, Elsie, was very ill, could do nothing less than come to the mansion-house and tender such consolations as he was master of. It was rather remarkable that the old Doctor did not exactly approve of his visit. He thought that company of every sort might be injurious in her weak state. He was of opinion that Mr. Fairweather, though greatly interested in religious matters, was not the most sympathetic person that could be found; in fact, the old Doctor thought he was too much taken up with his own interests for eternity to give himself quite so heartily to the need of other people as some persons got up on a rather more generous scale (our good neighbor Dr. Honeywood, for instance) could do. However, all these things had better be arranged to suit her wants; if she would like to talk with a clergyman, she had a great deal better see one as often as she liked, and run the risk of the excitement, than have a hidden wish for such a visit and perhaps find herself too weak to see him by-and-by.

The old Doctor knew by sad experience that dreadful mistake against which all medical practitioners should be warned. His experience may well be a guide for others. Do not overlook the desire for spiritual advice and consolation which patients sometimes feel, and, with the frightful *mauvaise honte* peculiar to Protestantism, alone among all human beliefs, are ashamed to tell. As a part of medical treatment, it is the physician's business to detect the hidden longing for the food of the soul, as much as for any form of bodily nourishment. Especially in the higher walks of society, where this unutterably miserable false shame of Protestantism acts in proportion to the general acuteness of the cultivated sensibilities, let no unwillingness to suggest the sick person's real need suffer him to languish between his want and his morbid sensitiveness. What an infinite advantage the Mussulmans and the Catholics have over many of our more exclusively spiritual sects in the way they keep their religion always by them and never blush for it! And besides this spiritual longing, we should never forget that

"On some fond breast the parting soul relies,"

and the minister of religion, in addition to the sympathetic nature which we have a right to demand in him, has trained himself to the art of entering into the feelings of others.

The reader must pardon this digression, which introduces the visit of the Reverend Chauncy Fairweather to Elsie Venner. It was mentioned to her that he would like to call and see how she was, and she consented,—not with much apparent interest, for she had reasons of her own for not feeling any very deep conviction of his sympathy for persons in sorrow. But he came, and worked the conversation round to religion, and confused her with his hybrid notions, half made up of what he had been believing and teaching all his life, and half of the new doctrines which he had veneered upon the surface of his old belief. He got so far as to make a prayer with her,—a cool well-guarded prayer, which compromised his faith as little as possible, and which, if devotion were a game played against Providence, might have been considered a cautious and sagacious move.

When he had gone, Elsie called Old Sophy to her.

"Sophy," she said, "don't let them send that cold-hearted man to me any more. If your old minister comes to see you, I should like to hear him talk. He looks as if he cared for everybody, and would care for me. And, Sophy, if I should die one of these days, I should like to have that old minister come and say whatever is to be said over me. It would comfort Dudley more, I know, than to have that hard man here, when you're in trouble,—for some of you will be sorry when I'm gone,—won't you, Sophy?"

The poor old black woman could not stand this question. The cold minister had frozen Elsie until she felt as if nobody cared for her or would regret her,—and her question had betrayed this momentary feeling.

"Don' talk so! don' talk so, darlin'!" she cried, passionately. "When you go, Ol' Sophy'll go; 'n' where you go, Ol' Sophy'll go: 'n' we'll both go t' th' place where th' Lord takes care of all his children, whether their faces are white or black. Oh, darlin', darlin'! if th' Lord should let me die fus', you shall fin' all ready for you when you come after me. On'y don' go 'n' leave poor Ol' Sophy all 'lone in th' world!"

Helen came in at this moment and quieted the old woman with a look. Such scenes were just what were most dangerous, in the state in which Elsie was lying: but that is one of the ways in which an affectionate friend sometimes unconsciously wears out the life which a hired nurse, thinking of nothing but her regular duties and her wages, would have spared from all emotional fatigue.

The change which had come over Elsie's disposition was itself the cause of new excitements. How was it possible that her father could keep away from her, now that she was coming back to the nature and the very look of her mother, the bride of his youth? How was it possible to refuse her, when she said to Old Sophy, that she should like to have her minister come in and sit by her, even though his presence might perhaps prove a new source of excitement?

But the Reverend Doctor did come and sit by her, and spoke such soothing words to her, words of such peace and consolation, that from that hour she was tranquil as never before. All true hearts are alike in the hour of need; the Catholic has a reserved fund of faith for his fellow-creature's trying moment, and the Calvinist reveals those springs of human brotherhood and charity in his soul which are only covered over by the iron tables inscribed with the harder dogmas of his creed. It was enough that the Reverend Doctor knew all Elsie's history. He could not judge her by any formula, like those which have been moulded by past ages out of their ignorance. He did not talk with her as if she were an outside sinner, worse than himself. He found a bruised and languishing soul, and bound up its wounds. A blessed office,—one which is confined to no sect or creed, but which good men in all times, under various names and with varying ministries, to suit the need of each age, of each race, of each individual soul, have come forward to discharge for their suffering fellow-creatures.

After this there was little change in Elsie, except that her heart beat more feebly every day,—so that the old Doctor himself, with all his experience, could see nothing to account for the gradual failing of the powers of life, and yet could find no remedy which seemed to arrest its progress in the smallest degree.

"Be very careful," he said, "that she is not allowed to make any muscular exertion. Any such effort, when a person is so enfeebled, may stop the heart in a moment; and if it stops, it will never move again."

Helen enforced this rule with the greatest care. Elsie was hardly allowed to move her hand or to speak above a whisper. It seemed to be mainly the question now, whether this trembling flame of life would be blown out by some light breath of air, or whether it could be so nursed and sheltered by the hollow of these watchful hands that it would have a chance to kindle to its natural brightness.

——Her father came in to sit with her in the evening. He had never talked so freely with her as during the hour he had passed at her bedside, telling her little circumstances of her mother's life, living over with her all that was pleasant in the past, and trying to encourage her with some cheerful gleams of hope for the future. A faint smile played over her face, but she did not answer his encouraging suggestions. The hour came for him to leave her with those who watched by her.

"Good-night, my dear child," he said, and stooping down, kissed her cheek.

Elsie rose by a sudden effort, threw her arms round his neck, kissed him, and said, "Good-night, my dear father!"

The suddenness of her movement had taken him by surprise, or he would have checked so dangerous an effort. It was too late now. Her arms slid away from him like lifeless weights,—her head fell back upon her pillow,—a long sigh breathed through her lips.

"She is faint," said Helen, doubtfully; "bring me the hartshorn, Sophy."

The old woman had started from her place, and was now leaning over her, looking in her face, and listening for the sound of her breathing.

"She's dead! Elsie's dead! My darlin' 's dead!" she cried aloud, filling the room with her utterance of anguish.

Dudley Venner drew her away and silenced her with a voice of authority, while Helen and an assistant plied their restoratives. It was all in vain.

The solemn tidings passed from the chamber of death through the family. The daughter, the hope of that old and honored house, was dead in the freshness of her youth, and the home of its solitary representative was hereafter doubly desolate.

A messenger rode hastily out of the avenue. A little after this the people of the village and the outlying farm-houses were startled by the sound of a bell.

One,—two,—three,—four,—

They stopped in every house, as far as the wavering vibrations reached, and listened—

—five,—six,—seven,—

It was not the little child which had been lying so long at the point of death; that could not be more than three or four years old—

—eight,—nine,—ten,—and so on to fifteen,—sixteen,—seventeen,—eighteen — — —

The pulsations seemed to keep on,—but it was the brain, and not the bell, that was throbbing now.

"Elsie's dead!" was the exclamation at a hundred firesides.

"Eighteen year old," said old Widow Peake, rising from her chair. "Eighteen year ago I laid two gold eagles on her mother's eyes,—he wouldn't have anything but gold touch her eyelids,—and now Elsie's to be straightened,—the Lord have mercy on her poor sinful soul!"

Dudley Venner prayed that night that he might be forgiven, if he had failed in any act of duty or kindness to this unfortunate child of his, now freed from all the woes born with her and so long poisoning her soul. He thanked God for the brief interval of peace which had been granted her, for the sweet communion they had enjoyed in these last days, and for the hope of meeting her with that other lost friend in a better world.

Helen mingled a few broken thanks and petitions with her tears: thanks that she had been permitted to share the last days and hours of this poor sister in sorrow; petitions that the grief of bereavement might be lightened to the lonely parent and the faithful old servant.

Old Sophy said almost nothing, but sat day and night by her dead darling. But sometimes her anguish would find an outlet in strange sounds, something between a cry and a musical note,—such as none had ever heard her utter before. These were old remembrances surging up from her childish days,—coming through her mother from the cannibal chief, her grandfather,—death-wails, such as they sing in the mountains of Western Africa, when they see the fires on distant hill-sides and know that their own wives and children are undergoing the fate of captives.

The time came when Elsie was to be laid by her mother in the small square marked by the white stone.

It was not unwillingly that the Reverend Chauncy Fairweather had relinquished the duty of conducting the service to the Reverend Doctor Honeywood, in accordance with Elsie's request. He could not, by any reasoning, reconcile his present way of thinking with a hope for the future of his unfortunate parishioner. Any good old Roman Catholic priest, born and bred to his faith and his business, would have found a loophole into some kind of heaven for her, by virtue of his doctrine of "invincible ignorance," or other special proviso; but a recent convert cannot enter into the working conditions of his new creed. Beliefs must be lived in for a good while, before they accommodate themselves to the soul's wants, and wear loose enough to be comfortable.

The Reverend Doctor had no such scruples. Like thousands of those who are classed nominally with the despairing believers, he had never prayed over a departed brother or sister without feeling and expressing a guarded hope that there was mercy in store for the poor sinner, whom parents, wives, children, brothers and sisters could not bear to give up to utter ruin without a word,—and would not, as he knew full well, in virtue of that human love and sympathy which nothing can ever extinguish. And in this poor Elsie's history he could read nothing which the tears of the recording angel might not wash away. As the good physician of the place knew the diseases that assailed the bodies of men and women, so he had learned the mysteries of the sickness of the soul.

So many wished to look upon Elsie's face once more, that her father would not deny them; nay, he was pleased that those who remembered her living should see her in the still beauty of death. Helen and those with her arrayed her for this farewell-view. All was ready for the sad or curious eyes which were to look upon her. There was no painful change to be concealed by any artifice. Even her round neck was left uncovered, that she might be more like one who slept. Only the golden cord was left in its place: some searching eye might detect a trace of that birth-mark which it was whispered she had always worn a necklace to conceal.

At the last moment, when all the preparations were completed, Old Sophy stooped over her, and, with trembling hand, loosed the golden cord. She looked intently, for some little space: there was no shade nor blemish where the ring of gold had encircled her throat. She took it gently away and laid it in the casket which held her ornaments.

"The Lord be praised!" the old woman cried, aloud. "He has taken away the mark that was on her; she's fit to meet his holy angels now!"

So Elsie lay for hours in the great room, in a kind of state, with flowers all about her,—her black hair braided as in life,—her brows smooth, as if they had never known the scowl of passion,—and on her lips the faint smile with which she had uttered her last "Good-night." The young girls from the school looked at her, one after another, and passed on, sobbing, carrying in their hearts the picture that would be with them all their days. The great people of the place were all there with their silent sympathy. The lesser kind of gentry, and many of the plainer folk of the village, half-pleased to find themselves passing beneath the stately portico of the ancient mansion-house, crowded in, until the ample rooms were overflowing. All the friends whose acquaintance we have made were there, and many from remoter villages and towns.

There was a deep silence at last. The hour had come for the parting words to be spoken over the dead. The good old minister's voice rose out of the stillness, subdued and tremulous at first, but growing firmer and clearer as he went on, until it reached the ears of the visitors who were in the far, desolate chambers, looking at the pictured hangings and the old dusty portraits. He did not tell her story in his prayer. He only spoke of our dear departed sister as one of many whom Providence in its wisdom has seen fit to bring under bondage from their cradles. It was not for us to judge them by any standard of our own. He who made the heart alone knew the infirmities it inherited or acquired. For all that our dear sister had presented that was interesting and attractive in her character we were to be grateful; for whatever was dark or inexplicable we must trust that the deep shadow which rested on the twilight dawn of her being might render a reason before the bar of Omniscience; for the grace which had lightened her last days we should pour out our hearts in thankful acknowledgment. From the life and the death of this our dear sister we should learn a lesson of patience with our fellow-creatures in their inborn peculiarities, of charity in judging what seem to us wilful faults of character, of hope and trust, that, by sickness or affliction, or such inevitable discipline as life must always bring with it, if by no gentler means, the soul which had been left by Nature to wander into the path of error and of suffering might be reclaimed and restored to its true aim, and so led on by divine grace to its eternal welfare. He closed his prayer by commending each member of the afflicted family to the divine blessing.

Then all at once rose the clear sound of the girls' voices, in the sweet, sad melody of a funeral hymn,—one of those which Elsie had marked, as if prophetically, among her own favorites.

And so they laid her in the earth, and showered down flowers upon her, and filled her grave, and covered it with green sods. By the side of it was another oblong ridge, with a white stone standing at its head. Mr. Bernard looked upon it, as he came close to the place where Elsie was laid, and read the inscription,—

CATALINA

WIFE TO DUDLEY VENNER

DIED

OCTOBER 13TH 1840

AGED XX YEARS.

A gentle rain fell on the turf after it was laid. This was the beginning of a long and dreary autumnal storm, a deferred "equinoctial," as many considered it. The mountain streams were all swollen and turbulent, and the steep declivities were furrowed in every direction by new channels. It made the house seem doubly desolate to hear the wind howling and the rain beating upon the roofs. The poor relation who was staying at the house would insist on Helen's remaining a few days: Old Sophy was in such a condition, that it kept her in continual anxiety, and there were many cares which Helen could take off from her.

The old black woman's life was buried in her darling's grave. She did nothing but moan and lament for her. At night she was restless, and would get up and wander to Elsie's apartment and look for her and call her by name. At other times she would lie awake and listen to the wind and the rain,—sometimes with such a wild look upon her face, and with such sudden starts and exclamations, that it seemed as if she heard spirit-voices and were answering the whispers of unseen visitants. With all this were mingled hints of her old superstition,—forebodings of something fearful about to happen,—perhaps the great final catastrophe of all things, according to the prediction current in the kitchens of Rockland.

"Hark!" Old Sophy would say,—"don' you hear th' crackin' 'n' th' snappin' up in Th' Mountain, 'n' th' rollin' o' th' big stones? The' 's somethin' stirrin' among th' rocks; I hear th' soun' of it in th' night, when th' wind has stopped blowin'. Oh, stay by me a little while, Miss Darlin'! stay by me! for it's th' Las' Day, maybe, that's close on us, 'n' I feel as if I couldn' meet th' Lord all alone!"

It was curious,—but Helen did certainly recognize sounds, during the lull of the storm, which were not of falling rain or running streams,—short snapping sounds, as of tense cords breaking,—long uneven sounds, as of masses rolling down steep declivities. But the morning came as usual; and as the others said nothing of these singular noises, Helen did not think it necessary to speak of them. All day long she and the humble relative of Elsie's mother, who had appeared as poor relations are wont to in the great crises of life, were busy in arranging the disordered house, and looking over the various objects which Elsie's singular tastes had brought together, to dispose of them as her father might direct. They all met together at the usual hour for tea. One of the servants came in, looking very blank, and said to the poor relation,—

"The well is gone dry; we have nothing but rain-water."

Dudley Venner's countenance changed; he sprang to his feet and went to assure himself of the fact, and, if he could, of the reason of it. For a well to dry up during such a rain-storm was extraordinary,—it was ominous.

He came back, looking very anxious.

"Did any of you notice any remarkable sounds last night," he said,—"or this morning? Hark! do you hear anything now?"

They listened in perfect silence for a few moments. Then there came a short cracking sound, and two or three snaps, as of parting cords.

Dudley Venner called all his household together.

"We are in danger here, as I think, to-night," he said,— "not very great danger, perhaps, but it is a risk I do not wish you to run. These heavy rains have loosed some of the rocks above, and they may come down and endanger the house. Harness the horses, Elbridge, and take all the family away. Miss Darley will go to the Institute; the others will pass the night at the Mountain House. I shall stay here, myself: it is not at all likely that anything will come of these warnings; but if there should, I choose to be here and take my chance."

It needs little, generally, to frighten servants, and they were all ready enough to go. The poor relation was one of the timid sort, and was terribly uneasy to be got out of the house. This left no alternative, of course, for Helen, but to go also. They all urged upon Dudley Venner to go with them: if there was danger, why should he remain to risk it, when he sent away the others?

Old Sophy said nothing until the time came for her to go with the second of Elbridge's carriage-loads.

"Come, Sophy," said Dudley Venner, "get your things and go. They will take good care of you at the Mountain House; and when we have made sure that there is no real danger, you shall come back at once."

"No, Massa!" Sophy answered. "I've seen Elsie into th' ground, 'n' I a'n't goin' away to come back 'n' fin' Massa Venner buried under th' rocks. My darlin' 's gone; 'n' now, if Massa goes, 'n' th' ol' place goes, it's time for Ol' Sophy to go, too. No, Massa Venner, we'll both stay in th' ol' mansion 'n' wait for th' Lord!"

Nothing could change the old woman's determination; and her master, who only feared, but did not really expect the long-deferred catastrophe, was obliged to consent to her staying. The sudden drying of the well at such a time was the most alarming sign; for he remembered that the same thing had been observed just before great mountain-slides. This long rain, too, was just the kind of cause which was likely to loosen the strata of rock piled up in the ledges; if the dreaded event should ever come to pass, it would be at such a time.

He paced his chamber uneasily until long past midnight. If the morning came without accident, he meant to have a careful examination made of all the rents and fissures above, of their direction and extent, and especially whether, in case of a mountain-slide, the huge masses would be like to reach so far to the east and so low down the declivity as the mansion.

At two o'clock in the morning he was dozing in his chair. Old Sophy had lain down on her bed, and was muttering in troubled dreams.

All at once a loud crash seemed to rend the very heavens above them: a crack as of the thunder that follows close upon the bolt,—a rending and crushing as of a forest snapped through all its stems, torn, twisted, splintered, dragged with all its ragged boughs into one chaotic ruin. The ground trembled under them as in an earthquake; the old mansion shuddered so that all its windows chattered in their casements; the great chimney shook off its heavy capstones, which came down on the roof with resounding concussions; and the echoes of The Mountain roared and bellowed in long reduplication, as if its whole foundations were rent, and this were the terrible voice of its dissolution.

Dudley Venner rose from his chair, folded his arms, and awaited his fate. There was no knowing where to look for safety; and he remembered too well the story of the family that was lost by rushing out of the house, and so hurrying into the very jaws of death.

He had stood thus but for a moment, when he heard the voice of Old Sophy in a wild cry of terror:—

"It's th' Las' Day! It's th' Las' Day! The Lord is comin' to take us all!"

"Sophy!" he called; but she did not hear him or heed him, and rushed out of the house.

The worst danger was over. If they were to be destroyed, it would necessarily be in a few seconds from the first thrill of the terrible convulsion. He waited in awful suspense, but calm. Not more than one or two minutes could have passed before the frightful tumult and all its sounding echoes had ceased. He called Old Sophy; but she did not answer. He went to the western window and looked forth into the darkness. He could not distinguish the outlines of the landscape, but the white stone was clearly visible, and by its side the new-made mound. Nay, what was that which obscured its outline, in shape like a human figure? He flung open the window and sprang through. It was all that there was left of poor Old Sophy, stretched out lifeless, upon her darling's grave.

He had scarcely composed her limbs and drawn the sheet over her, when the neighbors began to arrive from all directions. Each was expecting to hear of houses overwhelmed and families destroyed; but each came with the story that his own household was safe. It was not until the morning dawned that the true nature and extent of the sudden movement was ascertained. A great seam had opened above the long cliff, and the terrible Rattlesnake Ledge, with all its envenomed reptiles, its dark fissures and black caverns, was buried forever beneath a mighty incumbent mass of ruin.

CHAPTER XXXI

MR. SILAS PECKHAM RENDERS HIS ACCOUNT

The morning rose clear and bright. The long storm was over, and the calm autumnal sunshine was now to return, with all its infinite repose and sweetness. With the earliest dawn exploring parties were out in every direction along the southern slope of The Mountain, tracing the ravages of the great slide and the track it had followed. It proved to be not so much a slide as the breaking off and falling of a vast line of cliff, including the dreaded Ledge. It had folded over like the leaves of a half-opened book when they close, crushing the trees below, piling its ruins in a glacis at the foot of what had been the overhanging wall of the cliff, and filling up that deep cavity above the mansion-house which bore the ill-omened name of Dead Man's Hollow. This it was which had saved the Dudley mansion. The falling masses, or huge fragments breaking off from them, would have swept the house and all around it to destruction but for this deep shelving dell, into which the stream of ruin was happily directed. It was, indeed, one of Nature's conservative revolutions; for the fallen masses made a kind of shelf, which interposed a level break between the inclined planes above and below it, so that the nightmare-fancies of the dwellers in the Dudley mansion, and in many other residences under the shadow of The Mountain, need not keep them lying awake hereafter to listen for the snapping of roots and the splitting of the rocks above them.

Twenty-four hours after the falling of the cliff, it seemed as if it had happened ages ago. The new fact had fitted itself in with all the old predictions, forebodings, fears, and acquired the solidarity belonging to all events which have slipped out of the fingers of Time and dissolved in the antecedent eternity.

Old Sophy was lying dead in the Dudley mansion. If there were tears shed for her, they could not be bitter ones; for she had lived out her full measure of days, and gone —who could help fondly believing it?—to rejoin her beloved mistress. They made a place for her at the foot of the two mounds. It was thus she would have chosen to sleep, and not to have wronged her humble devotion in life by asking to lie at the side of those whom she had served so long and faithfully. There were very few present at the simple ceremony. Helen Darley was one of these few. The old black woman had been her companion in all the kind offices of which she had been the ministering angel to Elsie.

After it was all over, Helen was leaving with the rest, when Dudley Venner begged her to stay a little, and he would send her back: it was a long walk; besides, he wished to say some things to her, which he had not had the opportunity of speaking. Of course Helen could not refuse him; there must be many thoughts coming into his mind which he would wish to share with her who had known his daughter so long and been with her in her last days.

She returned into the great parlor with the wrought cornices and the medallion-portraits on the ceiling.

"I am now alone in the world," Dudley Venner said.

Helen must have known that before he spoke. But the tone in which he said it had so much meaning, that she could not find a word to answer him with. They sat in silence, which the old tall clock counted out in long seconds; but it was silence which meant more than any words they had ever spoken.

"Alone in the world. Helen, the freshness of my life is gone, and there is little left of the few graces which in my younger days might have fitted me to win the love of women. Listen to me,—kindly, if you can; forgive me, at least. Half my life has been passed in constant fear and anguish, without any near friend to share my trials. My task is done now; my fears have ceased to prey upon me; the sharpness of early sorrows has yielded something of its edge to time. You have bound me to you by gratitude in the tender care you have taken of my poor child. More than this. I must tell you all now, out of the depth of this trouble through which I am passing. I have loved you from the moment we first met; and if my life has anything left worth accepting, it is yours. Will you take the offered gift?"

Helen looked in his face, surprised, bewildered.

"This is not for me,—not for me," she said. "I am but a poor faded flower, not worth the gathering of such a one as you. No, no,—I have been bred to humble toil all my days, and I could not be to you what you ought to ask. I am accustomed to a kind of loneliness and self-dependence. I have seen nothing, almost, of the world, such as you were born to move in. Leave me to my obscure place and duties; I shall at least have peace;—and you—you will surely find in due time some one better fitted by Nature and training to make you happy."

"No, Miss Darley!" Dudley Venner said, almost sternly. "You must not speak to a man, who has lived through my experiences, of looking about for a new choice after his heart has once chosen. Say that you can never love me; say that I have lived too long to share your young life; say that sorrow has left nothing in me for Love to find his pleasure in; but do not mock me with the hope of a new affection for some unknown object. The first look of yours brought me to your side. The first tone of your voice sunk into my heart. From this moment my life must wither out or bloom anew. My home is desolate. Come under my roof and make it bright once more,—share my life with me,—or I shall give the halls of the old mansion to the bats and the owls, and wander forth alone without a hope or a friend!"

To find herself with a man's future at the disposal of a single word of hers!—a man like this, too, with a fascination for her against which she had tried to shut her heart, feeling that he lived in another sphere than hers, working as she was for her bread a poor operative in the factory of a hard master and jealous overseer, the salaried drudge of Mr. Silas Peckham! Why, she had thought he was grateful to her as a friend of his daughter; she had even pleased herself with the feeling that he liked her, in her humble place, as a woman of some cultivation and many sympathetic points of relation with himself; but that he *loved* her,—that this deep, fine nature, in a man so far removed from her in outward circumstance, should have found its counterpart in one whom life had treated so coldly as herself,—that Dudley Venner should stake his happiness on a breath of hers,—poor Helen Darley's,—it was all a surprise, a confusion, a kind of fear not wholly fearful. Ah, me! women know what it is,—that mist over the eyes, that trembling in the limbs, that faltering of the voice, that sweet, shame-faced, unspoken confession of weakness which does not wish to be strong, that sudden overflow in the soul where thoughts loose their hold on each other and swim single and helpless in the flood of emotion,—women know what it is!

No doubt she was a little frightened and a good deal bewildered, and that her sympathies were warmly excited for a friend to whom she had been brought so near, and whose loneliness she saw and pitied. She lost that calm self-possession she had hoped to maintain.

"If I thought that I could make you happy,—if I should speak from my heart, and not my reason,—I am but a weak woman,—yet if I can be to you—— What can I say?"

What more could this poor, dear Helen say?

"Elbridge, harness the horses and take Miss Darley back to the school."

What conversation had taken place since Helen's rhetorical failure is not recorded in the minutes from which this narrative is constructed. But when the man who had been summoned had gone to get the carriage ready, Helen resumed something she had been speaking of.

"Not for the world. Everything must go on just as it has gone on, for the present. There are proprieties to be consulted. I cannot be hard with you, that out of your very affliction has sprung this—this—well—you must name it for me,—but the world will never listen to explanations. I am to be Helen Darley, lady assistant in Mr. Silas Peckham's school, as long as I see fit to hold my office. And I mean to attend to my scholars just as before; so that I shall have very little time for visiting or seeing company. I believe, though, you are one of the Trustees and a Member of the Examining Committee; so that, if you should happen to visit the school, I shall try to be civil to you."

Every lady sees, of course, that Helen was quite right; but perhaps here and there one will think that Dudley Venner was all wrong,—that he was too hasty,—that he should have been too full of his recent grief for such a confession as he has just made, and the passion from which it sprung. Perhaps they do not understand the sudden recoil of a strong nature long compressed. Perhaps they have not studied the mystery of *allotropism* in the emotions of the human heart. Go to the nearest chemist and ask him to show you some of the dark-red phosphorus which will not burn without fierce heating, but at 500°, Fahrenheit, changes back again to the inflammable substance we know so well. Grief seems more like ashes than like fire; but as grief has been love once, so it may become love again. This is emotional allotropism.

Helen rode back to the Institute and inquired for Mr. Peckham. She had not seen him during the brief interval between her departure from the mansion-house and her return to Old Sophy's funeral. There were various questions about the school she wished to ask.

"Oh, how's your haälth, Miss Darley?" Silas began. "We've missed you consid'able. Glad to see you back at the post of dooty. Hope the Squire treated you hahnsomely,— liberal pecooniary compensation,—hey? A'n't much of a loser, I guess, by acceptin' his propositions?"

Helen blushed at this last question, as if Silas had meant something by it beyond asking what money she had received; but his own double-meaning expression and her blush were too nice points for him to have taken cognizance of. He was engaged in a mental calculation as to the amount of the deduction he should make under the head of "demage to the institootion,"—this depending somewhat on that of the "pecooniary compensation" she might have received for her services as the friend of Elsie Venner.

So Helen slid back at once into her routine, the same

faithful, patient creature she had always been. But what was this new light which seemed to have kindled in her eyes? What was this look of peace, which nothing could disturb, which smiled serenely through all the little meannesses with which the daily life of the educational factory surrounded her,—which not only made her seem resigned, but overflowed all her features with a thoughtful, subdued happiness? Mr. Bernard did not know,—perhaps he did not guess. The inmates of the Dudley mansion were not scandalized by any mysterious visits of a veiled or unveiled lady. The vibrating tongues of the "female youth" of the Institute were not set in motion by the standing of an equipage at the gate, waiting for their lady teacher. The servants at the mansion did not convey numerous letters with superscriptions in a bold, manly hand, sealed with the arms of a well-known house, and directed to Miss Helen Darley; nor, on the other hand, did Hiram, the man from the lean streak in New Hampshire, carry sweet-smelling, rose-hued, many-layered, criss-crossed, fine-stitch-lettered packages of note-paper directed to Dudley Venner, Esq., and all too scanty to hold that incredible expansion of the famous three words which a woman was born to say,—that perpetual miracle which astonishes all the go-betweens who wear their shoes out in carrying a woman's infinite variations on the theme, "I love you."

But the reader must remember that there are walks in country-towns where people are liable to meet by accident, and that the hollow of an old tree has served the purpose of a post-office sometimes; so that he has her choice (to divide the pronouns impartially) of various hypotheses to account for the new glory of happiness which seemed to have irradiated our poor Helen's features, as if her dreary life were awakening in the dawn of a blessed future.

With all the alleviations which have been hinted at, Mr. Dudley Venner thought that the days and the weeks had never moved so slowly as through the last period of the autumn that was passing. Elsie had been a perpetual source of anxiety to him, but still she had been a companion. He could not mourn for her; for he felt that she was safer with her mother, in that world where there are no more sorrows and dangers, than she could have been with him. But as he sat at his window and looked at the three mounds, the loneliness of the great house made it seem more like the sepulchre than these narrow dwellings where his beloved and her daughter lay close to each other, side by side,— Catalina, the bride of his youth, and Elsie, the child whom he had nurtured, with poor Old Sophy, who had followed them like a black shadow, at their feet, under the same soft turf, sprinkled with the brown autumnal leaves. It was not good for him to be thus alone. How should he ever live through the long months of November and December?

The months of November and December did, in some way or other, get rid of themselves at last, bringing with them the usual events of village-life and a few unusual ones. Some of the geologists had been up to look at the great slide, of which they gave those prolix accounts which everybody remembers who read the scientific journals of the time. The engineers reported that there was little probability of any further convulsion along the line of rocks which overhung the more thickly settled part of the town. The naturalists drew up a paper on the "Probable Extinction of the *Crotalus Durissus* in the Township of Rockland." The engagement of the Widow Rowens to a Little Millionville merchant was announced,—"Sudding 'n' onexpected," Widow Leech said,—"waälthy, or she wouldn't ha' looked at him, —fifty year old, if he is a day, *'n' ha'n't got a white hair in his head.*" The Reverend Chauncy Fairweather had publicly announced that he was going to join the Roman Catholic communion,—not so much to the surprise or consternation of the religious world as he had supposed. Several old ladies forthwith proclaimed their intention of following him; but, as one or two of them were deaf, and another had been threatened with an attack of that mild, but obstinate complaint, *dementia senilis*, many thought it was not so much the force of his arguments as a kind of tendency to jump as the bellwether jumps, well known in flocks not included in the Christian fold. His bereaved congregation immediately began pulling candidates on and off, like new boots, on trial. Some pinched in tender places; some were too loose; some were too square-toed; some were too coarse, and didn't please; some were too thin, and wouldn't last;—in short, they couldn't possibly find a fit. At last, people began to drop in to hear old Doctor Honeywood. They were quite surprised to find what a human old gentleman he was, and went back and told the others, that, instead of being a case of confluent sectarianism, as they supposed, the good old minister had been so well vaccinated with charitable virus that he was now a true, open-souled Christian of the mildest type. The end of all which was, that the liberal people went over to the old minister almost in a body, just at the time that Deacon Shearer and the "Vinegar-Bible" party split off, and that not long afterwards they sold their own meeting-house to the malecontents, so that Deacon Soper used often to remind Colonel Sprowle of his wish that "our little man and him [the Reverend Doctor] would swop pulpits," and tell him it had "pooty nigh come trew."—But this is anticipating the course of events, which were much longer in coming about; for we have but just got through that terrible long month, as Mr. Dudley Venner found it, of December.

On the first of January, Mr. Silas Peckham was in the habit of settling his quarterly accounts, and making such new arrangements as his convenience or interest dictated. New-Year was a holiday at the Institute. No doubt this accounted for Helen's being dressed so charmingly,—always, to be sure in her own simple way, but yet with such a true lady's air, that she looked fit to be the mistress of any mansion in the land.

She was in the parlor alone, a little before noon, when Mr. Peckham came in.

"I'm ready to settle my accaount with you now, Miss Darley," said Silas.

"As you please, Mr. Peckham," Helen answered, very graciously.

"Before payin' you your selary," the Principal continued, "I wish to come to an understandin' as to the futur'. I consider that I've been payin' high, very high, for the work you do. Women's wages can't be expected to do more than feed and clothe 'em, as a gineral thing, with a little savin', in case of sickness, and to bury 'em, if they break daown, as all of 'em are liable to do at any time. If I a'n't misinformed, you not only support yourself out of my establishment, but likewise relatives of yours, who I don't know that I'm called upon to feed and clothe. There is a young woman, not burdened with destitute relatives, has signified that she would be glad to take your dooties for less pecooniary compensation, by a consid'able amaount, than you now receive. I shall be willin', however, to retain your services at sech redooced rate as we shall fix upon,—provided sech redooced rate be as low or lower than the same services can be obtained elsewhere."

"As you please, Mr. Peckham," Helen answered, with a smile so sweet that the Principal (who of course had trumped up this opposition-teacher for the occasion) said to himself she would stand being cut down a quarter, perhaps a half, of her salary.

"Here is your accaount, Miss Darley, and the balance doo you," said Silas Peckham, handing her a paper and a small roll of infectious-flavored bills wrapping six poisonous coppers of the old coinage.

She took the paper and began looking at it. She could not quite make up her mind to touch the feverish bills with the cankering coppers in them, and left them airing themselves on the table.

The document she held ran as follows:

Silas Peckham, Esq., Principal of the Apollinean Institute,
   In Account with Helen Darley, Assist. Teacher

Dr.		Cr.	
To Salary for quarter ending Jan. 1st, @ $75 per quarter	$75.00	By Deduction for absence, 1 week 3 days	$10.00
		" Board, lodging, etc., for 10 days, @ 75 cts. per day	7.50
		" Damage to Institution by absence of teacher from duties, say	25.00
		" Stationery furnished	43
		" Postage-stamp	01
		" Balance due Helen Darley	32.06
	$75.00		$75.00

ROCKLAND, Jan. 1st, 1859

Now Helen had her own private reasons for wishing to receive the small sum which was due her at this time without any unfair deduction,—reasons which we need not inquire into too particularly, as we may be very sure that they were right and womanly. So, when she looked over this account of Mr. Silas Peckham's, and saw that he had contrived to pare down her salary to something less than half its stipulated amount, the look which her countenance wore was as near to that of righteous indignation as her gentle features and soft blue eyes would admit of its being.

"Why, Mr. Peckham," she said, "do you mean this? If I am of so much value to you that you must take off twenty-five dollars for ten days' absence, how is it that my salary is to be cut down to less than seventy-five dollars a quarter, if I remain here?"

"I gave you fair notice," said Silas. "I have a minute of it I took down immed'ately after the intervoo."

He lugged out his large pocket-book with the strap going all round it, and took from it a slip of paper which confirmed his statement.

"Besides," he added, slyly, "I presoom you have received a liberal pecooniary compensation from Squire Venner for nussin' his daughter."

Helen was looking over the bill while he was speaking.

"Board and lodging for ten days, Mr. Peckham,—*whose* board and lodging, pray?"

The door opened before Silas Peckham could answer, and Mr. Bernard walked into the parlor. Helen was holding the bill in her hand, looking as any woman ought to look who has been at once wronged and insulted.

"The last turn of the thumbscrew!" said Mr. Bernard to himself. "What is it, Helen? You look troubled."

She handed him the account.

He looked at the footing of it. Then he looked at the items. Then he looked at Silas Peckham.

At this moment Silas was sublime. He was so transcendently unconscious of the emotions going on in Mr. Bernard's mind at the moment, that he had only a single thought.

"The accaount's correc'ly cast, I presoom;—if the' 's any mistake of figgers or addin' 'em up, it'll be made all right. Everything's accordin' to agreement. The minute written immed'ately after the intervoo is here in my possession."

Mr. Bernard looked at Helen. Just what would have happened to Silas Peckham, as he stood then and there, but for the interposition of a merciful Providence, nobody knows or ever will know; for at that moment steps were heard upon the stairs, and Hiram threw open the parlor-door for Mr. Dudley Venner to enter.

He saluted them all gracefully with the good-wishes of the season, and each of them returned his compliment,— Helen blushing fearfully, of course, but not particularly noticed in her embarrassment by more than one.

Silas Peckham reckoned with perfect confidence on his Trustees, who had always said what he told them to, and done what he wanted. It was a good chance now to show off his power, and, by letting his instructors know the unstable tenure of their offices, make it easier to settle his accounts and arrange his salaries. There was nothing very strange in Mr. Venner's calling; he was one of the Trustees, and this was New Year's Day. But he had called just at the lucky moment for Mr. Peckham's object.

"I have thought some of makin' changes in the department of instruction," he began. "Several accomplished teachers have applied to me, who would be glad of sitooations. I understand that there never have been so many fust-rate teachers, male and female, out of employment as doorin' the present season. If I can make sahtisfahctory arrangements with my present corpse of teachers, I shall be glad to do so; otherwise I shell, with the permission of the Trustees, make sech noo arrangements as circumstahnces compel."

"You may make arrangements for a new assistant in my department, Mr. Peckham," said Mr. Bernard, "at once,—this day,—this hour. I am not safe to be trusted with your person five minutes out of this lady's presence,—of whom I beg pardon for this strong language. Mr. Venner, I must beg you, as one of the Trustees of this Institution, to look at the manner in which its Principal has attempted to swindle this faithful teacher whose toils and sacrifices and self-devotion to the school have made it all that it is, in spite of this miserable trader's incompetence. Will you look at the paper I hold?"

Dudley Venner took the account and read it through, without changing a feature. Then he turned to Silas Peckham.

"You may make arrangements for a new assistant in the branches this lady has taught. Miss Helen Darley is to be my wife. I had hoped to have announced this news in a less abrupt and ungraceful manner. But I came to tell you with my own lips what you would have learned before evening from my friends in the village."

Mr. Bernard went to Helen, who stood silent, with downcast eyes, and took her hand warmly, hoping she might find all the happiness she deserved. Then he turned to Dudley Venner, and said,—

"She is a queen, but has never found it out. The world has nothing nobler than this dear woman, whom you have discovered in the disguise of a teacher. God bless her and you!"

Dudley Venner returned his friendly grasp, without answering a word in articulate speech.

Silas remained dumb and aghast for a brief space. Coming to himself a little, he thought there might have been some mistake about the items,—would like to have Miss Darley's bill returned,—would make it all right,—had no idee that Squire Venner had a special int'rest in Miss Darley,—was sorry he had given offence,—if he might take that bill and look it over——

"No, Mr. Peckham," said Mr. Dudley Venner, "there will be a full meeting of the Board next week, and the bill, and such evidence with reference to the management of the Institution and the treatment of its instructors as Mr. Langdon sees fit to bring forward will be laid before them."

Miss Helen Darley became that very day the guest of Miss Arabella Thornton, the Judge's daughter. Mr. Bernard made his appearance a week or two later at the Lectures, where the Professor first introduced him to the reader.

He stayed after the class had left the room.

"Ah, Mr. Langdon! how do you do? Very glad to see you back again. How have you been since our correspondence on Fascination and other curious scientific questions?"

It was the Professor who spoke,—whom the reader will recognize as myself, the teller of this story.

"I have been well," Mr. Bernard answered, with a serious look which invited a further question.

"I hope you have had none of those painful or dangerous experiences you seemed to be thinking of when you wrote; at any rate, you have escaped having your obituary written."

"I have seen some things worth remembering. Shall I call on you this evening and tell you about them?"

"I shall be most happy to see you."

This was the way in which I, the Professor, became acquainted with some of the leading events of this story. They interested me sufficiently to lead me to avail myself of all those other extraordinary methods of obtaining information well known to writers of narrative.

Mr. Langdon seemed to me to have gained in seriousness and strength of character by his late experiences. He threw his whole energies into his studies with an effect which distanced all his previous efforts. Remembering my former hint, he employed his spare hours in writing for the annual prizes, both of which he took by a unanimous vote of the judges. Those who heard him read his Thesis at the Medical Commencement will not soon forget the impression made by his fine personal appearance and manners, nor the universal interest excited in the audience, as he read, with his beautiful enunciation, that striking paper entitled "Unresolved Nebulæ in Vital Science." It was a general remark of the Faculty,—and old Doctor Kittredge, who had come down on purpose to hear Mr. Langdon, heartily agreed to it,—that there had never been a diploma filled up, since the institution which conferred upon him the degree of *Doctor Medicinæ* was founded, which carried with it more of promise to the profession than that which bore the name of

Bernardus Caryl Langdon.

CHAPTER XXXII

CONCLUSION

Mr. Bernard Langdon had no sooner taken his degree, than, in accordance with the advice of one of his teachers whom he frequently consulted, he took an office in the heart of the city where he had studied. He had thought of beginning in a suburb or some remoter district of the city proper.

"No," said his teacher,—to wit, myself,—"don't do any such thing. You are made for the best kind of practice; don't hamper yourself with an outside constituency, such as belongs to a practitioner of the second class. When a fellow like you chooses his beat, he must look ahead a little. Take care of all the poor that apply to you, but leave the half-pay classes to a different style of doctor,—the people who spend one half their time in taking care of their patients, and the other half in squeezing out their money. Go for the swell-fronts and south-exposure houses; the folks inside are just as good as other people, and the pleasantest, on the whole, to take care of. They must have somebody, and they like a gentleman best. Don't throw yourself away, but have a good presence and pleasing manners. You wear white linen by inherited instinct. You can pronounce the word *view*. You have all the elements of success; go and take it. Be polite and generous, but don't undervalue yourself. You will be useful, at any rate; you may just as well be happy, while you are about it. The highest social class furnishes incomparably the best patients, taking them by and large. Besides, when they won't get well and bore you to death, you can send 'em off to travel. Mind me now, and take the tops of your sparrowgrass. Somebody must have 'em,—why shouldn't you? If you don't take your chance, you'll get the butt-ends as a matter of course."

Mr. Bernard talked like a young man full of noble sentiments. He wanted to be useful to his fellow-beings. Their social differences were nothing to him. He would never court the rich,—he would go where he was called. He would rather save the life of a poor mother of a family than that of half a dozen old gouty millionnaires whose heirs had been yawning and stretching these ten years to get rid of them.

"Generous emotions!" I exclaimed. "Cherish 'em; cling to 'em till you are fifty, till you are seventy, till you are ninety! But do as I tell you,—strike for the best circle of practice, and you'll be sure to get it!"

Mr. Langdon did as I told him,—took a genteel office, furnished it neatly, dressed with a certain elegance, soon made a pleasant circle of acquaintances, and began to work his way into the right kind of business. I missed him, however, for some days, not long after he had opened his office. On his return, he told me he had been up at Rockland, by special invitation, to attend the wedding of Mr. Dudley Venner and Miss Helen Darley. He gave me a full account of the ceremony, which I regret that I cannot relate in full. "Helen looked like an angel,"—that, I am sure, was one of his expressions. As for her dress, I should like to give the details, but am afraid of committing blunders, as men always do, when they undertake to describe such matters. White dress, anyhow,—that I am sure of,—with orange-flowers, and the most wonderful lace veil that was ever seen or heard of. The Reverend Doctor Honeywood performed the ceremony, of course. The good people seemed to have forgotten they ever had had any other minister,—except Deacon Shearer and his set of malecontents, who were doing a dull business in the meeting-house lately occupied by the Reverend Mr. Fairweather.

"Who was at the wedding?"

"Everybody, pretty much. They wanted to keep it quiet, but it was of no use. Married at church. Front pews, old

Doctor Kittredge and all the mansion-house people and distinguished strangers,—Colonel Sprowle and family, including Matilda's young gentleman, a graduate of one of the fresh-water colleges,—Mrs. Pickins (late Widow Rowens) and husband,—Deacon Soper and numerous parishioners. A little nearer the door, Abel, the Doctor's man, and Elbridge, who drove them to church in the family-coach. Father Fairweather, as they all call him now, came in late with Father McShane."

"And Silas Peckham?"

"Oh, Silas had left The School and Rockland. Cut up altogether too badly in the examination instituted by the Trustees. Had removed over to Tamarack, and thought of renting a large house and 'farming' the town-poor."

Some time after this, as I was walking with a young friend along by the swell-fronts and south-exposures, whom should I see but Mr. Bernard Langdon, looking remarkably happy, and keeping step by the side of a very handsome and singularly well-dressed young lady? He bowed and lifted his hat as we passed.

"Who is that pretty girl my young doctor has got there?" I said to my companion.

"Who is that?" he answered. "You don't know? Why, that is neither more nor less than Miss Letitia Forrester, daughter of—of—why, the great banking-firm, you know, Bilyuns Brothers & Forrester. Got acquainted with her in the country, they say. There's a story that they're engaged, or like to be, if the firm consents."

"Oh!" I said.

I did not like the look of it in the least. Too young,— too young. Has not taken any position yet. No right to ask for the hand of Bilyuns Brothers & Co.'s daughter. Besides, it will spoil him for practice, if he marries a rich girl before he has formed habits of work.

I looked in at his office the next day. A box of white kids was lying open on the table. A three-cornered note, directed in a very delicate lady's-hand, was distinguishable among a heap of papers. I was just going to call him to account for his proceedings, when he pushed the three-cornered note aside and took up a letter with a great corporation-seal upon it. He had received the offer of a professor's chair in an ancient and distinguished institution.

"Pretty well for three-and-twenty, my boy," I said. "I suppose you'll think you must be married one of these days, if you accept this office."

Mr. Langdon blushed.—There had been stories about him, he knew. His name had been mentioned in connection with that of a very charming young lady. The current reports were not true. He had met this young lady, and been much pleased with her, in the country, at the house of her grandfather, the Reverend Doctor Honeywood,—you remember Miss Letitia Forrester, whom I have mentioned repeatedly? On coming to town, he found his country-acquaintance in a social position which seemed to discourage his continued intimacy. He had discovered, however, that he was a not unwelcome visitor, and had kept up friendly relations with her. But there was no truth in the current reports,—none at all.

Some months had passed, after this visit, when I happened one evening to stroll into a box in one of the principal theatres of the city. A small party sat on the seats before me: a middle-aged gentleman and his lady, in front, and directly behind them my young doctor and the same very handsome young lady I had seen him walking with on the sidewalk before the swell-fronts and south-exposures. As Professor Langdon seemed to be very much taken up with his companion, and both of them looked as if they were enjoying themselves, I determined not to make my presence known to my young friend, and to withdraw quietly after feasting my eyes with the sight of them for a few minutes.

"It looks as if something might come of it," I said to myself. At that moment the young lady lifted her arm accidentally in such a way that the light fell upon the clasp of a chain which encircled her wrist. My eyes filled with tears as I read upon the clasp, in sharp-cut Italic letters,

E. V. They were tears at once of sad remembrance and of joyous anticipation; for the ornament on which I looked was the double pledge of a dead sorrow and a living affection. It was the golden bracelet,—the parting-gift of Elsie Venner.

THE END

One